COUNTERTRANSFERENCE

COUNTERTRANSFERENCE

edited by
Lawrence Epstein, Ph.D. and
Arthur H. Feiner, Ph.D.

for
the William Alanson White
Psychoanalytic Society

New York ● Jason Aronson ● London

ISBN: 0-87668-378-2

Library of Congress Catalog Number: 79-51929

Manufactured in the United States of America

CONTENTS

Part II
THE THERAPIST'S USE OF COUNTERTRANSFERENCE

Part III
COUNTERTRANSFERENCE WITH PARTICULAR
TYPES OF PATIENTS

ACKNOWLEDGMENTS

The idea for this volume was conceived at an executive committee meeting of the William Alanson White Psychoanalytic Society in 1976. To all the members of this committee: Drs. Amnon Issacharoff, president; Marylou Lionells, treasurer; Lawrence Epstein, secretary; and Anna M. Antonovaky, president-elect, who encouraged us to produce and edit this work, we will be forever grateful. It is under the aegis of the Society that this book is published.

The William Alanson White Psychoanalytic Society is the organization of graduates from the William Alanson White Institute of Psychiatry, Psychoanalysis and Psychology. The Institute was founded in 1943 by Drs. Harry Stack Sullivan, Clara Thompson, and Erich Fromm, and carries on the training of psychoanalysts drawn from the professions of psychiatry and clinical psychology. It is a center for progressive thinking in psychoanalysis, requiring of its students the highest standards.

Our gratitude goes to Helen Ekstein, who, despite innumerable responsibilities at the Institute, handled the correspondence with the authors, typed the manuscripts, and sorted out many details; to Lori Feiner, who also was helpful with many sections of the manuscript, to Michael Farrin for his editing of our introduction, and to Joan Langs, who aided in more ways than can be enumerated. And, of course, Roz and Alice.

Some of the papers in this volume were first published in *Contemporary Psychoanalysis,* Journal of the William Alanson White Psychoanalytic Society and the William Alanson White Institute. Amnon Issacharoff's "Barriers to Knowing in Psycho-analysis" appeared in Volume 12, No. 4, 1976; a version of Arthur H. Feiner's "Countertransference and the Anxiety of Influence," Volume 13, No. 1, 1977; Earl G. Witenberg's "The Inner Game of Psychoanalysis," Volume 13, No. 3, 1977; Lawrence Epstein's "The Therapeutic Function of Hate in the Countertransference," Volume 13, No. 4, 1977; Peter L. Giovacchini's "Pervasive Delusion: A Countertransference Dilemma," Volume 13, No. 4, 1977; Edward S. Tauber's "Countertransference Reexamined," Volume 14, No. 1, 1978; L. Bryce Boyer's "Countertransference Experiences with Severely Regressed Patients," Volume 14, No. 1, 1978; Joyce McDougall's "Primitive Communication and the Use of Countertransference," Volume 14, No. 2, 1978; Donald Meltzer's "Routine and Inspired Interpretations," Volume 14, No. 2, 1978; Amnon Issacharoff's and Winslow Hunt's "Beyond Countertransference," Volume 14, No. 2, 1978; Robert Langs' "Adaptational-Interactional Dimension of Countertransference," Volume 14, No. 4, 1978; Leon Grinberg's "Projective Counter-Indentification and Countertransference," Volume 15, No. 1, 1979; and Lawrence Epstein's "On the Therapeutic Use of Countertransference Data with Borderline Patients," Volume 15, No. 1, 1979.

INTRODUCTION

Freud's earliest remarks on the identification of countertransference occur in that famous paragraph whose second sentence begins "We have become aware of the 'counter-transference,' which arises in [the physician] as a result of the patient's influence on his unconscious feelings ... "; there the requirement is stated that the analyst "begin his activity with a self-analysis and continually carry it deeper while he is making his observations on his patients" (Freud 1910, pp. 144, 145). Two years later Freud wrote that the analyst "must turn his own unconscious like a receptive organ towards the transmitting unconscious of the patient.... [S]o the doctor's unconscious is able ... to reconstruct [the patient's] unconscious ... " (Freud 1912, pp. 115, 116). These two thematic strands — countertransference as a hindrance, and the doctor's use of his own unconscious to understand the patient — have intertwined, like a double helix, throughout the historical development of psychoanalytic conceptions of countertransference. And, we might add, of its theory of treatment itself.

Racker (1953) in Argentina; Winnicott (1949), Heimann (1950), and Little (1951) in England; and in the United States Fromm-Reichmann (1950), Mabel Blake Cohen (1952), Thompson, Crowley, and Tauber (1952), and Tauber (1954) have made several significant contributions to the issue. These analysts turned to the *data* of countertransference to seek a better understanding of the patient in the ongoing process of psychoanalysis. We specifically focus in this introduction on the seminal contributions of Heimann (1950), Little (1951, 1957), Winnicott (1949), and Racker (1953). True, the Balints (1939) had commented on the analyst's subtle influence on the patient's transference, Horney (1939) had likened the countertransference to an aspect of the analyst's characterology, and Sharpe (1947) had mentioned both conscious and unconscious aspects of countertransference. But it was Heimann, Little, Winnicott, and Racker who actually broke through the prevailing classical view that countertransference was simply a hindrance to effective psychoanalytic work. Their ideas concerning the therapeutic usefulness of countertransference data have foreshadowed all subsequent developments, and their papers are even today the most widely quoted in the literature. Racker's elaboration of countertransference theory, and of the use to which countertransference data may be put in clinical practice, remains probably the most comprehensive and original contribution by any single author.

We will consider also the polar classical position of Annie Reich (1951, 1960, 1966), who holds to the view that, ultimately, countertransference is a hindrance to the work. Finally, we will review some of the bases for resistance to the continued scientific study of the use of countertransference in both the classical and the interpersonal schools.

Note that more than thirty years passed before Freud's position, that countertransference was little more than a hindrance, was effectively challenged. During the late forties and early fifties marked interest in countertransference emerged throughout the psychoanalytic community. The challenge took the form of respecting the antitherapeutic aspects of countertransference while sensing the possibility that by its study analysts could derive and formulate interventions which might enhance the therapeutic process. We shall return to this issue when we discuss the possible reasons why the challenge and reformulation of the classical concept of countertransference had to wait this long. First let us review the ideas of the seminal quartet.

Paula Heimann

In her brief paper, "On Countertransference" (1950), Heimann offered several revisions of the concept. First she extended the term to include all the feelings that the therapist experiences toward his patient, no longer restricting it, as did Freud, to the pathological components of the therapist's response. She went on to remark that

> the aim of the analyst's own analysis . . . is not to turn him into a mechanical brain which can produce interpretations on the basis of a purely intellectual procedure, but to enable him, to *sustain* the feelings which are stirred in him, as opposed to discharging them (as does the patient), in order to *subordinate* them to the analytic task in which he functions as the patient's mirror reflection. [p. 82]

She considered "the analyst's emotional response to his patient within the analytic situation . . . one of the most important tools for his work. The analyst's countertransference is an instrument of research into the patient's unconscious" (p. 81).

She therefore recommended that the analyst's evenly hovering, freely working attention to the patient's associations be extended as well to the doctor's own emotional responses. Echoing Freud (1912), she wrote, "Our basic assumption is that the analyst's unconscious understands that of his patient. This rapport on the deep level comes to the surface in the form of feelings which the analyst notices in response to his patient, in his 'counter-transference' " (p. 82).

Thus Heimann, freeing herself of the popular view of countertransference as "bad" and consequently a barrier to understanding, turned her attention to its potential value in furthering the analytic work.

While most analysts would reject Heimann's perhaps overstated conclusion that the countertransference is "the patient's *creation*" and "part of the patient's personality" (p. 83), there are those who describe typical clinical situations in which this may be nearly true. In this volume Spotnitz (chapter 14), discussing the "narcissistic countertransference," and Grinberg (chapter 8), elaborating on "projective counteridentification," present such situations.

Finally, when it came to what the therapist should do with his countertransference, Heimann was quite explicit. It should not be communicated to the patient, she advised, but should be used as a source of insight into the patient's conflicts and defenses. This remains the widespread view among analysts of almost all schools, especially when working with the more integrated patient (see Langs 1976, Sandler 1976, and Feiner, chapter 5).

Margaret Little

In her 1951 paper as well as in another appearing in 1957, Little placed the analyst's countertransference at the center of the therapeutic work with severely disturbed patients. It is the countertransference, she wrote, which often has to do the work.

She observed that these patients are often successfully treated by beginning therapists who are not afraid to allow their unconscious impulses a considerable degree of freedom, and by experienced analysts who trust their unconscious impulses. She recommended that when an interpretation has been mistimed or wrongly emphasized, the analyst should admit his error to the patient and — unless this is contraindicated — explain its origin in his unconscious countertransference. And, she commented, this is essential for the progress of the analysis and contributes to the patient's developing confidence in the honesty and good will of an analyst who is also seen as having the right to make mistakes. Furthermore, it demonstrates the universality of transference in all relationships.

Little pointed out that not only does the therapist hold up a "mirror" to the patient; the patient in turn holds one up to the therapist. In addition to his fantasies about the analyst, the patient often becomes aware of real feelings in the analyst even before the analyst himself is fully aware of them. She noted that "what comes [from the patient] may on occasion be a piece of real counter-transference interpretation for the analyst" (1951, p. 39).

Thus in her 1951 paper Little extended the Balints' suggestion (1939) as to the analyst's influence on the patient's transference and introduced a view that subsequently has been elaborated by Robert Langs, both in this volume (chapter 4) and elsewhere (1976). That view is that the patient is indeed exquisitely sensitive to, and influenced by, the therapist's unconscious countertransference as well as by his deliberate interventions. Harold Searles has also developed this theme throughout his writings (1958, 1978, and chapter 13).

Little also noted that the act of interpreting transference actually contains an implicit denial that the analyst is behaving as had the earlier parental figure.

In her 1957 paper, Little commented that the severely disturbed patient constantly tests the analyst to see whether he has sufficient ego strength to deal with his own instinct tensions. If this reveals that the analyst cannot successfully manage his own tensions, the patient will be shattered. This statement presaged Bion's view (1962, 1963, 1970) that the analyst must function as an active container and metabolizer of the patient's projective identifications and projected inner contents. This view has also influenced Kernberg (1965) and several of the writers in this volume, in particular, Issacharoff (chapter 1), Langs (chapter 4), Feiner (chapter 5), Grinberg (chapter 8), Fordham (chapter 9), McDougall (chapter 12), and Epstein (chapter 16).

In this paper, Little went even further in her recommendations for the communication of the therapist's countertransference reactions to severely disturbed patients. She wrote that the analyst must feel free to react, even primitively and spontaneously at times, since this type of patient needs to experience the analyst as one human being with whom it is possible to have genuine contact. It is essential therefore that this patient discover that the analyst can bear the patient's tensions as well as their discharge, and that there are some things that even the analyst cannot stand. A patient's paranoid anxiety, Little advised, can be relieved only in a direct way, through the experience of the analyst as a human, that is, a limited being. This point is further elaborated by Epstein (chapter 10). In this connection, Spotnitz (1969, 1976) and Searles (1958, 1978) have recommended that therapists selectively communicate feelings induced in them by schizophrenic and borderline patients.

D.W. Winnicott

Winnicott's pithy "Hate in the Countertransference" (1949) dealt with several core issues. He distinguished the idiosyncratic from the therapeutically useful in countertransference, classifying its phenomena as follows:

1. Abnormality in countertransference, and set relationships and identifications that are under repression in the analyst. . . . It is evident here, that the analyst needs more analysis. . . .
2. The identifications and tendencies belonging to an analyst's personal experiences and personal development which provide the positive setting for his analytic work and make his work different in quality from that of any other analyst.
3. . . . the truly objective countertransference, or . . . the analyst's love and hate in reaction to the actual personality and behavior of the patient based on objective observation. [p. 195]

Winnicott then suggested, anticipating Little (1951) —

that if an analyst is to analyze psychotics or antisocials he must be able to be so thoroughly aware of the countertransference that he can sort out and study his *objective* reactions to the patient. These will include hate. Countertransference phenomena will at times be the important things in the analysis. [p. 195]

"A main task of the analyst is to maintain objectivity," he stressed, adding that "a special case of this is to hate the patient objectively" (p. 196). He then went on to discuss how certain patients repeatedly arouse intense hate in the analyst and to indicate that for these patients the evocation of hatred in the other is part of a maturational process. As was characteristic of him, Winnicott made his point succinctly: "If the patient seeks objective or justified hate he must be able to reach it, else he cannot feel he can reach objective love" (p. 199).

We might summarize Winnicott's achievement in this essay as follows:

1. He went far beyond the traditional view of countertransference as hindrance, making an excellent case for its therapeutic usefulness.

2. He indicated that countertransference was useful as a source of information not only about the patient, but about the ongoing process of the analysis as well.

3. He emphasized that the analyst's intense countertransference feelings, when "objectively" evoked by the patient, may be needed as feedback, and that this need for feedback is nothing less than a maturational need.

4. He noted the analyst's need to detoxify intense countertransference feelings so as to be able to continue functioning constructively with his patient.

Winnicott's schema of the objective and subjective components of the countertransference is utilized in this volume by Spotnitz (chapter 14), Marshall (chapter 17) and Epstein (chapters 10, 16). An elaboration of the therapeutic usefulness of hate appears in chapter 16.

Heinrich Racker

Racker's papers concerning countertransference appeared in English-language psychoanalytic journals between 1953 and 1958 (the Spanish originals had begun to appear somewhat earlier), and were collected in his *Transference and Countertransference* (1968).* In these papers Racker attempted to penetrate the countertransference experience to its depths, illuminating its meanings in detailed patient-therapist transactions and formulating interpretations based on this understanding. He has delineated the normal predispositions shared by analysts, any of whom under certain conditions can find themselves in the emotional position of the child vis-à-vis the patient-parent. Racker termed this complex of predispositions and its manifestations the *countertransference neurosis,* implying that it is as natural and normal a development in the analyst in response to his patient as is the transference neurosis in

* For a complete review of Racker's work, from which some of this material was derived, see Hunt and Issacharoff (1977).

the patient. In this volume Issacharoff (chapter 1) and Feiner (chapter 5) develop this theme. In 1949, when Racker presented his paper on the countertransference neurosis, and for many years thereafter, the popularly accepted conception among classical analysts (e.g., A. Reich 1951, see below) was that the normal ego state of the analyst should be hovering, contemplative and emotionally neutral. The occurrence of strong emotions in response to a patient would be considered, according to this position, an aberration signifying a pathological problem within the analyst. Racker's notion of countertransference neurosis rejects this view. To him the countertransference neurosis is inevitable and, once understood and accepted as such, yields easily to self-analysis.

Even those instances in which the analyst finds himself in the child position can illuminate the patient's ongoing transference. Once the analyst has identified his own emotional state, he is able to consider the questions: Why have I fallen into this position now? What has this to do with the analytic process? What internal self and object relations might the patient be enacting with me? Do my feelings indicate that he needs my love, or that he wants to triumph over me? Is the patient from the position of his child-self relating to me as if I were his superego? Do my feelings indicate that he wants me to punish, or criticize, or demean him? Thus, to Racker, the totality of the therapist's countertransference, even though it may be dominated by idiosyncratic or even pathological components, is likely to yield significant information about the patient's immediate ego state.

Unfortunately Racker did not present his ideas as clearly as we have stated them here. He wrote in a Freudian-Kleinian meta-psychological framework that does not make for easy reading (see Hunt and Issacharoff 1977). We believe, however, that our translation of Racker's *experience-distant* terminology into *experience-near* language (Kohut 1978) accurately reflects his thought.

Racker's classification of countertransference reactions is systematic, precise, and, above all, clinically useful. He distinguishes between direct and indirect countertransference. Direct countertransference is a response to the patient. Indirect countertransference is a response to an emotionally significant other person outside the therapeutic setting. This might, for example, be anyone whose good opinion of the therapist's work with the patient the therapist might be concerned about. It might be someone in the professional community, a referral source, a supervisor, or a training committee at a psychoanalytic training institute. It could be anyone who knows the patient, colleague, relative, or friend.

Racker further differentiated direct countertransference into two processes: *concordant identifications* and *complementary identifications*. Concordant identifications are empathic responses to the patient's thoughts and feelings. In Racker's language they are identifications with the patient's ego or id. In the case of complementary identifications, the analyst finds himself in the emotional position of some projected (unwanted) part of the patient's self or superego. For example, the therapist might find himself in an adversary position vis-a-vis the patient. He might experience himself as persecuted by the patient or might even feel punitive, a reaction typical with violent-prone patients (King 1976). Racker uses Klein's theory of projective identification to account for complementary identifications in the therapist. Projective identification is an unconscious, primitive, aggressively self-preservative operation involving two stages, splitting and projection. In this way, according to the theory, the patient rids himself of either a toxic introject or some unwanted part of himself, and then identifies the therapist with the split-off aspect of his personality. The therapist may then experience these feelings and impulses toward the patient. He is likely also to feel pressured to engage in counterprojective processes toward the patient. If, for instance, the therapist is made to feel like a bad person, his normal inclination will be to see the patient as bad. Racker remarks that such reactions follow the *lex Talionis* ("eye for an eye, tooth for a tooth"). By restraining his own inclination to follow the Talionic principle, containing the patient's projected impulses and feelings, and then addressing these contents analytically, the therapist will be in a favorable position to understand the transference-countertransference matrix and formulate an interpretative intervention. Racker assumes the universality of the Talionic principle as well as of projective identification, thereby linking the unconscious processes in the patient with those in the therapist. As such they become fundamental to his understanding of countertransference processes and his conceptualization of countertransference theory. In this volume projective identification is used to account for a variety of countertransference phenomena in the papers by Issacharoff (chapter 1), Meltzer (chapter 6), Grinberg (chapter 8), McDougall (chapter 12), Boyer (chapter 15), and Epstein (chapter 16).

With numerous clinical vignettes Racker illustrates how the analyst's concordant and complementary identifications with the patient may be addressed as data providing important clues concerning the self-experience of the patient, and his experience of his internal and early objects. According to Racker, therefore, countertransference is the most reliable guide to knowing what, in the patient's communications or behavior, the analyst should respond to at any given moment. Even countertransference reactions of great intensity may serve as aids to understanding. While Little and Winnicott have underscored the inevitability of such intense reactions in response to disturbed patients and even recommended the selective communication of such reactions, it was Racker who first showed how these reactions may be used as tools to develop a more trenchant understanding of the patient. This view is radically at odds with the conventional orthodox emphasis on the therapist's intense emotional reactions as pathological, and has been developed by Kernberg (1965) with borderline patients, and by Searles (1979) and Spotnitz (1969, 1976) with both psychotic and borderline patients. It is the predominant view of most of the chapters in this volume.

A careful scrutiny of Racker's work reveals the caution in his recommendations concerning what the therapist should *do* with his countertransference reactions. He recommended that the analyst first develop an understanding of the patient's internal processes in the here and now, and that he then use the countertransference as an aid in formulating appropriate interpretations. Racker was cautious concerning the direct communication of countertransference reactions, but did not rule it out. He advised, however, that "we need extensive and detailed study of the inherent problems of communication of countertransference." Gitelson (1952) too, recommended communicating countertransference only when necessary to further the analysis.

We turn now to one classical position on countertransference, most eloquently represented by Annie Reich (1951), a position decidedly at odds with those we have discussed.

Reich (1951, 1960, 1966) sharply rejects the notion that countertransference can in any way be used as a therapeutic tool, either as data for understanding the patient or for communication. The second of her three papers on countertransference (1960), "Further Remarks on countertransference," is a strong polemic against the

position advanced by Heimann, Little, and Racker. Reich states that
to use the analyst's emotional responses and countertransference
manifestations to understand the patient is really "a substitute for
empathy." In her 1950 paper, Heimann had presented a clinical
example of how she came to understand her countertransference
reaction of worry and anxiety in response to a patient. Her eventual
formulation was that this was the counterpart of the patient's
sadistically tinged fantasies about the analyst, who was seen as a
defective object. To this Reich comments that —

> Something interfered with the process of immediate intuitive
> understanding. The analyst reacted to the patient's striving
> with an emotional response of her own. She did not just 'know'
> that the patient was involved in an acting out of his
> transference, since she failed to identify with him and to detach
> herself again from such trial identification. For this process she
> substituted a *retranslation* of her own feelings into those of the
> patient.

To Reich, then, Heimann is converting a fault into a virtue. She
does not, however, consider the possibility that Heimann's understanding of her countertransference might have enhanced the
therapeutic process.

Reich stands on firmer ground when she attacks Little's
recommendations for the free expression of countertransference
feelings with disturbed patients:

> But such therapeutic endeavors are not psychoanalysis, even
> though they may be based on the fundamental insights of
> analytic psychology.... Any differentiated subtle understand-
> ing of the interaction of the various psychic structures; any
> detailed careful analysis of defense; any effort to analyze ego
> pathology and correct it is left behind. Instead, there is an
> attempt to work directly with the id and to exert immediate
> influence upon the object relations. Such an approach
> disregards Freud's most important formulation concerning the
> therapeutic aim of analysis: "Where id was, there shall ego be."
> Therefore, no lasting effect can be expected from these
> methods. [pp. 393-394]

However, her argument is arbitrary and mechanistic, omitting any consideration of a possible integration of the two positions. In fact, Little carefully detailed the usefulness not only of the communication of countertransference reactions, but of interpretations as well, and stressed that countertransference revelation or the direct impact of the analyst's emotions can break "through the wall of resistance when interpretation is to no avail." Tauber (chapter 3) has elaborated this position.

While Reich writes of countertransference as a "prerequisite" of psychoanalysis, her attack on its therapeutic usefulness does not distinguish between countertransference as an inner experience, to be digested, scrutinized, clarified, understood, and subsequently harnessed for therapeutic understanding, and countertransference as directly, impulsively enacted or discharged. She rejects intense countertransference experience as ipso facto pathological. She states patently,

A neutralized cathexis of the patient is *never* relinquished. Thus, the analyst *never* loses sight of the patient as a separate being and at *no time* feels his own identity changes. This enables him to remain *uninvolved*. [p. 391, italics ours]

Thus, the analyst is simply not supposed to have intense emotional reactions to the patient, and, note, is supposed to remain *uninvolved*. This disregards Freud's recognition that the analyst has feelings toward his patients and conflicts aroused by them (Sandler et al. 1973). Though respectful of Heimann's "honesty" about countertransference, Reich acerbically comments that countertransference "as such is not helpful." She then remarks, "But the readiness to acknowledge its existence and the ability to overcome it is."

Reich firmly rejects Racker's conjecture that the countertransference is dominated by the *lex Talionis*, as well as the idea that typical countertransference reactions may arise in response to a patient's covert processes. She states that "all such notions about a typical content of countertransference represent schematizations and a narrowing down of the beautiful variety of psychic functioning." The usefulness of what Reich calls "free countertransference," as a tool for understanding the patient is arbitrarily dismissed.

Reich's arguments are not based on empirical considerations, nor does she recommend any further scientific study of countertransference for its potential therapeutic uses. We do not believe that Reich's views are currently shared by the majority of classical analysts. Those who hold that strong emotional reactions are necessarily due to empathic failures based on the therapist's psychopathology are far fewer now than they were in 1960. The view that countertransference reactions can be useful for understanding the patient seems to be gaining acceptance, especially in working with psychotic and borderline patients, among analysts of various orientations. In this volume Tauber (chapter 3) considers the classical "anti-countertransference" position to be an unconscious countertransference reaction. It is also true that techniques involving the direct communication of countertransference reactions continue to be widely rejected or are, at best, viewed with considerable scepticism (Langs 1976).

During the last few years, interest in countertransference as a valuable component in psychoanalysis and psychoanalytic psychotherapy has increased markedly among the various psychoanalytic schools. Professional journals abound with papers on the subject. Definitions, however, still vary, with at least three conceptions currently in use: (1) the *totalistic conception*, in which *all* feelings and attitudes of the therapist toward the patient are considered countertransference; (2) the *classical conception*, in which countertransference is viewed as the unconscious resistive reaction of the analyst to the transference of the patient, or parts of the patient, and as containing both neurotic and nonneurotic elements; and (3) the view of countertransference as the natural, role-responsive, necessary *complement or counterpart* to the transference of the patient, or to his style of relatedness.

We can, moreover identify four working orientations to countertransference, that is, the way in which countertransference is actually used by different therapists:

1. Countertransference is attended to when "difficulties arise," when the therapist experiences emotional disturbances, or disturbances of attention or concentration. Such interferences are then subjected to self-analysis.

2. Interferences in the analyst's efforts caused by disturbances in the analyst's emotional state are studied primarily in order to gain an understanding of the patient's contribution.

3. The totality of the countertransference is used as essential data for understanding the patient in the here and now. Accordingly, the

countertransference is frequently considered when formulating interventions and strategies. Interventions may be restricted to interpretations; countertransference fantasies may be directly communicated to the patient; or induced countertransference feelings may be communicated "as needed" by the patient. This orientation usually includes the view that the therapist's internal silent processing of countertransferential disturbances is essential to the further integration of the patient. This is seen as especially important with the more disturbed patient.

4. Countertransference inevitably infiltrates the patient's unconscious processes. Such infiltrations must be constantly monitored by studying the patient's associations and responses, and subsequently interpreted.

Considering the career of countertransference within psychoanalytic history, we note two nodal points: the flurry of interest surfacing in the late forties and early fifties, and now its resurgence in the seventies. The question naturally occurs to us, Why the long and almost unbroken history of resistance among psychoanalysts to the study of countertransference? Although Freud initially treated transference as an obstacle to treatment and then shifted his view to involve it as a useful tool in the psychoanalytic effort, he never traced a similar path with countertransference. Bird (1972) reminds us that Freud considered transference "a mental structure of the greatest magnitude" (p. 274). In "An Autobiographical Study" (1925), Freud wrote that transference "is a universal phenomenon of the human mind ... and in fact dominates the whole of each person's relations to his human environment" (p. 42). But, Bird writes sadly, Freud never followed this idea up, an idea he had in fact introduced as early as his postscript to the case of Dora (1905). Bird points out that Freud, in his "Analysis Terminable and Interminable" (1937), "an otherwise masterful discussion of difficulties contributed by the individuality of the analyst, ... fails almost completely to direct these difficulties to their most obvious source, the countertransference" (p. 275). For thirty years Freud toyed with but never thoroughly worked through his own conception of transference-countertransference phenomena. Yet despite his never changing his mind about countertransference being a hindrance, requiring mastery through analysis on the part of the analyst, he did, as we have remarked, offer at various times those subtle and exciting suggestions concerning the value of the analyst's unconscious processes to analytic work. Hence his statement that the analyst —

> must turn his own unconscious like a receptive organ towards
> the transmitting unconscious of the patient. He must adjust
> himself to the patient as a telephone receiver is adjusted to the
> transmitting microphone. Just as the receiver converts back
> into sound waves the electric oscillations ..., so the doctor's
> unconscious is able, from the derivatives of the unconscious
> which are communicated to him, to reconstruct that uncon-
> scious, which has determined the patient's free associations.
> [Freud 1912, pp. 115-116]

And again:

> everyone possesses in his own unconscious an instrument with
> which he can interpret the utterances of the unconscious in
> other people. [Freud 1913, p. 320]

These are typical of the way Freud hinted at what might be a
fruitful area for discovery. And so again we must ask why, from 1912
to 1950, interest in these kinds of complex processes lagged, and
why it took another twenty years to resurface. Racker (1953)
provides some insight here.

> The lack of scientific investigation of countertransference
> must be due to rejection by analysts of their own countertrans-
> ferences — a rejection that represents unresolved struggles
> with their own primitive anxiety and guilt. These struggles are
> closely connected with those infantile ideals that survive
> because of deficiencies in the personal analysis of just those
> transference problems that later affect the analyst's counter-
> transference. These deficiencies in the training analysis are in
> turn partly due to countertransference problems insufficiently
> solved in the training analyst.... Thus we are in a vicious circle
> but we can see where a breach must be made. We must begin
> by revision of our feelings about our own countertransference
> and try to overcome our own infantile ideals more thoroughly,
> accepting more fully the fact that we are still children and
> neurotics even when we are adults and analysts. Only in this
> way — by better overcoming our rejection of countertrans-
> ference — can we achieve the same result in candidates.

The insufficient dissolution of these idealizations and underlying anxieties and guilt-feelings leads to special difficulties when the child becomes an adult and the analysand an analyst, for the analyst unconsciously requires of himself that he be fully identified with these ideals. I think that it is at least partly for this reason that the Oepidus complex of the child toward his parents, and of the patient toward his analyst, has been so much more fully considered than that of the parents towards their children and of the analyst towards the analysand. For the same basic reason transference has been dealt with much more than countertransference.... [pp. 130-133]

It might well be that Racker's analysis of the unconscious resistance to an evolving understanding of countertransference data is more generally applicable to classical analysts than to analysts of less orthodox schools. Harry Stack Sullivan and Erich Fromm, two of the founders of the William Alanson White Institute, stressed as early as the late thirties and early forties the limits and fallibility of the analyst in his participation with his patient. What is important to grasp is that the much-criticized "egalitarian" attitudes of the neo-Freudians, the "democratizing" of the analytic situation by members of the interpersonal and other less orthodox schools, did not have their origins simply in the ideologies and value systems of theoreticians. The "political" overtones — what has been characterized as typically American antiauthoritarian attitudes in the consulting room — were actually less relevant than the epistemological ones.

When Sullivan (1953) introduced the concept of participant observation in the late 1930s, he was already paying homage to the influences of other scientific disciplines on his thinking. Einstein's notion of the significance of the position of the observer (that it influences the nature of the data), Heisenberg's principle of indeterminacy (the act of observation influences the data), and the operationalism of American pragmatism — to all of which Sullivan had been exposed — funneled into his one-genus hypothesis, that is, that we are all more simply human than otherwise. The impinging demands of his therapeutic work with schizophrenics was still another important factor. Sullivan, together with Fromm-Reichmann (1950), "humanized" the therapist. That is, they pointed to the significance of the analyst as a real object. They rejected the

orthodox "mirror" concept as the analyst's only function, not
because it was based on an inadequate theory of technique but
because they believed that the opacity of the mirror-analyst and the
separation of the patient's affectivity from the analyst's were
impossible to maintain in light of the recognition of a field of forces
in the consulting room. The idea was also advanced that awareness
and confrontation of the myth of the analyst's anonymity actually
furthered the work (Fromm-Reichmann 1950, Cohen 1952).

Accordingly, Fromm (1947), for whom the analyst was a "rational
authority," rejected the idea that anyone, simply by virtue of being
an analyst and having undergone a training analysis, is the possessor
of superior mental health. Freud had touched on this in his "Analysis
Terminable and Interminable" (1937, p. 247). In supervision and in
seminars Fromm repeatedly stressed that the temptation to believe
the fiction of the analyst's superiority could only lead the analyst into
the major pitfall of the profession, that is, unconscious despair.
Fromm believed that psychoanalysts must face endlessly in
themselves the same regressive forces others are heir to, and he
therefore advised that analysts engage in lifelong self-analysis. This
was the same advice that Freud offered in 1910 (and later in 1937),
but Fromm went beyond the need to gain mastery over "complexes,"
or the "abrasiveness" of the de-repressed. He was concerned lest
those forces insidiously erode an analyst's potential for growing and
living fully.

Candidates in training, at the William Alanson White Institute and
elsewhere, have traditionally been encouraged to scrutinize and
discuss openly their countertransference reactions in seminars and
in supervision. This kind of openness to countertransference
perhaps approaches the monitoring function originally recommended by Freud (1910). But this reasonable concern with the
protection of the patient from the potentially damaging effects of
the analyst's inner processes and their products, a concern shared by
all serious analysts, lends itself, unfortunately, to restricting the aim
of studying countertransference to a simple uncovering of the
analyst's residual pathology. We view this tendency as the "rational
factor" which has impeded research into the data of countertransference. It has been extremely difficult to make the shift from
regarding the analyst's emotional or affective reactions as errors
from which the patient naturally needs to be protected, to regarding
these responses as significant data with a potential for illuminating

the therapeutic situation. And Freud's ambivalence on this point certainly did not help.

Some of the factors that have reawakened the profession's interest following the period of dormancy from the 1950s to the 1970s have been neatly and tersely commented on by Witenberg (chapter 2). He writes: "As one views society as a whole, one sees increasing openness and candor in all sectors.... a diminution in the power of authority — whether it be religious or secular.... The breakdown of institutions such as the family ... has been accompanied by a spate of literature that analyzes authority roles." And he further credits the "growing maturity of psychoanalysis" as well as "the widespread acceptance in the field of the fact that each of us can potentially be the other."

What impresses us here is Witenberg's easy, relaxed use of the phrase "the growing maturity of psychoanalysis." For it was not too long ago that the death knell was being tolled for psychoanalysis. Long considered inadequate for schizophrenics and other patients with primitively, poorly organized personality structures (such as the borderline and the narcissistic character disorders), psychoanalysis (including psychoanalytic psychotherapy) has had to struggle just to maintain its position as treatment of choice for the neuroses and the more moderate character disabilities. Its protracted and sometimes virtually interminable treatment situations, with sometimes limited but costly results, had occasioned disillusionment and cynicism among therapists and patients alike. Young therapists and their patients were increasingly attracted to the human potential movement and to the more abreactive forms of therapy encouraged by the movement's popularity. These therapists provoked an intensity of affective experience and held out the promise of quick and easy cure. As Freud (1910) had noted in another context, such hopes and promises of quick and lasting results were bound to be disappointed. Despite the growth during the sixties and seventies of these alternative forms of treatment, many younger therapists are turning again to the hard work of psychoanalysis and psychoanalytic psychotherapy for training, and many patients are returning for treatment. In addition, psychoanalysis and psychoanalytic psychotherapy have been emerging more and more strongly as the treatment of choice for those very patients for whom it was so long considered ineffectual, that is, patients with poorly organized personality structures. What strikes us here as significant and germane is that almost everything written about the treatment of such patients includes a great deal on or relating to the subject of countertransference (Giovacchini, chapter 10).

This is hardly surprising. Throughout the history of psychoanalysis analysts have addressed themselves to the question of what is curative in the process. Friedman (1978) has delineated the continuing development of the analytic theory of treatment and the analytic concept of curative factors. The two milestones of this history, according to Friedman, are the Marienbad Conference of 1936 and the Edinburgh Conference of 1961. Both meetings focused on elucidating the curative factors, which were assumed to be (1) *introjection*, which is concerned with the taking in from the analyst and the analytic process the necessary healthy replacements for old and now unhealthy aspects of experience; (2) *attachment*, which refers to the quality of the analytic relationship, the medium in which introjection and all other analytic procedures take place; and (3) *insight* via interpretation, by which unconscious processes are made conscious so that mastery over them can be achieved. Interest in countertransference is kindled whenever analysts turn their attention to the relationship between themselves and their patients and begin to notice what the patient takes in. With the new emphasis on fields of forces, interpretation taken alone, which betrays a dichotomous subject-object conception, is devalued. This is not to demean the importance of interpretation and interpretative intervention, but as analysts turn to the question of *what* is being interpreted, under what *conditions*, and by *whom* and *how* it is being received, the issue of countertransference comes to the forefront. Not simply a misplaced "empathy" or "trial identification," as Reich (1966) would have it, countertransference plays the same role in the attachment of analyst to patient as transference does in the attachment of patient to analyst. Fulfillment of the promise implicit in Freud's Dora postscript (1905) requires that countertransference be studied scientifically, as the effective ally in the analytic process it can become when recognized for what it is. And so the double helix of Freud's views — countertransference as hindrance and as therapeutic instrument — forces itself upon us today more insistently than ever.

In general we seem to have become more receptive to the idea that in relation to our patients we are more similar than different in kind (Sullivan 1953). We have also been made aware of the fact that our more intense countertransference reactions are usually generated by the more severely distrubed type of patient. Thus, countertransference is now seen as a normal, natural interpersonal event, rather than as an idiosyncratic pathological phenomenon. This has facilitated the shift from viewing countertransference reactions solely as a hindrance, to viewing them for their potential value in understanding the patient and the therapeutic relationship, and in formulating interventions which deepen and intensify the psychoanalytic process.

The question of what is most useful about countertransference seems to us to pose one of the more interesting challenges in psychoanalysis today (Sandler 1976; Moeller 1977; Feiner, chapter 5). As a radical and refreshing change of orientation in the performance of our task, it stimulates us intellectually as well as technically. The implications are far-reaching. Today's emphasis has shifted from the therapist's suppression of self in the clinical situation to his viewing himself as a genuine coparticipant in an ongoing process. This enables us to be more vivacious and less elitist in our work with our patients and furthermore promises better therapeutic results, all of which makes our work not only more exciting, but more exacting and gratifying as well (Wolstein 1959, 1973).

The authors collected here portray the full scope and depth of contemporary psychoanalytic thinking on the subject of counter-transference. While it is evident that each develops his discussion according to his own particular theoretical persuasion, taken as a whole the chapters are marked less by theoretical differences than by common evolutionary trends. Despite the history of internecine warfare among the various schools, psychoanalysts by and large seem to be arriving at a consensus regarding their own contribution in the consulting room.

We see, for instance, an increasing convergence and integration of the intrapsychic and interpersonal field orientations, points of view which were, some years back, evidently polarized. Freud alluded to such an integration in 1912, but only today are the internal processes of patient and analyst being examined for the impact each has on the other. The chapters that follow examine the various aspects of countertransference and develop the role these have come to play in each author's current work with patients. To this end the volume is replete with clinical examples. Among the themes and issues addressed are the following:

1. How to differentiate those components of the patient's reactions resulting from the impact of the analyst's unconscious countertransference; and how to recognize those conditions under which infiltrations may likely occur.

2. How to differentiate components of the countertransference which derive directly from the patient's contribution from those which emerge from the idiosyncratic and/or pathological features of the analyst.

3. Theories of the role that ego-splitting and unconscious projective and introjective processes play in transference and countertransference reactions.

4. The therapeutic functions of the analyst as "container" (not "receptacle") of the patient's projections, and of the analyst's resistances to the patient's unconscious efforts to nullify the bipersonal situation by means of penetration, fusion, incorporation, or modification of the field.

5. The therapeutic function of the patient as "container" of the analyst's unconscious countertransference projections.

6. Countertransference data as the basis for understanding the patient's unconscious communication of impulses, affects, fantasies, and conflicts.

7. Countertransference data as the key to understanding ongoing resistances and split self, split-object relationships.

8. The phenomenology, theory, and management of the average, expectable variations in countertransference reactions, including those disturbances in attention and concentration which may be generated by different personality organizations of the patient, specifically the borderline, narcissistic, and psychotic states and organizations, and the structural neuroses.

9. The integration of countertransference data in the formulation of interventions and strategies, for example, interpretation, confrontation, interpersonal transactions, joining techniques, the

judicious sharing of countertransference reactions, emotional communications, and so on.

We assume that this volume is not the last statement in this area. In fact, we hope it serves as a stimulus to further research. If the perceptive work collected here makes the impact we intend, we trust others will be encouraged to write about countertransference with even greater precision and in a way that will broaden our understanding.

REFERENCES

Balint, A., and Balint, M. (1939). On transference and countertransference. *International Journal of Psycho-Analysis* 20:223-230.

Bion, W. (1962). *Learning from Experience.* New York: Basic Books. Reprinted in *Seven Servants.* New York: Jason Aronson, 1977.

_____(1963). *Elements of Psychoanalysis.* New York: Basic Books. Reprinted in *Seven Servants.* New York: Jason Aronson, 1977.

_____(1970). *Attention and Interpretation.* London: Tavistock. Reprinted in *Seven Servants.* New York: Jason Aronson, 1977.

Bird, B. (1972). Notes on transference: universal phenomenon and hardest part of analysis. *Journal of the American Psychoanalytic Association* 20:267-301.

Cohen, M. B. (1952). Countertransference and anxiety. *Psychiatry* 15:231-243.

Freud, S. (1905). Fragment of an analysis of a case of hysteria. *Standard Edition* 7:3-122.

_____(1910). The future prospects of psycho-analytic therapy. *Standard Edition* 11:139-152.

_____(1912). Recommendations for physicians practising psychoanalysis. *Standard Edition* 12:109-120.

_____(1913). The disposition to obsessional neurosis. *Standard Edition* 12:313-326.

_____(1925). An autobiographical study. *Standard Edition* 20:3-74.

_____(1937). Analysis terminable and interminable. *Standard Edition* 23:209-253.

Friedman, L. (1978). Trends in the psychoanalytic theory of treatment. *Psychoanalytic Quarterly* 47:524-567.

Fromm, E. (1947). *Man For Himself.* New York: Holt, Rinehart and Winston.

Fromm-Reichmann, F. (1950). *Principles of Intensive Psycho-therapy*. Chicago: University of Chicago Press.

Gitelson, M. (1952). The emotional position of the analyst in the psycho-analytic situation. *International Journal of Psycho-Analysis* 33:1-10.

Heimann, P. (1950). On countertransference. *International Journal of Psycho-Analysis* 31:81-84.

Horney, K. (1939). *New Ways in Psychoanalysis*. New York: W. W. Norton.

Hunt, W., and Issacharoff, A. (1977). Heinrich Racker and Counter-transference theory. *Journal of The American Academy of Psychoanalysis* 5:95-105.

Kernberg, O. (1965). Notes on countertransference. *Journal of the American Psychoanalytic Association* 13:38-56.

King, C. (1976). Counter-transference and counter-experience in the treatment of violence prone youth. *American Journal of Orthopsychiatry* 46:43-52.

Kohut, H. (1978). *The Restoration of the Self*. New York: International Universities Press.

Langs, R. (1976). *The Therapeutic Interaction*, Volume 2. New York: Jason Aronson.

Little, M. (1951). Countertransference and the patient's response to it. *International Journal of Psycho-Analysis* 32:32-40.

_____(1957). 'R' — The analyst's response to his patient's needs. *International Journal of Psycho-Analysis* 38:240-254.

Moeller, M. L. (1977). Self and object in countertransference. *International Journal of Psycho-Analysis* 58:365-374.

Racker, H. (1953). The countertransference neurosis. *International Journal of Psycho-Analysis* 34:313-324. Reprinted in *Transference and Countertransference*. New York: International Universities Press, 1968.

_____(1957). The meanings and uses of countertransference. *Psychoanalytic Quarterly* 26:303-357. Reprinted in *Transference and Countertransference*. New York: International Universities Press, 1968.

_____(1968). *Transference and Countertransference*. New York: International Universities Press.

Reich, A. (1951). On countertransference. *International Journal of Psycho-Analysis* 32:25-31.

_____(1960). Further Remarks on countertransference. *International Journal of Psycho-Analysis* 41:389-395.

Part I

THE CONCEPT
OF COUNTERTRANSFERENCE

Reich, A. (1966). Empathy and countertransference. In Reich, *Psychoanalytic Contributions*, pp. 344-360. New York: International Universities Press. 1973.

Sandler, J. (1976). Countertransference and role-responsiveness. *International Review of Psycho-Analysis* 3:43-47.

Sandler, J., Dare, C., and Holder, A. (1973). *The Patient and the Analyst*. New York: International Universities Press.

Searles, H. (1958). The schizophrenic's vulnerability to the therapist's unconscious processes. *Journal of Nervous and Mental Disease*. 127:247-262.

———(1978). Psychoanalytic therapy with the borderline adult. In *New Perspectives on Psychotherapy with the Borderline Adult*, ed. J. Masterson. New York: Brunner/Mazel.

Sharpe, E. (1947). The psychoanalyst. *International Journal of Psycho-Analysis*. 28:1-60.

Spotnitz, H. (1969). *Modern Psychoanalysis of the Schizophrenic Patient*. New York: Grune and Stratton.

———(1976). *Psychotherapy of Preoedipal Conditions*. New York: Jason Aronson.

Sullivan, H. S. (1953). *The Interpersonal Theory of Psychiatry*. New York: W. W. Norton.

Tauber, E. (1954). Exploring the therapeutic use of countertransference data. *Psychiatry* 17:331-336.

Thompson, C., Crowley, R., and Tauber, E. (1952). Symposium on countertransference. *Samiksa* 6:205-228.

Winnicott, D. (1949). Hate in the countertransference. *Through Paediatrics to Psycho-Analysis*, pp. 194-203. New York: Basic Books, 1958. Reprinted from *International Journal of Psycho-Analysis* 30:69-75.

Wolstein, B. (1959). *Countertransference*. New York: Grune & Stratton.

———(1973). The new significance of psychoanalytic structure. In *Interpersonal Explorations in Psychoanalysis*, ed. E.G. Witenberg. New York: Basic Books.

Chapter 1

BARRIERS TO KNOWING

AMNON ISSACHAROFF, M.D.

I have been reading and thinking about the use of the self in the treatment situation for some time now.[1] The question I want to address myself to has, I believe, important implications for the theory of technique in psychoanalysis. One way I can formulate this question is: *What processes can give us the feeling that we know something about the patient and about ourselves?*

I will first present a brief historical view of a body of writing dealing with the therapist's emotional reactions towards the patient. I will then address myself to the question I have posed, particularly as it affects the gathering of knowledge in the analytic process, approaching it from three points of view. First, I will present my view of countertransference and its use in treatment. Here the focus will be on the therapist's attitude toward his own feelings. Secondly, I will deal with the technical issue relating to anonymity and neutrality in structuring the analytic process, and their importance in facilitating analytic objectivity. It is my contention that without that structuring and objectivity, the indiscriminate use of countertransference material becomes reminiscent of the dangers of "wild analysis." Finally, I will discuss greed. Greed is a feeling with which

1. This is a slightly edited version of the Presidential address, presented to the William Alanson White Psychoanalytic Society May 19, 1976.

I want to thank Dr. L. Epstein for his help in clarifying my thinking in this paper.

we are all more or less familiar, and one which tends to be repressed because it is unacceptable in our culture. It will serve as an example of an emotional reaction that, when unconscious or repressed, may spark defenses which may interfere with the normal need to know in the analytic process.

GROWING INTEREST IN COUNTERTRANSFERENCE

Although Freud defined the term countertransference in 1910, his writings contain only two explicit references to it, and subsequently there was very little research done in this area for the next forty years.

Freud's first reference (1910), consisted of a single paragraph, stating that the analyst is limited by his own neurotic conflicts, and advising continuous self-analysis. The other, more extended discussion (Freud 1915) deals with the temptation a male analyst might feel in response to the erotic transference of a female patient. In this paper, the analyst's feelings are seen as normal and treated sympathetically, with no implication that neurosis in the analyst is involved.

Freud's comments on the analyst's feelings toward his patient were not as incisive as his observations on the transference phenomenon. It almost seems as if he shied away from public comments on this matter. After all, psychoanalysis was not part of the "establishment" at that time. It was still sensitive and highly vulnerable to its numerous detractors.

When, in 1937, Freud advised that analysts return periodically to analysis themselves, his stated reason was the unavoidable effects of transference on treatment. Here Freud seems to use the term transference as a two-pronged phenomenon, emanating simultaneously from the patient and the analyst in a pervasive and continuous fashion.

After this, until Heinrich Racker's first paper in 1948, countertransference was treated rather dismissively as a problem arising from the analyst's conflicts. Appropriately enough, H. S. Sullivan, in developing the theoretical basis of the interpersonal approach to psychiatry, represented the most important exception during those forty years. That trend was described by Frieda Fromm-Reichman in 1950:

Recently the significant vicissitudes of the psychiatrist's relationship to his patients has been brought increasingly into the focus of the therapeutic attention... H. S. Sullivan has introduced the term "parataxis" instead of "transference" and "countertransference."

She further stated that

The psychiatrist who is trained in the observation and inner realization of his reactions to the patient's manifestations can frequently utilize these reactions as a helpful instrument in understanding otherwise hidden implications in the patient's communications. Thus, the therapist's share in the reciprocal transference reactions of a doctor and patient in the wide sense of the term may furnish an important guide in the conduction of the psychotherapeutic process [pp. 5-6].

Here Frieda Fromm-Reichman expressed what I think is the prevalent modern view of countertransference. Some authors call this the "totalist" approach, contrasting it to the more classical position. The latter defines countertransference as a hindrance emanating from unconscious unresolved conflicts in the analyst. The "totalists" view countertransference as a continuous phenomenon in which a great many, though not all, of the therapist's reactions are in response to the actual situation as well as to the patient's transference. In the totalists' view, these responses can be useful in understanding the patient and the interpersonal situation.

Around 1950, there was suddenly an explosion of an idea. It was not a new idea, but it emerged with great vigor in different parts of the world, reminding one of Unamuno's (1895) concept of "intrahistory." Unamuno compared humanity to an ocean where waves emerge at different points simultaneously and swell the entire surface, an idea that is basically an extension of the idea of the collective unconscious. Around 1950, waves of the idea of countertransference rose in Argentina with Racker (1948), in England with Winnicott (1949) and P. Heimann (1950), and in the United States with Fromm-Reichman (1950), Karen Horney (1939), and Clara Thompson (1952).

In 1952 Thompson, Crowley, and Tauber published their "Symposium in Countertransference." Tauber, in 1954, explored the use of the analyst's dreams to clear the "parataxic field." This daring way of entering the interlocking system of transference counter-transference distortions represented what Thompson, in her introductory comments to Wolstein's book on *Transference* (1964), defined as the democratization of analysis and the increasing interest in the role of countertransference in therapy.

This is the main thrust of Wolstein's (1964) subsequent develop-ment of the interactional essence of the parataxic field. And fifteen years ago, in 1961, another presidential address was dedicated to this topic, countertransference. Zaphiropoulos' (1961) description of tender hearts and martinets, reflecting stereotyped personality and theoretical orientations, remains a valid observation today.

THE ANALYST'S LIVING RESPONSE

Like the patient, with his basic and profound resistance to becoming an observer of his own transference distortions, we analysts require a constant reawakening of interest in observing our own countertransference and in studying its implications in training, research, and therapy. Furthermore, countertransference is our most precise and reliable guide to knowing what in the patient's communication and behavior we should respond to at the moment.

There is no "normal" emotional state for the therapist. Indeed, as Racker (1968) emphasized, his inner state is continuously and profoundly responsive to the patient and to what the patient is saying and doing. Racker observed specific correlations between transference and countertransference, and emphasized the power of countertransference either to impede the analytic task or to facilitate the understanding of important aspects of the inter-personal neurosis (*la neurose-a-deux*) that often emerges in the analytic situation (although, one hopes, with different intensities in the two participants).

Racker's work not only described the therapist's responses as natural and even inevitable; it also emphasized the importance of the analyst's emotional reaction to the analytic situation as a measure of the reality of both participants' interpersonal and intrapersonal situation.

Countertransference is the living response to the patient's emotional situation at a given moment. And some analysts, like Searles, even believe that it may be therapeutic to communicate these living responses, feelings, or fantasies to the patient spontaneously. I, on the contrary, do not consider that desirable. I believe that the analyst, by first being aware of his responses, should control his behavior, and delay what he chooses to communicate until he can intervene from a position of understanding.

Analytic understanding presupposes objectivity. Objectivity can only be achieved by the self-analysis of the countertransference and by the preservation of anonymity and neutrality. These are essential characteristics in the role of the analyst.

It is a commonly held technical assumption that the analyst fosters transferential attitudes by preserving a mantle of anonymity. Therefore, he does not reveal his opinions about extra-analytic matters or facts about his past or present. We remember Freud's definition of the analyst as a blank screen to gather the transference. And without carrying this injunction to an extreme, most present-day analysts do continue to manipulate, in more or less subtle ways, this secretiveness about their social personae. By removing the cover of opinions, biographical events and accidents that give coloring to our person, we allow the patient to compare, on different levels of consciousness, his past experiences with the analytic relationship. We also know that how much the analyst reveals about himself is not as important as how he responds to his patient's curiosity, dependency needs, separation reactions, and acting out. These responses allow the patient to develop, early in the treatment, a fairly good idea of how the analyst responds in ordinary human situations.

This knowledge may be partial because the analyst, by maintaining the role of biographical anonymity, tries to screen out of the relationship that part of his personality that is not compatible with his values as an analyst. There may also be many other facets of the analyst's personality which are irrelevant to the relationship to the patient — they just don't enter into it.

I have tried up to this point to express the reasons for my agreement with the increasing number of analysts of all persuasions who see countertransference as a useful instrument in analysis. Now I will speculate on how neutrality of affect and anonymity on the part of the analyst may contribute to a fuller expression of the epistemophilic impulse (the impulse to seek knowledge and to explore the world around oneself).

THE ROLE OF ANONYMITY AND NEUTRALITY

Both transference and countertransference, that is, the parataxic field, make of the analytic process an obstacle course. I believe that the analyst may facilitate the pursuit of knowledge by remaining neutral and anonymous.

In fact, I believe that without the preservation of anonymity and neutrality in the analyst, it is impossible to conduct an analysis. If the analyst loses his neutrality, and therefore his anonymity, what transpires between him and the patient is not a psychoanalytic inquiry. For example, if the analyst, through the intricate network of the parataxic field, comes to feel strong like or dislike for some solution in living that the patient has come to accept as natural for him, he may express his reaction. His patient realizes that his analyst has a strong bias for or against him. The analyst cannot remain anonymous under those circumstances.

Perhaps I should make it clear here that anonymity and neutrality are useful only as tools to explore the psychic reality of the patient. They do not preclude the multiple ways in which the analyst validates the patient's ordinary business of being a member of our society.

If the therapist's bias arises from countertransferential responses, and if the reasons for that bias remain disassociated, then the analyst's response to his patient ceases to be neutral. By that I mean simply that any comment or interpretation made under the influence of an unanalyzed bias is necessarily one-sided. It will interfere with an exploration of the full picture with the patient.

I hope I do not seem to be arguing for neutrality of affect or neutrality in regard to value judgments. I am arguing for the neutrality that is a process of ego control. Reacting in a disassociated way, without an observing ego, eliminates distance, and distance is necessary for psychological awareness. When the analyst preserves his neutrality and refrains from identifying with any particular aspect of the patient he can maintain his objectivity, and react if and when he chooses.

If the analyst becomes a capricious adversary or ally, the patient cannot examine and recognize the conflictual aspects of his ambivalence. For this is one of the principal axioms of the analyst's activity: to allow his patient to recover parts of himself that, in the parataxic field, were projected and deposited on the analyst. These projected parts may be some disassociated and rejected aspect of the self that is then incarnated outside, or a narcissistic reflection of a highly valued aspect of the self. The interpretive activity of the analyst allows the patient to recover and tolerate his ambivalence about what he considers good and bad about himself. And the analyst, by detoxifying himself of the patient's projections, can retain his role, including his capacity to remain anonymous and neutral.

PROJECTIVE IDENTIFICATION

It is evident from the foregoing that I believe that the concept of projective identification as a mechanism makes a substantial contribution to the interplay between transference and counter-transference. Basically, this mechanism consists of an empathic recognition of some aspect of the self in another person. Some say that it is more than a recognition, it is a transposition. However, there is another step. This recognition becomes an attribution. The other person becomes the sole proprietor of that familiar aspect and, because of it, a person of particular significance. The interpersonal situation that this mechanism creates is the self, minus one particular attribute, and a significant other, plus that attribute. The economy of this interchange defines the setting of a parataxic mode of experience.

A striking result of this phenomenon is that where one person attributes to another certain characteristics, the other may respond as though he has them. Sometimes the recipient of the projections, the analyst, may actually have those traits. At other times a potential may be activated by a continuous and powerful transferential stimulation. When that situation becomes fixated over a period of time, we have the basic ingredient for the development of transference neurosis and, at times, its counterpart, countertransference neurosis.

When this occurs, the parataxis is mutual. And in the field thus created, the analyst reciprocates the projection to balance the economy of the interchange.

When the particular aspect of the self that the patient projects into the analyst has the characteristic of a parental object, the analytic situation may resemble, transferentially, the early parent-child relationship. However, the situation becomes more complex when the projected aspect is a unit of experience of the patient as a child.

In this transferential situation an aspect of the early parent-child relationship may be reenacted, but in reverse. That is, the patient may retain the internal parental object and relive its particular attributes in the context of congruent character defenses. He then projects onto the analyst the corresponding child aspect. This peculiar transposition may evoke powerful childlike feelings in the analyst, which are not compatible with his values as an analyst. The complexity of these subtle manipulations in which two unconscious constellations encounter each other and interchange objects by means of projection and introjection can be described in different theoretical systems and languages. The axis transference counter-transference emphasizes the system as a whole where changes in both poles of the dyad are the therapeutic aim.

The basic instrument of this change is analytic neutrality, which I will define as the continuous attempt on the part of the analyst to identify the mechanisms of projection and splitting that the patient uses to solve the conflicts in his internal world. To be successful in this complex task, the analyst must wage a continuous battle on two fronts. He must recognize the projected parts with which the patient identifies him (projective identification). And he must identify within himself the parts of the patient that he has incorporated and even, perhaps, enacted (introjective identification).

These elusive terms, projective identification and introjective identification, are not readily incorporated in our lexicon. Levenson (1972) called them "too alien and mystical," although he described in quite familiar terms the process enacted by these mechanisms when he observed that:

> the relationship between the patient and therapist in any given session is a homologue of the context of the session. If they talk about the patient's problem with his mother, they will enact between them some of the very problems under discussion. Knowing the content of a session, one could predict the direction and outcomes of the transferential exchange.

And, I would add, the countertransferential exchange.

Let me give you a brief example of how these two basic mechanisms (projective identification and introjective identification) influenced a transaction where transference and countertransference were the predominant issue. In this case, my affective participation created a situation typical of a lack of neutrality. This incident occurred in the treatment of a borderline patient who uses an inordinate amount of projective identification in all his significant interpersonal relationships. During the previous few weeks the atmosphere during the sessions had been marked by some joviality, storytelling, and a reluctance (shared by both participants) to dwell on "deep" matters. My rationale as an analyst was that by maintaining a benign atmosphere, I could alleviate the toxicity of his highly persecutory internal objects. But my lulled analytic sense was rudely awakened by his announcement that, due to financial considerations, he would have to stop treatment at the end of the month.

I reacted to his curt dismissal with anger and told him he was treating me with contempt. He rejected this accusation indignantly, and asked me if I needed his money to survive.

This patient had inherited a very sizable fortune and was not engaged in a gainful occupation, although he pursued his highly developed intellectual interests. He was a Ph.D. engaged in research but his activities were not considered serious enough by a close relative, who had assumed a parental role during the patient's childhood after his real father had committed suicide. This relative managed the patient's financial affairs. A day before the session reported, he had admonished the patient about them, reminding him, in effect, of his childlike dependency. During the session an inversion of these roles took place. He saw me as the easygoing analyst who would not engage him in a steadfast and bloodletting treatment. In identification with his guardian, he projected his "nonserious" part on me and proceeded to dismiss me.

For me, the most important question was to understand how I had been seduced into abandoning my analytic role and not taking him seriously. I realized that during the preceding hours we had colluded to create a light atmosphere. His subsequent encounter with his guardian had only repeated his experience of not being taken seriously. Both his guardian and I were induced to maintain the role of benevolent but contemptuous protector. By asking me if I needed his money, he was able to reverse these roles.

In this example, we can observe the following mechanisms:

In the patient: (1) Projective identification. The patient projects his "contemptible child" part on me. (2) Introjective identification. The patient identifies with the introjected contemptuous relative.

In the analyst: (1) Projective identification. The analyst projects his critical superego on the patient, feeling that he had colluded in creating a "nonworking" atmosphere. (2) Introjective identification. The analyst identifies with the "contemptible child" part of the patient and reacts defensively.

THERAPEUTIC FUNCTION OF SELF-ANALYSIS AND NEUTRALIZATION OF THE COUNTERTRANSFERENCE

In this fragment we see the patient projecting part of himself onto the analyst, and the analyst accepting it by introjective identification, thereby facilitating a situation where the patient is, in a way, divided into two. One part of him is in the analyst; and one part of him, he retains. As long as that situation stands, it is impossible for the analyst to maintain an objective neutrality or to remain anonymous. He becomes a known adversary, with quite specific qualities emanating from both the internal world of the patient and from the reality of the analytic experience. Here an interpretation, formulated as a statement or a series of goal-directed questions that enable the patient to move toward similar conclusions, permits him to link his internal reality and the analytic reality. That is, the process of clarification should confirm the accuracy of the patient's perception as well as the distortion in emphasis. By establishing the connection between inner experiences and the reality of the analytic situation, the analyst acknowledges the patient's knowledge of what is essentially real in the analytic relationship.

A previous and crucial step in this interpretive process is the self-analysis of the countertransference. A respected and trusted colleague may enormously facilitate this process, which can be quite painful at times.

Only to the extent that the analyst can sense the resonance in his own internal world to the focused beams of feelings emanating from the patient can he reflect them back. He must be able to identify within himself these same conflicted feelings that the patient desperately tries to polarize between them. Only then will he be able to formulate the necessary interpretation and provide the understanding that restores the internal integrity of the patient, allowing him to accept his ambivalence — the conflicts of his internal objects. Also (and this is a fundamental condition for the successful continuation of the analysis), by making that integrative interpretation, the analyst reacquires the neutrality of his affect. He is not siding affectively with any part of the patient. He is not incorporating what the patient disowns. He makes a statement that provides a balance in the conflict between internal objects. His is a neutral statement that doesn't take sides.

This allows the patient to retain the richness of his feelings and gradually to control them, rather than being controlled by them. In other words, we hope that repetition of such integrative interpretations will more and more enable the patient to tolerate his ambivalence, and this defines the primary function of the interpretive activity of the analyst. At the same time, the analyst retains his neutrality of affect. He is no longer dominated by the projection and no longer dominated by the affects the projection induces in him.

Here is a quotation from Freud which seems to be a clear example of his abandonment of neutrality. In "Analysis: Terminable and Interminable," published in 1937, Freud made the following statement:

> At no point in one's analytical work does one suffer more from the oppressive feeling that all one's efforts have been in vain and from the suspicion that one is "talking to the winds" than when one is trying to persuade a female patient to abandon her wish for a penis...

Nacht (1965), commenting on the same statement, observed that what makes the analysis interminable is the perpetuation of the transference neurosis due to the analyst's need to "persuade" the patient into a cure that is perceived by the patient as castrating. For Nacht, the transference neurosis becomes necessary to ward off the dangerous cure. We can see Freud's urging the patient to abandon her wish for a penis as a countertransference reaction on different levels.

1. There is identification with the patient's superego, provoking castration anxiety in him as well as an attempt to actually inhibit the patient. This attitude may have the unintended beneficial side effect, in patients with healthier egos, of encouraging a defiant and assertive attitude that may restore the symbolic penis, or power to influence the world.

2. Or, there is identification with the unconscious guilt of the patient due to her hateful and destructive attitude towards the breast symbolized by the penis. The urging can be seen as an attempt to repair the fantasized damage to the breast-penis.

3. It can also be seen as an attempt on the analyst's part to uphold social values and preserve social order. The analyst reacts unconsciously and, at times, consciously to attempts made by the patient to subvert the balance of power between the sexes. Clara Thompson (1943) pointed to these cultural factors in "penis envy" in women.

Citing Nacht (1965) again: "The avowal of painful feelings and fruitless effort give evidence of an affective participation far removed from the neutrality of an analyst. The patient cannot fail to be aware of it, and transference reactions are necessarily influenced thereby."

Let me give you another example where the patient projected onto me the part of him that felt like a deprived and angry child. It was a rather common situation, one in which the analyst can be quite receptive to that projection.

This patient had paid me at the beginning of every month for two and a half years. This month, he had not paid me. A likely reaction to this breach of contract was to accuse the patient of acting out, particularly when he kept me waiting and forced me to raise the issue. It is difficult under those circumstances to protect analytic objectivity from feelings of frustrated greed. However, I knew about his anxious wait for a promotion and the increasing feeling of futility and helpless anger as the days went by. By reversing roles and making me wait, he seemed to recover some ego strength from anal-sadistic sources. The parataxic field was marked by trans-ferential aggression that induced countertransferential confusion and helplessness at first, followed by frustrated greed and annoyance.

If the analyst does not decontaminate himself of these bad feelings before interpreting the patient's acting out, the likely result is that the patient will maintain the projective split. A correct interpretation without neutrality of affect will not reduce the splitting that makes the patient angry and punishing. I forgot what I said but I do remember that the inner clarity I reached was helpful in decontaminating the field of bad feelings. And there was no further need to bore each other with our frustrations.

Actually, we can see this whole process as one of constant contamination and decontamination. The analyst lets himself be contaminated by the patient's projections. We can call this the empathic step. Then he proceeds to decontaminate himself. This second step involves self-analysis and an active attempt to recover a neutral stance by helping the patient reintegrate his projected parts.

Up to this point I have examined the role of self-analysis of the analyst's reaction to his patient and its essential role in shedding some clarity on what evolves in the analytic situation. I have also asserted that that clarity may be further facilitated by the preservation of neutrality in the analyst.

THE ANALYST'S UNCONSCIOUS GREED

Now I will examine greed and the defensive reaction that it provokes in the analyst as an example of what ordinarily inhibits the pursuit of knowledge in analysis. I believe that conflict around curiosity and the need to know is a particularly good example of how both patient and analyst may renounce the analytic task to avoid painful confrontations with these deep-seated unconscious feelings.

Developmentally, as Klein (1963) has pointed out, the origin of the epistemophilic instinct concurs with the emergence of aggressive tendencies at their maximal strength. This appears to be a genetically coded determinant that defines the structure of our human condition and is not necessarily explainable. Throughout life this association remains strong, and often fruitful, as in the aggressive pursuit of knowledge in all areas of human endeavor. At other times, as Freud (1913) wrote: "the desire for knowledge in particular often gives one the impression that it can actually take the place of sadism in the mechanism of the obsessional neurosis."

The stage of development when these aggressive tendencies manifest themselve is also the time when oral gratification, directed at the mothering person, is the most important aim. Her body is the chief source of gratification of these oral aims as well as of the infant's exploratory activities. She is an object to suck, pinch, bite, and press oneself against — a wonder of different textures, flowing nectar, and soothing sounds. She is a field to explore, full of surprises, some moist and soft, some rough and startling — a world of satisfactions and frustrations. And to master the anxiety produced by this world of contrasts and contradictions, the infant begins to feel the need to know. He begins to have thoughts, and to think.

One can also assume that the need to know may be increased by a nonanxious mother. That is, in an atmosphere of optimal anxiety, the aggressive component may be summoned to envelop a desire for knowledge. If, however, frustration is a prevalent occurence, the aggressive component of the epistemophilic instinct may become a strong sadistic component, and guilt is likely to exert an inhibitory function. Hence, the need to know becomes intertwined with aggression and guilt. The search for knowledge then induces the fear of destroying. And fear of retaliation may loom so large that it may impair forever the desire for knowledge as a whole.

One of the common problems in analysis is the intensified deprivation that the analyst suffers, provoking in him an inordinate amount of greed as a compensatory mechanism. The pursuit of knowledge, when severely thwarted and impatient of being confined, arouses powerful and insatiate longings in the analyst.

Greed, an instinctive solution to what is denied and seen as valuable, is one of the most primitive and powerful reactions which may create severe conflicts when it clashes with established cultural values. In the countertransferential situation created by this conflict, the analyst may resort to defenses that run opposite to the analytic pursuit of knowledge about the patient's psychic reality, as well as his own. The greedy impulses and the defenses against them can recreate the fear of destroying what is considered valuable and desirable, to the detriment of the analytic task.

It may sound from what I just said that every single analyst at one time or another is going to be driven by inordinate amounts of greed. This is exactly what I mean.

To elucidate further, arousal of greed in the analyst occurs as a result of the patient's withholding of whatever is "valuable" for the analysis. And the stronger the greed that has to be suppressed, the smaller the capacity to bear frustration and to maintain an empathic link with the patient. Under these circumstances, the acquisition of knowledge, motivated by greed, is precarious. The eager analyst pursues things wonderful, instead of things true, and his fervent desire colors them with ambivalent light. His anxiety over losing the coveted objects is matched only by the fear that his greed will destroy them.

This is especially true during the long pull of analysis. The patient who withholds information, desire for change and love for the analyst, has a regressive influence on the analyst. The permanent state of partial deprivation (inherent in the analytic situation for both participants) makes inevitable the resurgence of rapacious tendencies which, if brought to awareness, help the analyst to understand his ambivalent attitudes toward his patient. His search for knowledge is culturally sanctioned and role-sanctioned. Not to pursue it entails failure of responsibility and ensuing guilt. To pursue it, however, may revive greedy impulses experienced as destructive toward the patient or, at the level of his own internal objects, as hateful and aggressive towards the depriving aspect of parental images.

We know that analysts have, more often than not, a depressive predisposition. When our work is stimulating, the depressive core recedes and we are alive in relation to the patient. We know how difficult it is to treat depressives that withhold that necessary stimulus. In his personal life an analyst can be at times a destructive, sadistic person. But in his relationship to his patient, he can indicate how much he values the opposite of this, if the masochistic maneuvers of the patient are not stronger than the analytic challenge they pose. For we know that in any routine analysis the good intentions of the analyst do not prevent the eruption at some crucial moments of some strongly suppressed feelings. This may be particularly true when the patient's behavior tends to elicit feelings that are not compatible with his values as an analyst. Greed is a case in point.

The most common defense against the potentially uncontrollable aspects of greed in the analyst is the reinforcement of what seem to be acceptable rules of behavior: respect for the patient's defenses, and an implicit pseudoacknowledgment of his right to privacy.

The resulting collusion between the analyst and his patient to suppress the emergence of knowledge from the analytic field allays different anxieties. The self-ideal of the analyst is protected by the suppression of inordinate avarice, and persecutory anxieties therefore diminish. The patient, on the other hand, may experience some relief in seeing the chase temporarily suspended.

When the two participants find themselves in such an uncomfortable relationship, the stalemate is solved by the tacit agreement to abandon the exploration of psychic reality.

A patient whose intense ambition and high achievements had a libidinal charge so powerful that it practically excluded any other concern from our exploration may serve as a good example. His singleminded dedication to success made him curious only for knowledge that could make him function better in the rarified and murderously competitive corporate environment. I felt deprived of pursuing more leisurely paths and had often a stakhanovian sense of my analytic labor.

On one occasion, he was describing his working lunch hours. Almost as a side comment, he mentioned his pleasure at combining fun and important work in catering to special VIPs. Hungry for some diversity, I seized upon the opportunity to look into the hidden, fun-loving part of his personality. I was only conscious of my analytic intentions, but I found myself greedily asking him for details of the decor of the sumptuous lunch clubs he was describing.

One in particular caught my fancy, as he described it, located high over Park Avenue, with a French chef and staff, a hushed environment, with widely separated tables fit for highly confidential conversations. As I kept pressing him for more and more details, he finally paused and quite seriously asked me: "Would you like me to take you for lunch sometime, Doctor?"

An appropriate ending to this anecdote, and to this presentation, is to quote once more from Freud (1913): "It is not without good reason, however, that I have maintained that every man possesses in his unconscious an instrument by which he can interpret the expressions of the unconscious of another."

References

Freud, S. (1910). The future prospects of psycho-analytic therapy. *Standard Edition* 11:139-151.

———(1913). The predisposition to obsessional neurosis. *Standard Edition* 12:311-326.

———(1915). Observations on transference-love. *Standard Edition* 12:157-173.

———(1937). Analysis terminable and interminable. *Standard Edition* 23:216-253.

Fromm-Reichman, F. (1950). *Principles of Intensive Psychotherapy.* Chicago: University of Chicago Press.

Heimann, P. (1950). On countertransference. *International Journal of Psycho-Analysis* 31:31-83.

Horney, K. (1939). *New Ways in Psychoanalysis.* New York: W.W. Norton.

Klein, M. (1963). *Psychoanalysis of Children.* London: Hogarth Press.

Levenson, E.A. (1972). *The Fallacy of Understanding: An Inquiry into the Changing Structure of Psychoanalysis.* New York: Basic
Books.

Nacht, S. (1965). Criteria and techniques for the termination of analysis. *International Journal of Psycho-Analysis.* 46:107-116.

Racker, H. (1948, 1953). The countertransference neurosis. *International Journal of Psycho-Analysis* 34:313-324.

———(1968). *Transference and Countertransference.* New York: International Universities Press.

Tauber, E.S. (1954). Exploring the therapeutic use of countertransference data. *Psychiatry* 17:331-336.

Thompson, C.M. (1943). Penis envy in woman. *Psychiatry* 6:123-125.

———(1952). Countertransference. *Samiksa* 6:205-211.

———(1964). Introduction. In *Transference: Its Structure and Function in Psychoanalytic Therapy,* ed. B. Wolstein. New York:
Grune & Stratton.

Thompson, C.M., Crowley, R.M., and Tauber, E.S. (1952). Symposium on countertransference. *Samiksa* 6:205-228.

Unamuno, M. de (1895). *En Tormo al Casticismo. Ensayos.*

Winnicott, D.W. (1949). Hate in the countertransference. *International Journal of Psycho-Analysis* 30:69-75.

Wolstein, B. (1964). *Transference: Its Structure and Function in Psychoanalytic Therapy.* New York: Grune & Stratton.

Zaphiropoulos, M.L. (1961). Tender hearts and martinets: Some varities of Countertransference. Presented to the William Alanson
White Psychoanalytic Society, March 16, 1961. Unpublished.

Chapter 2

THE INNER EXPERIENCE
OF THE
PSYCHOANALYST

EARL G. WITENBERG, M.D.

What are the factors determining the growing study of counter-transference phenomena?

As one views society as a whole, one sees increasing openness and candor in all sectors. But this has been a mixed blessing, as it has brought with it a diminution in the power and prestige of authority, whether religious or, as with the physician, secular. The breakdown of sexual standards and of such institutions as the family has occasioned a spate of literature analyzing authority roles. And once analyzed, they are never again the same.

Couple the social pressures — "man is the plaything of social forces defying both his will and his lethargy" (Schwartz 1976) — with the growing maturity of psychoanalysis and you have pressure on the profession to be more open. The widespread acceptance in our field of the fact that each of us is potentially the other makes us aware of how similar we can be to our patients. We are all more accepting of human frailties than we used to be. It is openly acknowledged that professionals recognize how impossible it is to be a "blank mirror" or to be absolutely neutral at all times. With the increasing diversity of the patient population (as indications for psychoanalysis have broadened), has come the realization of the utility of countertransference reactions. The use of face-to-face treatment added to the frequency of countertransference and brought it into fuller use. The seated patient does notice more than the recumbent and does have more of an impact on the analyst.

In the realm of theory, disillusionment with the explanatory force of metapsychology (after all, a theory about a theory) led to a push toward a theory of treatment independent of metapsychology. Once one starts to formulate a theory of treatment, one begins to realize that man taken in isolation is a fiction.

One analyst who enabled us even to consider countertransference was Harry Stack Sullivan. His focus on the field between patient and analyst, and his concept of the analyst as participant observer, opened doors for the study of countertransference phenomena. Much work remained to be done following his great insights, although he did lay the underpinnings for studying the exact nature of the analytic field. The *Samiksa* papers of Thompson, Crowley, and Tauber (1952) rapidly followed. Mabel Blake Cohen (1952) discussed at some length the issue of countertransference, seeing it essentially as a response to anxiety in the analyst. When the anxiety and its derivatives are recognized and understood, then the countertransference is clear. Tauber's (1954) paper on the constructive use of the analyst's dreams about the patient added a new dimension to the thinking about this issue. In my Miami paper (1976), I pointed out how the analyst's experience and acceptance of countertransference phenomena have broadened indications for the treatment of narcissistic and borderline personalities. There are numerous papers in the classical mode which have been mentioned elsewhere and I will not dwell upon them.

THE ALLOCENTRIC ATTITUDE AND COUNTERTRANSFERENCE

I will comment now on some aspects of the psychoanalytic situation which are germane to countertransference and the analyst's inner experience. First is the kind of attention or attitude that I consider fundamental to psychoanalysis. I consider it so because it presupposes the analyst's capacity to become interested in the totality of any object, without interference from his own needs. This attitude provides a richness based on his capacity to emancipate himself temporarily, during the course of the analytic session, from being dominated by the needs he shares with other animals, that is the capacity to suspend his need for gratification and to perceive the world around him, not in terms of how it might be used to gratify those needs but in its own right. This openness on the part of the analyst toward his patient is the type of attitude Ernest Schachtel (1959) labeled *allocentric*. He said:

> The few examples described of shifts in perceptual modes and the resulting differences in perceptual experience demonstrate the inseparable connection between total attitude and perceptual mode. Because of the unique importance of allocentric perception as the highest form of perception reached in phylogenetic and in human ontogenetic development, the question of the *attitude linked with allocentric perception* deserves our special attention now.
>
> I shall designate this attitude as the *allocentric attitude*. From the descriptions of allocentric perception it has already become apparent that this attitude is one of *profound* interest in the object, and complete openness and receptivity toward it, a full turning toward the object which makes possible the direct encounter with it and not merely a quick registration of its familiar features according to ready labels. The essential qualities of the interest in the turning toward the object are its *totality* and *affirmativeness*. The totality of interest refers both to the object in which the perceiver is interested and to the act of interest. The interest concerns the *whole object*, not merely a partial aspect of it; and the perceiver turns toward the object with *his entire being*, his whole personality, i.e. fully, not just with part of himself. The act of interest is total and it concerns the totality of its object. Indeed, one is the function of the other. If one turns to the object with only part of his total being, e.g. with a certain appetite (hunger, sex), or to use it for some specific purpose, then one is interested only in certain aspects of the object. On this hinges the often observed fact that the object, the world, reveals itself to the man only according to the degree and quality of the interest he takes in it.

For heuristic purposes I will call anything other than the allocentric attitude countertransference. Those who prefer the term *hovering attention* to the allocentric attitude may use that. But there

is an absence of neutrality in both these concepts. In hovering
attention there is receptivity; and in allocentric attention there is a
totality and affirmativeness with the openness of attention. Others
have described similar attitudes with different metaphors. Erich
Fromm has described the analyst as the sand on the beach over
which and through which the water runs, though without altering
the sand permanently. Alberta Szalita views it as similar to the
spectator at a play who watches the action and comments on it. For
countertransference may interfere with openness on the part of the
analyst. Its presence implies that somehow his needs are entering the
analytic field where they now command attention, so that the
analyst does more than "hover," is more than "receptive," or acts
beyond the role of the "commenting spectator," all to the detriment
of the analytic work. I am suggesting that any change in this type of
allocentric attitude may be labeled countertransference.

Intercurrent life processes in the analyst will of course influence
this attitude, as will such vicissitudes of life as health problems, one's
own analysis, or difficulties with a job, a family, a mate, a parent, or
a sibling. These are part of the hazards of being human as well as of
being an analyst. By and large most analysts handle these variations
well, but sometimes they overload the analytic situation and make
for mischief. For many it is a relief to be able to see patients at times
like these, to recognize that although one is helpless about some
events in one's life it does not interfere with the ability to attend
properly to one's patients. It is helpful, and to some extent healing, to
be able to know that one can work, that one's professional identity is
intact. However, there are two major reservations to the utility of
working during times of personal distress, when concurrent
personal events might interfere with the proper attitude of attention:
(1) there may be an undue need for the patient, who may for
neurotic reasons in the analyst be seen as important, in order to deny
this personal distress; (2) if one has not fully accepted one's own
frailty, and is, for example, waiting for the result of a G.I. series or an
EKG, a state of anxiety and depletion may result that will interfere
with attention. I know of one incident very like this. An analyst had
recently become aware of the possibility of a cardiac problem. As
cardiac problems go, it was a minor one without any particular
implications for his longevity or even for restriction of activity. For
various appropriate reasons, he had so informed some of his
patients. A few weeks after this communication, one patient who
had a tachycardia (that had been mentioned in the treatment only

two or three times in the previous three years) began to complain of paroxysms regularly in the treatment situation, interrupting her verbal productions so as to press on her carotid. In one session there were three such episodes. The analyst reacted internally with some boredom, futility, drowsiness, and later, he realized, some anxiety. He was puzzled by this but was by and large inattentive to the matter.

He began to have a series of dreams which had to do with the death of his father from arteriosclerotic heart disease a number of years previous. He also realized the implications for himself. This process required three sessions of personal analysis for him. It was only after he was clear about this self-involvement that he could go back to encounter, with the patient, the issues around her need to "bug" him, her anger at him, her fear of death, and her wish to be identified with him. This illustrates what I think is a failure in one of the basic aspects of allocentric attention — the attempt to understand the patient by a trial identification. We might ask, How does one understand what another person is saying? One temporarily puts oneself in the other's shoes, and then comments on what is subjectively perceived. The unattended anxiety involved in this analyst's trial identification (others have called it *empathic* or *sympathetic identification*) resulted in the series of affects of boredom and futility, and that change in state of consciousness, drowsiness. This instance of countertransference was obviously not related directly to the patient's productions; nor were they, when integrated by the analyst, directly productive for the patient. *Another step was required.* The analyst had to become aware that his own anxieties had contaminated the data he was receiving from the patient and had resulted in his retreat to a state of self-absorption. Of course, had he been able to attend to his anxieties and fears during the actual analytic session with his patient he would have been able to work more therapeutically.

Another, more severe example of an analyst's untoward response would be falling asleep in the patient's presence. The one time I have fallen asleep in the analytic session was immediately after a male patient reported a dream which involved violence to his older brother. His associations led him back to a time in adolescence. I suddenly was awakened by the patient. I do not want to elaborate further on the transaction between us; that is for another study. However, in searching myself for reasons for my altered state of consciousness, I came in touch with feelings about my relationship with my younger brother, who had died when I was six years old. In my own analysis, I had had some inkling of unfinished business around my deceased sibling; but I had to wait until this incident to get in touch with a fuller elucidation and grasp of the matter.

Discussion

From the description of these two incidents one can see how intercurrent issues in the life of the analyst may interfere with the analytic position; one also sees how unresolved anxieties in one's past life are triggered off in the analytic situation during the trial identification phase. Falling asleep and rageful anger toward a patient actually may be viewed as transference reactions to the patient, as Crowley has suggested (Thompson et al. 1952). But I am classifying them as countertransference reactions because of the way they arise and because of the light they throw on our attitude in the analytic situation. As felicitous as the attitude of allocentric attention is, we are undefended in it. We are at the mercy of the push and pull of the patient; we are also at the mercy of our inner tensions and anxieties. As we resonate to the productions of the patient we are sharply attuned to our inner feelings, thoughts, reveries, etc.

There are many factors in the life situation of the analyst that interfere with the ability to attend to the patient in an analytic mode. There are certain obvious extraneous distractions, such as noise in the street, the ringing of the telephone, and even such things as New York's famous blackout. There is one other factor I should like to include here because it happens so frequently that it fails to attract the notice it deserves. That is the overscheduling of patients. While there is probably an objective daily limit to the number of patients to whom we can give our undivided attention, we often fail to specify this to ourselves. The inevitable tension and fatigue of over-scheduling depletes our resources; we are therefore more vulnerable to the pull of anxiety and cannot as easily maintain an analytic stance. Notice the difference between your feelings when you are with the last patient (on an overscheduled day) and the first one on that same day.

Usually, when things are going well in an analysis, I do not elaborate or integrate my inner feelings. I have only a faint perception of them. I am attempting to identify temporarily with the communication of the patient. I put myself in the situation the patient is describing. I scan the material for any lacunae in the narrative. That is one way of locating the presence of unattended or dissociated material. Sometimes I find I am having a feeling that reciprocates the behavior (verbal and nonverbal) expressed by the patient, for example, protectiveness, annoyance, guilt. These reciprocal feelings give me a sense of how other people react to the patient in similar contexts. I know in this way the reactions of parents and friends, a mode of knowing very similar to Winnicott's "objective countertransference" (1949). So temporary identification, reciprocal responses and resonating go on. And I say what I see. What I say is dependent on my subjective perception.

It is only when the work is bogged down that I attend closely to my feelings. How do I know the work is bogged down? There is a repetitious quality to the material and to the style. I see the "same" person each time, the communication is the "same." I feel the "same." I get bored, distant, passive (all ways I have of coping with anxiety). When the work goes well, I see a "different" person each time. W. R. Bion comments that when he does not recognize a patient when he comes in the door, he knows the patient is really in analysis.

In my opinion analyses bog down when the demarcation between the real and the unreal aspects of the treatment become fuzzy for both patient and analyst. The context of an analysis is unreal and contrived to an extent; it is staged that way. We, for example, inform patients that they can say anything with impunity from criticism, rancor, etc. Nowhere else in the world is this true! And, where else does one get the undivided attention of another over so protracted a period? For most patients the transference is not alive enough. They tend to explain their actions and reactions to the analyst on the basis of the reality of the interaction in the consulting room. Most analysts have a problem with this too. They tend to explain what look like transference reactions as being related to their real personalities, feelings, or attitudes to the patient. That is, they explain the patient's repetitive behaviors by their own feelings.

ANALYSIS AND THE "AS IF" EXPERIENCE

I want to comment about how real an analysis is; and how real the experience is for the analyst. In the course of looking at and listening to the totality of the other person, we put ourselves into those situations the patient describes, a scene with a mate, a family quarrel, etc. As long as we are aware that it is *as if* we are there, there is no great problem with shifting back to the allocentric mode. We will even stop (metaphorically) and examine in minute detail the phenomena which catch our mind's eye. It is only if there is anxiety about this curiosity concerning these partial phenomena, or if we do not know about our need to be there, that there will be any difficulty in shifting back to the allocentric attitude. What this inattention to our unawareness of our specific needs in stopping at the scene does is make the experience *too* real for us. It is that we *are* there in the scene; it is not *as if* we are there. The same issue is of course true for the patient. If he does not ultimately see the transference as an "as if" experience the analysis cannot work. The cutting edge for change is the realization that one is bringing along into a new situation old feelings — and they seem unreal. I am emphasizing here the temporary nature of the shift in the analyst's attitude in order for him to know what the patient is saying in detail. Once that is more than temporary, the reality of the experience is too total and not "as if," as part of a more total involvement with the patient. These are the roots of the countertransference phenomena in those situations where trial identifications misfire. There is another phenomenon worth describing. When I attend a patient, I may find myself admiring, being annoyed by, being bored by the patient. In the scenes that he is describing, I am, so to speak, in a role reciprocal to his. Sandler (1976) has in fact referred to this type of countertransference reaction as "role-responsiveness." I find myself introducing this phenomenon by pointing out that the patient might expect such a response under such and such a circumstance. If this response becomes too prolonged or too real, I will communicate my attitude at that moment in a way that hopefully protects his (and my own) self-esteem. I have never been impressed with the facilitation of the work by naked displays of rage or temper.

What about cognition and cognition theory in all this? Sometimes I feel we're on the right track when the theory comes into my mind after the patient has formulated something. Most of the time I attempt to listen theory-free.

I would like to comment particularly about the perception of transference phenomena. The recognition comes that the same sequence and the same affect recur time and time again with the patient. And I have a recurrent reciprocal response which doesn't feel like me. Then I ask, Who am I at this moment to this person? It then becomes clear it is as if I am mother, father, whoever, to this person in this context. Analysis of the transference, making it explicit, has also to be *as if*, or no analysis will occur. The same is true for reliving memories. They are *not* relived; again it is *as if* they were relived. I want to note again the change from the allocentric attitude when the subjective experience is accompanied by anxiety and an untoward response. It is an active looking-at, with a receptivity and acceptance. It is participatory to this extent; it is neutral only in the judgmental sense.

OPTIMAL DISTANCE

Passions of any kind shared between analyst and patient over a prolonged period of time indicate that something other than analysis is going on. By this I mean passions displayed in other than an "as if" category. Love, hate, sex, indifference, admiration akin to awe, are all signs that something other than analysis is occurring. Those analysands who cluster around their analyst, beware! Those analysts who socialize almost exclusively with their analysands, take heed! Analysis is work and it demands a work relationship. The rule of thumb for me about socialization is this: If I'm not feeling like an analyst, that is, having to listen with the particular analytic stance, I will socialize. Work and socialization are two different experiences for me. To understand and to be understood are probably the most basic human qualities there are. We develop them in our work and in our social relationships. However, in no relationship outside of analysis are the transference issues made explicit in this *as if* way. We know more details of the inner life of our patients than do their mates. But we know them only in the particular context of analysis.

On those occasions when we notice the difference between the social behavior of our patients (as experienced in couple interviews, family interviews, group therapy, society meetings, or house visits) and their analytic behavior, we are obliged to ponder the reasons for this difference and discuss it with the patient. The reverse is also true; hopefully, they will tell us about such differences in ourselves. My point is that there are inevitable constraints on the nature of the relationships with our patients because of the context of the analytic relationship and because of the reasons for our being together in the treatment room.

And yet there are feelings that do arise in the analyst; there are flights of fancy, altered states of consciousness, feelings of vagueness and unclarity. They all are useful in identifying some aspect of the processes in the patient. One analyst related the following about listening to a new patient (it was the third time they had met). He was bored and suddenly found himself having the fantasy of playing cowboy with the patient, who responded with the fact that he had spent most of his childhood doing that. What fell into place at this moment was the man's slight accent (a Texas drawl in a New Yorker) and his monotonous imitation of a cowboy's monosyllabic speech. I remember the annoyance I often felt at a patient's bad grammar. "Between she and I" was his favored gaff. Under some inquiry this turned out to be his way of depersonalizing an experience. Despite his Phi Beta Kappa and Alpha Omega Alpha keys, he had not noticed this defense against the experience.

You can now see that I am opting for a kind of distance from the patient. And I believe that there is an optimum distance that is determined by the patient in a good professional encounter. For example, a patient expressed with some annoyance the other day at how clinical I was, meaning how little concerned I seemed to be. She had problems in reality, practical problems with time, money, etc., and I would not comment on them except to ask her questions. She was quite accurate, I pointed out. Then I also pointed out that she had veiled the follow-up of certain points in secrecy; furthermore, she had given far from complete information about the actual data. She had failed to spell out the actual transactions involved. So it behooved us to look further at her characteristic need for secrecy. My point is that one cannot have a full interchange when there are powerful resistances operating. Some analysts might recommend expressing their annoyance at the resistance once it appeared on the scene. I tend to wait. If I am aware of how the patient is functioning, I am not annnoyed. In this case, we discussed the patient's difficulty in giving full data about other areas in living — family, sexual, and professional. The need for secrecy and privacy had been unveiled. So we were now bringing up an old friend; what at one point had been out of awareness was not a matter of conscious withholding. And it was beginning to trouble her, particularly since she had benefited from prior work when she had lifted the veil. The fact that it was troubling her more than it was troubling me was all to the good. After all it was her life.

For me to have a larger stake in her life than she had would not only be inappropriate but would also prevent her from developing and growing in her own way. In this instance her associations led her to episodes in her life where openness about wishes (e.g., about appearance, dress, etc.) with her mother had led to disaster (e.g., dresses that were not suitable, hairdos that were not becoming). She had to keep her innermost wishes from others, but also from herself. My countertransference response to the holes in her presentation ranged from accurately pointing out the incompleteness to experiences of boredom and drowsiness (having to do with internal frustration and anger, as I would discover after sessions in which they occurred). I have seen too many analyses founder on the analyst's being more interested in having a patient than on the patient's wanting to be a patient. There is an introductory period, of varying length for each patient, in which the specifics of the motivation have to be clarified for each problem.

GOALS OF ANALYSIS

What I have been trying to formulate above are the ways the analyst is actor, spectator, and dramatist. In this way I have expanded the metaphor used by Levitt (1976): "The psychoanalyst is somewhat like Racine who enclosed the irrationality of passions in a concise chaste, rational dramatic form that reflects, for us, the measured harmony of Louis XIV's Versailles Gardens." What are the goals in all this self-scrutiny in this peaked self-consciousness? It helps us to be "fully present" or interhuman, as Martin Buber would say, or to approach an allocentric stance. But the achievement of self-awareness and self-interest are not enough. Margaret Rioch, in a forthcoming book (1978), states it this way: "If the learning stops here [i.e., with self-interest] self-awareness becomes self-aggrandizement and corruption of the new priesthood has begun. The search for [psychological] security and personal happiness is like the search for material wealth."

To avoid banality, which more than venality is the poison in the treatment process, it is necessary to recognize the spiral of self-awareness to self-aggrandizement. To arrive at a modicum of personal security and of personal happiness is enough. Without some profound dedication to a loss of preoccupation with one's "precious self," treatment is not "different from conversion to a new set of rules and regulations." The caveat for analysis is that everything that goes on in your heads and bodies is important to know; it is essentail that you use it to facilitate the patient's self-awareness. To share it in its entirety with the patient (or, as some would say, to dump it on him) is neither necessary nor desirable.

Helping people "to be better adjusted," "to get along better," "to relate better," "to cure the phobia," "to lower the anxiety," "to get out their anger and other feelings" are goals with which a lot of psychotherapists are satisfied, and I do not think there are pragmatic issues that may make these goals necessary for some of the people we see. But again I would stress the importance of the patient arriving at these goals explicitly and by himself. For me the goal toward which I am eager to work with the patient is to help him, in Clara Thompson's words, "to be what he might have been if such and such had not happened in his life." Terms like *psychological rebirth* or *satori* are not operational enough for me. We will not change biology or chemistry, only psychology. I can offer the patient a self-awareness which will do him good only if he will eventually *be* able to forgo his self-interest for another.

And so the purpose of learning about ourselves, about our responses to patients, of setting up a stage on which the drama of a patient's life may be lived, of being dramatist, spectator, and actor in our treatment rooms, is so that someone else's awareness may be expanded, so that someone else is more acutely aware of his genuine self-interest than he was previously. He will know himself as others know him and may be able to help others.

References

Cohen, M.B. (1952). Countertransference and anxiety. *Psychiatry* 15:231-243.

Levitt, H.H. (1976). Psychoanalysis, artist, and critic. *Contemporary Psychoanalysis* 12:140-143.

Rioch, M. (1978). Untitled manuscript.

Sandler, J. (1976). Countertransference and role-responsiveness. *International Review of Psycho-Analysis* 3:43-47.

Schachtel, E.G. (1959). *Metamorphosis*, New York: Basic Books.

Schwartz, E. (1976). *Washington University Alumni News.*

Tauber, E.S. (1954). Exploring the therapeutic use of countertransference data. *Psychiatry* 17:331-336.

Thompson, C.M., Crowley, R.M., and Tauber, E.S., (1952). Symposium on countertransference. *Samiksa* 6:205-211.

Winnicott, D. (1949). Hate in the countertransference. *International Journal of Psycho-Analysis* 30:69-74.

Witenberg, E.G. (1976). To believe or not to believe. *Journal of the American Academy of Psychoanalysis* 4:433-445.

Chapter 3

COUNTERTRANSFERENCE REEXAMINED

EDWARD S. TAUBER, M.D.

SCIENTIFIC LIMITATIONS OF THE CLASSICAL POSITION

I wish to discuss my misgivings about the construct of countertransference as originally formulated and then to examine how my thoughts have evolved in respect to this problem.

The classical formulation troubled me because I accepted the validity of the need to correct unconstructive intrusions by the therapist into the therapeutic transaction but also intuited that the correction could lead to an impoverishment of therapeutic experience. While not certain that this challenge would be construed as valid to others, I believed an unacknowledged scientific controversy was emerging. I expressed myself on this topic in an article entitled "Exploring the Therapeutic Use of Countertransference Data" (Tauber 1954). The issues as I saw them then, are expressed in the introductory passage of this article:

This paper is designed to illustrate the fact that countertransference phenomena may under certain circumstances afford an opportunity to evoke new material about the patient, the analyst, or the relationship, and that they may be used therapeutically to increase mutual spontaneity. The author

59

believes that there is a real need for developing a scientific method to utilize contructively the negative components introduced by the therapist in the treatment situation and to determine which of these components are worthy of mutual exploration. According to classical psychoanalytic theory, countertransference reactions represent unanalyzed portions of the therapist's personality which either transparently or unwittingly interfere with the treatment situation. These reactions may be due to blind spots, private needs, irrelevant attitudes, biases, or moral prejudices; and they call for a change to a more productive orientation, necessitating their analysis. This is the basis in psychoanalytic theory for recognizing that any person engaged in intensive psychotherapeutic work with others needs a training analysis — a recognition which represents one of the most valuable discoveries in psychoanalysis.

It seems to me, however, that this emphasis on the negative value of countertransference reactions, important as it is, has tended to preclude the possibility of using these very reactions for achieving therapeutic goals. That is, the analyst may be so concerned with avoiding countertransference reactions that he does not take time to fully examine the content (or implications) of the reaction. In this way, for instance, he may deliberately try to forget a dream he has had about a patient; or he may fail to mention to a supervisor some fleeting thought he has had about the patient. In other words, there is a taboo on everything which vaguely resembles countertransference reactions, and only the grossest type are explored even in supervision. Eventually the gross countertransference phenomena tend to diminish; the more subtle ones remain, but are probably handled by selective inattention. This taboo has the harmful effect of inhibiting the analyst from recognizing the creative spontaneous insights that may occur to him in a dream, or in making use of a marginal thought or a slip of the tongue.

It is my impression that the analyst takes in more about the patient than he realizes; that there may be special reasons for the analyst's inability to bring some of his unconscious grasp of the patient into his own conscious awareness; and that by discussing some of the countertransference fragments, both the analyst and the patient may find out that the analyst has a richer understanding of the patient which can be put to good use in the exploratory process of analysis.

The very nature of the analytic setting is such that the analyst plays a relatively passive role and maintains an incognito. Many patients seem to respond to this setting by presenting an incognito of their own. Such a patient may give the analyst no clues even for suspecting that his behavior in therapy really represents only a small part of his total functioning and way of living. As a result, both the analyst's taboo on countertransference attitudes and the patient's subtle incognito limit the amount of potentially useful information for analytic progress. [Thus] the analytic procedure [seems to require] a constant infusion of new materials, fresh appraisals, and a challenging reconsideration of issues in the light of provocative data. Otherwise, the analysis can become stagnant, and the so-called (accredited) standardization of the procedure and the established scientific postulates can themselves become (legitimate) targets of the patient's resistance. This, of course, does not imply that the countertransference reactions should be construed as license for acting out with the patient but only that mutual exploration of their significance can open up more areas of development in the therapeutic situation.

With this as a hypothesis, I have discussed openly with several patients for mutual clarification dream material of mine that involved them, and also some fleeting fragments of an instructive nature.

CONSTRUCTIVE USE OF THE ANALYST'S SELF: THERAPEUTIC SPONTANEITY

These notes represented a first published statement of how I envisaged my mode of engagement as therapist. Daring to violate the traditions operated essentially in the field of dreams, where I shared certain of my own dreams (reported in the article). I encouraged free association of both participants, and did not hesitate to speak up first.

Although I am not certain under what conditions I chose to conduct such experiments, my decision was guided by how safe it seemed to me to discover the meaning of my dreams of patients.

I have always been interested in dreams as a means of increasing therapeutic traction and for many years conducted dream seminars attempting to encourage a respect for the value of immediacy of response and spontaneity. The student has to come in touch with himself and use himself and acknowledge his own participation in therapy. I was convinced over time that the constructive use of the self was a sine qua non and an important measure of the therapist's talent. Furthermore, the restraint suggested by traditional technique could make for difficulties in that insensitive passivity devitalizes treatment.

Where are we so far with this puzzle? Is there a satisfactory answer, or are we asking the wrong questions? As far as I am concerned, no satisfactory light has been shed on this issue. Adherents of the traditionalist persuasion and so-called revisionists have tackled it from their respective biases. We are all in somewhat the same spot as the anonymous gifted Russian author who was deputized to write about the elephant - - he chose the intriguing title "The Elephant — Does It Exist?" I am inclined to say: Countertransference — does it exist? If it exists, what is it? Where is its true habitat? Is it today what it was years ago? Has natural selection modified it or does it retain its pristine morphology?

I believe that there is a partial answer to the conundrum. I believe we are actually dealing with two different animals. This strikes me as more than a metaphor. We are dealing with two different processes beclouded by our failure to note that fact. To continue the naturalistic metaphor, these two animals, if you will, are of the same genus but of different species. Thus, they are closely related but coexist poorly in the same habitat. How we avoid unwisely intruding into the therapeutic situation and how we achieve constructive entry into that interpersonal arena comprises the two species of challenges. Each process may operate separately and/or conjointly.

Spontaneity, often misconstrued as unwise intrusion by classicists, can have positive effects if productively employed. The classical position advocates constructive restraint, but the neoclassical approach, in addition, strongly advocates constructive use of the self — namely therapeutic spontaneity.

Let me retain the terminology, countertransference, for each and simply call one negative and the other positive. Eventually, if what I am attempting to sort out is valid and acceptable, new or more appropriate taxonomic labels will be appropriate.

I believe we are working with an unwitting and also false assumption in our study of negative countertransference. The assumption is that one can eliminate negative countertransference effectively by the recognition of the objections to it. But something more is required.

All psychoanalysis is a journey into scientific adventure for both participants. Secession from the life of the mind as protection against intellectualization is a distinction an analyst must learn.

The psychoanalytic inquiry is not different in nature from any scientific inquiry. It is this to me indisputable fact which makes therapy so challenging, exciting and open to defeat. How many of us are prepared to face the challenge of discovery. Many of us have never even considered the implicitness of the assignment. Yet any human engagement of any depth calls for the durable scientific curiosity of the participants. I am implying an effective searching set toward what is unknown, not an intellectualizing exercise. How prepared are we as therapist and patient to tolerate the pain, the uncertainty and the possibility of defeat? If one cannot tolerate the uncertainty, often unrecognized since not tested, the outcome may be disappointing. This creative necessity is a tall order for therapist and patient. More is asked of us as analysts, if my hypothesis is correct, than of the medical profession. A well-trained, alert, conscientious physician can learn what is known about his speciality and is supported by the canons of modern medical knowledge. More need not be asked of him. By the nature of the analytic challenge just described, the analyst comes more or less quickly into touch with his own primitive omnipotence, his deeper anxieties, his frustration and rage, and so on. I have to add, parenthetically, in anticipation of being misunderstood, that the comparison is not intended to suggest that the role of the physician and surgeon is an easy one, and that none of the human passions, frailties, and other private claims ever enter his world.

Now we come to the heart of the problem. How we envisage the problem and what we do about it in practice will be determined by our views on the nature of man and his involvement with others, the claims he makes on himself, for himself, from others and with others. These factors must shape the configuration of his therapeutic mode. A thoroughgoing grasp of these elements and their interrelationships can only be partially glimpsed and must be at the roots of much controversy among therapists with regard to theories of therapy and appropriate therapeutic intervention. It would seem that the "choice" of therapeutic posture must depend upon what is comfortable to the therapist, and the conditions which best fulfill his productive use of himself. Ambiguous and ill-defined though these conditions be, perhaps only limited modifications of the self are possible. That is to say, the analyst must operate in a way that best fits his adaptive capacities. Genetic constitutional factors and temperment influenced and acted upon by social mileu; selective factors with respect to learning, what we "consent" to learn, what is blocked and how and by whom we are taught all flow together in mysterious ways. That some therapists and some patients seem to be better suited to each other or otherwise is recognized but extremely difficult to foresee or predict or articulate. Many elements may make it possible or impossible at certain times to effect productive growth.

What I have just described constitutes the background for understanding positive countertransference. This idealized concept implies that the analyst can empathize with verbal and nonverbal processes. It implies that an affective unconsciously organized process in the analyst can engage the inner experience of the patient, that the patient is able to "talk" with the analyst, that the patient is allowed, encouraged to "know" the analyst. I believe that something of this order occurs in a productive interpersonal interaction; that we may not satisfactorily understand how this process takes place does not gainsay the operation of such phenomena. Many therapeutic engagements never achieve this level of engagement. One cannot reliably predict when it is possible to have openness and how much can be tolerated by the participants. To discuss this topic is most difficult because we cannot specify or articulate the processes involved. We are in a field of great uncertainty at such time. Tolerating the tension is important. I am not describing ecstatic states, states of intoxication, otherworldliness, or advocating mystic attitudes. I do not believe true relatedness makes one elite, superior, or need be a special gift; however, sometimes, like talent or giftedness, rational skepticism is not out of order. How this type of experience relates to mystical experience, parapsychology, or Oriental philosophy I do not claim to know nor do I believe myself able to make assertions about the connection between a genuine analytic experience and any other kind of experience. True mutual creative experience has to occur, is not easily achieved, and is more infrequent than we would desire. No other form of psychotherapy approaches the best in the analytic experience. It guarantees little but can be profound. How this is learned and brought about is no easier to explain than creative experience in any other art or science. There are no books on when to share a thought or feeling and when it is truly wise to wait and see. The art of silence is not in contention. Unresponsiveness and blindness to the interaction are as unfruitful as insensitive manipulation and intrusion; neither should serve as acceptable tools of therapeutic technique. The failures of constructive traction arise out of a combination of incompetence, which may or may not be healed, and inflexible neurotic claims on the other, which also may or may not get resolved.

I now wish to explore present-day views on negative countertransference. But before doing so, let me restate the problem: destructive input, either arising *de novo*, that is, from the therapist's fear of scientific creativity or his exaggerated neurotic claims, or both, is pitted against potential constructive input.

The specific hypothesis is:

The classical position is itself a countertransference phenomenon. It is the therapist's fear of using himself and is directed against the therapeutic transaction; it indirectly discourages the patient's confidence and daring in respect of his own contribution. The rationalization of the fear is not recognized as such and the technique of passivity is given honorific status because it is traditionally and uncritically accepted.

The distinction between constructive silence and therapeutic inertia is not challenged so long as the therapist sticks to the book. Waiting for the patient to "come forth with his unconscious" is what is considered correct, yet what is taking place in the therapist, whether he intrudes or not, is vital to the therapeutic interaction. Perhaps we know no way to teach therapeutic traction, and when it is learned we still cannot follow the pathways leading to its development. Yet is has to develop for therapy to improve.

SEARLES' POSITION ON COUNTERTRANSFERENCE

In the present period the literature on countertransference explores its operation primarily where the patient sample is schizophrenic, ambulatory schizophrenic or borderline. In an immensely valuable paper entitled "Psychoanalytic Therapy with Schizophrenic Patients in a Private-Practice Context," Searles (1976) notes that "for the most part they [schizophrenic patients] call for modes of participation on the analyst's part which are appreciably, and often strikingly, different." In brilliant fashion, he reveals how

his own methods are at variance with the classical technique. He
makes a powerful case for forthrightness, for spontaneity and for
avoiding emotional evasiveness. The tremendous challenge of
dealing with very disturbed persons deeply and inescapably shakes
the foundations of our self-concepts and forces us to resolve
questions of human existence. These challenges are less apparent in
dealing with neurotics but they are there.

Although my experience in private practice does not entitle me to
speak authoritatively about schizophrenics, I venture to suggest that
his (Searles') position on countertransference has the power of rich
generality. It seems to encompass problems therapists deal with
irrespective of diagnostic category. Whatever he has said about the
conscious and *particularly unconscious* processes released in the
therapist during the therapeutic transaction, namely, strivings for
omnipotence, envy, murderous rage, self-pity, despair, disappointment with the patient's progress; all these trends evoked by the
patient's accusations, passive aggression, savagery, and contempt
can and do occur in muffled tones, so often poorly appreciated by
the participants in the seemingly more unchallenging atmosphere
with the neurotic.

How we victimize patients is also more difficult to bring into
sharp relief when we treat neurotics. I suspect, or better, hope that
my desire to see greater generality in these processes arises from an
educated respect for unifying principles. These issues are difficult to
discuss and formulate with effective penetration, partly because I
have said nothing that calls for argument; who is against unifying
principles, provided the search for certainty is not merely an
inability to tolerate uncertainty. What appeals to me about Searles'
engagement with himself and his patient is his ability to sort out
unwitting postures of therapists, locating false assumptions as to
what constitutes therapy differentiating it from artifactual help,
albeit sincere and well-intentioned. We cannot escape ourselves.
This does not leave us condemned or judged, nor does it encourage
relativism. What I regard as countertransference is when I feel and
behave as I should or ought rather than as I am. I would like to
achieve attitudes as therapist which do not develop because they
should or ought so to develop. Maybe I cannot achieve that degree
of constructive spontaneity, but that is what I want for myself. I
cannot say how such a phenomenon occurs and is nurtured. I have
thought for a long time that what strongly blocks us is a profound
unease in dealing with love, affection, and tenderness in our work;

we have acknowledged the need to deal with anxiety, hate, rage and so on, but we are unclear about and evasive with love, affection, and tenderness than other human affects. We are unhappily yearning to receive and give. The subject matter is so treacherously difficult we have no comfortable language to ruminate about it with our colleagues. In terms of a reliably productive therapeutic transaction, we suspect it must be somewhere, but what, where, how and when? Is this something for our fictitious Russian author to write about? "Does it exist?" Searles (1976) touches on this (p. 399). He writes: "He (the patient) is also trying once again to cure the sick parent whom in his childhood he was unable to cure. This aspect of the patient's genuine loving therapeutic devotion toward the parents and toward subsequent transference figures such as the analyst himself is the dimension of this work which is of greatest current interest to me."

I have found this dimension of the work in therapy of great interest to me for a long time. That the patient's living devotion is transference seems correct, but is this only transference? How does the analyst stand in this matter? Is the analyst's loving devotion only a countertransference phenomenon?

Despite the recognition that the classical position has important validity — constraint on the therapist's spontaneity can lead to falsification of true naturalistic interaction. Can one actually delete the therapist's spontaneity and approximate the goals of acquiring constructive relatedness? Can two people truly study only one of the two? Analysis is not directly similar to a nonanalytic relationship, yet it must be sufficiently similar in important ways otherwise it fails to actualize what the patient's goals are in his nontherapeutic world. The question is how can this analytic process approximate outside reality without the therapist's making pathological claims on the patient. Guarding against unconstructive intrusion is not sufficient to accomplish the mission. The atmosphere is impoverished and unnatural; the atmosphere may unwittingly recreate many of the destructive elements in the patient's past. The mystique, mystification, the authoritarian climate, the patient's obligation to tolerate emotional deprivation, the patient's obligation to conform to a theory — are these truly valuable modes of therapeutic technique?

My argument in regard to the classical tradition is not to degrade it but to respect its early beginnings. It was recognized that unwise intrusion could only interfere with what may uncomplicatedly emerge from the patient. If the patient were aided only by interpretation aligned with the postulations of the extant theory, it was hoped that this rationale could lead to cure. This was a beginning of vast importance — the first milestone. Subsequently, in some quarters the patient was invited into a therapeutic alliance characterized by participant observation: the therapist and the patient studied the patient — a second milestone. Then there were some who recognized that the therapist must enter the challenge of the patient's affective input — a set calling for new expertise, renewed courage and more clearly acknowledged undefensiveness. Perhaps one approach to countertransference is more congenial to one therapist's mode of operating while the other suits another therapist. Yet, in simple terms, the classical tradition "protects" the analyst and reduces the enrichment potential of the transaction. What I have styled the positive transference position can introduce error, and requires close monitoring of the influence of the therapist's input. Error is unavoidable and since reparations are often possible, this technique is closer to life — to the way life is lived. Error has to occur in order to sharpen what one is truly seeking to discover.

The mistake that I see the classicists make is their outspoken or tacit condemnation of those who wish to use themselves optimally, inferring thereby that such methods lead in the extreme to wild analysis or to lesser degrees of irresponsible attitude and behavior. What we are discussing here is not for a beginner's manual — it is a subject for serious mature colleagues who apply judgment and wisdom to their task and who are not involved in unconscionable, self-seeking tactics. I see the classical technique as unwittingly introducing a countertransference phenomenon by the therapist's failure to use himself in therapy in the fullest and most natural direction. The so-called "hovering" attitude is not enough. Nonengagement is the therapist's misuse of nonintrusion and may have its roots in neurotic anxiety.

If the therapist's unacknowledged need to feel grandiose, to express murderous rage, envy, hate, and his need to deceive himself by specious dedication — if these characteristics constitute countertransference, is it not equally true that fear of using his imagination, his sense of immediacy, his spontaneity are also harmful to the therapeutic transaction — in effect, a negative countertransference reaction?

REFERENCES

Searles, H. (1976). Psychoanalytic therapy with schizophrenic patients in a private practice context. *Contemporary Psychoanalysis* 12:387-406.

Tauber, E.S. (1954). Exploring the therapeutic use of countertransference data. *Psychiatry*, 17:331-336.

Chapter 4

THE INTERACTIONAL DIMENSION OF COUNTERTRANSFERENCE

ROBERT LANGS, M.D.

It is the basic purpose of this paper to outline, discuss, and synthesize a serious of clinical postulates regarding countertransference, developed through an adaptational approach to this dimension of therapeutic and analytic relationships. These postulates are based on clinical observations and an extensive review of the psychoanalytic literature (Langs 1976a,c), and were shaped with a view toward enhancing our understanding of the treatment interaction and with some stress on their pertinence to analytic and therapeutic technique.[1] The present investigation of countertransference is somewhat different than the prior explorations I have undertaken (1974, 1976a,c), in that I shall focus here almost exclusively on the interactional aspects of countertransference and shall concentrate on recent conceptions developed largely since those earlier publications — some of which have not previously been considered at all, either by myself or by others. I shall adopt an

1. The clinical observations and formulations to be developed in this paper are equally pertinent to psychotherapy and pyschoanalysis. Since almost all the prior literature on this subject is derived from the psychoanalytic situation, I will adopt that as my model for this presentation.

71

approach that concentrates on the delineation, elaboration, and clinical illustration of these postulates and, while the ideas presented here have been contributed to significantly by earlier writers, I will not provide an historical survey since I have done so in an earlier work (1976c). Without further introduction, then, I shall turn now to the basic definitions that we will need in order to define and comprehend the interactional dimension of countertransference.

BASIC DEFINITIONS

I shall proceed in outline form, offering only the essentials (the interested reader may find the elaborating literature in Langs 1973a,b, 1974, 1975a,b,c, 1976a,c, 1978a,b).

1. *The bipersonal field* (Baranger and Baranger 1966, Langs 1976a,c) refers to the temporal-physical space within which the analytic interaction takes place. The patient is one term of the polarity; the analyst is the other. The field embodies both interactional and intrapsychic mechanisms, and every event within the field receives vectors from both particpants. The field itself is defined by a framework — the ground rules of psychoanalysis — which not only delimits the field, but also, in a major way, contributes to the communicative properties of the field and to the anaylst's hold of the patient and containment of his projective identification.

Communications within the field take place along an interface determined by inputs from both patient and analyst, and possessing a variety of characteristics, including, among others, psychopathology, depth, and stability. The major interactional mechanisms in the field are those of projective and introjective identification, although other interactional defenses, such as denial, splitting, the creation of bastions (split-off sectors of the field; see Baranger and Baranger 1966), and additional unconsciously shared forms of gratification and defense are also characteristic. The major intrapsychic defenses are those of repression, displacement, and the other well-known classically described mechanisms.

2. The investigation of the communicative medium provided by the frame of the field and the communicative mode of each participant is essential for an understanding of the analytic interaction and therapeutic work. The basic communications from each participant occur verbally and nonverbally, through words

and actions serving a variety of meanings and functions. As a fundamental means of categorizing these communications, they can be classified as manifest content and as Type One and Type Two derivatives (Langs 1978a,b). The first term refers to the surface nature and meaning of a communication, while a Type One derivative constitutes a relatively available inference or latent theme extracted from the manifest content. In contrast, a Type Two derivative is organized around a specific *adaptive context* — the precipitant or instigator of the interactional and intrapsychic response — and entails definitive dynamic meanings and functions relevant to that context. Further, within a given bipersonal field, every communication is viewed as an interactional product, with inputs from both participants.

3. On this basis, we may identify three basic styles of communicating and three related forms of interactional field (Langs 1978a). The Type A style or field is characterized by the use of symbolic communications, and the bipersonal field itself becomes the realm of illusion and a transitional or play space. In general, the patient's associations can be organized around a series of specific adaptive contexts, yielding a series of indirect communications that constitute Type Two derivatives. These latent contents and themes fall into the realm of unconscious fantasy, memory, and introject on the one hand, and unconscious perception on the other. For the development of a Type A field, both patient and analyst must be capable of tolerating and maintaining a secure framework; in addition, the analyst must have the ability to offer symbolic interpretations of the patient's communications.

The Type B field or style is one in which action, discharge, and the riddance of accretions of psychic disturbance is central. The primary mechanism in this field is that of projective identification and living (acting) out, and both language and behavior are utilized as means of discharge rather than as vehicles for symbolic understanding.

While the Type A and Type B fields are positively communicative, each in its own way, the essential characteristic of the Type C is the destruction of communication and meaning, and the use of falsifications and impervious barriers as the main interactional mode. Here, language is used as a defense against disturbed inner mental contents. The Type C field is static and empty, and is further characterized by the projective identification of both emptiness and nonmeaning, finding its only sense of meaning in these efforts to destroy communication, links, and meaning itself. While resistances in the Type A field are characterized by the availability of analyzable derivatives, and those in the Type B field are amenable to interpretation based on the defensive use of projective identification, defenses and resistances in the Type C field have no sense of depth and possess a persistent, amorphous, and empty quality.

4. Within the bipersonal field, the patient's relationship with the analyst has both transference and nontransference components. The former are essentially distorted and based on pathological, intrapsychic unconscious fantasies, memories, and introjects, while the latter are essentially nondistorted and based on valid unconscious perceptions and introjections of the analyst, his conscious and unconscious psychic state and communications, and his mode of interacting. Within the transference sphere, in addition to distortions based on displacements from past figures (genetic transference), there are additional distortions based on the patient's current intrapsychic state and use of interactional mechanisms (projective distortions). Further, nontransference, while valid in terms of the prevailing actualities of the therapeutic interaction, always includes important genetic components — though essentially in the form of the actual repetitions of past pathogenic interactions (for details, see Langs 1976c).

The analyst's relationship with the patient is similarly constituted in terms of countertransference and noncountertransference. The former entails all inappropriate and distorted reactions to the patient, whatever their source, and may be based on displacements from the past as well as on pathological projective and introjective mechanisms. Factors in countertransference-based responses range from the nature of a particular patient, the quality and contents of his communications, the meaning of analytic work for the analyst, and interactions with outside parties — other patients and others in the analyst's nonprofessional and professional life.

The noncountertransference sphere of the analyst's functioning entails his valid capacity to manage the framework, to understand the patient's symbolic communications and offer meaningful interpretations, and a basic ability to contain, metabolize, and interpret symbolically the patient's projective identifications. There are a wide range of additional aspects of the analyst's valid and noncountertransference-based functioning which will not be detailed here (see Langs 1976c).

THREE INTERACTIONAL POSTULATES REGARDING COUNTERTRANSFERENCE

Postulate 1: As a dimension of the bipersonal field, countertransference (as well as noncountertransference) is an interactional product with vectors from both patient and analyst.

Among the many implications of this generally accepted postualte, some of which have not been specifically identified and discussed in the literature, I will consider those most pertinent to psychoanalytic technique and to the identification and resolution of specific countertransference difficulties. In this context, it is well to be reminded that countertransference-based interventions and behaviors are often not recognized as such by the analyst, due largely to the fact that countertransference is itself rooted in unconscious fantasies, memories, introjects, and interactional mechanisms. The adaptive interactional approach to countertransference greatly facilitates their recognition and resolution.

This initial postulate implies that each countertransference-based response from the analyst has a specific and potentially identifiable adaptive context. While this stimulus may reside in the personal life of the analyst or in his work with another patient, it most often entails stimuli from the relationship with the patient at hand and is, as a rule, evoked by the communications from the patient. Any unusual feeling or fantasy within the analyst, any failure by the patient to confirm his interventions (whether interpretations or management of the framework), any unusual or persistent symptom or resistance in the patient, or any regressive episode in the course of an analysis should alert the analyst to the possible presence of countertransference factors.

Value of interactional approach. The interactional approach proves to be of special value in these pursuits in three important ways: (1) by establishing the finding that the patient's communications and symptoms may be significantly derived from the countertransferences of the analyst; (2) by indicating that through the process of introjective identification the patient becomes a mirror and container for the analyst, in the sense that the patient's communications will play back to the analyst the metabolized introjects derived from his countertransference-based interventions (and his valid, noncountertransference-based interventions as well); and (3) by directing the search for the form and meaning of countertransferences to the sequential interactions of each session.

If we consider these sequential clues first, we may recognize that the immediate precipitant for the countertransference-based reaction can be found in the material from the patient that precedes the erroneous intervention (inappropriate silences, incorrect verbalizations such as erroneous interpretations, and mismanagements of the framework). While there is often a broader context to the countertransference-based intervention in the ongoing relationship between the analyst and his patient, and while there may be, as I have noted, additional inputs derived from relationships outside of the immediate bipersonal field, clinical experience indicates that these immediate adaptive contexts provide extremely important organizing threads for the detection and comprehension of the underlying countertransference fantasies. When dealing with a countertransference-based positive intervention (as compared to silence, which I could consider a negative intervention), it is, of course, the last of the patient's associations that prompts the analyst's response. If this communication is viewed within the overall context of the patient's material, and understood in terms of manifest and latent content, and if all of this is addressed in interaction with the manifest and latent content of the analyst's erroneous intervention, the amalgam provides important and immediate clues as to the nature of the analyst's underlying difficulty.

The interactional sequence. Thus, the interactional sequence for a countertransference-based response is (1) adaptive context (especially the stimulus from the patient at hand), (2) the analyst's erroneous reaction (positive or negative intervention, whether interpretation or management of the frame), and (3) response by the patient and continued reaction by the analyst. If countertransferences are to be understood in depth, they must be organized around their specific adaptive contexts, so the analyst may understand himself in terms of Type Two derivatives, including both unconscious fantasies and perceptions. Without such an effort, he would be restricted to an awareness of the manifest content of his erroneous intervention or to readily available inferences — both fraught with possible further countertransference-based effects.

This sequence also implies that the analyst may recognize the presence of a countertransference difficulty at one of several junctures — as the patient is communicating disturbing material, while he is intervening, or after he has intervened — and that this recognition may be based either on his own subjective reactions or on subsequent communications from the patient. Much has already been written regarding subjective clues within the analyst who has a countertransference problem, while less consideration has been given to those leads available from the patient; let us now examine these latter more carefully.

The bipersonal field concept directs the analyst to the investigation of his countertransferences when any resistance, defense, symptom, or regression occurs within the patient or himself. Since the adaptational-interactional view considers all such occurrences as interactional products, it generates as a technical requisite the investigation of unconscious factors in both participants at such moments in therapy. As a rule, these disturbances, when they occur within the patient (to take that as our focus), will have unconscious communicative meaning. In the presence of a prevailing counter-transference-based communication from the analyst, they will reflect the patient's introjective identification of this disturbance, his unconscious perceptions of its underlying basis, and his own realistic and fantasied metabolism of the introject. That patient's reactions to the disturbed intervention from the analyst may include exploitation, the creation of misalliances and bastions, and use of the intervention for the maintenance of his own neurosis (a term used here in its broadest sense), as well as unconscious efforts to detoxify the introject and cure the analyst.

In terms of the patient's associations and behaviors following and incorrect intervention, the interactional model directs us to the intervention itself as the adaptive context for the patient's subsequent association. In this way, the patient's material can, as a rule, be treated as Type Two derivatives in response to the particular adaptive context. I term these associations *commentaries* on the analyst's intervention, in that they contain both unconscious perceptions and unconscious fantasies.

Hierarchy of tasks for the analyst. It is here that we may identify a particular hierarchy of tasks for the analyst, based in part on the recognition that this discussion implies that the patient's association always take place along a *me-not-me interface* (Langs 1976c, 1978a) with continuous reference to self and analyst. Thus, valid technique calls for the monitoring of the material from the patient for conscious and unconscious communications related to the analyst before establishing those related to the patient; actually, the one cannot be identified without an understanding of the other. In addition, in both spheres — self and analyst — the analyst must determine the patient's valid perceptions, thoughts, and fantasies before identifying those that are distorted and inappropriate; here too, the identification of one relies on a comprehension of the other. Ultimately, of course, these determinations have as their most essential basis the analyst's self-knowledge, and especially his in-depth understanding of the conscious and unconscious meanings of his communications to the patient.

In the adaptive context, then, of the analyst's interventions, the patient's responsive associations are an amalgam of unconscious perceptions of the manifest and latent qualities of the intervention, on the one hand, and, on the other, their subsequent elaboration in terms of the patient's valid and distorted functioning. Thus, in addition to determining whether such associations truly validate the analyst's intervention by providing genuinely new material that reorganizes previously known clinical data (i.e., constitutes a *selected fact*, as Bion [1962] has termed it) and evidence for positive introjective identification, the analyst must also consider this material in terms of the patient's experience and introjection of his communication — valid and invalid. This introjective process takes place on the cognitive level as well as in terms of interactional mechanisms. The analyst must therefore be prepared to recognize that both cognitive-symbolic communications and projective identifications are contained in his interventions; in fact, he must be prepared to recognize his use of interventions as facades, falsifications, and barriers as well (see below).

This interactional approach enables the analyst to make full use of his patient's conscious and unconscious resources, and of the analysand as an unconscious teacher and therapist. The analytic bipersonal field is not, of course, designed primarily for such a use of the patient, but these occurrences are inevitable in every analysis, since countertransference can never be totally eliminated. In addition, in actuality, these experiences often have enormously therapeutic benefit for the patient (see Searles 1975), so long as the analyst has not deliberately misused the analysand in this regard, and is in addition capable of understanding and responding appropriately to the patient's curative efforts. In this respect, it is essential that the analyst make silent and unobtrusive use of his patient's introjection of his countertransference and of his additional therapeutic efforts on his behalf, responding without explicit acknowledgment and with implicit benefit. This latter implies the analyst's ability to follow the patient's leads and to benefit through

efforts at self-analysis based on the patient's unconscious perceptions and the therapeutic endeavors; it also requires a capacity to
acutally rectify — correct or modify — any continued expression of
the countertransference difficulty and to control most, if not all,
subsequent possible expressions. In addition, it may entail the
analyst's *implicit* acknowledgment of an error in technique and a
full analysis of the patient's unconscious perceptions and other
responses in terms that accept their validity — work that must in
addition address itself eventually to the patient's subsequent
distortions, and to the pathological misappropritions and responses
to these countertransference-based difficulties within the analyst.

*Postulate 2: The analyst's unconscious countertransference fan-
tasies and interactional mechanisms will influence his three major
functions vis-à-vis the patient: his management of the framework
and capacity to hold the patient; his ability to contain and
metabolize projective identifictions; and his functioning as the
interpreter of the patient's symbolic associations, projective identifications, and efforts to destroy meaning.*

A complementary postulate would state that the analyst's
countertransferences can be aroused by, and understood in terms
of, not only the patient's associations and behaviors, but also in terms
of the analyst's responses to the framework of the bipersonal field,
and to the holding and containing capacities of the patient.

While some analysts, such as Reich (1960) and Greenson (1972),
have questioned the invariable relationship between technical
errors and countertransference, my own clinical observations
clearly support such a thesis. However, virtually the entire classical
psychoanalytic literature prior to my own writings (see especially
1975b,c, 1976a,c, 1978a) considered as the sole vehicle of countertransference expression the analyst's erroneous verbal interventions,
especially his errors in interpreting. A number of Kleinian writers,
especially Grinberg (1962) and Bion (1962, 1963, 1965, 1970) have
also investigated countertransference influences on the analyst's
management of projective identifications and on his containing
functions. A full conceptualization of possible avenues of countertransference expression would include all these areas, as well as the
analyst's management of the ground rules and his capacity to hold
the patient.

As we have already seen in the discussion of the first postulate, the
adaptational-interactional view helps to deepen and render more

specific our understanding of the interplay between countertransference and the analyst's interpretive interventions. Not unexpectedly, it leads us to include missed interventions and inappropriate silences along with the expression of countertransference, and provides us extensive means for identifying, rectifying, and interpreting the patient's responses to these errors. Much of this has been discussed above, tends to be familiar territory for most analysts, and has been considered rather extensively in prior publications (see especially Langs 1976a,c); I will therefore restrict myself here to a consideration of those aspects of this postulate that have been relatively disregarded.

Management of ground rules. Perhaps the single most neglected arena for the expression of the analyst's countertransferences is that of his management of the ground rules — the framework of the bipersonal field. In part, because virtually every analyst has to this day been analyzed within a bipersonal field whose framework has been modified, the influence of countertransferences on the analyst's management functions has been virtually ignored by all. Nonetheless, I have garnered extensive evidence for the basic and necessary functions of a secure framework (Langs 1975c, 1976a, 1978a), demonstrating its importance in creating a therapeutic hold for the patient, in establishing the necessary boundaries between patient and analyst, and in affording the bipersonal field its essential open and symbolic communicative qualities.

However, the maintainance of a secure framework requires of the analyst a tolerance for his patient's therapeutic regression and related primitive communications, a renunciation of his pathological and countertransference-based needs for inappropriate gratification and defenses, and a capacity to tolerate his own limited regression and experiences of anxiety, which are inevitable under these conditions. Thus, because the management of the frame is so sensitively a function of the analyst's capacity to manage his own inner state, and to maintain his psychic balance, his handling of the framework is in part a direct reflection of the extent to which he has mastered his countertransferences. Further, because of the collective blind spots in this area and the sanction so implied, analysts will tend to monitor their verbal interventions for countertransference-based influences, while neglecting to do so in regard to their management of the frame. Clearly, any alternation in the framework can provide the analyst countertransference-based and inappropriate gratifications, as well as defenses and nonadaptive relief from anxiety and other symptoms; all possible deviations in the frame should therefore be explored for such factors (see Langs 1975c).

Three types of containing pathology: problems of countertransference. Interactionally, one of the analyst's basic functions is to receive contain, metabolize, and interpret the patient's projective identifications (interactional projections) and other interactional inputs. Due to underlying countertransferences, an analyst may be refractory to such containment and impervious to both the patient's communications and his interactional efforts. Much of this is based on what Bion (1962, 1970) has described as the container's dread of the contained, and which he has characterized as fears of denudation and destruction. An analyst may indeed dread the effects on himself of the patient's communications and projective identifictions, and may respond on a countertransference basis with nonlistening, with distancing or breaking the link with the patient (Bion 1959), or by undertaking active efforts to modify the patient's disturbing communications and projections — often through the use of irrelevant questions, distinctly erroneous interpretations, and sudden alterations in the framework.

A second form of countertransference-based disturbance in the analyst's containing function may occur in regard to the processing or metabolizing of the patient's projective identifications (see Langs 1976b). Grinberg (1962) has termed this *projective counteridentification:* a situation in which the analyst receives a projective identification, remains unconscious of its contents, meaning and effects, and inappropriately and unconsciously reprojects the pathological contents back into the patient — either directly or in some modified but detoxified form. Bion (1962) has termed this containing function the capacity for *reverie,* and has stressed the importance of the detoxification of dreaded and pathological projective identifications, leading to reprojections back into the patient that are far more benign than the original projective identifications. In my terms, this detoxification process entails the appropriate *metabolism* of a projective identification, the awareness in the analyst of its conscious and unconscious implications, and the symbolic interpretation of these contents in terms of defense-resistance functions and the revelation of pathological introjects. In this regard, countertransference-related anxieties, introjects, and disruptive fantasies may disturb the metabolizing and detoxifying process within the analyst, and may render him incapable of

becoming aware of the nature of the patient's projective identifications and unable to interpret them. Under these conditions, he will,
as a rule, pathologically metabolize the introject in terms of his own
inner disturbance, and reproject into the patient — through verbal
interventions and mismanagement of the framework — a more
terrifying and pathological projective identification than that which
orginated from the analysand.

A third type of containing pathology entails what I have described
as a pathological need for introjective identifications — a countertransference-based need to inappropriately and excessively contain
pathological introjects (Langs 1976a,b). This tends to be expressed
through provocative interventions — whether interpretive or in
respect to the frame — that are unconsciously designed as intrusive
projective identifications into the patient, intended to evoke
responsive pathological projective identifications from the analysand.
These analysts have a hunger for pathological expressions from their
patients, and find many means of inappropriately disturbing their
patients and generating ill-timed pathological projective identifications.

The analytic bipersonal field. The analytic bipersonal field is
designed for the cure of the patient, and for the analytic resolution,
through cognitive insight and implicit positive introjective identifications, of his pyschopathology. It has proved difficult for analysts
to accept that a valid and secondary function of the same bipersonal
field — valid only so long as it is, indeed, secondary — is that of the
analytic resolution of more restricted aspects of the analyst's
psychopathology. This idea is often misundertood to imply a belief
in the use of the patient and the analytic situation as a primary
vehicle for the cure of the analyst. Despite explicit disavowal of such
intentions, the recognition that this will inevitably be a second-order
phenomenon is viewed as exploitation of the patient, rather than as a
relatively silent and actually indispensable benefit that will accrue to
the well-functioning analyst. In the course of overcoming the many
resistances against accepting this postulate — more precisely, a
clinical observation — it has become evident that this attribute is an
essential component of the bipersonal field, and that it is unlikely
that the analyst could function adequately in its absence. Without it,
it would be virtually impossible for him to master the inevitable
anxieties and disturbances that will occur within him, as interactional products, in the course of his analytic work with each
patient. Their inevitable presence has not only a potential therapeutic

effect on his behalf, but also renders him a far more effective analyst for his patients.

The basic framework — the ground rules — of the psychoanalytic situation provides a hold, appropriate barriers, and the necessary communicative medium for analyst as well as patient. This hold affords him a valuable and appropriate sense of safety, a means of defining his role vis-à-vis the patient, assistance in managing his inappropriate impulses and fantasies toward the patient (his countertransferences), and insures the possibility of his use of language for symbolic interpretations (it is therefore essential to his interpretive capacities).

Just as certain aspects of the analyst's behavior and stance are essential dimensions of the framework, the patient too offers a hold to the analyst. Such factors as the regularity of his attendance at sessions, his being on time, his payment of the fee, his complying with the fundamental rule of free association, his listening to and working over the analyst's interpretations, and his own adherence to the ground rules and boundaries of the analytic relationship contribute to a holding effect experienced by the analyst. Further, the patient will inevitably serve as a container for the analyst's projective identifications — both pathological and nonpathological — a function through which, once again, the analyst may implicitly benefit.

As for the influence of countertransference in these areas, these may derive from undue or pathological (instinctualized: aggressivized or sexualized) holding needs, and an unconscious fear of, or need to repudiate, the patient's hold, a dread of the patient as container, and an excessive need to utilize the patient's containing capacities. These countertransference influences are manifested through the analyst's mismanagement of the frame, his erroneous interventions, his failures to intervene, and, overall, through conscious and unconscious deviations in the analyst's central commitment to the therapeutic needs of the patient. The analyst who inordinately requires a rigid and unmodified frame will be intolerant of his patient's alterations of that frame; these may take the form of latenesses, missed sessions, necessary requests to change the time of an hour because of changed life circumstances, unnecessary requests for such changes in schedule, and a variety of gross and subtle efforts to alter the basic ground rules of analysis — such as efforts to engage the analyst in conversation after an hour.

It is my empirically derived conclusion (Langs 1975c, 1976a,c) that it is the analyst's main responsibility to maintain, to the extent feasible, the framework intact in the face of all inappropriate efforts at deviation. I am therefore in no way advocating conscious — or unconscious — participation in inappropriate modifications of the frame. I wish to stress, however, that analysts with pathological needs for a rigid frame — in contrast to the necessary rigorous frame (Sandler, in Langs et al., in press) — will have difficulty in recognizing those rare valid indications for an alteration in the framework (e.g., a suicidal emergency), a change that is in essence a revised version of the basic framework without its destruction or defective reconstitution. In addition, such an analyst will have a great deal of difficulty in dealing with his patient's efforts to modify the framework and in recognizing such endeavors as a crucial adaptive context for the organization of the analysand's subsequent material. He also will have major problems in understanding the unconscious implications of these intended or actual alterations in the frame, and in carrying out effective, relevant analytic work. Further, he will dread those interpretations to his patient that might generate moments of hostility and rejection, and which might unconsciously prompt the patient to modify in some way his usual, implicit hold of the analyst.

The pathological container. Those analysts for whom the patient's inevitable hold generates a threat, whether related to fears of intimacy, instinctualization of the patient's holding capacities in terms of seductive and aggressive threats, or the dread of the necessary and therapeutic regression evoked by such a hold, unconsciously will make efforts to disturb the patient's holding capacities. It seems evident that the patient derives a degree of implicit and necessary gratification in regard to his capacity to safely hold the analyst, a satisfaction that is not unlike those derived from his unconscious curative efforts on the analyst's behalf (Searles 1965, 1975, Langs 1975b, 1976a,c). Thus, the repudiation on any level of the patient's appropriate holding capacities not only generates active countertransference-based inputs into the bipersonal field, but also denies the patient a form of growth-promoting gratification that forms an important complementary means of achieving adaptive structural change, in addition to the more generally recognized means derived from affect-laden insights and inherent positive introjective identifications. It is evident too that the analyst's need to repudiate the patient's appropriate hold will prompt him to generate interventions and mismanagements of the framework designed unconsciously to disturb that holding function, create artificial and undue distance, and erect pathological and inappropriate barriers between himself and the patient.

Every analyst at some time in the course of an analytic experience, and a number of analysts in the course of much of their work with all of their patients, will be burdened by countertransference pressures that prompt the inappropriate use of the patient as what I have termed a *pathological container* for his own disturbed inner contents (Langs 1976a). At such junctures, the analyst's interventions are not primarily designed for the meaningful insight of the patient and for the appropriate maintenance of the framework, but instead unconsciously function as efforts at projective identification as a means of placing into the patient the analyst's burdensome psychopathology and inappropriate defensive needs. And while, as I have mentioned above, the patient can indeed accrue adaptive benefit from his own unconscious capacities to function as a pathological container for the analyst's projective identification and from his curative efforts on the analyst's behalf, such gains are dangerously intermixed with the destructive aspects of such interactions. These include the overburdening of the patient with the analyst's pathology to a degree that evokes a pathological regression that not only will be difficult to manage and interpret, but also may be essentially misunderstood by the analyst who has unconsciously evoked the regressive process and who maintains his unconscious disturbed needs for the patient's containing ability. Failures by the patient to contain the analyst's pathological projective identifications, and to metabolize them, however unconsciously, toward insights for the analyst, will be unconsciously resented by the analyst, and will considerably complicate the analytic interaction. The influence on the patient of the pathological introjects generated by the analyst also may be quite destructive, and may in a major way reinforce the patient's own pathological introjects and defenses. In large measure, such an interaction may constitute the repetition of an important past pathogenic interaction which helped to generate the patient's emotional problems in his formative years.

On the other hand, the analyst may dread any even momentary and limited use of the patient as a container — not only for his pathological projective identifications, but for his valid interventions as well. Under these conditions he will experience an extreme constriction in his capacity to interpret to the patient and excessive anxiety in communicating freely to him, however consciously these interventions are founded on a wish to be appropriately helpful. Often, the dread of containing the patient's projective identifications is based on conscious and unconscious fears of being driven crazy by the patient, and related fears of psychic disintegration or loss of control; fears of similar effects on the patient may inhibit the analyst's necessary projective communications to the analsysand.

Postulate 3: Countertransferences have a significant influence on the communicative properties of the bipersonal field, and on both the analyst's and the patient's style of communicating.

It is evident that the communicative style of the analyst (and of the bipersonal field of which he is a part) is a function of a wide range of factors, the most immediately obvious being inborn tendencies; acute and cumulative genetic experiences; personality and character structure; ego resources; ego dysfunctions; intrapsychic conflicts; unconscious fantasies, memories, and introjects; and the overall extent of emotional health or psychopathology. The focus here on the influence of countertransference is, then, an attempt to delineate simply one vector among many that coalesce to effect a particular communicative style and field.

Ideal mode of communication: Type A. Initial clinical evidence suggests that the ideal analyst basically employs the Type A mode of communication, with its essential symbolic qualities, and that he has a capacity to manage the framework of the analytic situation in order to create with the patient a potential field for a Type A communicative interaction. Such an analyst would undoubtedly, from time to time, and based on many factors, momentarily shift to the Type B, action-discharge mode of communication and to the Type C, barrier-negation mode. He would, however, through his own awareness and through communications from his patient, be capable of recognizing these shifts in communicative style, of self-analyzing their underlying basis, of rectifying their influence on the patient and the therapeutic bipersonal field, and of interpreting to the patient his conscious and unconscious perceptions of this communicative shift and its unconscious meanings and functions.

Type B mode. In contrast to the Type A therapist, the Type B therapist experiences repeated difficulty in deriving symbolic formulations of his patient's associations and in generating symbolic interpretations. While his conscious intentions may well be to offer such interventions — there is considerable lack of insight within analysts in regard to their communicative mode — his use of language will be unconsciously aimed at projective identification into the patient and internal relief-producing discharge. While at times patients may undoubtedly derive some type of symptom relief from such therapeutic interactions — based primarily on relatively benign projective identifications from the analyst and on positive self-feelings derived from unconscious curative efforts and containing responses to his pathology — such gains are not embedded in valid cognitive insights and modulating, positive introjective identifications. As a result, they are quite vulnerable to regression and are without the necessary substantial foundation characteristic of lasting adaptive structural change. In addition to their use of verbal interventions that function interactionally as pathological projective identifications, these analysts are quite prone to unneeded modifications of the framework which similarly serve their needs for pathological projective identification, action, and discharge. Elsewhere (Langs 1976a,c) I have designated as *misalliance and framework cures* the noninsightful, unstable symptom relief, in either patient or analyst, that may be derived in a Type B communicative field.

Type C mode. The analyst who is prone to a Type C communicative style will seldom be capable of a truly symbolic interpretation. His verbal interventions make use of language not primarily as communication, but as a form of noncommunication and as an effort to destroy meaning. These analysts make extensive use of the psychoanalytic cliche and, unconsciously, their interventions and mismanagements of the framework are designed to destroy the communicative qualities of the bipersonal field and to render it frozen and static. Based on the massive defensive barriers and falsifications offered by these analysts, patients will from time to time experience symptom relief through reinforcement of their own Type C communicative style or through the development of impermeable defensive barriers that momentarily serve as a protection against disruptive underlying contents — fantasies, memories, and introjects. This type of *misalliance cure* (Langs 1975b, 1976a, c) may well account for a large percentage of symptom relief among present-day psychotherapeutic and psychoanalytic patients, and within their therapists and analysts as well.

The Type A therapist will, of course, tend to be rather comfortable with a Type A patient, and will be capable of interpreting his communications. Countertransference-based anxieties may occur because of the regressive pressures that he experiences in a Type A field and, in addition, will arise when the communications from the Type A patient touch upon areas of continued vulnerability. With a Type B patient, he will be capable of containing, metabolizing, and interpreting his patient's projective identifications, though countertransference difficulties may intrude when these projective identifications are massive or touch upon areas of excessive sensitivity. Some Type A analysts experience discomfort with the action-prone, projectively identifying Type B patient, and will experience difficulties in containing, metabolizing, and interpreting their interactional projections.

A Type C patient may be quite boring to the Type A analyst, who will consciously and unconsciously experience the envy, destruction of meaning, and attack on the analyst's ability to think and formulate that is characteristic of these patients. The Type A analyst may be vulnerable to these qualities of the negative projective identifications of these patients, and he may also have difficulty in tolerating their use of massive, impenetrable, and uninterpretable defensive barriers. Still, he is in the best position to identify the qualities of a Type C communicative style and to patiently interpret the primary defensive aspects. In addition, he is best prepared to tolerate, contain, and interpret the underlying psychotic core of these patients.

While clinical evidence indicates that it is possible to conduct a successful analysis with a Type B or Type C patient (Langs 1978a), it appears likely that the reverse is not true: Type B and Type C analysts cannot be expected to generate bipersonal fields characterized by an openness of communication, the use of symbolic language, the rendering of symbolic interpretations that lead to cognitive insight and mastery, and the interactional experience of positive projective and introjective identifications — all culminating in adaptive structural change and growth for the patient. While, as I have noted above, Type B and Type C analysts may indeed afford their patients periods of symptom relief, and while these may on occasion structuralize and lead to the disappearance of symptoms, the underlying basis for these symptomatic changes are infused with pathological mechanisms and are quite vulnerable to regressive pressures. There can be no substitute for a personal analysis and for the self-analytic efforts designed to master a given analyst's propensities for the Type B and Type C communicative modes.

In concluding this delineation of interactional postulates related to countertransference, two points implicit to this discussion deserve to be specified. First, in virtually every countertransference-based intervention there is a nucleus of constructive intention and effect. While in general, this kernel of valid effort is by no means sufficient to compensate for the hurt and damage done by a countertransference-based intervention — effects that may range from the relatively modifiable to the quite permanent — this positive nucleus often can be used as a center of constructive therapeutic work during the therapeutic interludes evoked by the consequences of an unconscious countertransference fantasy or introject. Second, it follows from this observation, and from more general clinical impressions, that considerable insightful analytic work can prevail throughout the rectification-analysis phase of such countertransference-dominated interludes. Thus, we must maintain a balanced view of the effects of the analyst's countertransferences: to some degree, they damage the patient and reinforce his neurosis (a term I again use here in its broadest sense), and thereby perpetuate or even intensify his psychopathology; in addition, however, so long as the countertransference-based effects are recognized, rectified, and fully analyzed with the patient — and of course, subjected to self-analysis by the analyst — these experiences also can provide extremely moving, insightful, positive introjective moments for both patient and analyst.

CLINICAL VIGNETTE

I will now present a single condensed vignette as a means of illustrating these postulates. Because of my commitment to total confidentiality regarding my direct work with patients, this material will be drawn from a supervisory seminar. While this approach is somewhat limiting in the area of countertransference, the interested reader will find additional data in several recent publications (Langs 1976a, b, 1978a); most important, he should have ample opportunity to clinically document these postulates in his own therapeutic endeavors.

Mr. A. was married, in his mid-thirties, depressed, and afraid of growing old and dying. Early in his analysis, during sessions in which his analyst took notes and intervened largely in terms of questions and reflections of the patient's anxiety about initiating treatment, the patient seemed concerned with a certain deadness in the analytic situation: it was, he said, like talking into a tape recorder. He spoke a great deal of tennis, of the homosexual discussions of his closest male friend, and of his fears of divorce, despite feelings that his marriage was killing him. His wife, he said, often loses control and acts crazy; she is overdependent on him. He also expressed wishes that he could invent a machine that could do psychoanalysis. He spoke of friends who fared poorly in analysis, and the analyst suggested that the patient had doubts about his own treatment. The patient disagreed, but said, however, that he wanted it to be quiet and peaceful, like smoking pot. He was not afraid of talking about homosexuals, though he felt that a physician who worked for him had many such fears.

In the next session, he reported a dream in which he found himself in bed with two women. Earlier that day, he had lingered at his tennis club after one of the members had died of a heart attack or sudden stroke. Mr. A. had fantasies of dropping dead on the tennis court, but spoke instead of feeling quite alive and interested in some medically related research in which he and a male friend were engaged.

The analyst asked the patient how he felt in the dream and inquired about other details. The twosome reminded the patient of a harem and of how he often thinks of other women during intercourse with his wife. He thought of a madam in a movie who had been destructive toward the girls who worked for her, and added that he never understood women and feared them. Further questions along these lines by the analyst led to additional allusions to discussions with friends about homosexuality and to curiosity about what was going on in the analyst's mind. When he plays tennis, the patient said, he thinks of nothing — his mind is blank. The analyst pointed out that the patient seemed frightened of his thoughts concerning homosexuality, but that having two women at one time could hardly be called "homosexual." In response, Mr. A. wondered why he comes to analysis at all. When his friends told him that homosexuals hate women, he panicked; these women were his slaves. He spoke of his hatred for his mother and of his close relationship with a research physician, and wondered what he saw in him; he was always involved with other men; it would be awful to be homosexual.

In the next hour, Mr. A. reported a dream of being late for his session. He was standing outside his analyst's office. The analyst came out to move his car and everybody started to laugh. His tire hit a rock, which then hit a taxicab and disabled it. A black woman got out of the cab and called the analyst crazy; he then pushed the cab around because it couldn't go. In associating, the patient alluded to the previous session and how analysis was a dangerous field because the wrong people can influence you. He feels constricted in what he says while on the couch. The dream followed tennis. He can't be close with anyone; he fights with his wife; everything he does brings him unhappiness.

The analyst asked a series of questions related to the manifest dream, and the patient spoke of how his friends and father think that he is crazy for coming to analysis, though in the dream people are calling the analyst crazy. His father accuses him of trying new things and dropping them. After some rumination, the patient spoke of feeling constricted in the sessions and of possible envy of the analyst; he had to arrange his life in keeping with the analyst's schedule. The analyst responded that the patient skips out in the dream, but the patient rejoined that it was the analyst who had been late — not he. He said he recognized that he is not the analyst's only patient and that the analyst's life does not center around him, as is true for himself in relation to the analyst. If he missed an appointment, he mused, would the analyst lie down? That would be reversing their roles and would make the analyst the crazy one. The analyst responded that the patient seemed afraid of being laughed at, and the patient agreed, suggesting again that the whole thing was a big reversal. The analyst emphasized again that the dream reflected the patient's fears of being laughted at, criticized, and going crazy.

The patient was late for the next session and spoke of a friend who had become a college professor; the patient felt guilty that he had not taken the right path for his own life. There were further references to being crazy, to being in analysis, and to the static qualities of his marriage. The research center at which the patient had done his postgraduate work was probably going to close because it could not get enough funds or students. Many of the staff had died, and the patient spoke of a fear of cancer that he had felt since beginning his analysis. He had had gastrointestinal symptoms; his mother was always preoccupied with gynecological problems; and at his engagement party he had suffered food poisoning. When his father had had his recent surgery, the patient had experienced an intense fear of dying. His father was seldom available when Mr. A.

was a child and would never play tennis with him. Mr. A. recalled several accidents in his childhood, and spoke considerably of his father's disinterest, coldness, and lack of care; if he had been different, the patient would have realized his potential far more than he had. His mother, on the other hand, would get hysterical to the point that no one could talk to her; she was only concerned when he was hurt.

At this point, the analyst suggested that the patient write a short biography of himself for the analyst. Without responding directly, the patient continued to associate: he could always make his mother cry and yet she never hated him as did his father, who held grudges.

In the next hour the patient reported that he had not written the biography; he hadn't had time. He spoke of his research physician friend who had come to Mr. A.'s office to get some downers (sleeping pills) that the patient kept on hand. This doctor was a man worried about aging, and yet Mr. A. still idealized him. He was, however, beginning to see new things and maybe this doctor friend was becoming more human. He felt at any rate that he was more honest with himself than this other man was, and Mr. A. was thinking of leaving the area. He wondered if he should get a nursemaid for his infant daughter and spoke again of his tennis club. He wished his wife would be more aggressive and wondered how women ever develop into good mothers. If he left her, he said, she'd fall apart, and all the time he spends with his men friends interferes with his love for her. So much of this had happened since he started analysis, and it came up too because he'd been talking to his physician friend about that analytic jargon about homosexuality and castration anxiety. His friend felt that analysis is actually insignificant and that one day Mr. A. would have a gnawing pain somewhere, and they'd open him up and find something that would mean that everything would soon be over. Mr. A. would sometimes think about childhood and sex, but not about his parents in that respect. He said he felt he should have read more before he came into analysis, and here the analyst noted that the patient seemed to be looking for some kind of guidelines. The patient said that analysis is like an examination, and he spoke of his secret purchase of nudist magazines. His parents never talked about sex. He had his first sexual relations quite late in life; it was a difficult experience and he had trouble getting an erection and had considered turning on with some kind of drug.

The patient's unconscious perceptions. I will focus here solely on those aspects of this material that are pertinent to this discussion.

The early fragments of this material are in part an unconscious response to the analyst's note-taking and questions — nonanalytic work with manifest contents. At the time this material was presented, the supervisee indicated some sense of confusion with this patient and stated that the note-taking was an effort to get a better idea about what was going on in this analysis; it was also based on a wish to discuss this case with colleagues. The patient's unconscious perceptions and experiences of the note-taking serve us well in attempting to define its unconscious implications, especially those related to the analyst's countertransferences: the analyst is not alive, but a tape recorder and analytic machine; his wife loses control and acts crazy; craziness is connected with homosexuality; his wife is excessively dependent; and there is worry about a physician who worked for the patient.

I will take this as sufficient commentary on the note-taking, and will not attempt to trace out its implications in the additional clinical material. We can therefore pause here and suggest that the note-taking did indeed serve as a significant adaptive context for the patient's associations. It is a meaningful organizer of these communications from the patient, which may be viewed as symbolic in nature and largely in terms of Type Two derivatives: disguised unconscious perceptions of, and fantasies about, the analyst. Much of this falls into the realm of unconscious perceptiveness, and conveys possibly valid unconscious fears, motives, and needs within the analyst that have prompted him to take notes — motives of which the analyst was largely unaware, if we are to take his justifications as reflecting the extent of his insight into himself. It would be difficult here to identify and establish the patient's own unconscious homosexual anxieties and fantasies, fears of losing control and going crazy, and needs for mechanical protective devices, since he can justifiably project and conceal them within the analyst's own evident similar anxieties, efforts at inappropriate gratification, and pathological defenses, expressed, however unconsciously, through the note-taking.

The patient's communicative mode. In terms of the postulates developed here, I also would suggest that this patient is making extensive efforts at Type A communication and toward the development of a Type A bipersonal field. The analyst, for his part, both through the alteration in the framework reflected in his note-taking and through his use of noninterpretive interventions — questions directed at the surface of the patient's associations — is utilizing a Type C mode of communication and is endeavoring to create a static, surface-oriented, falsifying communicative field. While there are, in this material, occasional efforts by the analyst at projective identification which I will soon consider, many of his interactional projections are attempts to place a sense of emptiness and void into the patient, and to develop impenetrable, cliched defenses — the negative type of projective identification characteristic of the Type C field. The main hypothesis, then, is to the effect that the note-taking and the surface-oriented interventions are unconsciously designed by this analyst to satisfy his own needs for a Type C barrier and, actually, to destroy the patient's openness to symbolic communication — to the expression of anxiety-provoking contents that are too disturbing for this analyst.

This hypothesis is supported by the patient's material, and while under other conditions these associations might well reflect the patient's own need for a Type C field, here the data suggest that this is not at all the case: the patient seems to be making repeated efforts at Type A communication, and his allusions to Type C mechanisms appear to be based on introjective identifications with the analyst.

The patient's associations, then, support the formulation that the note-taking and questioning unconsciously reflect impairments in the analyst's capacity to safely hold the patient and to contain the patient's projective identifications. The analyst's behaviors also convey his inappropriate needs to be held by the patient and for the patient to contain his anxieties — implications to which the patient is quite sensitive. On a communicative level, these interventions reflect an unconscious effort by the analyst to modify this potential Type A field into a Type C field in which he would feel better held and safer, especially in regard to disturbing communications and projective identifications from the patient.

The very act of writing down every word from the patient, with its striking containing and incorporative qualities, reflects a dread of actually containing in an affective way the patient's projected contents and a distinct incapacity to metabolize them toward interpretation. Instead, much as the patient unconsciously perceives the therapist's interventions — in respect to the frame and verbally — the note-taking is an effort to deaden the analytic situation, to make it mechanical, and to render it static. The mention of the tape recorder, and the later reference to a psychoanalytic machine, are metaphors of the analyst's containing functions rendered inanimate, probably because of inordinate fears of the patient's projective identifications — the container's fear of the contained (Bion 1962). To state this another way, in terms of the patient's unconscious perceptions and Type Two derivative communications, the therapist fears being driven crazy by his patient and his material, and attempts a Type C mode of expression and set of defenses in a massive effort to seal off this potential craziness and to prevent the contained contents from destroying him — a formulation quite in keeping with an earlier delineation of the Type C field and its function (Langs 1978a).

Among these terrifying contents and projective identifications, those related to latent homosexual themes, uncontrolled destructiveness, and annihilation seem most prominent. While, as I pointed out earlier, the patient may well have intense anxieties in each of these areas, for the moment these formulations apply very directly to the analyst. These countertransferences and their manifestations must be rectified in actuality, and the patient's responses to them analyzed, before the latter's own disturbances could surface in derivative and analyzable form in this bipersonal field. The patient himself refers to the conditions of this field, in which the communicative interface, and the elements of psychopathology it contains, has shifted toward the analyst by referring to efforts to put himself in the analyst's shoes and the reference to role reversal. The analyst's unneeded deviations in the frame and inappropriate interventions unconsciously express his countertransferences and his wish to have the relevant contents contained by the patient and in a sense, therapeutically modified.

The psychoanalytic cliche. In this context, the analyst's intervention that the patient seemed to have many doubts about treatment may be seen as what I have termed a *psychoanalytic cliche* — a psychoanalytically derived generalization based on manifest content or Type One derivatives that primarily serves to destroy the true underlying meaning of the patient's communications, and to substitute a defensive falsification (Bion 1965, 1970, Langs 1978a). The patient's response to this intervention, in which he referred to feeling peaceful when he smoked pot, reflects again the unconscious obliterating qualities of the analyst's interventions — a characteristic of almost all the interventions described in this vignette — and suggest in addition that the patient's own propensities toward the Type C mode are being intensified in this therapeutic interaction.

The patient rather wisely concludes this hour with a further allusion to the underlying homosexual anxieties unconsciously shared by both himself and the analyst.

In a general way, the analyst confirmed aspects of this formulation in indicating that he was having a difficult time understanding the patient's material and that he was feeling somewhat anxious about the patient's pathology and the initial course of this analysis. These conscious feelings and thoughts are related to the analyst's difficulty in holding this patient and in containing his projective identifications; they also suggest a countertransference difficulty related to the patient's hold of the analyst. In some way, this patient's material and reactions were not providing the analyst a sense of safety. But rather than tracing out the sources of the analyst's discomfort, he turned to note-taking as a means of artificially and mechanically (how well the patient senses this!) providing himself with a holding device and a containing substitute that will protect him from the postulated dreaded inner destruction — denudation and annihilation, as Bion (1962, 1970) terms it.

The framework cure. In addition, it may well be that the analyst's sense of dissatisfaction regarding the hold that he is experiencing in this analytic interaction has been intensified, rather than reduced, by his own alteration in the framework: his note-taking. Unconsciously, analysts tend to have anxieties in regard to their need to take notes, their anticipation of presenting such material to colleagues and exposing their vulnerabilities, and their use of what I have termed *framework cures* (Langs 1975c, 1976a, c) to resolve underlying countertransference problems. The note-taking itself is often distracting. The entire constellation, conscious and unconscious, actually disrupts the analyst's sense of security rather than enhancing it.

Impaired holding. In evaluating the next hour, it would appear that in addition to continuous specific precipitants (the analyst's note-taking and erroneous interventions — questions and generalizations) there was a specific and related adaptive context in the patient's outside life: the death of a member of his tennis club. This day residue can be readily related not only to the patient's fears of death, but also to his unconscious perception of similar anxieties in the analyst — based on earlier material not presented here. However, in the actual session, these day residues were not integrated with the dream, which appears to have been a response to these precipitants; instead the analyst chose to focus on the manifest content of the dream and to its postulated role as a defense against homosexual fantasies and anxieties.

Keeping to ideas relevant to this presentation, it would appear that interventions of this kind, offered without a specific adaptive context and in terms of manifest content and Type One derivatives — the direct reading of a manifest dream and limited associations for latent content, rather than the use of an adaptive context to generate dynamically meaningful Type Two derivatives — characteristically serve to reinforce the Type C, falsified, and static qualities of the bipersonal field. As this session illustrates, such interventions almost always are designed to avoid a specific adaptive context which connects on some level to the patient's relationship with the analyst, and usually they are designed to cover over the patient's unconscious perceptions of the analyst's countertransference-based interventions. This approach facilitates an emphasis on the patient's pathology, and on his unconscious fantasies rather than his unconscious perceptions, and often deals with anxieties extraneous to the analytic relationship; it is a major form of defensiveness in respect to the influence of the analyst's countertransferences on the analytic interaction, the bipersonal field in which it occurs, and the analysand.

Interventions of this type are experienced by patients in terms of an impaired sense of holding, and especially as a reflection of the analyst's refractoriness in regard to his containing functions. Here, the unconscious communication from the analyst is to the effect that death, and especially sudden death, is to be denied, rendered nonexistent, and split off into a bastion of the bipersonal field (Baranger and Baranger 1966). A more general and widespread effort at obliteration may follow, creating a Type C field.

To some extent, these hypotheses are supported by the patient's response to the analyst's general interpretation of the patient's concerns about homosexuality and the dream of the two women as defensive in this regard. The patient rightly wonders why he comes to analysis at all, implying that if important meanings are to be destroyed in the analytic bipersonal field, effective analytic work will be impossible. There are also further indications of his doubts regarding the analyst's capacity to contain, manage the frame, and interpret, and, in respect to his stress on underlying homosexual anxieties, it might be asked whether these are primarily the analyst's concerns, and whether as such they serve as a deflection from more disturbing worries.

In the following hour, the patient had a dream that he immediately linked to the previous session. In terms of the patient's associations, it alludes to the analyst's craziness and his fear of doing damage — and by implication, of being damaged. The patient comments on the dangers of being an analyst, a point quite pertinent to the present discussion. He also describes his sense of constriction in the sessions, conveying both the extent to which the Type C mode is being imposed upon him and his unconscious perceptions of the analyst's own needs to constrict. It is then that the patient refers to his envy of the analyst and his security. On one level, this alludes to the analyst's envy of the patient, who feels secure enough to communicate his unconscious fantasies, introjects, memories, and anxieties — a communicative mode that is quite difficult or perhaps even impossible for this analyst.

It is also noteworthy that when the analyst attempts to suggest that the dream reflects the patient's wish to leave analysis, the patient points out that it is the analyst who had the problem in the dream — a formulation in keeping with the assessment of this material being offered here. It is in this context that the patient implies the projection into himself by the analyst of the wish that patient become therapist in this bipersonal field — the reversal of roles. The analyst's rejoinder is to emphasize the patient's paranoid feelings and anxieties, partially, it seems, to deny his own concerns and partially to projectively identify them into the patient as well.

In the next hour, the patient was late and the analyst felt concerned about the course of the analysis. Patients frequently respond to failures in the analyst's holding, containing, and interpretive capacities with disruptions in the framework that impart to the analyst a sense of being held poorly and a related sense of disturbance.

Container's fear of the contained. The hour itself begins with direct and indirect allusions to having made a mistake in entering analysis. The patient then returns to the theme of death and his own fear of cancer — an image that would suggest, in the context of this discussion, both the patient's dread of containing the analyst's pathological projective identifications and the analyst's comparable fear. It is a metaphor of the container's fear of the contained, and is the reprojection of the analyst's pathological projective identifica-

tion in a form that is further imbued with toxicity and destructiveness. The patient's reference to food poisoning conveys similar
implications.

The interactional qualities of this material is supported by the
patient's reference to his own fears, as well as those of his mother,
and his allusion to his father's surgery. Unconsciously, he then
reprimands the therapist for his insensitivity and distance, but sees it
as an alternative to utter loss of control — hysteria.

It was at this point in the session that the analyst experienced an
intense sense of disquietude and concern about the patient's
pathology and asked him to write a biography. Consciously, he had
been concerned about the dream of the previous hour, in which he
had appeared undisguised, and while he wondered whether this was
an indication of some type of countertransference difficulty, most
of his thoughts related to anxieties about serious underlying
pathology in the patient. The request for the biography was made
by the analyst as another effort to learn more about the patient in
order to understand his pathology more clearly.

Once again, we will allow the patient's response to guide us in
evaluating this intervention — another alteration in the frame. First,
he did not write the biography, and he soon spoke of a physician
friend who asked him for some sedatives. This consciously idealized
physician was now being seen as human and vulnerable, and in some
sense, as dishonest with himself. Here we have a metaphor for the
analyst's projective identification into the patient of his own
anxieties and need for noninsightful, artificial, drug-based relief. It
is the patient who is to offer a healing reprojection — the pill or the
biography — to relieve the analyst of his inappropriate anxieties.
The danger, as the patient puts it in Type Two derivative form, is
that the analyst might fall apart; the dread is of something deadly
inside. Exhibitionism, voyeurism, sexual impotence, and homosexuality are all implied as related anxieties and themes.

At this point in his presentation, the analyst was able to describe
some unresolved anxieties regarding death. He soon realized that
the request of the patient that he write a biography was an effort to
undo the anxieties by creating a permanent, indestructible record of
the patient with which he — the analyst — could reassure himself. It
is interesting that this patient refused to serve as a pathological
container for the analyst's anxieties, at least on this level, and that he
also refused to join in the sector of misalliance and in the framework
cure offered by the analyst. Apparently recognizing unconsciously

that the biography was an effort at artificial communication and an effort to erect a barrier to the disturbing contents that were emerging in this analysis, the patient unconsciously communicated these perceptions to the analyst and became engaged in additional unconscious efforts at cure — largely through a series of insightful unconscious interpretations related to the analyst's need to obliterate, his wish for the patient to serve him as a nursemaid and good mother, his homosexual and bodily anxieties, and his fears of death, containing, and sexuality.

While considerably more could be said in regard to this vignette, I will conclude this discussion by suggesting that only a series of self-insightful efforts directed toward resolution of the analyst's underlying countertransference difficulties, and the actual rectification of his difficulties in holding, containing, interpreting, and creating a Type A rather than a Type C communicative field — and the full interpretation of the patient's unconscious perceptions, introjections, and reactions to these inputs by the analyst — could redirect the interface of this bipersonal field to the pathology of the patient, and provide him a Type A communicative medium and an opportunity for insightful therapeutic work.

CONCLUDING COMMENTS

I will not attempt a comprehensive discussion of these postulates regarding countertransference, nor will I endeavor to delineate further the special advantages of viewing countertransference as an interactional product of the bipersonal field. I shall conclude by simply emphasizing the importance of an adequate and full listening process, of a validating clinical methodology, and of self-knowledge in applying these concepts regarding countertransference in the clinical situation, and more broadly in the expansion of psychoanalytic knowledge.

As many other analysts have noted (Langs 1976a), transference was first seen by Freud as the major enemy and obstacle to psychoanalysis, and only later recognized as its greatest ally — a quality that is by no means fully appreciated even to this day, so that the patient as the enemy and as resisting dominates the analyst's unconscious images, while the patient as ally and as curative is still far less appreciated. Similarly, with an even greater sense of dread, countertransference was first viewed as an enemy to analytic work;

and while Freud never specifically acknowledged its constructive aspects, later analysts have indeed attempted to do just that. There has been a recent trend toward identifying the constructive dimensions of countertransference, and these very much deserve to be put into perspective.

However, it is well to conclude this discussion with a recognition that despite the many parallels between transference and counter-transference (in their narrowest sense), there are important differences. While both are inevitable in the course of an analysis, transference manifestations are absolutely vital to the analytic work and are bound to be a major component of the patient's constructive experiences with the analyst and of his unconscious communications to him. By contrast, it is essential that countertransference expressions be kept to a reasonable minimum, that they not dominate the experiences and communications of the analyst, and that they not overfill the bipersonal field. However human such expressions are, and however meaningful the rectification and analysis with the patient may be, countertransference-based communications do traumatize the patient to some degree and these effects must be fully appreciated. It can be seen, then, that a properly balanced view of countertransference is extremely difficult to maintain. It is my hope that the present paper has enabled the reader to develop a more senitive conception of this most difficult subject.

References

Baranger, M., and Baranger, W. (1966). Insight and the analytic situation. In *Psychoanalysis in the Americas,* ed. R. Litman, pp. 56-72. New York: International Universities Press.

Bion, W. (1959). Attacks on linking *International Journal of Psycho-Analysis* 40:308-315.

―――― (1962). *Learning from Experience*. New York: Basic Books. Reprinted in *Seven Servants*. New York: Jason Aronson, 1977.

―――― (1963). *Elements of Psycho-Analysis*. New York: Basic Books. Reprinted in *Seven Servants*. New York: Jason Aronson, 1977.

―――― (1965). *Transformations*. New York: Basic Books. Reprinted in *Seven Servants*. New York: Jason Aronson, 1977.

Greenson, R. (1972). Beyond transference and interpretation. *International Journal of Psycho-Analysis* 53:213-217.

Grinberg, L. (1962). On a specific aspect of counter-transference to the patient's projective identification. *International Journal of Psycho-Analysis* 43:436-440.

Langs, R. (1973a). The patient's view of the therapist; reality or fantasy? *International Journal of Psychoanalytic Psychotherapy* 2:441-431.

———(1973b). *The Technique of Psychoanalytic Psychotherapy,* vol. 1. New York: Jason Aronson.

———(1974). *The Technique of Psychoanalytic Psychotherapy,* vol 2. New York: Jason Aronson.

———(1975b). Therapeutic misalliances. *International Journal of Psychoanalytic Psychotherapy* 4:77-105.

———(1975c). The therapeutic relationship and deviations in technique. *International Journal of Psychoanalytic Psychotherapy* 4:106-141.

———(1975a). The patient's unconscious perception of the therapist's errors. In *Tactics and Techniques in Psychoanalytic Therapy, Volume II: Countertransference,* ed. P. Giovacchini. New York: Jason Aronson.

———(1976a). *The Bipersonal Field.* New York: Jason Aronson.

———(1976b). On becoming a psychiatrist: discussion of "Empathy and intuition in becoming a psychiatrist" by Ronald J. Blank. *International Journal of Psychoanalytic Psychotherapy* 5:255-279.

———(1976c). *The Therapeutic Interaction.* 2 vols. New York: Jason Aronson.

———(1978a). Some communicative properties of the bipersonal field. *International Journal of Psychoanalytic Psychotherapy* 7:89-161.

———(1978b). Validation and the framework of the therapeutic situation. *Contemporary Psychoanalysis* 14:98-124.

Langs, R. et al. (in press). *Psychoanalytic Dialogues III: Some British Views on Clinical Issues.* New York: Jason Aronson.

Reich, A. (1960). Further remarks on counter-transference. *International Journal of Psycho-Analysis* 41:389-395.

Searles, H. (1965). *Collected Papers on Schizophrenia and Related Subjects.* New York: International Universities Press.

_____ (1975). The patient as therapist to his analyst. In *Tactics and Techniques in Psychoanalytic Therapy, Volume II: Countertransference,* ed. P. Giovacchini. New York: Jason Aronson.

Chapter 5

COUNTERTRANSFERENCE AND
THE ANXIETY OF INFLUENCE

ARTHUR H. FEINER, Ph.D.

> But since she pricked thee out
>   for women's pleasure
> Mine by thy love and thy
>   love's use their treasure
> — *Shakespeare*

I agree with those analysts who believe that they "themselves regularly develop transference reactions to their patients, including periods of transference neurosis, and that these transference reactions play an essential part in the analytic process" (Bird 1972).[1] Notwithstanding the position one takes with regard to a grasp and application of the concept "countertransference," most analysts

1. This is an expanded and modified version of a paper that was originally published in *Contemporary Psychoanalysis*, Volume 13, Number 1, 1977. Some of the additional material has appeared elsewhere. The phrase *the anxiety of influence* is the title of Harold Bloom's book (1973) on critical theory in poetry.

The "she" in the epigraph refers to Nature. It is the naturalness, the inevitability, of the phenomena described here that I wish to emphasize.

I want to thank Drs. D. Ehrenberg, L. Epstein, A. Issacharoff and N. Stockhamer who helped me clarify some of the highly condensed ideas presented in this paper; and Clara Rabinowitz who, a long, long time ago, stimulated my thinking along these lines.

agree that along with its mate, "transference," it is the most significant aspect of the psychoanalytic process; and their concurrent analyses the sine qua non of psychoanalytic practice. It has been commented by others that difficulties in the management of the transference derive from the management of the countertransference (Levenson, Feiner, and Stockhamer 1976). But it is not that simple. Despite the surfeit of papers, symposia, and commentary on this important topic, since Freud (1910) first wrote of his discovery with characteristic amazing lucidity, there has been a good deal of disagreement, and perhaps even confusion, as to what Freud originially intended. There is little consensus as to how countertransference develops, what its contents consist of, and how it is used (if at all). In fact, there are several definitions of countertransference.

THREE VIEWS OF COUNTERTRANSFERENCE

There is the position of those who view countertransference as a counterpart or complement of the transference of the patient, that is, part of a necessary, natural unity, reflexive in quality. There is also a view, similar to the early classical conception, which considers countertransference as the unconscious reaction of the analyst, and which includes neurotic and nonneurotic components. Finally, there is the totalistic conception, in which *all* feelings and attitudes of the doctor toward the patient fall under the countertransferential rubric.

That there are several definitions is not at all difficult to understand. After all, Freud was not entirely consistent in the few specific references he made to his early discovery, during the forty-odd years he wrote and developed his ideas. Furthermore, did not other contributors find their own thinking imbricated with their conceptions about countertransference as awareness of it evolved along with changes in other areas of pyschoanalysis?

Attitudes about countertransference do differ with regard to its derivation, its content, and its applicability. We inevitably seem to have followed, or at least paralleled Freud's struggle to wrench out of himself the intricate insights about psychoanalysis. Bird (1972), remarking on the creative leap that Freud (1905) took in the postscript to the case of Dora, in which Freud states succinctly that transference was in fact the key to psychoanalysis, suggests that Freud spent four and a half fateful years between the original writing of the manuscript, in 1900, to publishing it with its postscript in 1905, working out his own transference. And it was this, "the development, the discovery and then the resolution within himself of the complexity of transference neurosis that constituted the actual center of his self analysis ... that was the beginning of analysis as we know it" (Bird 1972). We too have learned about the discovery of countertransference via the impingement of our patients (more "real" than our reading), recognized its power, tried to identify its development, and now attempt some resolution, within ourselves, of it conflictual issues.

FREUD'S SENSITIVITY TO THE INTERPERSONAL

Whatever we discern in Freud, or even read into his work, for example, his early 1910 paper in which he stated:

We have become aware of the 'counter-transference,' which arises in [the physician] as a result of the patient's *influence* on his unconscious feelings.... We have noticed that no psychoanalyst goes further than his own complexes and resistances permit and we consequently require that he shall begin his practice with a self-analysis and *continually carry it deeper while he is making his own observations on his patients.* [Italics mine.]

Or take his 1912 essay, in which he remarks about the analyst that —

he must turn his own unconscious like a receptive organ toward the transmitting unconscious of the patient ... adjust himself to the patient as a telephone receiver is adjusted to the transmitting microphone. Just as the receiver converts back into soundwaves the electric oscillations ... *so the doctor's unconscious is able, from the derivatives of the unconscious which are communicated to him, to reconstruct the unconscious,* which has determined the patient's free associations. [Italics mine.]

it does seem evident that he was very much aware of the *interactive* implications of his great discovery, transference. But he never quite gave up the notion that countertransference was indeed a hindrance, a "transference" of the analyst's infantile impulses and feelings to the patient. It seems self-evident that if we view the course of an ordinary analysis as the analysis of repressed material, that is, the uncovering of infantile conflicts, it would follow naturally that the analysis of "hindering" countertransference would be the analysis of remnants of unconscious infantile conflicts in the analyst. However, if we begin to change our view as to what *is* analysis, or what analysis is *about*, or what is *analyzable* in the patient, we begin to see how a conceptualization of the content of countertransference changes.

CHANGING VIEWS IN THE 1950s

A different way of seeing the origin of countertransference content begins with Racker's 1953 paper which was a significant bridge to an interpersonal position. His early work points to the analyst as an interpreter of unconscious processes, and the *object* of them as well. In this view, "countertransference may help, distort or hinder the (analyst's) perception. Or ... the perception may be correct but ... may provoke neurotic reactions which impair interpretive capacity ... As object, the countertransference affects his (the analyst's) manner and his behavior."

A radically new contribution was made during the 1950's by Fromm-Reichmann (1950) and Sullivan (1953). Stemming from the inherent demands of their work with schizophrenics, the new point of view had two aspects, among others. First emphasis was placed on a broader, more encompassing concept of past-in-present. That is, transference/parataxic processes were no longer seen by Sullivan or Fromm-Reichmann as mechanistic repetitions of early oedipal struggles, but were now viewed as having derived from *all* aspects of infancy and childhood, not even necessarily from entanglements with parents. Significant others no longer referred rigidly to mother and father. The quality of the relationship with a significant other, real or in fantasy, the evoked self-image from the past, continued in the present, were more important than the labels ascribed to the figures. The second aspect of this new interpersonal position lay in reminding the analyst that he was after all, essentially human, as was his patient, and thus his contribution to the analytic field was not simply his observing methodology and his technique of inquiry. Instead, the new view insisted that his participation, as expert in a field of inquiry, involved his total person. That is, *his* past-in-present evidently influenced the field. And to the extent that he remained aware of this (through his continued self-analysis) so did his effectiveness improve. Accordingly, countertransference was seen in this light. However, whether from infancy, for example, in the early personifications of good-me, bad-me, and not-me (Sullivan 1953), or in the later oedipal context, analysts still tended to view the *content* of countertransference solely as aspects of unresolved conflicts, or repetitions of past relationships, emerging inappropriately during the analysis.

Now there are two types of transferences (and hence countertransferences). There is the "primal" transference, that is, the general latent craving, in all, for an omnipotent, all-giving, all-gratifying "mother." True, this transference is shaped by the evolution of each phase of development but it remains, nevertheless, an emergent potential in all of us, when the conditions are appropriate (Stone 1961). We see this in patients as underlying their desires for "free" treatment, unconditional love and interest; or their search for, and fascination with fusion (of course, with its attendant anxieties). It is as though an attempt were being made to *re-create* or reconstitute, *in the body of the analyst,* the parent of earliest infancy or even before, so that "she" is utterly available, and her interior space utterly and freely accessible.

The other type of transference is a relatively integrated phenomenon, reflective of character traits, habitual attitudes and expectations, deriving from those relationships that were of significance throughout life (Stone 1961). In terms of its *earliest* conception, it is thus evident that there are two equivalent types of countertransference.

Heimann's 1950 paper was the landmark in the change of our conceptualization of the content of countertransference. While Heimann suggested that countertransference referred to *all* the feelings which an analyst may experience towards the patient, she warned succinctly that since the analyst has had a training analysis, he consequently should be able to sustain those feelings which are stirred up in him instead of discharging them. Therefore, the analyst can subordinate his feelings to the analytic task in which he functions as a significant participant. Therapists who are indeed moved, or influenced or prevailed upon *to do* something instead of sustain (and reflect on) feelings, invariably do the wrong thing (if it is other than inquire). I would guess that, historically, this is one of the reasons that countertransference (as "induced" by the patient) was seen for so long as a hindrance and taboo. Certainly with a hindrance-taboo concept the pristine purity of the transference relationship, and the Cartesian attitude of the patient-as-object, that is, something out there to be analyzed, can be maintained. And in this sense, that the therapist can be induced (Epstein, chapter 13, this volume), or evoked to do something other than analyze, the early warnings of Freud are remarkably appropriate. The great contribution which Heimann made was that she showed clearly that the reaction of the analyst may usefully be the first clue to what is going on in the patient.

Tauber (1954) did reiterate this latter theme, implying that while the actual content of countertransference was based on some unresolved issue in the analyst, that it came into being via the *absorption* of something from the patient. Tauber states, "the analyst takes in more about the patient than he realizes" (Tauber 1954). Tauber echoed Heimann except that his was an interpersonal frame of reference. True the direct revelation of the analyst's thought processes to the patient, which Tauber (1954) advocated, may be (though not necessarily) an imposition, an invasion or intrusion. It is here that there is a necessity for the validation of the method by meticulously evaluating the patient's responses (Langs 1976a).

So first we had the development of the concept of countertransference as originating from the repressed data of the analyst's instinctual life, and taboo and dangerous because it is a block to understanding. Then we had a view of countertransference as emanating from the characterology, the quality of relatedness of the analyst, still taboo and dangerous, and consequently a hindrance to be removed (Horney 1939, Sullivan 1953). Finally, we have two similar views of countertransference as emerging from certain aspects of the self as participant in the therapeutic context, receptive to the patient's presentations of himself, and *now* seen as a clue to understanding the patient and eminently useful (Heimann 1950, Tauber 1954).

Margaret Little's "'R,' — The Analyst's Total Response to His Patient's Needs" (1957), contains the following statement:

We have to recognize the same paradox that we find in other areas of life is there too in analysis — that the same thing can also be dangerous ... unless ... the analysis, as far as the analyst's share in it is concerned depends on the extent to which

> the analyst's world in which he lives is a sane and friendly one
> ... i.e. how far he has been able to deal with his own paranoid
> anxieties and his depression — anxieties that are inseparable
> from the work that he is doing. ... Countertransference ... at
> first like transference ... was regarded as ... dangerous and
> undesirable, but nevertheless unavoidable. *Nowadays it is*
> *even respectable!* [Italics mine.]

There is a bounty of ideas in this terse comment. It would lead me
far afield to discuss all of them. However, I must take note of Little's
phrase, "how far he has been able to deal with his own paranoid
anxieties and his depression anxieties *that are inseparable from the*
work he is doing." [Italics mine.] In her extension of Freud's note on
the abrasiveness of the patient's derepressed material (Freud 1937),
Little seems to be anticipating my suggestions here about the anxiety
of influence.

Actually Little's position had been presaged one year earlier in a
paper by Money-Kyrle (1956), in which the analytic task was
defined as one during which

> the patient's state of mind is absorbed through the medium of
> the association the analyst hears, and the postures he observes
> so that the analyst recognizes it as expressing some pattern of
> his own [that is, the analyst's] unconscious work or fantasy
> which in turn is reprojected on the patient in the act of
> formulating the interpretation.

He remarked that what "keeps the process going is the analyst's
repeated acts of recognition and that such a pattern of absorbed
emotion expresses such and such a fantasy in *his own* unconscious."
[Italics mine.] And what causes a break in this relationship is a failure
in this recognition. Countertransference is seen here as *emerging*
from the structure of the analyst's personality as a normal
phenomenon. The analyst usually perceives this as a breakdown, or
failure, in his recognition of what is going on in the patient.

In a footnote, Money-Kyrle commented that

> how exactly a patient does succeed in imposing a fantasy and
> its corresponding affect upon his analyst in order to deny it in
> himself is a most interesting problem ... the communication
> can be of a preverbal and archaic kind — similar perhaps to

that used by gregarious animals in which posture or call of a single member will arouse a corresponding affect in the rest. In the analytic situation, a peculiarity in communications of this kind is that at first sight they do not seem as if they had been made by the patient at all. The analyst experiences the affect as being his own response to something. The effort involved is in differentiating the patient's contribution from his own.

Thus we see Money-Kyrle retaining the idea that the precipitate for the countertransference phenomenon lies in the patient's presentation, but that countertransference per se no longer necessarily derives from the repressed or dissociated aspects of the analyst's characterology. Now it is viewed as part of the inevitable response of his "normal" personality structure to the patient's interaction with him. Money-Kyrle attributes this to two interests on the part of the analyst. One is concern for the patient's welfare, as a function of the analyst's need for reparation, and the other is his natural tendency to see the patient as standing for the child in himself. What is most significant about this position is that it makes the countertransference response part of the *natural* interactive process between patient and analyst. Furthermore, Money-Kyrle comments that the analyst "is most concerned with the unconscious child in the patient ... and because this child so often treats the analyst as parent, the analyst's unconscious can hardly fail to respond in some degree by regarding the patient as his child." Add this to Money-Kyrle's idea that the analyst naturally sees the patient "as standing for the child in himself," and we begin to have a view of countertransference that is essentially interpersonal, and interactive, and rooted clearly in the simple but remarkable one genus hypothesis of Sullivan (1953), that we are "much more simply human than otherwise." What Sullivan had in mind had to do with an understanding of "human identities" or "parallels," that is, the old aphorism "nothing human is alien to me." Racker (1953) also referred to what he called "concordant" countertransference, in which there is a recognition on the part of the analyst "of what belongs to another as one's own." Of course, Freud (1912) had hinted at this when he remarked that one man's unconscious can be used to interpret another's.

COUNTERTRANSFERENCE AS
REFLEXIVELY ROLE-RESPONSIVE

This is at considerable remove now from a concept of countertransference as dangerous or undesirable; it is now considered appropriate, useful, and even valuable. Yet these views still retain the idea that the triggering of its occurence in the analyst comes *from* the patient. It would lead one to see countertransference "induced" or "evoked" in the analyst by the patient. This still falls short of conceptualizing as part of a truly *inter*personal, *inter*-penetrating process. A shift in this direction has occurred in the thinking of Sandler (1976), who writes:

> My contention is that the analyst's overt reactions to the patient, as well as in his thoughts and feelings, what can now be called his 'role responsiveness,' shows itself not only in his feelings but also in his attitudes and behavior as a crucial element in his 'useful' countertransference.

That is, there is a part which is usable and a part which is not (derived from the analyst's pathology), and they are "role-responsive." Sandler goes on to emphasize that the role relationship of the patient in analysis, at any particular time, consists of a role in which he casts himself, and complementary role in which he casts the analyst (at that particular time). The patient's transference would thus represent an attempt by him to impose an interaction, and interrelationship between himself and the analyst (Sandler 1976). In addition to the overt responses of the analyst, which indicate his blind spots and or his own pathology reflected in his particular reaction or attitude to the patient, Sandler suggests:

> That very often the irrational response of the analyst which his professional conscience leads him to see entirely as a blind spot of his own, may sometimes be usefully regarded as a compromise formation between his own tendencies and *his reflexive acceptance of the role which the patient is forcing on him.*

In this position Sandler rejects completely the idea that counter-transference or all countertransference responses of the analyst are due to what the patient has imposed on him, finding little use in the terms "projection," "externalization," "projective indentification," or the phrase "putting parts of oneself into the analyst." It seems to Sandler that a complicated system of unconscious cues, both given and received, is involved. Moeller's (1977) position is quite similar.

But does the patient really "force" anything on the analyst? After all, the patient moves, like all, with his best foot forward. It is the analyst's responsibility to recognize what the patient "needs" to maintain any relationship. And this will recreate the content of the session in a homologous way (Levenson 1972).

Klauber (1972) had asked earlier what sort of "secret loving and secret hating" have patient and analyst needed to make their relationship viable. The loving and understanding situation of analysis, he wrote, to some extent rests on a social contract. However understanding an analyst may be, Klauber reminded us, most analysts do begin to feel a sense of irritation if the patient dares to dally more than twenty seconds on his way out the door. And, as he put it, it is a great burden to an analyst to have to work with a patient with whom one does not sympathize. But it is not the analyst's tendency to aggression which provokes the irritability that is fundamental to his anxiety. The analyst's anger, Klauber wrote, is his response in the face of a task required, which he finds difficult, if not impossible (Klauber 1972). Klauber informs us that the interpretation is a technique of agreeing to a verbal formula, which has as its goal the reduction of psychic tension between analyst and patient, and this, an acute need for the patient, is a chronic need for the analyst and requires constant attention. It is in this space, between patient and analyst, along this dimension of tension, to which Money-Kyrle alludes, and where Klauber and Sandler have focused their attention. It is along here that we must move for a still firmer grasp of that part of the analyst's responsiveness.

THE ANALYST'S ANALYSIS AS PRIMARY

I am almost ready to say that the *key to the analysis of the patient resides in the analysis of the analyst, during the analysis.* This notion is the ultimate extension of Freud's (1910) idea that the analyst carry his self-analysis deeper while working with the patient, and dispenses with the difficulty of differentiating what is usable from what is not.[2] This goes beyond that which is reasonably expectable from a training analysis.

In the course of his own analysis, like any patient, the analyst comes to deal in general with two interrelated issues: the ambivalences of the past and a reinvestment in relatedness. Out of the analysis of the paradoxes of the past, real or imagined hurts are laid to rest or at least are forgiven, and understood as part of the reciprocal humanity in which we all find ourselves. We learn, as the aphorism goes, not to throw out the baby with the bath water. Our reinvestment in relatedness comes along with this so that cynicism, one of our most painful and debilitating human feelings, is rendered dormant but never eliminated. Cynicism refers to that misanthropic attitude or feeling that denies, churlishly, hopelessly, the possibility of the goodness of motives, events, things, etc. I want to differentiate here the significance of cynicism from any other issue that would be routinely analyzed in a training analysis. In the sense in which I am using the concept, cynicism is most crucial.

The analyst (now analyzed as part of his training) fulfills his task in keeping with his new view of his past, himself, and others. And as he is concerned with the growth of people (respecting the process as the surgeon respects living tissue) he sees his patient repeating variations of images or personifications of himself, images that he in his own analysis had to reformulate and reintegrate. His effectiveness as analyst keeps his potential cynicism, every ready to emerge, dormant. It is here where the patient's analysis, and the analyst's ongoing self-analysis in the analytic consulting room collide. Any deviation from the analytic process is an aberration, and it implies the ineffectuality of the analyst who suffers the reemergence of his latent cynicism, amid the situations calling out dormant images of himself. Cynicism is a most painful human feeling. (Some analysts use the term "despair" for what I am referring to; our differences are

2. Actually the usable ("normal") and unusable ("neurotic") elements in the analyst's character structure form an indissoluble integrated unity. It may not be simply an academic point to separate these components (see Grinberg, chapter 18, this volume), but I do not want to suggest that neurotic feelings (e.g., anxiety) cannot be helpful signals if we recognize them as such and, as Freud advised, master them. Hence, my suggestion that the analyst's self-analysis is primary. As Moeller (1977) points out, what is more important than trying to separate the normal from the neurotic in the analyst is whether his countertransference response has been understood, and consequently utilized for productive understanding, that is a creative, or process-enhancing response.

essentially semantic.) We live with the perennial necessity of creating the ambivalent illusion that we can make contact, that we can reunite or reintegrate with the available and utterly accessible "mother's" body, but progressively transmuted or transformed into a current, working, loving relationship — that such things can be. Indeed, they are. But more often, real things, because of the vicissitudes of life, are destroyed. A person dies or moves away, a relationship is betrayed, analytic work is frustrated: something happens. Our grief and mourning processes help us maintain the illusion that: "Well, next time around it will be okay" because the disillusionment stirs up the ancient, archaic cynicism which is the most painful feeling that a human being can experience. We run from that. The dialectic of hopefulness[3]-cynicism is, I believe, the emotional counterpart to our confronting the realities of the paradoxical "mother," the "giver" and "taker" of life, the potential presence and absence of all things, their unavailability, their inaccessibility.

All psychoanalysis, all psychology, all life can be seen in the dialectic of presence and absence. For example:

> A poem begins because there is an absence. An image must be given for a beginning, so that absence is ironically called a presence. Or, a poem begins because there is too strong a presence, which needs to be imaged as an absence, if there is to be any imaging at all [Bloom 1977].

Presence and absence are interrelated and cannot be separated. But can there be an excess of presence and an excess of absence? Apparently. Surely an excess of presence is experienced as intrusion, and an excess of absence as loss. A reasoned, reflective effort is needed on the part of the patient to tolerate an absence, and to differentiate it from loss. The same is true for the analyst. Still, only the absence of the object can be that stimulus for imagination and thinking, for psychic creativeness and aliveness (Green 1977).

SACRIFICES OF THE ANALYST

Participant observation is a most demanding experience, against which the more integrated, gratifying aspects of the analyst's life are

---

3. I am trying to convey, with this half of the dialectic, "euphoria-in-connection."

marshalled, so that he has to struggle constantly, invoking his *love for the process*, not to be pulled out of the room and away from the analytic task. For example, analysts who have second offices in their homes, know the subjective difference between "impersonal noise" and "personal noise." The clack of a wife's heel in another room, the slam of a door by a child returning from school, the phone ringing in the kitchen, however dulled or subdued, are far more distracting than the shriek of a fire engine or police siren. Thus, one sacrifice the analyst makes is to try to sever, temporarily, his personal connections for the sake of that hour. There are, unfortunately, analysts who use the process for their own gratifications, but this can be seen as an unresolved aspect of the problems that evidently were not worked through in training analyses (Racker 1953). I am not addressing myself to this issue.

There seems to be four analysts in any consulting room. Analyst Number One is the man or woman who is earning a living in this way. He owns the room, sets the fees, arranges the schedule, etc. He has a family, children, friends and colleagues, a bank account , a mortgage, insurance, and bills to pay. Number two is the professional who has taken training as an expert, has some skill and is expected to develop it and use it by taking patients in therapy. Number three is that fantasy analyst who will be created and recreated by the patient into what he or she needs to make the relationship viable *at any one moment*. This creation is not imposed on or tacked *onto* the particular analyst, it is simply created, because it is necessary. My point is that Number two must confront Number one, proceed to analyze Number three and understand *him*. We all know this is not an easy or simple task (Bird 1972). And Number four is still another analyst who holds out future potential, future possibilities. I refer to him as the "hope" analyst. He is present at all times, and no matter how Number three appears to be persecuted or persecuting, denigrated or denigrating, even destroyed, by the patient. Number four will *always* be rescued or repaired. He is always defended by the patient in some way as a sort of sanctuary, where destructive forces are forbidden entry. For example, there may be unconscious appropriate attempts, on the part of the patient, to cure what is perceived as the analyst's pathology or his errors (Langs 1976b), so the Number four remains intact and available and hopeful. For if this analyst is not there, there can be no hopefulness, no therapy, and cynicism rules the day. I want to distinguish this "hopefulness" from the issues of "hope" which Harold Boris (1976) writes about so eloquently, and which, if I understand him, has to do with definitions of self, as contrasted with anticipation of satisfactions. The two are related but not the same.[4]

Each analyst has to introduce Number two into the room, by getting Number one out as quickly as possible. This is where his sacrifice begins, and it cannot be successfully handled unless Number one's existence is acknowledged and confronted. If Number one is not faced honestly, he creeps petulantly in the shadows, ready to make his incessant demands heard.

I suppose too, there are patient counterparts, for example, the "ten o'clock" who is engaging, the "eleven o'clock" who is difficult, and so on. This would refer to Patient Number 1. Patient Number 2 is the person in need who comes to therapy. Number 3 represents whatever goes on in the analyst's unconscious, out of his own necessities, elaborated by his own definition of himself as analyst (e.g., Money-Kyrle 1956). And Number 4 represents the rational possibility that one could be a helpful analyst. Number 4 has got to be there, so that the patient might get well.

One typical and common dysphoric feeling that analysts have is the resentment that is experienced during termination. It is part of the analyst's need for the patient to express some special kind of gratitude for the analyst's risk-taking. This expected undying gratitude goes far beyond rational gratitude and objective remuneration, the success of the analysis, even the joy or the exultation in the intimacy achieved. Despite the reasonableness of the patient's actual gratefulness, no amount can satisfy our innermost need for it, a need in all of us (I mean this literally — and see it as deriving from our own "primal" transference) since no one outside of us knows the painful, sacrificial, hazardous side of our analytic efforts (Bird 1972). In the same way, it could be expected that a patient in a *successful* analysis, during the termination phase, might denigrate the analysis, the analyst, or himself and the world around him. This kind of degrading attack too comes from the deepest recesses of the patient and is the natural emergence of cynicism. Like the analyst, the patient had risked exposure in an attempt at a creative

4. I am aware that my scheme for the multifaceted aspects of analytic interaction must seem clumsy at best, but may facilitate a grasp of the complicated nature of the analytic field confronting every analyst. Writings about the "working alliance" or "therapeutic alliance," have tended to gloss some of the issues presented here.

reinvestment and now resents having to give up the process, since his cynicism hides just beyond the door.

Analysis leaves its scars; the truism that it cannot cure the past but only lay it to rest in a forgiveable way, is never more poignant than in the moment-to-moment countertransferential responsiveness of the analyst to his patient. This may be coincident with anxiety, not what we ordinarily consider anxiety, but anxiety nevertheless. It is from the anxiety, reactive to the influence of this calling out, that the analyst swerves, sometimes with a deviant technique, barriers to knowing (Issacharoff, Chapter 1), pseudostupidity, and ultimately the reification of his patient, himself, or the process (Feiner 1970).

Differentiating the patient's contribution from the analyst's own response to it is part of the initial analysis of countertransference. To the extent that the analyst can accomplish this task, so does he enhance the process.

In this sense then the analyst's self-analysis is primary. The patient, in that respected separateness and differentiation, a differentiation from the analyst's self in his ongoing self-analysis, is protected from boundary invasions, and other intrusive interactive processes that impose upon him a matrix for living not of his own making. Furthermore, in this way the patient's ultimate "real" individuality is assured to the extent that his idiosyncratic view of himself and his development is at all possible. But this anxiety of influence is terribly compelling and demands immediate surcease. It is in the analyst's failure to reduce it, or the defensive maneuvering against it, that the aberrations of the psychoanalytic process occur.

THE ANALYST'S NEED TO BE ORIGINAL

The patient does reach us with his presentation of himself, with his necessary "secret lovings and secret hatings." Yet we have secrets of our own as analysts, and one of them is our need to be original. I do not mean originality in content, that is, the crisp, evocative, sometimes pungent, trenchant interpretations that brilliantly flash before patient and analyst, illuminating what may be a dark or foggy landscape. In fact, this kind of endeavor is more often than not a defensive swerving. Most interpretative work is simple, sometimes just mundane, always appropriate to the patient's concern and his adaptive context (Langs 1976b). The scintillating, associational build-up in the analyst, however intriguing and entertaining, may be utilized by him quietly, internally, in formulation or in building toward an intervention, but is better left unsaid. I am referring to our need to be our own persons, our own selves, in connection with the other (the patient) at the same time. It is not that we subordinate this originality to the task, but that in the artifactual relationship we know as psychoanalytic, this originality is only permitted to emerge in an analytic way. We need to be ourselves. And in connection with a patient, we thereby become analytic selves. That is, the analysis gives the self its form. When the patient imposes his influence upon us, we naturally bridle, in reciprocity. In response to the influence, "complementary needs are resolved or aggravated, patterns of activity are developed or distinguished and foresight of satisfaction or rebuff is facilitated" (Sullivan 1953). This, I believe, derives from our earliest struggle with the dialectic of separation and connection, and I think it is in this sense that Sandler (1976) assumes a "natural" role reflexivity on the part of the analyst.

Again, as Heimann (1950) long ago pointed out, if we have been analyzed during our training we do not simply discharge feelings. However, we can do something original. When we have reminded ourselves of the *analytic* connection, and that within that we can realize ourselves, our response can serve an original purpose. If the patient has presented greed, envy, his necessity to prevail or his difficulty in tolerating loss, as issues in his motivation, then what we begin to see in our original swerve, we can identify as the original motive in ourelves. When we do this we can respond, and our response — not a discharge of reciprocal emotion or a defense against it — becomes a counter-communication about the patient himself or how he has been or is being experienced. To conceptualize our response simply as counter emotion evades the possibility of our real genuine sensitivity.

COMMUNICATING COUNTERTRANSFERENCE DATA AND THE ANXIETY OF INFLUENCE

There are several constructive ways to communicate counter-transference responses to the patient, or to my way of thinking, preferring Bloom's (1975) phrase: to clear some imaginative space of our own.

One of the more obvious ways of responding to the influence of the patient is to scrutinize the content of a fantasy, or the feelings aroused in the analyst coincident with the patient's presentation, or even that which takes place in him later in the day. The relationship between, or among, the elements of the fantasy, or between these elements and the analyst himself, clues him to the patterned issues extant in the patient. I tend to prefer this, asking myself how it is that I'm having such and such a fantasy and feeling at this particular time. Not a discharge but a reflective process, the quality is sometimes obvious, sometimes obscure (e.g., with radical shifts in the analyst's posture or muscle tension). However obscure, hints about the patient are there. If these are ignored defensively, treated as though they are simply "caused" by the patient, or if it is assumed they are nothing but "hindrances," reflective solely of unanalyzed aspects of the analyst's unconscious, little is gained. But if they are treated as imaginative responses, an awareness of the *interrelationship of the parts* of the fantasy can be of immense help in facilitating the necessary intimacy.

I suppose most analysts sympathetic to this outlook make some sort of gesture which is a combination of these, sometimes content, sometimes feeling, sometimes structure. I would guess that stylistic preference for the analyst is largely an aesthetic issue, determined as much by his own feelings of comfort with a technical style as by the issues presented by the patient. And there is still another way to communicate an analyst's fantasy to a patient. I once heard (on film) Searles say to a schizophrenic woman that he fantasized her stealing into his bedroom at night and stabbing him with a stiletto. I also sensed the audience immediately divide itself into two camps. Those who felt what they took in themselves to be compassion for the woman emitted what I perceived as a collective boo. Those who, I believe, were asserting at that moment that schizophrenia presented the extreme in dehumanization, isolation, growth inhibition, and that its effect was paralyzing to patient and analyst, seemed to me to cheer Searles' effort. In this latter view, like St. George and the dragon, spontaneity demonstrated, at least, the validity of risking with another one's own inner thought processes. At best, the comment might have imaged precisely the woman's murderous impulses, and implicitly lay the groundwork for a later psychogenetic interpretation.

One explanation would be that the therapist "took in" aspects of his patient and elaborated them in his own way. (Langs 1976b).

Later, I wondered if I could or would have done the same, had I had the same fantasy with that woman. I then thought that after connecting the fantasy with our immediate conversation, I might have said to the woman that I had just gotten the idea that "you must have been furious with a man, maybe your father, whom you loved so very much, for turning away from you *to* your mother. But that you might have wanted to protect your mother more, and let more of the craziness out on your father, which would be a way of sacrificing yourself, which, indeed, you continue to do" (Feiner and Levenson 1968). I might have said all that, or part of it, and in effect it would have been an *interpretation* of my own fantasy (perhaps even incorrect). It would have shifted the thrust of the communication in the direction of a conjunctively nonautistic symbolizing process, not leaving the patient to do that work alone. A disquisition of the role dialectics of the therapist as healer or hero, to which I allude here, would require another paper. Suffice to state that no hero could be effective unless his efforts were colored by compassion. Heroic, interpretive interventions assume their healing potential in a sensitive compassionate setting. Heroics without compassion is a kind of adventuristic dandyism, as compassion that is blind would be a maudlin, unreliable "mothering." One more point: A careful monitoring and analyzing of the analyst's concurrent fantasies, even postural changes (Feiner 1974), makes him his own unconscious supervisor. If "listening" to the patient for his or her unconscious attempts at rectification of the therapist's errors is useful (Langs 1976b), the effort directed at the therapist himself can only add to the efficaciousness of the work.

Some other examples may help clarify this. Simple and usual are sexual fantasies, the elements of which may have to do with interpenetration in intimacy, intrusion, invasion, violation, thrust and reception, ecstatic connection; or even skin-to-skin contact, warmth, cuddling, holding, suckling and so on — that is, anything as much as genital sexual pleasure itself. Or, this example: A mature man tells a banal anecdote of childhood, which, he remarks seriously and confidentially, he has been too embarrassed to tell anyone. At age nine, after having been promised he could go rabbit hunting with his father, he is forbidden by his mother. He comments that this is a terribly painful memory, one that he has never shared with anyone, even though he knows it is a common enough story. Neither he nor the therapist have the foggiest notion as to why this is experienced by him the way it is, except for the evident disappointment and letdown. Nor is there any indication why the patient is relating this historical anecdote at this time. There had been no overt disappointment or letdown in the analysis thus far. The patient rambles on, seemingly getting nowhere and shedding little light, and the therapist finds himself bored, thinking about the difference between a surgeon's fee for a recent operation and the actual compensation from an insurance company. The analyst is aware of his own aggression (the patient is boring), and of his having turned it against himself (his felt experience of boredom and the fantasy). There is no question about the patient's fee, which the analyst believes is reasonable and fair. He then queries the patient whether he thinks of the letdown as an *assault*, and whether the patient believed he had *paid* too high a price for his composure. With a sudden, remarkable voice change from a high-pitched, strident staccato, to a low-pitched, sombre tone the patient then comments that in some ways his parents treated him as an adult, but it was clear to him that it was only at their discretion, and that this incident "*cut so deeply* as to render [him] a social basket case." (The implications of cutting-repair of the therapist, possibly evoked by the patient's desultory, dull presentation, which the analyst took unconsciously as an assault for analytic impotence or error, and the insured compensation for this, that is, the fee, were entertained by the analyst but not explored at this time. Nor was examined the possibility that the patient was imploring the analyst not to repeat the parental transgression.)

There is another truism, which is that we never understand. Through the graciousness of our patients we get to know ourselves a little better. It is through the patient's presentation of himself and our response to it that we are given this opportunity. The resultant knowledge, given back to the patient, in the patient's own metaphors, is what is meant by the transformation or re-creation of the patient's data, now in the shapely language of interaction. This is largely an aesthetic (or sensual) issue rather than one of hermeneutics (Levenson 1972).

To let ourselves be influenced to respond to the patient's presentation of himself as he would have us respond without our deliberation, is to find ourselves unwittingly replicating a system not of our making. This replication of the patient's system in the therapy room is continuous, and not only under the conditions of anxiety.

The structure of the relationship between patient and analyst in any particular session is a homolog of the content of the session (Levenson 1972).[5] This may indeed gratify the patient, in the sense that any response is possibly gratifying. Although somewhat inevitable, it is antithetical to the analysis, since analysis must be accomplished in an ambience of deprivation. If it is inevitable, then how is it possible for change to take place? The question is answered implicitly with another question. How do we keep the analysis going expansively for the patient and analyst? How do we facilitate inquiry, leading up to interpretive intervention? The result of our dealings with the anxiety of influence — the reciprocal struggle between that role we are forced to focus on and the repetitive patterns of the patient's need to force it upon us — results in something new. It is only in the act of interpenetration that any newness comes about. Neither defensive swerving nor abject submission results in any creative product. The analyst struggles to maintain his analytic identity within the framework of his countertransference and this gives the impetus for change (see footnote 5).

THE CONNECTION WITH CLASSICISM

Now why, today, have we come full circle and returned to the same place Freud came to in 1910, after that great creative leap of his in that magnificent postscript of 1905? We return, not mechanistically, not simply to repeat what has already been done, but in a parallel way, ready to *wrench out of ourselves things necessary*, in the same way as Freud, but with our own newly

5. Levenson's thrusting work (1972) in the organismic paradigm, which stresses isomorphic patterning, perspectivism, and equifinality, is not concerned with countertransference as such. I believe Levenson views the concept as more properly belonging to earlier paradigms, e.g., the mechanistic or the communicational. Levenson advises analyzing "the entire choreography" of a session (or several in sequence). "One analyzes not the ego defects or the acting out, not the failure of communication or the therapist's countertransference, but the entire piece of living theatre" (p. 158). The analyst's ability, he writes, to be "immersed . . . and then . . . work his way out" of the system, "makes the therapy" (p. 174). To me, then, analysis is ultimately about analysis; and change results from the patient's emergent choices. These choices follow a return to an experience of confusion and ambiguity, a return to the emotional turbulence (Bion 1977), the undifferentiatedness, that sense of diffusion in the patient, when choices are made — must be made.

evolved vision. And yet, underneath the adulation, is it just possible that something else is also at work? Is it just possible that, in our ephebic trembling, we dread becoming absorbed by Freud, at one with him, only to lose ourselves? It is not only our curiosity, but also our anxiety, our concern over the power of his influence, that drives us, in our own interpersonal way in renewing our connection with him.

THE ANALYST AS STRONG POET

And is this not the rational way (as with our patients), to keep a firm connection with the classical base but to swerve, as need be, to keep our own perceptive identities? This is how science advances. Each new conceptual scheme embraces the phenomena explained by its predecessors and adds to them. The danger in our need to differentiate ourselves is that we will handle our anxiety about the influence in a defensive way, or not handle it at all, and make no creative response whatsoever. If a patient's neurotic way of life and the communications he makes about it are seen as his "creative" or even "poetic" statements attempting to swerve himself from *his* precursors, then that swerving away, on the part of the therapist, that clearing of imaginative space, becomes a corrective gesture which makes change possible. Without swerving, both patient and therapist are doomed to idealization, imitation, and "weakness." The therapist, like the poet, may retain the precursor's terms, using them in an independent or even heretical sense. (Much, not all, of neo-Freudianism is like this). There may be in addition a breakaway from the precursor in the spirit of self-abasement, particularly in the face of the precursor's rigidity, refractoriness, and perceived obdurateness. There may be self-purgation and, ultimately, solitude. In these moments the patient and the therapist are total strangers to each other. (Ex-analysts dissatisfied with their analysts, or their analyses, find new "religions.") Finally, there may be resolution and reconstruction in which a therapist's interaction is completely open to the patient, and in which the patient's statements are now included with his within a new structural framework, and the patient's spirit suffused within the new.

To end this essay I want to refer directly to the concept and the words that have informed this paper's position and title.

I believe psychoanalytic issues parallel those of poetry (hence the

epigraph). "Poetic history," Harold Bloom writes, is "indistinquish-
able from poetic influence, since strong poets make that history by
misreading one another, so as to clear imaginative space for
themselves. . . . Weaker talents idealize; figures incapable of imagination appropriate for themselves. But nothing is got for nothing,
and self appropriation involves the immense anxieties of indebted-
ness, for what strong maker desires the realization that he has failed
to create himself?" (Bloom 1973). Substitute psychoanalysis and
psychoanalysts at will. And for "strong poets" read, Freud, Sullivan,
and Fromm. With our patients, my point is, we are stronger "poets."
We must grapple with them as precursors, as they in their neurotic
ways of living grappled with theirs, and clear some space for
ourselves. Our "misreading" provides the insight (that is, what they
take "in") so that they can change (Bloom 1975).

References

Bion, W. (1977). Emotional turbulence. In *Borderline Personality
Disorders,* ed. P. Hartocollis. New York: International Univer-
sities Press.
Bird, B. (1972). Notes on transference. *Journal of the American
Psychoanalytic Association* 20:267-301.
Bloom, H. (1973). *The Anxiety of Influence.* New York: Oxford
University Press.
――― (1975). *A Map of Misreading.* New York: Oxford University
Press.
――― (1977). Wallace Stevens: *The Poems of Our Climate.* Ithaca:
Cornell University Press.
Boris, H. (1976). On hope. *International Review of Psycho-Analysis*
3:139-150.
Feiner, A. (1970). Toward an understanding of the experience of
inauthenticity. *Contemporary Psychoanalysis* 7:64-83.
――― (1974). Discussion. *Contemporary Psychoanalysis* 10:80-85.
Feiner, A., and Levenson, E. (1968). The compassionate sacrifice.
Psychoanalytic Review 55:552-573.
Freud, S. (1905). Fragment of an analysis of a case of hysteria.
Standard Edition 7:3-122.
――― (1910). The future prospects of psycho-analytic therapy.
Standard Edition 11:139-151.
――― (1912). Recommendation to physicians practising psycho-
analysis. *Standard Edition* 12:109-120.

———— (1937). Analysis terminable and interminable. *Standard Edition* 23:209-253.

Fromm-Reichmann, F. (1950). *Principles of Intensive Psychotherapy.* Chicago: University of Chicago Press.

Green, A. (1977). The borderline concept. In *Borderline Personality Disorders,* ed. P. Hartocollis. New York: International Universities Press.

Heimann, P. (1950). On countertransference. *International Journal of Psycho-Analysis* 31:81-84.

Horney, K. (1939). *New Ways in Psychoanalysis.* New York: W.W. Norton.

Klauber, J. (1972). On the relationship of transference and interpretation in psychoanalytic therapy. *International Journal of Psycho-Analysis* 53:385-391.

Langs, R. (1976a). *The Therapeutic Interaction.* 2 vols. New York: Jason Aronson.

———— (1976b). *The Bipersonal Field.* New York: Jason Aronson.

Levenson, E. (1972). *The Fallacy of Understanding.* New York: Basic Books.

Levenson, E., Feiner, A., and Stockhamer, N. (1976). The politics of adolescent psychiatry. In *Adolescent Psychiatry,* vol. 4, ed. S. Feinstein and P. Giovacchini. New York: Jason Aronson.

Little, M. (1957). "R"—The analyst's total response to his patient's needs. *International Journal of Psycho-Analysis* 38:240-254.

Moeller, M.L. (1977). Self and object in countertransference. *International Journal of Psycho-Analysis* 58:365-374.

Money-Kyrle, R. (1956). Normal countertransference and some of its deviations. *International Journal of Psycho-Analysis* 37:360-366.

Racker, H. (1953). The countertransference neurosis. *International Journal of Psycho-Analysis* 34:313-324. Reprinted in *Transference and Countertransference.* New York: International Universities Press, 1968.

———— (1957). The meanings and uses of countertransference. *Psychoanalytic Quarterly* 26:303-357. Reprinted in *Transference and Countertransference.* New York: International Universities Press, 1968.

Sandler, J. (1976). Countertransference and role-responsiveness. *International Review of Psycho-Analysis* 3:43-47.

Stone, L. (1961). *The Psychoanalytic Situation.* New York: International Universities Press.

Sullivan, H.S. (1953). *The Interpersonal Theory of Psychiatry.* New
    York: W.W. Norton.
Tauber, E. (1954). Exploring the therapeutic use of countertrans-
    ference data. *Psychiatry* 17:331-336.

Chapter 6

ROUTINE AND INSPIRED INTERPRETATIONS

DONALD MELTZER, M.D.

This paper is one of a series of studies, essentially personal, which have grown out of and are therefore an extension of the investigation of the nature of the psychoanalytic process which I reported in my book (1967). In that work I left rather empty the description of the interpretive function of the analyst as one of his modes of particpation in the therapeutic relationship, since it was not central to the main theme. This centered on the process and its evolution seen as arising essentially in the unconscious of the patient. But it is probably true that any analysis which really taps the passions of the patient does the same for the analyst and promotes a development which can further his own self-analysis. Insofar as this is true, the main industrial hazard of this work lies in the danger of the transference-countertransference process taking a turn in the direction of perversion and thus becoming antitherapeutic for both members of the undertaking.

The analyst's great safeguard against this lies in the method and its basic technique, any breach of which should serve as a warning bell that the countertransference requires special scrutiny. This subject was deeply investigated and reported in the 1950s, especially by members of the British Society. These studies dealt mainly with

129

countertransference behavior and emotion, and thus extended in a more detailed way the concept of "wild analysis" described by Freud. These authors described, one might say, bits of wild analysis embedded in a matrix of correct procedure. But the difficult task of investigating the intrusion of the analyst's unanalyzed psychopathology into his understanding of the phenomenology of the consulting room is, perhaps necessarily, left untouched since it entrenches itself unobtrusively in the guise of theoretical formulation, the hidden passions only emerging as the irrational heat of talmudic debate and society politics.

One reason for this vulnerability of analysts lies in the incompleteness of our methodology, which still leaves such vagueness in our formulation of technique that a great gap necessarily exists between what analysts can describe, what they think occurs, and what occurs in fact. Wilfred Bion has been revealing his own grapplings with this problem, perhaps most movingly in his recent *Attention and Interpretation* (1970), and much of what I have to report seems to me to make an assault on the same citadel from a somewhat different direction. As Bion uses his extraordinary capacity for reverie to investigate his experience of analytic work, I wish to use my special interest in dreams. But in this instance I do not mean my own dreams, but those of the patient which hold up a mirror to the analyst.

Like our other categories of offspring, patients in states of projective or other types of narcissistic identification with the analyst hold up a Fun Fair type of mirror, full of distortions and exaggerations no doubt, but revealing the truth in caricature. This becomes particularly germane to our present problem when the narcissistic identification is taking the form, early in an analysis, of premature attempts at self-analysis. I wish to use an instance of this sort and a dream which accompanied it to probe a particular problem concerning the interpretive work of the analyst.

TWO MODES OF INTERPRETIVE ACTIVITY

This problem relates, as I say, to the interpretive activity of the analyst, as a personality function, and not primarily to the interpretation itself, although I hope to show that it has far-reaching consequences for the form as well as the content of the interpretion.

I am going to employ a polarizing concept for investigating the range of analytic interpretive activity by assuming two extreme types; in one of these the analyst listens and observes the behavior of the patient, which comes to assume a pattern or Gestalt in his mind to which he then applies certain aspects of his theoretical equipment in an explanatory way; at the other extreme the analyst, exposed to the activities of the patient, has an experience which is essentially personal, which he then uses, with the aid of his theoretical equipment, to explore the meaning of the relationship going on at that moment in his room. I am going to call these two extremes "routine" and "inspired" interpretation, respectively. I have chosen these two terms because of the implications, of dullness on the one hand and megalomania on the other, since these are indeed the respective dangers of the two extreme poles of interpretative activity. The clinical instance I will present shows just this transition, from a routine to an inspired activity, along with its dangers.

The second part of the paper will then use these understandings to investigate the significance of this differentiation between routine and inspired interpretation for the evolution of the psychoanalytic process, with special reference to the penetration of the depressive position, the formation of the combined object in psychic reality, the influence of the experience of this object on the weaning process, and the implication of all this for the patient's character and capacity for further development by the aid of self-analysis.

CLINICAL MATERIAL

In the third year of analysis the evidence strongly suggested that this young man's rigid narcisstic organization, which had been built up from early in childhood around a very exclusive relationship to a cousin who later accompanied him through boarding school, was finally giving way a bit to the dominance of his object relations. The struggle against this had been manifest very strikingly in the transference during the previous year's work. Once the beauty of the internal mother had been restored from its earlier delapidated state she seemed, in her isolation, to begin to demand with increasing insistence a husband worthy of her, and no one but "Daddy" would do. The patient's infantile search for alternate objects and relationships to satisfy her was externalized in an interesting obsessional investigation which fell into three categories of preoccupation with the transference situation: the first was a search for a therapeutic method superior to psychoanalysis; the second for a man of greater stature than Freud; and the third for evidence of an analyst whose writings reflected comprehension superior to his own analyst's.

In all three instances his search foundered on the same rock, namely, the realization of his own limitations in knowledge and judgment. Unwillingly, he gradually surrendered to the emotionality of the transference experience of being a child with "the best mummy and daddy in the world," that is, best for him because they were his own.

When he began to be gripped by this experience of being substantially without grievance to set against unworthiness and guilt related to neglect, delinquency, and perversity, a great urgency came upon him to dispel these incipient depressive pains before ever they were suffered. This he attempted to do by a combination of sparing, premature independence and manic reparative achievement, both inside and outside the analytic situation. One of the consequences was a striking change in his cooperation. Previously he had been above reproach on the surface; he lay on the couch, presented his dreams and associations in a beautiful and free way, and waited politely for the analyst to "do his stuff." He was a good "client" and naturally felt it his prerogative to assess the quality of the goods, variously praising, criticizing, gently admonishing. But his other prerogative was to judge the limits of his privacy, and, so long as this was not challenged as secrecy, all went smoothly, no sullen silences, no sense of grievance.

But now he was eager that there should be no secrecy, or rather no cause for it either in behavior or in fantasy. In addition he showed a disposition to help with the interpretative work, was keen to finish the analysis as soon as possible to give some other sufferer a chance. From "seeming good" he now became a "really good" patient, the only trouble being that his motives were largely defensive in respect of depressive mental pain. If his analytic house had rising damp and he was eager to sell it, the reason was not to cheat some unsuspecting buyer but because he hated the cost of the repairs. He could live in a tent!

In this context, being an intelligent and sensitive man with a sense of the truth if not yet a love for it, he began to notice that there was somehow a difference between his own interpretations and those offered by the analyst. It was not so much that his were not "correct," if this term could be used for their being in basic agreement with the analyst's. In fact he was rather good observer and translator of behavior and dream language into the theories with which he was now fairly familiar, but it was all a bit like schoolboy Latin. But after all, Freud himself had likened the first phase of dream analysis to translating Livy! He noticed that when he gave an interpretation himself it seemed somehow to stop everything, to put a lid on it, like conversation-stoppers of the "just-human-nature" type. On the contrary, when the analyst interpreted, and often in a way that seemed no different in content to his own ideas about the material, it had a different effect. It took the lid off; it increased the excitement; it was tinged with pain.

The relevance of all this to the infantile transference was not clear at the time, except in its broad outlines: why was he inferior to mummy and daddy; why did his wee-wees not make babies and his buttocks not give milk? But the quality of his feelings of perplexity seemed rather mysterious. On Thursday he came complaining of having slept very badly. All night long he had felt an incipient diarrhea, but on the toilet nothing came; a bit of flatus, a mushy stain. This he associated with an incident at age twelve when he had soiled his pajamas in the night and his somewhat harsh mother had been "incredibly understanding." But it also seemed to link in a puzzling way with an insistent recollection of his early student days in music composition when he first disovered how virtually impossible it was to make up a melody "of one's own." In the night this somehow had turned into a ruminative attempt to hold together in his mind a certain note and one a semi-tone lower, but without success.

The patient agreed that the events of the night must be related to the transference and contain some reexperience of infantile suffering: of inability to control either his feelings (expressed in bodily terms, the incipient diarrhea) or his objects (the inability to hold the two notes together in his mind), along with some recognition of creative incapacity, and thus inferiority (the inability to make a melody "of his own"). To the Friday session he brought the following dream:

He and the analyst seemed to be sharing a hotel room which was overlooked by rooftops filled with people. At one point the analyst seemed to be squatting over the patient, saying something like, "In fact you have never actually seen my anus." The patient felt a mixture of intense emotions. On the one hand he felt embarrassed that the people across the way would surely see this as a homosexual relationship. But even more acute was a feeling of triumph over the analyst, who was apparently quite unaware that behind him was a mirror which enabled the patient to look directly between his buttocks. These appeared huge and muscular, like a Japanese wrestler's.

The patient connected the dream with an important occurrence of puberty. His father had come into his bedroom early one morning and sat down on the bed, looking a bit amusedly at the patient's disarranged pajamas, but after a few moments silence had left. At the time he had experienced this in the light of a common experience of tentative homosexual approaches made to him by older boys at boarding school. Later he had wondered if his father had wanted to broach the subject of masturbation but had lost his nerve. He also linked the dream with one-way screens used both for psychological research and for sexual perversions. His own interpretation was that he was accusing the analyst of having been trumphant over him the previous day. Perhaps he was having his revenge by accusing the analyst of a type of showing off that revealed his anal homosexuality. But perhaps he was mistaken, as with his father. It was a weekend theme with which we were fairly familiar and I could not add much to the interpretation. But I was disturbed by an insistent image that had arisen before my eyes as I had been listening to the dream, namely of Velasquez's "Rokeby Venus," in which the goddess is visualized from behind, reclining and gazing into a mirror held up to her by an infant Cupid and in which her face, looking rather thoughtful, is depicted.

Although this painting seemed irrelevant to the patient's dream, as he had never mentioned it, still it was a surprise to me as I had not seen the picture for some years myself. But I had several reasons to pay attention to it: the patient is knowledgeable about art; the beauty of the mother's back was a prominent feature of his dream life and early recollections. I therefore asked him if he thought the dream could have anything to do with this famous painting and was relieved to be told that in fact it had been the subject of discussion at a dinner party a few nights ago. But how did this throw any light on the dream?

First of all we could recognize the transpositions: the patient is in the position of the goddess, the analyst in that of Cupid, and the people on the rooftops see it as the painter. At this point it merely seemed that the patient's dream had made a caricature of the painting in which he accuses Velasquez of being a pornographer and voyeur who doesn't even realize how he reveals his perversity. That is just the same as the patient's interpretation of the dream and probably quite right at some level. But if we follow this line, it is Cupid who is the main target of ridicule. What about the Japanese wrestler bit? They don't in fact wrestle naked but wear a very nappylike loincloth. Is there here a revenge on the mummy who is "incredibly understanding" about the baby's dirty bottom? But in the painting Venus is supposed to be looking at herself. Why then is her face visualized in the mirror? Must she not in fact be looking at the painter with that shadowy, absorbed expression? Certainly not at Cupid's bottom! Rather Cupid is facilitating the relationship of admiring and thoughtful contemplation between goddess-mummy and artist-daddy. The iconography of a madonna-and-child shows through from its classical facade and we are reminded of "Las Meninas" or of Vermeer's "Artist in his Studio."

A routine Friday session caught fire at this moment and we plunged into a new area in the transference, namely the patient's begrudging of his admiration to objects whose riches of admiration for one another was already too great for him to bear without overpowering envy. He was not going to be the loving Cupid boy who potentiated this admiration but a dirty-bottomed mother who attacked them and a sly little girl who intruded and spied upon their intimacy. In childish limitation of imagination the parents' pleasure in their creative combination to procreate and rear their children is seen as indistinguishable from the mutual admiration conspiracy of two children admiring one another's urination and defecation! We could see more clearly now that the patient's self-analytic efforts were not merely inadequate due to inexperience but because of heavy contamination by infantile omnipotence in the service of defense against depressive anxieties. His pregenital bisexuality was trying to make poo-poo babies from his wee-wee and feed them with his mushy diarrhea milk and keep all the admiration for himself. Or does the dream reveal a sharp insight into the analyst's megalomania and self-admiration regarding his artistic and creative way of doing psychoanalysis, and writing papers about it? Or both? Can more precise formulation of methodology assist the analyst in his self-analytic efforts to answer such a question? Or must he wait somewhat helplessly for the proof-of-the-pudding in the future course and outcome of the work?

EXPLANATION AND EXPLORATION: PEDAGOGY AND COMRADESHIP

Every Interpretation is a Type of Action-in-the-Countertransference.

The medical tradition behind psychoanalysis has been very naturally conducive to an orientation of analyst toward patient which tends to confuse the therapeutic alliance with the transference-countertransference situation. While truly it is more like teacher-to-pupil than doctor-to-patient in many respects, still we are inclined to assume that we are helping the patient or analysand to traverse developmental territory familiar to us from our own personal experience, be it ever so idiosyncratic in its manifest content or particular permutation of emotions, fantasies, and defense. Consequently we are bound to acknowledge that we are limited by the boundaries of our self-knowledge. This Virgil-leading-Dante model seems to me, however, to be applicable to only one aspect of the interpretive work, namely, to whatever degree of contact and communication we are able to hold with the infantile structures of the patient's mind. In that sense every interpretation, insofar as it is explanatory of the infantile tranference is also a type of action-in-the-countertransference. At best this concretely parental activity may be nurturing to the mind, ready for sacrifice, tolerant and tender. In the face of resistance it cannot but feel to the patient quite the contrary: overbearing, paternalistic, intolerant, demanding.

Within this area of the interpretive work we are doing a task of introducing order, restoring linkages, unscrambling confusion, and finding a notion for anchoring the unconscious experience in consciousness for the purpose of memory. It is a great service and facilitates the evolution of the transference by reconstituting the conflicts which had been prevented from finding resolutions because of the excessive operation of mechanisms of defense that lessened the mental pain below the levels necessary for development. This is one way of formulating it and probably as good as another.

To this aspect of the interpretive work I have introduced the term "routine" in order to stress both its reliance on past experience and its danger of dullness. It is as much a part of the therapeutic alliance as is the patient's behavior and verbalization that produces the material for analytic scrutiny, but insofar as the patient's behavior of cooperation also always harbors the element of acting-in-the-transference, so does the analyst's explanatory communication harbor an element of acting-in-the-countertransference. When a "good" transference-countertransference is ascendant, the glow of family happiness fills the room, always tinged with mutual idealization. Such a glow would have arisen for a while in the session reported had I given my agreement to the patient's interpretation, perhaps augmenting it with some reviewing and linking with earlier material and a bit of reconstructive comment on aspects of the patient's childhood relationships and development. It might have produced a happy Friday and a good return to the work on Monday. As it was, the patient went away quite stirred up and produced an awful week of what I hoped was negative therapeutic reaction.

What is the Advantage to Interpretation?

Now, I can well imagine an analysis proceeding like this very well indeed, with the transference evolving and the patient being cured of his symptoms and even making some headway in his character development. I have no doubt that the problem that we penetrated, which changed the dream from what might have come to be called the "anus in the mirror" dream, as a landmark of working through, to the "Rokeby Venus" dream as a beachhead to new developements in the analysis, would have found its way into unmistakable expression in the patient's material sooner or later. What then is the advantage of psychoanalytic interpretation? Does it risk the stability and safety of the process merely in the hope of saving time?

If we were to say that the most desirable aim of an analysis was not only to accomplish what has been adumbrated above and equip the patient with the self-analytic means of preserving his gains but also to place him in possession of tools which might continue his development after the termination of the formal analysis, what sort of basis in indentification processes would this involve? Clearly it would require, in our theoretical terminology, an integration of his adult bisexuality in introjection identification with the combined object. What qualities in the work of the analyst would be necessary in order for him to carry the transference of this combined object sufficient to the establishment of it by introjection into the patient's internal world?

Virgil-leading-Dante model of analysis. In order to answer this I am going to ask you to join me for a moment in a fantasy in order to alter the model of the psychoanalytical procedure which I have called the Virgil-leading-Dante model. Since psychoanalysis cannot agree with the church in seeing an external and unified inferno-purgatorio-paradiso in which all humans participate after death but rather an individual one in which each person operates in his dreamlife and unconscious fantasies during life, our model would be altered in this way. Virgil, having explored to some extent his own inner world, offers to help Dante do the same on the assumption that the corridors of these regions in each lie parallel, allow for communication, and are generally congruent in their content though far from identical. Dante would of course be distrustful of the assumptions and of Virgil's reliability, while the latter would be frightened of the heavy responsibility. But the companionship would attract them. Each time, as they proceeded, Dante would describe his findings and Virgil would reply with his understanding of the equivalent scene in his own corridor. At one point Dante says, "I have a Japanese wrestler bending over me and I can see his anus in a mirror." Virgil is puzzled because he expected around that bend to meet his father sitting by his bedside, but instead he finds himself holding a mirror for his mother while his father paints her portrait. He didn't even know his father could paint nor had his mother ever seemed so dazzlingly lovely. He also feels confused about himself and had the insistent idea that his name is Leopold Bloom! Clearly he is lost. He's never been in this corridor before. But he is a bit reassured when his unseen companion answers to the name of Daedelus.

Interpretation arising as a consequence of abandoning memory and desire. This is surely the type of experience that Freud was referring to when he wrote, "It remains for the future to decide whether there is more delirium in my theory than I should like to admit or whether there is more truth in Schreber's delusions than other people are prepared to believe." I think this must be the kind of experience that is an everyday occurrence with Bion (1970), which he describes as the consequence of abandoning memory and desire. My own point of view tells me that it is the necessary state for being able to carry the transference of the combined object, of that type of internal companionship which promulgates an atmosphere of adventure in which comradeship develops between the adult part of the patient's personality and the analyst as creative scientist. This would deserve the name of therapeutic alliance, implying therapeutic possibilities for both parties to the adventure. Perhaps, when an analyst's training in the craftsmanship of psychoanalysis has ripened into virtuosity, these moments of potential adventure begin to arise quite naturally. By seizing them he may foster in himself the tendency for moments such as Bion describes to arise again and again, moments of deep contact with his own combined object and the possibility of striving toward identification. But he probably risks everything and few of us could do that very often. Still, perhaps being able to do it even on rare occasions may be enough to enable us to carry the transference of the patient's combined object, for after all, we are never really required to be as good as the objects we are temporarily representing in the transference.

DISCUSSION

Inspired Interpretation Involves the Abandonment of the Pedagogic Position

Having now presented the two poles of interpretive activity, routine and inspired, the question must arise: are they really distinct from one another or am I really only describing something that exists on a gradient involving more or less unconscious or intuitive contribution to the intellectual process of formulation? It will have been noticed in my description of routine interpretive activity I said, "the analyst listens and observes the behavior of the patient, which comes to assume a pattern or Gestalt in his mind." Is not this "comes to assume" an unconscious, intuitive, and therefore inspired process? No, it is not what I mean by inspired. I think it is generally agreed that psychoanalytical work cannot be done by the conscious intellect alone but that any true understanding is based on intuition and not mere decipherment. I am probably trying to make the same distinction that Bion (1970) makes between knowledge and knowledge "about" something. He writes, "The 'act of faith'" (which he is encouraging the analyst to achieve by the discipline of avoidance of memory and desire) "has no association with memory or desire or sensation." It has a relationship to thought analogous to the relationship of *a priori* knowledge to knowledge. . . . It does not by itself lead to knowledge 'about' something, but knowledge 'about' something may be the outcome of a defence against the consequences of an 'act of faith.'"

To put in my own words, and of course I am not in the least certain that it is at all similar to the 'act of faith,' I mean by inspired interpretation a statement that has no explanatory significance (Could this dream have anything to do with the "Rokeby Venus"?) but involves the analyst in abandoning his pedagogic position vis-á-vis the infantile structures of the patient's personality in favor of one of comradeship with the adult part of the patient in an adventure that involves risking the whole analysis.

This risk to the analysis is shown very clearly in the dream, which, at one level, certainly accuses the analyst of a type of homosexual seduction through showing off his superior knowledge of sexuality ("In fact you have never actually seen my anus"). If this accusation were well founded, its natural implication would be that the analyst was about to lead the patient away from the sphere of his good objects into a perversion of the parent-child relation. In the psychoanalytic setting this would mean to abandon the basic method and aims of analysis for a wild "adventure" in the realm of mutual sexual excitation. What more likely form could this take than for the analyst to become inspired with new insights and to develop new techniques that would present themselves in his mind as scientific advances? In other words, were an analyst to yield to his megalomania in this way and embody inspiration as a part of his own method in error, he would also be risking his mental health. The material I have presented is intended to emphasize this problem by leaving the question unresolved in the reader's mind.

DEATH OF THE BREAST

The paper thus far has been an addendum to Chapter VIII of *The Psycho-Analytical Process*, on the Analytic Work. Because it is in a sense so idiosyncratic, because it is exemplified by a single complicated instance and, above all, because it deals with matters on the fringe of the method where creativity tips over into megalomania and wild analysis, a further effort is required. This effort, if it is to succeed, must lend the matter in hand significance for the psychoanalytical method in general by demonstrating the relevance to the process of this particular mode of functioning by the analyst which I have chosen to call inspired interpretation. In that sense what is to follow is an addendum to Chapter V of *The Psycho-Analytical Process,* on the Weaning Process.

At the time of writing that section, in 1965, the matter was still perhaps too close to the bone and my experience of carrying analysis to satisfactory termination too limited to speak with confidence. Twelve years later I feel better able to fill with meaning the concept "death of the breast" which I could only indicate at the time. I wrote: "The depressive situation, at bottom the death-of-the-breast, runs thread-like through all the material now. Attention to the analyst's physical and mental state, the urge to differentiate the person of the analyst in the outside world from the transference figures projected by psychic reality, and sensitivity to intrusion upon the psycho-analytic process from without, all become intensified, or may appear for the first time" (p. 47). I described also the increased preoccupation with the reproductive aspects of the parental sexuality and the expectation of the next baby and how the struggle against possessive jealousy in this area is directly related to the struggle to integrate split-off parts of the infantile structure, especially the more destructive parts. I added, "As yet we know relatively little, beyond what Melanie Klein has given us in 'Envy and Gratitude', about this process in relation to the most split-off parts of all, namely envious destructive parts, and, even more obscure, schizophrenic parts. One can, however hardly imagine such advanced steps in integration being accomplished outside the setting of formal analysis to begin with, and without the greatest danger, of somatic disease in the first instances and schizophrenic episodes in the second."

Richness of Therapeutic Alliance Makes Weaning Difficult for Both Partners

If we may put these considerations to one side for a moment, I would now return to our concept of inspired interpretation and its relation to the establishment of the combined object in order to describe its special significance for the weaning process in psychoanalysis. In my experience the richness of combination of the parental couple in psychic reality in respect of beauty, goodness, strength, and creativity stands in direct relation to the richness of the comradeship that emerges in the therapeutic alliance and is thus a function of both partners' capacities to abandon themselves to the adventure of pushing beyond therapy for the patient's psycho-pathology into the unknown of character development for both. Were it not for the depressive problem of the "others" who are in need of treatment and its relation to the "next baby" in psychic reality, there might be no need, in fact, to bring an analysis to termination. But the weaning is required, not merely desired, on this account. The objects must have their freedom just as the self must be free to follow its own separate development under-their-aegis and not merely to follow-in-their-footsteps.

But in proportion to this richness the weaning takes on an agonizing quality for both partners which I will now try to describe. The breast as part-object, which will die for the child internally and rise like the Phoenix from its ashes for the next baby, acts as prototype; it sets in motion a process of grief and anxiety which reawakens all those processes, past and expected in relation to external figures, including the analyst and the patient himself. Where parents and other beloved persons have already died this pain is acutely rekindled. But a combination of sparing tendencies, introjective identification and infantile tendencies to projective identification with the dying breast conspire to produce a current of death-anxiety which may reach a crescendo at times in episodes of dying. These episodes have a sufficient hypochondriacal undertone to coopt the symptomatology of deceased loved ones.

Abandonment of the Pedagogic for the Comradely Relationship Induces Doubt and Anxiety

Even when experience has deprived such events of any quality of surprise for the analyst, the anxiety and doubt which they engender for patient and analyst alike cannot be avoided. Because the richness of the experience has been a derivative of the abandoment of the pedagogic for the comradely relation in the adventure, a terrific current of mutual distrust as well as self-distrust seems to arise. The patient harbors suspicions that the analyst is mad, that he has se-duced the analyst out of the path of proper conduct, that he has undermined his stability, that a surreptitious reversal of values has corrupted the work and turned it into a perversion of the model of his most pathological excursions, prior to the treatment. The analyst suspects that his judgment is disturbed, that he is killing the patient, that megalomania has crept into his work and separated him from his mentors and colleagues, that some serious deficiency in his own analysis is being relentlessly repeated, that psychoanalysis is, after all, just the tautological system of self-deception that its most virulent critics claim.

This buffeting by doubt and anxiety, which commences usually once a date for termination is broached, does in my experience continue for some time with lessening intensity up to termination and for some considerable time after.

To return now to the question of the integration of the most split-off parts and their attendant dangers, I am of the opinion that this process can never be completed. Aspects of envious destructiveness in the infantile levels of the mental structure which are bound directly to the id, (unlike the adult part of the personality which has only an indirect relation to impulse through introjective identification processes) are required to remain outside the sphere of good objects. Their virulence can never be very accurately assessed. The fear must always remain that, either by insidious means or as sudden eruptions, they will attack the sanity and physical health.

It is precisely this fear of the split-off parts in patients and analyst alike which enters with such force to seed the pain of the weaning process with acute distrust. It is my contention that the richness of the analytic experience as a whole is bound up with the richness of the combined object which it assists to take shape, perhaps for the first time in the life of the particular patient. This paper offers as its main thesis that this richness has its source in the degree to which the pedagogic collaboration is replaced by an adventuresome comradeship at adult level. Since this requires an abandoment of the beaten track of routine interpretation at times, perhaps of the type Bion describes as the "act of faith" induced by the relinquishment of memory and desire, it is fraught with dread of incursion by the split-off parts. This becomes most acute in the period of working toward termination.

The foregoing exposition has laid emphasis quite naturally on the consequences and dangers of undertaking to make inspired interpretation a part of the method of work with a particular patient. I do not think that the opportunity for this mode of work arises with every patient nor do I see it as a possibility with most patients until the analysis is well advanced. Clearly therefore I am talking about something that is different from Bion's attitude and method. I think that creativity as an individual characteristic is an extreme rarity and cannot be achieved by any specific discipline. But for people of lesser capabilities moments of inspiration do arise and, if seized and weathered with some courage, can lead on to other moments. In my own experience these moments arise particularly when the collaboration with the patient has reached a good level of trust and understanding so that instances of comradeship can take place and the beaten track can be abandoned for a bit. But the buffeting of doubt and anxiety is quite severe, as I have explained.

What then are the consequences of retreat from these opportunities? I think that we fail the particular patients with whom such occasions arise and afford them a less rich experience, a diminished likelihood of being able to carry on the type of self-analytic work after the termination that can hold promise of further progress in integration. For the analyst the consequences must be a similar limitation in the development of his independence in psycho-analytical thought and method, curtailment of discovery and reluctance to reveal his work to others.

ADDENDUM

The body of this paper was written in 1972 and was read to the British Psycho-Analytical Society, where is was received in a friendly but uneasy way. The patient himself heard about it through a friend, realized it was about his material and asked to read it. I agreed; he was pleased with it and found that its content corresponded to his recollection — and all hell broke loose! Over the next two years he abandoned his career in music, gave himself up to a latent perversion, was left by his wife, became relatively indigent, failed to attend sessions, did not pay his bills in analysis or elsewhere, and lost most of his friends. But oddly enough his relationship with his mother became closer and more dependent, his admiration for his father and grief at his death intensified, and he threw himself gradually into a new career in which his knowledge of music was employed. But his expectations of genius and creativity were gone and became replaced by a desire to be useful and to earn his living.

It was striking over the next four years, as the perversion was relinquished and the analysis merely ticked over in a semi-interupted state, to see these changes in character appear. The grievance about the Japanese wrestler dream (his) and the Rokeby Venus dream (mine) and about the paper which strengthened his tormenting doubts about psychoanalysis and my practice of it, seemed gradually to give way to affection for both. Who has to forgive whom is still not clear but is no longer so important. It is perhaps of special interest, apropos the beauty of the mother Venus's back, that this man was not breast-fed but sucked his thumb until puberty — secretly. It was an item of both triumph and guilt toward his parents, who had trustingly-stupidly celebrated his overcoming the habit by his own account. The grievance about not being fed at the breast has been conscious as long as he has known of it.

Whether this has been a successful analysis or a catastrophe I still cannot say. But that it has had a profound influence on my own development is certain. I can feel within myself a clear and paradoxical call and joke: "Analysts of the world dis-unite. You have nothing to lose but your self-idealization."

References

Bion, W. (1970). *Attention and Interpretation*. London: Tavistock. Reprinted in *Seven Servants*. New York: Jason Aronson, 1977.

Meltzer, D. (1967). *The Psycho-Analytical Process*. London: Heinemann.

Chapter 7

BEYOND COUNTERTRANSFERENCE

AMNON ISSACHAROFF, M.D.
WINSLOW HUNT, M.D.

> Truth is incessant invention since it contradicts itself, since only the provisional is true, only what can be shared.
>
> — *Edmond Jabes*

THE ORGANIZING FUNCTION OF AN INTERPRETATION

We think of psychoanalysis as an exploration of the mind of the analysand, a search in which we find in him ideas, emotions, motives, which have been there all along but of which he had been heretofore unaware. In its genetic aspect, we imagine the analysis as a recovering of memories which have been stored in the unconscious. An interpretation is a way of pointing to something just below the surface, so that the patient can them find it in himself. Our imagery has been much influenced by Freud's fondness for analogies with archeology.

We are coming to realize that that way of conceiving the process is naive, but are having difficulty replacing it with another model which is truer to reality and yet conceptually clear and usuable. We do know that memory is not a matter of passive storage, comparable

147

to documents in an archive or data in a computer, and that the "information retrieval system" of the mind transforms that which it retrieves. An interpretation does more than just *find* something. We now speak of the *organizing function* of an interpretation. (Loewald 1960)

Perhaps the following story, taken from Isak Dinesen's (1937) autobiography *Out of Africa* will illustrate what we have in mind by this "organizing function": Jogona, a Kikuyu native on Dinesen's farm is involved in a legal matter, the resolution of which requires that an account be written down of a part of his own life, that part connected with his adopted son, who had recently died in an accident. The Kikuyu do not possess a written language.

> Two days later Jogona came back early in the morning, when I was at my typewriter, and asked me to write down for him the account of his relations to the dead child and its family. ... I wrote his statement down for him. It took a long time, for it was a long report of events more than six years old, and in themselves extremely complicated. Jogona, as he was going through it, continually had to break off his tale to think things over or to go back in it and reconstruct it. He was, most of the time, holding his head with both hands, at moments gravely slapping the crown of it as if to shake out the facts. Once he went and leaned his face against the wall, as the Kikuyu women do when they are giving birth to their children ... it gave a lot of complicated circumstances and irrelevant details. It was not surprising to me that Jogona had found it difficult to recollect, it was more surprising that he should be able to recollect the facts at all. ... When Jogona had at last come to the end of his tale, and I had got it all down, I told him that I was now going to read it to him. ... When I read out his own name, 'And he sent for Jogona who was his friend and who lived not far away,' he swiftly turned his face to me and gave me a great fierce flaming glance, so exuberant with laughter that it changed the old man into a boy, into the very symbol of youth. ... Such a glance did Adam give the Lord when He formed him out of dust and breathed into his nostrils the breath of life, and man became a living soul. I had created him and shown him himself: Jogona Kanyagga of life everlasting. ... The document became Jogona's great treasure ... Jogona made a little leather bag for it, embroidered with beads, and hung it on a strap around his

neck. . . . Once again when I had been ill, and was for the first
time again out riding, he caught sight of me at a distance, ran
after me a long way, and stood by my horse all out of breath, to
hand me his document. At each reading his face took on the
same impress of deep religous triumph, and after the reading
he solicitously smoothed out his paper, folded it up and put it
back in the bag. The importance of the account was not
lessened, but augmented with time, as if to Jogona the greatest
wonder about it was that it did not change. The past that had
been so difficult to bring to memory, and that had probably
seemed to be changing every time it was thought of, had here
been caught, conquered and pinned down before his eyes. It
had become History: with it there was now no variableness
neither shadow of turning [pp. 118-124].

It would be farfetched to consider that the memories out of which
a coherent life story was eventually constructed were isolated and
half-forgotten for defensive reasons. They were simply not
organized, because their possessor did not belong to a society
accustomed to think of careers, curricula vitae, biography. The
story also illustrates how gratifying it is for us to have our
experiences articulated and fashioned into a meaningful whole.

Every significant work of art acts *as an interpretation* on the one
who uses it, enabling him to find in himself experiences of which he
was previously less fully aware. It also does more, it defines,
organizes, and expresses some previously inchoate, unstructured
conglomerate of experience, perhaps something even too formless
to be called "an experience." It creates a new experience and adds
something new to the self of the experiencer. In that too it resembles
an interpretation.

A psychiatrist, seeing a depressed middle-aged man for the
first time, wanted to give the patient something helpful in that
initial interview to deepen the patient's very limited knowledge
of himself. The man was in a traveling episodic business and
met many people, some of whom he quite liked. But before a
relationship could really develop, he had to move on. The
doctor related, aloud, to the patient, his depression and his way
of life. Since the patient was Jewish he told him he should "sit
Shivah" for all the hopes and day-dreams aroused and then
frustrated by these transient contacts, for all the possibilities of

human sharing and closeness that he glimpsed but could not fulfill. The man was impressed and relieved, the previously inexplicable mood began to make sense and he felt understood. When the psychiatrist later knew more about his patient he could see what a very partial truth this initial formulation had been; there were other, much more important, sources of the depression.[1]

A formulation does not have to stand the test of time in order to be useful. Freud refers to this when, in discussing the possibility that a construction may be incorrect, he quotes Polonius "a bait of falsehood may catch a carp of truth."

A young man was in analysis because he could not work out a stable lasting relationship with a woman. He had been the middle of three sons, but unlike the other two in that he resembled the mother in coloring and physiognomy, while the oldest and youngest resembled the father. The father worked evenings, slept days, and was moody, irritable and worried about his health. The mother, vivacious, busy and assertive, was the dominant figure in the household. It was a generally well-ordered home, but the patient's childhood had been made miserable by beatings and sadistic teasing from the older brother, whom the usually effective mother was mysteriously unable to control. An important figure in the patient's life was the forceful family doctor, whose imperious, dogmatic style calmed the father's hyprochondrical anxieties. There was considerable contact with him over the years. He handled the children's illnesses adequately, although with unnecessary sarcasm and roughness, charged little or nothing for his services, and was treated with anxious deference by the mother.

At one point the analyst suggested that the patient had the fantasy of being himself the child of an affair between his mother and the doctor. This idea hit the patient with great force. "That never occurred to me, but now that you say it . . . why did I never think of it before . . . it may be no fantasy!" He became preoccupied with the possibility that he was really the

1. Personal communication Dr. Salvador Minuchin.

doctor's son and pursued various stratagems to seek out the truth. He was flooded with affect-laden memories, especially concerning experiences with his mother, who treated him as if he were the brightest child, destined for great things, was erotically seductive towards him and also abused him epecially through the older brother. He could become aware of how the mother had confused and unsettled him with highly ambivalent and inconsistent behavior, once he had a way to make sense of it. He realized that many of his own character traits were based on identification with the doctor. He had intentionally modeled himself on this man, thinking that a route to his mother's admiration. The idea that he was treated as he was because he was the carrier, for his mother, of an erotic, sado-masochistic, unfulfilled and guilty relationship, made it possible for him to bring together and into consciousness traumatic experiences that had been previously scattered and lacking any place in his conception of his existence. He eventually decided that he was in fact the biological son of the man he had all along considered his father, but he also knew that the emotional constellation described was nonetheless important and true, not just for him but for his parents as well.

A "NEW TRUTH"

The above examples could be said to illustrate the *integrating power* of an interpretation, but we prefer not to put it that way. To focus on the interpretation defers too much to the analyst's narcissism, *his* pride in *his* actions. After all, even the most clever interpretation has been "set up" by the patient who fed in to the analyst the material needed. For the patient the landmarks in a successful analysis may not be so much his analyst's brilliant interventions as those actions he himself has taken in order to improve his life. We need a new term for those organizing and facilitating syntheses that are created by both parties in a therapeutic relationship. We prefer to call such a synthesis a "new truth"—*new* not only because it did not exist before, prior to its creation by the patient-and-analyst, but also because we want the connotation that it is fresh for the present and meaningful only there, and *truth*, rather than reality, description, formulation, etc., because we want the implication of a valuable human statement of something central in the situation.[2]

Our central point is that an analysis does not only *discover* but *creates*. In the rest of this paper we will explore some implications of that fact.

The "beyond countertransference" of our title refers to our wish to be attentive to that which is created by *shared experience and understanding* in the ongoing analytic relationship and to go beyond a model which sees the patient as subject matter and the analyst as observer and reactor, a transference and something *counter* to it.

A young man was in group therapy and also in individual therapy. Shortly after the group had lost some members, but was still cohesive and functioning, he asked if the leader was planning to stop altogether what would seem to be too small a group. When asked what prompted the question, he proceeded to tell us what his analyst had said to him in a recent session. He quoted her to say that after having pondered and given much thought to the matter, she had come to the conclusion that he had been abandoned by his parents (psychologically) at the age of two. This statement made a profound impression on him. He described it as a Rosetta Stone that suddenly permitted him to make sense of a great many events in his life, including the fear of abandonment in the group situation and his reaction to it. There was no doubt about the enormous power that this reconstruction had on him.

The statement: "You were abandoned at the age of two" became the nucleus around which life experiences could be organized. A newly found truth gave meaning to his life. What had been heretofore fragmented experiences of abandonment and isolation became a coherent expression of his being in the world under the unifying and organizing concept of this truth.

Gershom Scholem, expressing the view of the medieval Kabbalists, saw the value of an organizing truth for human life. As a

---

2. Here we use the word *situation* in the sense of its usage in Sartre's existentialism, placing the emphasis onto the subject's role in creating his external reality and his way of experiencing it. "Sartre means by situation an active structuring of the world from the perspective of an engaged consciousness" (Danto 1975, p. 71).

speech-act, it brings form out of chaos. Or, as he put it, "God created Adam with the word 'emeth,' meaning 'truth,' writ on his forehead. In that identification lay the vital uniqueness of the human species, its capacity to have speech with the Creator and itself. Erase the initial *aleph* which, according to certain Kabbalists, contains the entire mystery of God's hidden name and of the speech-act whereby He called the universe into being, and what is left *meth*, 'he is dead'" (Scholem 1960, p. 179). The search for different levels of truth marks our human condition, particularly our need to put the successive truths we find into words that will contain them.

By emphasizing humanity's capacity to have speech with the Creator and itself, Scholem underlines the speech-act that attempts to convey truth by translating meaning into words. In therapy, this involves an interplay between patient and analyst that in itself influences the very subject under investigation. In the therapeutic situation, facts and feelings need to be transformed into words. The psychological process becomes a linguistic process. A translation takes place that decodes the inner experience of both participants in the therapeutic encounter. Our patient brought to his analyst a fragmented feeling of isolation and recurrent experiences of abandonment, as well as his precarious defenses to ward off the pain that the original abandonment had brought to his life. Her reconstruction created a *myth* that could give perspective to his life. The therapist's capacity to make that reconstruction is based on the possibility of recognizing something in her as well as in the patient.

When she says: "Your parents abandoned you when you were two," her aim is to structure the internal 'situation' of the patient. She is, in effect, inside of him, saying: "I know what happened to you. I recognize it, I am with you." A new reality is created in which the therapist and the patient are involved. And furthermore he will see her the next week or the day after tomorrow, he comes and he leaves. A new locus of control of an historical event has been created. The therapist has responded to the fragmented world of the patient with the need to integrate it and now he has control of the abandonment.

PAST TRUTHS GIVE WAY

By creating a new truth in the present, the truth of the past is necessarily changed. A truth of the past that is isolated from new developments is a rigid, unchangeable principle that affects the understanding of new realities in a disorganizing way. The present becomes stereotyped and fragmented because the myth of the past has to attack the reality of the present in order to maintain itself. A person with a rigid focus and fixed beliefs cannot grasp the totality of what he is living and therefore has to fragment what is going on in order to take it in through the distorting filter of his (transferred) view of the situation. To make sense of it, he has to destroy its true coherence.

Memories of the past tend to undergo a process of mystification. When the United States celebrated its bicentennial, each of many conflicting groups wanted to present its version of the American Revolution, that is, to promote that history which will most legitimize its claim in the present. In the individual, memories become woven into the self-image and play a role in structuring present action and imagining future possibilites. The psychiatrist-hypnotist,[3] Milton Erickson, has tried to use this fact for therapeutic purposes. One patient was a woman with low self-regard and an unhappy childhood. Dr. Erickson ignored her present life, but through hypnotic suggestion inserted into her memories of happy experiences with a loving father. The treatment is reported to have worked, to have increased her present self-valuation by giving her a personal myth-history of a happy, loved childhood.

TRUTH IN ANALYSIS AND TRUTH IN SCIENCE

All "new truths" in therapy are of equal standing. Some may be more helpful than others, bigger than others, but none are final. We wish to distinguish this concept, the "new truth" from the meaning of truth in the physical sciences. There it is believed that there is an ultimate and necessarily static truth. The history of science is one of increasing approximations to truth in an asymptotic progression. Science may never reach ultimate truth, but it gets closer, as Einsteinian physics is a better approximation than Newtonian physics. The "new truth" in therapy is of a different kind, more akin to the truth in art or literature. As in art there is no progress, at least not in the sense in which science progresses. An age can use the art of previous periods, but only as raw material, certainly not as a solid

---

3. Personal communication Dr. Salvador Minuchin.

platform on which one can stand while building the next level.

Art can be good or bad, and as each society or age creates its own art, it can do so well or poorly, but it is its own art. It is its own version of the world or its own way of life and these things can never be once and for all. The truth of psychoanalysis as science is like the truth of any science, it has a more or less well established structure and a growing edge. But in the analysis of an indivdual, truth is contingent, contingent on everything: the cultural setting, the two individuals, the past histories, their motives at the moment, their commitments and values and so on. Every painter paints roses as he sees them, and yet an art historian can date any rose within fifty years. Each religious mystic leaves society behind and goes off alone to find the ultimate ground of his existence, yet in historical perspective each is seen to be solidly within a specific, definable tradition. There is a certain sadness in realizing how transient are the truths that we create in the analytic process. They are true for that person at that time, they serve their purpose if they open up a path for learning, fresh experience, growth, and then are left behind, like a good mother. As Freud profoundly stated in his paper *On Transience* (1916), we can only value such creations if we can also mourn for their evanescence.

In science there is usually at any point in time one best formulation, or at least the issue between competing theories is in principle and generally in practice, resolvable. In art, life and analysis there are different ways to do it right. This has to do with the fact that human beings can hold the greatest variety of values, and can, and do, assign priorities to these values in almost all possible combinations and permutations. In science we have reached a consensus that one value has overriding importance: we agree to choose that formulation which best describes and predicts reality. In art, social relations, and the proper conduct of life, there is obviosly no such consensus. In analysis matters of value also enter in. It would be naive to imagine that the course of an analysis is not influenced by the analyst's fundamental view of what it means to be human, to lead a life, and of what is valuable and what is petty.

While human personality, as perceived by another, is not a Rorschach card, designed for maximum ambiguity, so that the observer is maximally forced to reveal his own personality in his way of perceiving it, neither is it a clear simple diagram, idiot-proof as we say, which can be understood in only one way. If we consider that every single thought, feeling and act is "over-determined" by the multiplicity of motives that enter into it and all this richness multiplied to make a total living person, and then picture the analyst, flooded with data but yet never knowing enough, trying to imagine the inner constellation of forces that makes the system move as it does, always unsure about what is fundamental and what is epiphenomenal, then we can realize that it is more like looking at an inkblot than we usually acknowledge and that the analyst's own personality must influence the way in which he brings order into all this, and in particular the way in which he visualizes the deep structure at any moment and overall. If we imagine that the patient, as he is about to arrive for the first session, is miraculously cloned into ten identical persons, and he (they) walk(s) into ten different offices, they will have ten different analyses, even theoretically, even under perfect conditions, apart from any practical matters, like errors in technique, analysts with headaches, etc.

But, the reader may object, we have enough on our hands just trying not to do it wrong, without bothering ourselves about different ways of doing it right. Yes, and in acknowledging that there is no single correct way to analyze, we imply no license, but rather would maintain the strictest level of dicipline, especially in maintaining open, radical freedom of imagination and willingness to hear anything, however disturbing. By imagining that there is an "only best way" one imposes on himself a cramping and unnecessary constraint and inhibits the full use of his own private talent and artfulness.

EXAMPLES FROM LITERATURE

Much modern literature has dealt with the issue of knowing the truth, especially the truth about ourselves, as we exist in society, in our closest relationships and as we evaluate the worth of our total lives. From this vast literature we wish to single out two plays, which particularly focus on truth in the self-image and in self-esteem, and on the therapeutic and destructive aspects of truth.

The Iceman Cometh

One is Eugene O'Neill's *The Iceman Cometh*. Set in New York in 1912, the play deals with a collection of more or less alcoholic habituees of a seedy bar, who cling to the security of the bar and of their group, comforting themselves with blown-up accounts of past exploits and full of rationalizations for their failure to go out in the world and confront challenges of their present lives. The group has one firm code—no one is to challenge the pipe dreams of another. Into this little world comes Hickey, a traveling hardware salesman, who is determined to free them all from their illusions about themselves and make them face up to their lives. With skill and perseverance he does in fact cut through their evasions and excuses, exposes the fears that keep them locked into Harry Hope's bar and even inspires them to make some feeble, unsuccessful attempts to change. In the end they are all more miserable than before. They have been stripped of their protective fantasies, their noses have been pushed into their weakness and failure and they are left with nothing but despair and whiskey. Hickey, it turns out at the end, has faced up to the truth of his life, that he is a mediocre cad, given to drinking and whoring, and living in a guilty tormented relationship with his saintly all-forgiving wife. He has acted to free himself from this hell. He has murdered his wife and called the police to take him in.

The play is enough to give truth a bad name. O'Neill offers no alternatives between pitiable self-delusion and a cruel destructive truth. The truth giver, Hickey, is a driven man himself and driven to forge the truth onto others. O'Neill allows us some distance from his characters, who are a rather special group living in circumstances unlike our own.

The Wild Duck

The other play we wish to examine, *The Wild Duck* by Hendrik Ibsen, has a more ordinary setting and deals with middle-class people involved in the usual pursuits of life.

The first act opens during a dinner party that Haaken Werle, a wholesale merchant and mill-owner, is throwing to celebrate the return of his son Gregers after seventeen years of absence. Invited to that party is Hjalmar Ekdal, Gregers' boyhood friend. During the evening Gregers discovers that his friend had married his father's former maid, Gina, and realizes that their daughter, Hedwig, had been fathered by the old Werle (his father) prior to their marriage.

Hjalmar and Gina had a stable marriage, working together in a photography business. Gina carried most of the practical burdens and Hjalmar, encouraged by their neighbor, Dr. Relling, spent most of his time dreaming about an invention, which gave him special status in the family. This mixture of fantasy and, at times, strenuous reality was working well enough until Gregers took it upon himself to bring out the truth by uncovering the past. Dr. Relling describes Gregers as suffering from an acute case of moralistic fever and tries to persuade him to desist from his new mission in life, which is to open his friend's eyes to the "truth." but nothing can deter Gregers in his zeal and his harsh literal truth finally destroys the warm human truth created by fifteen years of marriage. He brings chaos to the family and unnecessary pain to the innocent Hedwig, who finally commits suicide. This disaster was not Greger's intention, it was only the unintended result of his efforts to bring in the truth in order that Hjalmar and Gina can live up to the highest ideal of a "true marriage." Ibsen gives us enough materials to speculate about Gregers unconscious motivation to aim at this ideal state of affairs, particularly in his relationship with his father who, he felt, made his mother unhappy and caused her to die miserably. Gregers' goal was to free Hjalmar from all the lies and evasions he felt were smothering him, and to let Hjalmar forge a new way of life, based on a companionship in truth, with no more deception. Dr. Relling argues that he will only bring ruin to a good enough marriage and serious harm to their daughter.

Relling's prescriptions for the ills and imperfections of the world is to try to keep up what he calls "the vital lie," which is for him the animating principle of life. As an example, he describes how he made Molvik, a former divinity student and now a bombastic drunk, believe that his stupidity and lack of control was "demonic." That was Relling's remedy for Molvik to keep life going in him, to prevent him from giving in to self-contempt and despair. He cites other examples, including Hjalmar and his invention, and concludes that to deprive the average man of his vital lie would rob him of his happiness as well. The play concludes with Relling proclaiming that: "Life could be good in spite of all, if we could only have some peace from these damned shysters who come badgering us poor people with their 'summons to the ideal.'" The interplay between the two characters, Relling and Gregers, symbolizes the constant dilemma of illusion versus truth.

Relling, the practical philosopher, creates illusion in order to give *meaning* to life. Relling and Gregers are presented as polar opposites. One can say that Relling encourages madness and unreality but with kindly intent. Gregers' truth, on the other hand, is destructive and humanly false because it confuses literal truth with the "truth" of a human relationship. If biologically the older Werle was Hedwig's father, the subjective truth was different. To make a judgment about what level of reality is truer and, futhermore, to attempt to impose it in a self-righteous manner is a travesty that fanatics are well-known for. In a discussion of the play Dr. Szalita (1970) says: "Meddling irresponsibly in someone else's affairs is always a dangerous business. Yet it could be said that this is something we psychotherapists are engaged in as a profession, and who knows whether we always discharge our duties to the best interest of our clients? Hopefully, we learn to know our patients first and have enough tact to realize how much of the so-called truth the patient is able to integrate at a given moment, and what is more important, to what purpose we intend to put the given truth."

Freud's admonition that the psychotherapeutic endeavor is founded in truthfulness is a reminder of tendencies to "depart from this sure foundation." In his "Observations on Transference-Love" (1915) Freud observes that

When a man's life has become bound up with the analytic technique, he finds himself at a loss altogether for the lies and the guile which are otherwise so indispensable to a physician, and if for once with the best intentions he attempts to use them, he is likely to betray himself. Since we demand strict truthfulness from our patients, we jeopardize our whole authority if we let ourselves be caught by them in a departure from the truth.

As analysts we are against falsehood, and although this may coincide with our natural moral impulses, it can also be convincingly justified on therapeutic grounds. If the lie fails, that is, is discovered, it undermines the trust necessary for all intimate human relationships and if successful the lie undermines the patient's grasp of reality and hence his power to deal with it. A lie is a nodal point in a relationship based on contempt and exploitation. But if we are against falsehood, we are not moralistic about truth. Our sensitivity to our patient's needs, resistances, transference distortions, and in fact his total situation, makes us wary of untimely presentations to him of the truth as we happen to see it from our vantage point. Truth is an abstraction that has to be translated into interpersonal truthfulness. There is no truthfulness divorced from intention. As therapists, we may find in ourselves the polar tendencies represented by Gregers and Relling, or Hickey and the "dreamers." This is, we may want to encourage adventurous exploration in our patients, to reach beyond the prosaic and restrictive realities of their lives and wake them up to the realization that cherished beliefs must be laid to rest. Or, perhaps tired ourselves, we may want to share a world of fantasy with the patient, settle for comfort in the inner life, albeit there is some blurring of reality and rationalizations around the edges. We must walk a narrow path, neither entering into a folie-a-deux, however subtle, with the patient, nor yet crushing him with our vision, or version, of reality. In the actual treatment situation our conflict parallels, or may even be a response to, the same conflict in the patient, who asks himself, "How much of the truth do I really want to know?"

Our dilemma as analysts is how to reexamine the vital lie — which is really the old truth of the patient — without destroying him, how to make a bridge from the vital lie to the new vital truth. One of the indispensable ingredients in this bridge is our capacity for empathy. To be able to understand the patient "from inside" is an essential part of the therapeutic task. However, like any other tool, if misused, it may hinder rather than facilitate that task.

DANGER OF COUNTERTRANSFERENTIAL EMPATHIC REACTIONS

Szalita (1976) warns about the danger of the empathic reaction.[4] "The test of one's empathy is the capacity to relate to the sensitivity of the sufferer rather than to the magnitude of the misfortune." An empathic reaction may lead us to a never-never land where our own fantasies invade and populate the space between our capacity to observe and the psychical reality of our patient. We may relate more to the apparent magnitude of the patient's misfortune, particularly if it echoes a situation similarly experienced by us in the past. In interposing our empathic reaction we may misunderstand the

4. Some current usage implies that the emotional knowing of another in empathy is always correct, but Webster's (1953) definition gives "imaginative projection of one's own consciousness into another" and we follow this sense.

historical reality as well as the remembered, subjective truth of the patient. The emotional quality that we choose to emphasize in the patient's past experience may not be necessarily the only one, or the most decisive one that marked that particular experience for the patient. We can confuse feelings evoked in ourselves by the factual reality of the patient and attribute to him our own experience of our historical reality. Freud (1937) was confident that such transgressions of the psychological boundaries of the patient were not harmful because (after an incorrect reconstruction) the patient "will remain as though he were untouched." Perhaps Freud's optimism was based on the rarity of such occurrences in his own clinical practice. Internal reality, however, has different levels that are not mutually exclusive and "man enters into active possession of consciousness, into the active cognizance of reality, through the ordering, shaping powers of the language" (G. Steiner's [1975] paraphrase of Giambattista Vico). Influenced by our empathic reaction to the patient's story, through the ordering and shaping power of our language (in the interpretation or reconstruction), we may shape the representation of reality in the patient through a selective combination of his past experience and of ours.

The empathic or countertransferential reaction elicits a truth in ourselves that is not necessarily conducive to understanding where the patient is at the moment. It may serve as a general guide, but to define his precise experience, we need to corroborate our own creative, perhaps too creative, imaginings with his detailed memories.

CONSTRUCTIVE USE OF COUNTERTRANSFERENCE

The empathic recognition of some aspects of one's self in another person sets in motion an interpersonal event. In the course of it, persuasive forces may be mobilized to create a new "truth" through mutual validation of two historical truths (that of the patient and that of the therapist). This new "truth" is characterized by the selective inclusion of some aspects of the historical truths of both participants, and has a meaning in the context of the relationship between therapist and patient. This "new truth" is always subject to issues of the will, by which we mean that the "new truth" integrates the will of the therapist — which is to be helpful — and the will of the patient — which is to learn something useful for his life. We can contrast the helpfulness of the new truth with the destructive use of the truth, like Hickey's or Gregers' "truth." The very words which the therapist might use helpfully could be used by any angry husband or wife destructively, and thereby given a totally different meaning.

In our search for the truth that will allow our patient to free himself from a fixated internal reality, we attempt to sort out obstacles to a communication that will transcend the individual experience. For this purpose, we train ourselves in sorting out what in the patient's communication affects our capacity to understand his experience in his terms.

We constantly need to correct and adjust our capacity to listen while under the sway of emotional reactions that color what we hear. By extricating ourselves from countertransferential tides, to the best of our intention and knowledge, we give ourselves and our patient the best possible conditions of scientific objectivity that we can conceive at this time in the history of human communication. Partial and temporary identifications with the various aspects of the patient's experience are the road to objectivity. We allow the evocative value of the patient's experience to induce in us temporary identifications and reactions, while still maintaining a position from which we can return to objectivity. Objectivity is based on our capacity to maintain a neutral stance when confronted with a dilemma, a conflict or a request to take sides. This is what our patients constantly ask from us: to take their sides against their real or imaginary, past or present, tormentors. The kind of neutrality required in our role as therapists is not a neutrality of affects. We cannot help, neither should we avoid, responding empathically to our patients or even to their assumed tormentors. But, if we become capricious adversaries or allies of the patient at any particular moment, we may in fact allow the patient to manipulate us to accept a partial truth about himself. In that situation, a patient cannot examine or recognize the conflictual aspects of his ambivalence about what he considers good or bad about himself.

The self-analysis or nonjudgmental supervision of countertransference reactions allows the therapist to regain his objectivity and neutrality. This in turn creates the most favorable circumstances in which the patient can retrieve his ambivalent feelings toward his internal objects. This allows the patient to retain the richness of his feelings and gradually to control them, rather than being controlled by them. However, in our search for the truth we are constantly reminded that the language of ambivalence is necessarily vague and confusing; clarity is the reward of polarization.

We allow the patient to create in us his various emotions, attitudes, wishes, fears, and as we master each such experience, understanding how it expresses some force in the patient, we can come back to neutrality. A sailboat is turned this way or that by every wave or gust of wind, yet the sailor can each time bring it back onto its true course, and yet each wave has been felt and its force and direction taken into account.

Properly speaking, we never know anything of the external world in which the analysand lives. Except for special situations, our information all comes from the patient. The world is filtered and restructured in its passage through him. It is unnecessary and pejorative to say that he distorts the world, as if *we* could step outside our world and see reality as it is in itself. Rather it is just that the patient, like all of us, takes whatever it is out there and builds up from it his world. If we were really careful in our usage, we would never say, unless we had outside corroboration, "X happened to the patient in childhood," but always, "As he experienced it — or as he remembers it, X happened." Similarly we should rarely say, "The patient's mother is such and such," but rather "The mental representation of the patient's mother is . . ." But this is a truism and usually we do not bother with such matters, it being tedious and laborious to insert "as he experienced it" or "the mental respresentation of" into every other sentence. We have a general attitude of trust in the patient's reports and any possible discrepancy between the patient's version and what really happened is not an issue. Except with psychotic patients, where the inherent implausibility of a reported event will seize our attention, it is relatively rare that we catch ourselves up, begin to mentally insert the "as he experienced it," and become curious about what really happened. It is worth noting when, and in what circumstances this happens.

A patient, a young woman, would come in and complain of some mistreatment at the hands of a co-worker or friends. There was nothing implausible in the story, but the analyst felt skeptical, thought she was exaggerating and was generally annoyed with her and sympathetic towards her persecutor. In observing his reaction more closely, he realized that he felt badgered and cajoled into testifying to the nature of an event which he had not witnessed. In her tone and manner she was, as it were, tugging his sleeve and saying,"You know that this is right, don't you? You do see it my way of course. My feelings are justified, you must admit that. Don't be silent, come now, you must speak up for my side, etc."

When presented with this, she admitted that she herself was always plagued with doubts about how to interpret certain events. She feared that she was distorting things or thought she might have provoked the attack. She recalled that in childhood, whenever she had been in any conflict with a teacher or relation or playmate, her parents would take the other person's side. For instance, although Jewish she had gone to a very Christian school and had been subject to anti-Semitic sneers and to unfairness. When she reported these incidents to her parents, they denied that what she experienced had really happened, or twisted the story around so that it was really her fault. In adult life whenever she was ignored or attacked, that is, whenever she was in fact subject to another person's hostility, she could not fully grasp the situation, for she always heard an inner voice telling her that it hadn't really happened and anyhow she had caused it in the first place.

We have found it to be a general rule that whenever the analyst becomes preoccupied with what really happened, when he starts to doubt the patient, at that point the patient has grave doubts about his or her capacity to correctly perceive and interpret reality.

An analysis gets its energy from motivations stemming from both parties. On the patient's side, there is the wish to get well, to change and grow, to discharge the dammed-up emotions accumulated through past experience, to re-create the past, etc. From the analyst's side, in addition to the general need for object-relatedness and the varying motives that went into each analyst's choice of profession, there are certain specific but universal motives which help to bring the analyst to his calling and find gratificaton in it once he is there. We wish to call attention to two such motivations.

MOTIVATIONS SPECIFIC TO THE ANALYST

One is to overcome the fragmentation of one's personality, to master, and to enjoy the mastery of integrating scattered disparate and conflicted parts of the self. The entire process of analysis consists of bringing to consciousness disassociated parts of the self, tolerating and accepting them, and integrating them into a central self. The analyst participates in this not only as an active agent, helping to make it happen, but also more passively, as a coexperiencer. To follow Racker's terminology (1968) we can say that he coexperiences, via the "concordant identifications," the patient's self-experience or parts of it and through the "complementary identification" he experiences a part of what is, from the point of view of the patient's consciousness, the external world, namely, the unintegrated introjected objects. When the patient successfully uses the defense of projective identification, the analyst will take in, perhaps unwittingly or unwillingly, attitudes, emotions, beliefs, impulses of the analysand. If he is aware of what has happened, he can experience these contents, name them, find their proper locus in the patient's life and return them to the patient. He has been, for a time, the only experiencer of something that belongs to the patient's life. If he is unaware of what happened, he may carry around forever, like shrapnel, fragments of the patient's life.

For the patient, experiencing his conflicted self, the analyst's presence and knowledge of all of him may be like

> the sinewie thread my brain lets fall
> through every part

and he hopes that knowledge

> can tye those parts, and make mee one of all
> [Donne, 1633]

and in all this, parts of the analyst, of his life and his historical truth, are activated and resonate with what the patient experiences, so that the gradual integration involves him, too, and he also emerges changed, although less so than the patient.

The fear of going crazy is probably universal. It is closely interwoven with the fear of being completely abandoned and also, in particular with the fear of being, and being defined by others, as nonhuman. In the fear of going crazy, different elements are of special significance to different persons: some fear that speech or thought will become garbled or blocked, or there will be overwhelming experiences of terror, from which no one can rescue them; others fear that no one will believe or understand them; others, that they will do terrible things, etc. — but one aspect of most of these fears is that of being alone in one's own craziness. Everyone is aware of thoughts, feelings, impulses in himself that he or others might consider crazy. As analysts we are often able to make observations (on nonpsychotic patients) that reassure us that we are not alone in our strangeness or our nastiness.

A competent, likeable man in his early thirties, well integrated into society, had reached that point in his analysis and in his life when he was ready for intimacy and commitment and was seriously looking for a woman with whom he could share his life. Among the possibilities was a woman, intelligent, attractive, and well recommended by his friends, who thought herself also ready for marriage. The relationship progressed, but did not deepen. He found himself frustrated as he came up against a self-sufficiency and complacency, an unwillingness to change, a subtle but pervasive selfcenteredness, that left him with nothing to hold onto, and reminded him of his mother. In this context, in one session, he mentioned a newspaper account of the execution of a man for murder. He went on to tell the story in detail, killing by firing squad, body taken for autopsy, eyes taken out to use for corneal transplants, four bullet holes in the heart, skull sawed open, brains taken out, sliced into sections, etc. It was clear what he wanted to do to the woman who seemed to promise so much, but who came through with so little. The analyst felt a certain calm descend on him. He realized that he had just been told that his own capacity for hate and destructiveness was well within the boundaries of what is human.

We continuously recreate in analysis new situations that contain reciprocal elements of the historical truths of both participants. These refer to, but do not duplicate, their pasts. The truth that emerges from this interplay is a composite of reconstructions which are materially fictive. This fiction or invented narrative runs through the entire therapeutic process. The ineffable and elusive quality of what happens in the process is not subject to verification, even if witnesses are included. Self-knowledge, after all, derives understanding from autobiographical reconstruction at the service of one's needs. And these needs dictate the direction of the search, which, from session to session, finds itself swerving in two often diametrically opposite approaches. One attempts to reconstruct the past by pointing to what lies behind or beyond the verbal signs; the second attempts to demonstrate how these signs function in a current relationship. We know it is impossible to eliminate completely our subjectivity. What may be possible, perhaps, is to articulate further its subtle and pervasive role in our critical discourse about the truth.

CONCLUDING REMARKS

The formulations arrived at in the course of an analysis have a powerful organizing function. Even formulations which ultimately prove incorrect, assuming that they come from an open, exploratory attitude, can advance the process. Genetic interpretations or reconstructions not only unearth the past but also create a personal myth for the patient which guides him in the present.

These new formulations do not only discover, they also create. Even theoretically, there is no one best analysis of a patient. One influence on these formulations is the specific personality of the analyst. Even theoretically, it cannot be dispensed with.

Any such formulation, what we call the "new truth" in an analysis, is a synthesis of discovery and creation. In large measure, it is true in the way that a novel or poem is true, or a satisfactory life (in the sense that it is a creation and expresses a character). Such truth articulates, more or less adequately, a conjunction of inner and outer reality, a "situation" in Sartre's sense. It is to this extent unlike scientific truth, which asymptotically approximates to the truth and is not intrinsically contingent on the circumstances of its creation, although it may, or may not, be in time replaced by a yet closer approximation. The truth generated in an analysis — we are speaking here of the truth of the patient's life, not with the truth of psychoanalysis as science — is valid only for that time, place and circumstances; it is transient and contingent, inevitably and sadly so.

Because the analyst is aware of the contingent nature of his interpretations, he is not moralistic about the truth, he does not force it. He also is, or should be, humble in knowing that the only thing he can speak of with authority is the reality of the patient and *his* world, but not of anything concerning *the* world, that is, outer reality. A preoccupation in the analyst about what really happened usually reflects grave doubts in the patient regarding the intactness of his or her ability to perceive and correctly interpret reality.

Aside from the general need for object-relatedness, and the vagaries of countertransference which differ from analyst to analyst, there are certain universal motives which, from the analyst's side, fuel the analytic process. One of these is the need to integrate a fragmented self. Another is the need to reassure oneself that one is not alone in one's craziness.

References

Danto, A.C. (1975). *Jean-Paul Sartre*. New York: Viking Press.
Dinesen, I. (1937). *Out of Africa*. New York: Vintage Books, 1972.
Donne, J. (1633). *Poems of John Donne:* London: Oxford University Press.
Freud, S. (1916). On transience. *Standard Edition* 14:303-307.
_____ (1915). Observations on transference-love *Standard Edition* 12:159-171.
_____ (1937). Constructions in analyses, Standard Edition. 23:255.
Ibsen, H. *The Wild Duck*. New York: Bard-Avon, 1965.
Loewald, H. (1960). On the therapeutic action of psychoanalysis. *International Journal of Psycho-Analysis* 41:16-33.
O'Neill, E. *The Iceman Cometh*. New York: Vintage Books, 1957.
Racker, H. (1968) *Transference and Countertransference*. New York: International Universities Press.
Scholem, G. (1960). *On the Kabbalah and Its Symbolism*. New York: Schocken Books, 1965.
Szalita, A. (1970). Some questions for psychoanalysts: reflections on Ibsen's *The Wild Duck*. *Psychoanalytic Review* 57:587-598.
_____ (1976). Some thoughts on empathy. 18th Annual Frieda Fromm-Reichmann Memorial Lecture. *Psychiatry* 39:142-152.
Steiner, G. (1975). *After Babel: Aspects of Language and Translation*. London: Oxford University Press.

Chapter 8

COUNTERTRANSFERENCE AND PROJECTIVE COUNTERIDENTIFICATION

LEÓN GRINBERG, M.D.

In this paper I shall present a synthesis of the ideas which I have developed in various articles and books regarding the concept of "projective counteridentification." I first coined this term in 1957 to refer to a specific and differential aspect of countertransference, based on the unconscious analytic interaction between the patient and the analyst, and which is brought about by the particularly intense use of and psychopathic modality of the mechanism of projective identification of the patient. As a result of the pathological quality of this mechanism, the patient is able to induce different roles, affects and fantasies in the analyst, who unconsciously and passively feels himself "carried along" to play and experience them (Grinberg 1957).

PROJECTIVE IDENTIFICATION

I should like to refer briefly to the mechanism of projective identification.

This was described by Melanie Klein in her paper "Some Notes on Schizoid Mechanisms" (1946), and included in her hypotheses about

169

emotional development in the first months of life. It consists of an omnipotent fantasy that unwanted parts of the personality, and parts of internal objects can be split, projected, and controlled in the external object into which they have been projected.

Under normal conditions projective identification determines the empathic relationship with the object, not only because it allows one to put oneself in the place of the other and therefore understand his feelings better, but also for what it brings out in that person. The subject always produces some emotional reaction in the object. His attitude, the way he looks at the object, the way he speaks, what he says, or the gestures he makes, etc., means that there are always projective identifications at work. They stem from the various sources which bring them about which arouse the emotional responses related to the situation, for example, sympathy, anger, sorrow, hostility, boredom, etc. This usually happens, within certain limits, in all human relationships and forms the basis of communication. The object, in turn, also functions with his respective identifications, therefore producing an interchange.

Projective identification also plays a fundamental part in symbol formation.

The concept of the normal and the pathological are closely related to the greater or lesser predominance of aggressive impulses, to the degree of tolerance or intolerance of frustration, to the kind of contact with external and psychic reality, to the state of the ego functions, to the quality of the defense mechanisms and to the profound dynamics of the object links. Different modalities of projective identification will be at work in accordance with the predominance of one or other of the psychic states (Grinberg 1965).

The normal quality of later projective identification will also depend, in great measure, on the quality of the projective identifications with the first object relationships. It is not only important to know how the subject's projective identifications worked, conditioned by various fantasies and impulses, but also how the projective identifications from the first object worked and the type of reactions that emerged in the subject. Another factor important to bear in mind is that of the use (at a more organized level) of the mechanism of "adaptive or realistic control"[1] which

---

1. I differentiated between two levels of functioning of the mechanisms of obsessive control: one includes the more regressive aspects and corresponds to the widely known "omnipotent control," which is chiefly related to primitive states or

allows one control over the split parts, and those which have been projected away. The breakdown of this mechanism could bring about disturbances of varying degrees in the functioning of the ego vis-á-vis the object (Grinberg 1966).

The tendencies and fantasies which correspond to each of the libidinal stages will condition the appearance of projective identifications with oral, anal, urethal and genital contents, they will also bring about specific modalities towards the respective object relationships. Whichever stage predominates (because of fixation or regression) will naturally influence the contents of the fantasies included in the projective identifications. Those fantasies projected onto objects at the oral level are used for eating, sucking, biting or devouring, poison or destroying with flatus or excreta at the anal level; scalding and destroying with urine or its equivalents at the urethral level, etc.

It is essential to evaluate the quantity and the quality with which projective identifications intervene so as to determine the seriousness of the different clinical pictures. The situation is more serious if it coincides with an increase in sadism operating in each of the phases. It can also happen that, on certain occasions, projective identifications function with particular violence, as happens in the narcissistic, psychotic, and psychopathic personalities.

I should now like to present a classification of projective identifications (Grinberg 1965).

According to their qualities: Normal or realistic projective identifications, and pathological projective identifications (omnipotent, hypertrophic, with multiple splitting and "bizarre" objects, "explosive," etc.).

According to their orientations: Projective identifications directed towards the interior of an external object, towards the surface of the external object, towards an internal object, towards the body and different organs, etc.

According to their aims: Communicative, reparative, evacuative, controlling, destructive projective identifications, etc.

According to their contents: Projective identifications of aspects of the self (ego, superego, ego ideal, organs of perception, ego

---

psychotic conditions; the other comprises the most highly developed aspects and corresponds to what I termed "mechanism of adaptive or realistic control" to stress that they feature better adaptation and closer contact with reality and external objects. (Grinberg 1966).

functions, ideas, impulses, affects etc.). Projective identifications of internal objects.

According to their clinical modalities: Hysterical, phobic, perverse, psychopathic, obsessive, manic, paranoid, melancholoid, etc.

According to their effects on the subject: Empathy, relief, confusion, dependence, omnipotence, claustrophobia, etc.

According to their effects on the object: Empathy, reactivation of countertransferential feelings, reactions of projective counteridentifications.

Melanie Klein's papers, especially the one dealing with her concept of projective identification (Klein 1946), are sufficiently familiar to require no further commentary. Her paper "On Identification" (Klein 1955), constitutes, at present, one of the most complete studies of the contents and functioning of projective identification. According to her description, it implies a combination of the splitting mechanism, the subsequent projection of the split parts onto another person, with the ensuing loss of those parts to the subject, and an alteration of the object-perception process. This process is bound up with those processes that take place during the first three or four months of life (the paranoid-schizoid position), when the splitting mechanism is at its maximum height, with a predominance of persecutory anxieties.[2]

In pathology, projective identification consists in an omnipotent fantasy through which unwanted parts of the personality and internalized objects, with their attendant emotions, are split off, projected and controlled in the object towards which the projection is directed. As a result, the object is equated with what was projected onto him. This operates with utmost intensity during the earliest periods of life. It is important to scrutinize not only the different modalities of the subject's projective identifications as conditioned by his varied fantasies and impulses, but also those projective identifications of his parents and the kind of impact they made upon the subject.

PROJECTIVE COUNTERIDENTIFICATION REACTION

As I have pointed out (1959), projective counteridentification has

2. Freud, in *Group Psychology and the Analysis of the Ego* (1921), describes a type of projection very similar to the projective identification mechanism, when he

to do with a very specific aspect of the countertransference. It is important to stress this to demonstrate the difference between the response I have in mind and those countertransference reactions resulting from the analyst's own emotional attitudes, his neurotic remnants, reactivated by the patient's conflicts. I would like to describe, in a schematic form, the two processes which coexist in the analyst's mind so the difference is made clear.

1. In one the analyst is the active subject of the patient's introjective and projective mechanisms. In this process, three important phases can be described: (i) the analyst selectively introjects the different aspects of the patient's verbal and nonverbal material, with their corresponding emotional charges; (ii) the analyst works through and assimilates the identifications resulting from the identification of the patient's inner world; and (iii) the analyst (re)projects the results of this assimilation by means of interpretations (Fliess 1942).

2. On the other hand, the analyst can also be the "passive object" of the patient's projections and introjections. And two further situations may develop: (a) the analyst's emotional response may be due to his own conflicts or anxieties, intensified or reactivated by the patient's conflicting material; (b) the emotional response may be quite independent from the analyst's own emotions and appear mainly as a reaction to the patient's projections on him.

The second process presents for us considerable interest, especially in connection with the problem raised in this paper. In one phase, it is the analysand who, in an active though unconscious way, projects his inner conflicts upon the analyst, who in turn acts as a passive recipient of such projections.

The emphasis should be attributed to the extreme violence of the projective identifications of the analysand. I will show later in clinical examples how the particular intensity of this mechanism is usually related to traumatic infantile experiences, during which the patient suffered the effect of violent projective identifications.

Whenever the analyst has to meet such violent projective identifications, he may react in a normal way, that is, by properly interpreting the material brought by the patient and by showing him that the violence of the mechanism has in no way shocked him. Sometimes, however, the analyst may be unable to tolerate it, and he may then react in several different ways: (a) by an immediate and

points out the projection of the ego ideal of each of the members of the army on their commander.

equally violent rejection of the material which the patient tries to project into him; (b) by ignoring or denying this rejection through severe control or some other defensive mechanism (sooner or later, however, the reaction will become manifest); (c) by postponing and displacing his reaction, which will then become manifest with another patient; (d) by suffering the effects of such an intensive projective identification, and "counteridentifying" himself, in turn.

In fact, the specific response of the analyst will depend on his degree of tolerance.

When this counteridentification takes place, the normal communication between the analysand's and the analyst's unconscious will be interrupted. Then the unconscious content rejected by the analysand will be violently projected onto the analyst who, as the recipient of such projective identifications, will suffer its effects. And he will react as if he had acquired and assimilated the parts projected onto him in a "real and concrete way" (Grinberg 1956, 1959).

The analyst may have the feeling of being no longer his own self and of unavoidably becoming transformed into the object which the patient, unconsciously, wanted him to be (id, ego, or some internal object), or to experience those affects (anger, depression, anxiety, boredom, etc.) the analysand forced onto him. For this situation, I have proposed the term "projective counteridentification," that is, the analyst's specific response to the violent projective identification from the patient, which is not consciously perceived by the analyst. Even if the situation prevails only for a short time (although occasionally it may persist with ensuing danger) the analyst will resort to all kinds of rationalizations to justify his feeling of bewilderment (Grinberg 1962).

This concept has been affirmed by Bion (1961), who remarked that "the theory of countertransference offers only a partially satisfactory explanation because it deals with manifestation only as a symptom of the unconscious motives of the analyst and; therefore, *it leaves the patient's contribution without explanation. . . .* thanks to the beta screen *the psychotic patient is able to provoke emotions in the analyst*" (italics mine).

Bion also accepts the emergence of emotions in the analyst produced by the patient (through his projective identifications) and which are independent, up to a point, of the countertransference of the analyst. He goes on to state: "the use these patients make of words is more an action directed toward freeing the psyche from an increase of stimuli than a language."

To understand this last statement, it would be convenient to say a few words about the theory of alpha function, as Bion labels that function which allows the transformation of sensorial experiences into alpha elements which can be stored and used to form memories, oneiric thoughts, etc. They are those which permit dreaming, thinking, and maintaining the differences between the conscious and the unconscious. On the other hand, if the alpha function fails, beta elements appear, but they cannot be used to form thoughts; they contain undigested facts which can only be evacuated through projective identification and appear in the production of acting out. These theories offer a new contribution for the understanding of the thinking processes (Bion 1961).

Whenever the thinking function fails, for whatever reason, we suggest that it is replaced by projective identification which tends to free the psychic apparatus from the increase in tension.

DIFFERENCE BETWEEN COUNTERTRANSFERENCE AND PROJECTIVE COUNTERIDENTIFICATION

Based on the complementary series of Freud, Racker (1960) described a countertransferential disposition on the one hand, and present and analytic experiences, on the other, which leads to the resulting countertransference. He added that this joining of the present and the past, of reality and fantasy, of the external and internal, etc., makes a concept necessary which envelops the whole of the psychological response of the analyst, and he advised that the term countertransference should be used. Nevertheless, he made it clear that, at times, one may speak of "total countertransference" and differentiate and separate within that term one or other aspect.

Racker emphasized the existence of a "countertransference neurosis" where the "oedipal and preoedipal conflicts, along with pathological processes (paranoid, depressive, manic, masochistic, etc.), interfere with understanding, interpretation and the behavior of the analyst."

Racker made a particularly detailed analysis to two types of identification of the analyst with parts of the patient. Based on suggestions of H. Deutsch, he pointed out that the analyst, with his empathic tendency toward understanding everything which happens to the patient, is able to identify "each aspect of his own personality with its corresponding psychological part in his patient; his id with the patient's id, his ego with the patient's ego, his superego with the patient's superego, *accepting in his conscience these identifications*" (italics mine).

These are concordant or homologous identifications based, according to Racker, on introjection and projection, in the interaction of the external with the internal, with the recognition of the remote as his own — "this (you) is me" — and the association of his own with the remote — "that (me) is you." "Concordant identifications" would be a reproduction of the analyst's own past processes, which are being relived in response to the stimulus of the patient, bringing about a sublimated positive countertransference which determines a greater degree of empathy.

The second type of identification, called "complementary identifications" are the results of the identifications of the analyst with internal objects of the patient; the analyst feels treated like those internal objects and he experiences them as his own.

Racker also described a "concordant countertransference" where there is an approximate identity between parts of the subject and parts of the object (experiences, impulses, defenses); and a "complementary countertransference" where "an object relationship" can exist very similar to others, a true transference in which the analyst "repeats" earlier experiences. The patient now represents internal objects of the analyst.

It is here where I would like to outline the difference between Racker's countertransferential terms and my concept regarding "projective counteridentification."

To begin with, confusion only arises with regard to the difference between "projective counteridentification" and "complementary countertransference." "Concordant countertransferences" are related to the empathic link toward the patient, the desire to understand him and deal with identifications which are accepted in the analyst's conscience. It is worth mentioning that they almost depend on an active disposition on the analyst's part.

Let us therefore see what is the essential difference between "complementary countertransference" and "projective counteridentification." "Complementary countertransference" arises when the analyst identifies himself with the internal objects of the patient and experiences them as his own internal objects. Racker emphasizes the fact that the analyst repeats previous experiences in which the patient represents the internal objects of the analyst. The last experiences (which always and continuously exist) could be called "complementary countertransferences."

This countertransference reaction is therefore based on an emotional attitude which is due to neurotic remnants in the analyst, reactivated by the conflicts posed by the patient. It appears in the first situation of process (2), which I have described above, in which the analyst is the object of the patient's projections, e.g. the patient's internal objects; but he reacts countertransferentially because of his own anxieties and the reactivation of his own conflicts with his internal objects.

On the other hand, "projective counteridentification" corresponds to the second situation of process (2). The analyst's reaction stems, for the most part, independently of his own conflicts and corresponds in a predominant or exclusive way to the intensity and quality of the patient's projective identification. In this case, the origin of the process comes from the patient and not the analyst. It is the patient who, in an unconscious and regressive manner, and because of the specific functional psychopathic modality of his projective identification, actively provokes a determined emotional response in the analyst which the analyst will receive and feel in a passive way (Grinberg 1963a).

In "complementary countertransference" a reaction always arises which corresponds to the analyst's own conflicts. On the other hand, in "projective counteridentification" the analyst *takes onto himself* a reaction or a feeling which *comes from* the patient.

To clarify this point, I will use one of Racker's examples. It is the case of a patient who threatens the analyst with committing suicide. Racker (1960) writes:

The anxiety which such a threat sparks off in the analyst can lead to various reactions or defense mechanisms within him, e.g., a dislike of the patient. These feelings, the anxiety and the loathing, would be the contents of the "complementary countertransference." His awareness of dislike or loathing toward the patient can also bring about, at the same time, a guilt feeling in the analyst which can lead to desires of reparation and to the intensification of "concordant identification and concordant countertransference."

Now, if we analyze this extract we find both processes superimposed on each other or coexisting simultaneously. (This usually happens.) The analyst experiences anxiety in the face of the suicidal threat. In this anxiety, two main components are evident: one corresponds to the analyst's own anxiety due to the feeling of responsibility which he has, when confronted with the eventual danger of suicide of his patient which, at the same time, may represent one of the analyst's internal objects. (It can be the patient's internal object which is being experienced as one of the analyst's own internal objects.) This form of anxiety corresponds to a "complementary countertransference." On the other hand, the analyst takes onto himself the patient's specific anxiety which, through projective identification, the patient placed in him with the idea of the analyst controlling and eventually resolving it. This response of anxiety now forms part of "projective counteridentification." Later the analyst reacts with dislike (his own mechanism, belonging to "complementary countertransference") and guilt. If we analyze further this kind of guilt, we find that part of it has a persecutory characteristic, that is, "persecutory guilt" (Grinberg 1963b). This brings about the dislike for also having embodied (although in a partial way), the impotence and desperation of the patient and his fear of not being able to make reparation. Another part of this guilt belongs to the "depressive guilt" (Grinberg 1963b) which the patient is still not able to perceive or manage, and which, projected into the analyst, makes the analyst feel able to make reparation. These last considerations with regard to the patient's projection of the two types of guilt and the analyst's response, demonstrate how "projective counteridentification" works. However, it does not include the two qualities of guilt which the analyst may feel, due to his own conflicts which are reactivated by the material presented by the patient ("complementary countertransference").

Naturally, these processes are never pure nor are they isolated; they generally coexist in different proportions.

When mentioning other examples, Racker maintains that a transferential paranoid-depressive state of the patient corresponds to a "manic-countertransferential state" of the analyst, in the aspects of "complementary countertransference." He is implying the coexistence of the two mechanisms. The analyst may react manically because of his own conflicts which make him feel strong or dominant when confronted by a depressed object; or because he has taken onto himself the manic and triumphant attitude of the patient which, due to the special use of projective identification has "placed" him in that position.

Through "complementary countertransference" each analyst identifying himself with his patient's internal object will react in a personal way according to the type and nature of his own conflicts. Different analysts will react *differently* to the same situation, posed by a hypothetical patient. On the other hand, this hypothetical patient using his projective identification in a particularly intense and specific way could bring about the *same* counterfransferential response ("projective counteridentification") in different analysts. I had the opportunity to confirm this through the supervision of material of a patient who had been in analysis successively with various analysts.

In the way a transferential attitude begs a countertransferential response, a projective identification will also beg a specific projective counteridentification. Although the analyst introjects, albeit passively, this projective identification, what is important to recognize is that the specific reaction of the analyst is due to *the way* in which the patient projected, lodged, or "forced" into the analyst his projective identification.

Furthermore, the "projective counteridentification" will have different modalities related to the respective modalities of the projective identification, colored by the qualitative shading which gives it a functional specificity. Habitually, in all extraverbal communication, the type of functioning (degree and quality) of projective identification on the part of the patient does not go over the critical threshold of the analyst and the extraverbal message produces countertransferential resonance. It stimulates the response which could be received, controlled and verbalized with relative ease by the analyst. But, on certain occasions in which the degree and quality of the projective identification influence its functional modality in a special way, the result is that the extraverbal communication will pass over the critical threshold, producing "projective counteridentification." This threshold will depend on, in each case, the personality of the analyst, on his previous analysis, and the degree of knowledge or awareness he has regarding this phenomenon (Grinberg 1976).

I also think that sometimes the analyst, when faced with an excessive projective identification on the part of the patient may respond with a paranoid attitude which will bring about a counter-resistance and which will undoubtedly affect his work.

"Projective identification and counteridentification" phenomena are frequent in the analysis of narcissistic and borderline personalities, and give rise to a pathogenic interaction between the analyst and patient which is not easy to resolve. One might say that what was projected, by means of the psychopathic modality of projective identification, operates within the object as a parasitic superego which omnipotently induces the analyst's ego to act or feel what the patient wanted him to act or feel in his unconscious fantasy. I think that, to some degree, this is similar to the hypnotic phenomenon as described by Freud (1921) in which the hypnotist places himself in the position of the ego ideal and a sort of paralysis appears as a result of the influence of an omnipotent individual upon an impotent and helpless being. I believe the same idea applies, sometimes, to the process I am discussing. The analyst, unaware of what happened, may resort to all kind of rationalizations to justify his attitude or his bewilderment just as the hypnotized person does after executing hypnotic suggestions.

When the analyst is able to overcome this reaction, he may take advantage of this phenomenon so as to clarify some of the patient's unconscious fantasies and emotions, making an adequate interpretation possible.

FOUR CLINICAL EXAMPLES

Some clinical vignettes will serve as examples.
1. A male patient begins his session in the following way:

I feel very nervous today. I don't know how to describe it, but it is absolutely necessary that I do. I would like to tell you what I have discovered or what has been revealed to me [with great emotion]: It was so surprising the other day when the diarrhea stopped as a result of what you said to me . . . Besides I remember that something else you said gave me a physical stitch. Diarrhea is a physical process . . . Since you spoke, these words seem to produce a physico-chemical reaction in some or other of my nerve cells; but before that, when you think, there is also a transformation in other cells to the point where the voice comes from lungs, lips, tongue, etc., and a string of words which are now sound, vibrations, comes out. At this moment the receptive process begins in my ear, through various means until it becomes conscious listening. I ask myself if all those words, instead of being spoken by you, came from someone else, would they have the same therapeutic meaning? I think not. It is extremely important for me that those words came from Dr. Grinberg and no one else.

All this material was said with force and with a resounding voice which surprised me. It was not common for him to express himself like that and, therefore, I felt particularly attracted as much by what was said as the way it was said. Using as a guide my impression, I interpreted that he was trying to produce in me the same effect that he said I had had on him, and he tried to show me that that was his voice and no one elses which produced this special effect on me. That is to say that my interpretation was made showing his positive transference. I did not yet realize that it was only a defense against his deepest paranoid situation.

The patient goes on to say:

Now that we are talking about sound and listening, I would like to talk about music: it is divided into three basic parts, rhythm, melody and harmony which are undividedly joined together. I play jazz; in that we see rhythm and the harmony of the song we are playing. The melody is improvised. In modern jazz, the rhythm and the harmony are also improvised. I can improvise for hours on melodies with rhythm but I find it difficult to carry on a specific harmony. A melody in 8/4 time in the chord of A for four beats and the other four in A sharp is impossible for me. The same happens with written music; I cannot give the timing correctly to each note. On the other hand, when my music teacher played one of the pieces I was studying, I could play it after exactly by ear. In the session, for example, I find it difficult to adapt to the reality of time. I don't even know what time it is. It is as if I made my own time, which is different from your time. I can compare it to my inhibition in music; this specific harmony which we improvise is the kind which allows people who don't know each other to improvise a jam session.

While he was telling me all this, I did not fully understand what it was that was happening. I felt quite uneasy. I felt sorry that I did not understand sufficiently the theory and technique of music which I have always loved. I admired and envied his knowledge and apparent precision with which he described and explained it ... with its technical jargon, the relationship between rhythm, melody, and harmony. I felt the need to interpret it in his own words; it was a way of showing him that I could also play in the same field as he and which he knew so well.

My interpretation was that I represented the chord of A major and he the chord of A natural, but that between our beats there was no harmony and we needed to find a rhythm and a timing between the two of us which would harmonize so that we could improvise (free association) together in a common melody.

The interpretation was now spoiled; it only demonstrated a partial aspect and in a way different from what was essential. The important thing would have been to show him his envy and that he was really interested to discover which was my timing and which was my rhythm. The meaning of his deepest fantasy began to dawn on me and I payed attention to the following material.

The patient goes on:

> I don't know why I thought that one could do all kinds of tests to a patient; encephalograms, B.M.R.'s, a tape recording, a thermometer to take a temperature with, an oscilloscope to record sound waves; anyway the use of all those appliances so that you would have a better knowledge of the patient, both inside and out.

While I was listening to him I surprised myself with a parallel and simultaneous fantasy to have a metronome to regulate, control, and direct the time in him, that is to say, to have something which I already knew was lacking in him. I realized exactly at that moment of all the play of his unconscious fantasy contained in his intense projective identification and also "how" I "counteridentified" myself projectively with a partial aspect of his, full of envy, and anxiety. One of the major effects of my "projective counteridentification" was the blind spot of the paranoid content of his attitude and my having stressed instead the positive aspect of the transference. The patient used it in a defensive way to pacify the persecutor, which I represented. But that was only his defense because of his anxiety and panic due to the power he thought I had. My words not only cured him of his diarrhea but also they gave him a physical stitch. I was in possession of a secret which he envied and feared because I could do what I wanted with him. He wanted to take this over so that he could limit its danger and also so that he could dominate me at the same time. For this he needed both to know me and to control me. It was for this that he "took" me into his own field, acoustics and music. He made me feel, projectively, what he had felt with me. My feeling of dislike corresponded to his feeling of anxiety. My admiration and envy reflected similar feelings which he had felt, and my need to use his terminology and concepts was the equivalent of his desire to take onto himself my special terminology and concepts. My fantasy of the metronome, formed the response to his desire to use all kinds of medical apparatus so as to get to know me completely, that is to say, to control me. As a last resort, and as a transactional solution, he offered me his beat and timing in exchange for knowing mine.

2. In another case, a woman patient came to her first session fifteen minutes late. She lay down on the couch and then remained still and silent for a few minutes. After that she said she felt the same as she used to feel when passing an oral examination (which usually caused her great anxiety). Then she associated the analytic session with her wedding night when, even though she was feeling extremely frightened, she was told she looked like a statue.

I told her that what she felt was that she was having with me the same experience that she had had at her oral examinations and during her wedding night, because she feared I might deflower her, introduce myself into her to look at things and examine them. Here, too, she was behaving like a statue; the rigidity and stillness she showed at the beginning of her session were intended to disguise her anxiety, but also to prevent the actual possibility of being penetrated.

Although I realized that this interpretation of her paranoid anxiety was correct, I had the feeling that there was something wrong with it. Still, I could not understand the reason for such a feeling. I guessed that my interpretation had been rather superficial and that the facts I had pointed out to her were too near to her consciousness. I had to find out the deeper motives of her exaggerated fear of my going into her.

On the other hand, her initial attitude of stiffness had particularly attracted my attention, and I found myself, not without consider- able amazement, having the fantasy of analysing a corpse. A thought came at once into my mind, which took the form of a popular

Spanish saying: "she is trying to force the dead into me" (which meant that she wanted to burden me with the whole responsibility and guilt). This thought showed me my own paranoid reaction, aroused by the feeling that she was trying to project her fears into me, through projective identification.

Based on this countertransferential feeling, I told her that with her rigidity and silence perhaps she wanted to mean something else, besides the representation of a statue; perhaps she wanted to express in this way some feeling of her own, related to death.

This interpretation was a real shock to her; she began to cry and told me that when she was six years old her mother, who had suffered from cancer, had committed suicide. The patient felt responsible for her mother's death, because she had hanged herself in her presence, and it had been actually on account of her delay in warning the rest of the family that the death could not be prevented, as had been done in former attempts. She remembered having watched all the arrangements her mother made and being greatly impressed by them. Then she went out and waited for a long while (perhaps fifteen minutes, she said); only then did she run for help, but when her father came it was too late.

I had the feeling that with her corpselike rigidity the patient was not only trying to show that she carried inside a dead object, but also, at the same time, to get rid of it by projective identification. From that moment on, she wanted me unconsciously to take over the responsibility, to bear "the dead." As a defense against her violent projective identification, with which she tried to introduce into me a dead object, I reacted with my first interpretation, which in fact inverted the situation: she was the one who was afraid of my piercing her. Later on, I managed to grasp the actual meaning of the whole situation, I had a much clearer understanding of the deepest sources of her paranoid anxieties and gave her a correct and more complete interpretation.

3. The following example was given to me by a colleague.

This deals with an obsessive patient who had gone to the analyst to try to solve his great inhibition in studying and passing examinations.

Among his previous experiences he referred in a special way, to having had a very violent stepfather, who used to hit him extremely hard, doing it, on occasions, at the mother's request. He had felt, however, ill treated by everybody and in every way, in spite of his being a well disposed man. He said he had always been "kicked." As illustrative examples of his "victimization," he told of traumatic homosexual experiences which he had gone through with his elder brother and schoolmates who had harassed him continuously.

However, the most characteristic and remarkable aspect of this first session was the way which he told all this in shocking contrast to its contents. His language was pompous, in an irritatingly pedantic way, and he used a pseudo-technical terminology to tell of his experiences. He said he knew everything. He had read Adler, Jung, Freud and, according to him, he had also mastered different philosophical doctrines.

The countertransferential experience of the analyst was increasingly annoying and, at times, somewhat anxious. He felt he could not make headway with his interpretations because there was no room for them and, on the few occasions when he did manage, the reply was usually immediate and in terms of rejection, objection, or ridicule. As a clear demonstration of the absolute control with which the patient wished to be the dominant partner in the transference relationship, he used to interrupt his speech (since what was happening could not be called free association) in order to demand in an obligatory tone and in a self-satisfied way the opinion of the analyst: "How do you see all this?"

This situation repeated itself intensely in the following session. The patient commenced a new attack on the interpretations of the previous sessions using his now classical destructive techniques in order to nullify them. The analyst felt that his patient was getting to the end of what he had made into an "unbearable nightmare," as he described it. There was something more than dislike and frustration in his work. He felt the attitude of the patient to be one in which he mercilessly had decided to ill treat or destroy, one by one, all the interpretations.

If the analyst had given way to his own impulses, which were well controlled, he would have gotten up and kicked the patient. This fantasy was that which directed his subsequent interpretation expressed with decided annoyance showing in his voice, interrupting his patient brusquely and telling him: "Just a moment, you are behaving in a way which makes me want to kick you; just like your brother and the rest did. It's the way you seem to want the whole world to be against you."

After this intervention, the analyst thought the patient would not return. However, this did not happen and the analyst was able to see a decided change in the patient's attitude or behavior.

Evidently, the interpretation was disturbing to the analyst because of the enormous emotional content which the analyst demonstrated and this was especially reflected in the analyst's tone of voice, the way he said it, and the intention; an almost conscious wanting to convert the interpretation into the concrete substitute for the "kick." This was due, in a large part, as the interpretation indicates, to the fact that he was the passive receptor of the persecutory objects which the patient projected into him as a result of the strong repetitive compulsion to look for aggressions. At another level of the transference relationship, the patient identified himself with the aggressors, placing, through projective identification, his punished self into the analyst, in order to make him suffer what the patient himself had suffered. The purpose of the projection was that the analyst was not ony the depository of this suffering aspect, but changed it, giving it the quality of a reaction to counteract its masochistic meaning. This the analyst also did through the intervention.

4. In another example a student in psychoanalytic training came to his own analytic session after having analyzed a "difficult" patient. During the session with his own patient, the student had had the feeling of "killing himself," owing to his very active interpretations without obtaining any satisfactory result. He was depressed by his feeling of failure, and after communicating his experience and mood to his training analyst, he remained silent. While listening to his analyst's interpretations, which momentarily did not modify his state of mind, the student had the impression that the same situation he had been complaining about was being repeated, although with inverted roles. He realized that now it was his analyst who was "killing himself" to obtain some reaction from him, while he was acting in the same way as his patient had done. When, with some surprise, he communicated his impression to his analyst, the latter showed him that his behavior during the session had "compelled" (his own words) him to identify himself with the patient. The interpretation was then completed in this sense: the student envied his analyst for having better and easier patients (the student himself). A very intense projective identification had thus taken place, by means of which the student unconsciously wanted his analyst to experience his own difficulties. The student resorted to splitting, projecting his hampered and dissatisfied professional part onto the analyst, remaining with that part of himself identified with his own patient "who makes one work and does not gratify." The

training analyst had, in turn, "succumbed" to his patient's projection, and felt unconsciously compelled to "counteridentify" himself with the introjected part.

When this occurs — and this process is much more frequent than is usually believed — the analysand may have the magical unconscious feeling of having accomplished his own fantasies, by "placing" his parts on the object. This also may arouse in him a manic feeling of triumph over his analyst.

Several issues presented by Hanna Segal in her paper "Depression in the Schizophrenic" (1956) are closely related with the process I have called "projective counteridentification." These refer, especially, to the projection of the patient's depressive anxieties into the object (analyst) by means of projective identification, and to the specific response aroused in the analyst as a result of such identification. In Segal's words:

> Then one day as she was dancing around the room, picking some imaginary things from the carpet and making movements as though she were scattering something around the room, it struck me that she must have been imagining that she was dancing in a meadow, picking flowers and scattering them, and it occurred to me that she was behaving exactly like an actress playing the part of Shakespeare's Ophelia. The likeness to Ophelia was all the more remarkable in that, in some peculiar way, the more gaily and irresponsibly she was behaving, *the sadder was the effect, as though her gaiety itself was designed to produce sadness in her audience,* just as Ophelia's pseudo-gay dancing and singing is designed to make the audience in the theatre sad. [italics mine]

"Projective counteridentification" was successfully dealt with by Segal by integrating it in an adequate interpretation of her patient's attitude. She pointed out that the patient had put into the analyst all her depression and guilt, thereby transforming the analyst into the sad part of herself and, at the same time, into a persecutor, since she felt that the analyst was trying to push her unwanted sadness back into her.

Bion (1955) gives a clear example of the mechanism of projective counteridentification.

The patient had been lying on the couch, silent, for some twenty minutes. During this time I had become aware of a growing sense of anxiety and tension which I associated with facts about the patient which were already known to me from work done with him in the six-months he had already been with me. As the silence continued, I became aware of a fear that the patient was meditating a physical attack on me, though I could see no outward change in his posture. As the tension grew I felt increasingly sure that this was so. Then, and only then, I said to him: "You have been pushing into my inside your fear that you will murder me." There was no change in the patient's position, but I noticed that he clenched his fists till the skin over the knuckles became white. The silence was unbroken. At the same time I felt that the tension in the room, presumably in the relationship between him and me, had decreased. I said to him: "When I spoke to you, you took your fear that you would murder me, back into yourself; you are now feeling afraid you will make a murderous attack on me." I followed the same method throughout the session, waiting for impressions to pile up until I felt I was in a position to make my interpretations. *It will be noted that my interpretations depend on the use of Melanie Klein's theory of projective identification, first to illuminate my countertransference, and then to frame the interpretation which I give the patient.* [italics mine]

PROBLEMS DERIVED FROM COUNTERTRANSFERENCE AND PROJECTIVE COUNTERIDENTIFICATION IN THE SUPERVISORY SETTING

One of the most significant problems the supervisor has to tackle consists of the student's difficulties due to his countertransference. While this has already been discussed in a large number of papers, panels, and symposia on supervision, the most controversial issue has to do with the attitude the supervisor is supposed to assume toward the student's countertransference. General agreement has been reached in the sense that the candidate's countertransference problems should not be interpreted by the supervisors. Nevertheless, owing to its recurrence and intensity in students' work, discussion still goes on as to what should be the right posture for the supervisor.

Again I should like to point out the existence of two different categories of countertransference issues. One is related to those problems concerning countertransference itself. The other is concerned with what I have called projective counteridentification.

I believe it is necessary for the supervisor to be able to differentiate between the two categories when he encounters such issues during supervision. Countertransference has to be dealt with on the couch in the student's training analysis, projective counter-identification in supervision. When the candidate presents difficulties that stem mainly from his own conflicts the supervisor may refrain from making direct remarks, but point out the existence of difficulties and show how to aproach the dynamics of the patient. Some authors suggest making the situation explicit, advising that the candidate work it out in his analysis. However, this is questioned by others as potentially having a disturbing effect on the candidate.

The supervisor's task should then be to take care of the candidate's difficulties since it is in supervision that he could help the candidate become aware of a conflict or misunderstanding of which the student may not be conscious. When the candidate is thus disturbed, the supervisor has the advantage of available material which will disclose the cause for the problem. It is essential that the supervisor be able to illustrate from available clinical material, where, how and why the therapist has been liable to the projective counteridentification reaction.

The student can make the supervisor feel an emotional reaction of the same quality as the one the patient has aroused in him. If the supervisor has a full understanding of the genesis of his own affective response, he can, with greater ability, objectivity and experience, show the candidate the origin of the emotional reaction he experienced during the session with his patient.

Similar problems have been discussed by other authors, although from a different frame of reference, with different terminology. Sometimes, I wonder whether a good deal of disagreement between analysts is not more due to semantic differences rather than to conceptual ones. Arlow (1963) says, in reference to what I have termed projective counteridentification, that the therapist shifts from a role that consist of *reporting* the experience he has had with his patient to *experiencing* his patient's experience; the supervisor may find evidence that the candidate *enacts* an identification with his patient. Searles (1955) states that the relationship between patient and therapist is often revealed by the relationship between therapist and supervisor. He adds that the supervisor has a spectrum of emotional phenomena — as the therapist and the patient have theirs — which often throw light on classical countertransference reactions and at times are highly informative reflections of the therapist-patient relationship. He calls them part of a "reflection process" to stress their source and points out that they can be a decisive clue to obscure difficulties which emerge in the therapist-patient relationship. Searles suggests that unconscious identification is one of the processes involved in the genesis of this phenomenon.

When discussing a case at supervision, the supervisor may have the feeling that the anxieties and defenses of the therapist, while reporting the session, are an unconscious way of communicating something that occurs with the patient, which the student's own anxiety prevents him from describing to the supervisor. The supervisor can be more easily aware of the nature of the problem not only because his knowledge and experience are wider, but also because he is more emotionally detached.

Hora (1957) accounts for this kind of phenomena in the following way: "The supervisee unconsciously identifies with the patient and involuntarily behaves in such a manner as to elicit in the supervisor those very emotions which he himself experienced while working with the patient but was unable to convey verbally." He further on adds that "the therapist orally incorporates or introjects his patient in his endeavour to empathetically understand him. While on the conscious level the supervisee proceeds with the presentation of the factual data about the patient, unconsciously on a non-verbal level he communicates the affective aspects of his experience with the patient. This carries the dynamic aspects of the patient's personality make-up."

References

Arlow, J.A. (1963). The supervisory situation. *Journal of the American Psychoanalytic Association* 11:576-594.

Bion, W.R. (1955). Language and the schizophrenic. In *New Directions in Psycho-Analysis*, ed. M. Klein, et al., London: Tavistock.

———(1961). *Learning from Experience*. London: Heinemann. Reprinted in *Seven Servants* New York: Jason Aronson, 1977.

Fliess, R. (1942). Metapsychology of the analyst. *Psychoanalytic Quarterly* 11:211-227.

Freud, S. (1921). Group psychology and the analysis of the ego. *Standard Edition* 18:67-143.

Grinberg, L. (1956). Sobre algunos problemas de técnica psico-analitica determonados por la identificación y contraidentificacion proyectiva. *Revista de Psicoanalisis* 13:507-511.

―――― (1957). Perturbaciones en la interpretación motivadas por la contraidentificacion proyectiva. *Revista de Psicoanalisis* 14:23-28.

―――― (1959). Aspectos mágicos en la transferencia y en la contra-transferencia. *Revista de Psicoanalisis* 15:347-368.

―――― (1962). On a specific aspect of countertransference due to the patient's projective identification. *International Journal of Psycho-Analysis* 43:436-440.

―――― (1963a). Psicopatologia de la identificacion y contraidentifi-cación projectivas y de la contratransferencia. *Revista de Psicoanalisis* 20:112-123.

―――― (1963b). *Culpa y Depresion*. Buenos Aires: Ed. Paidos.

―――― (1965). Contribución al estudio de las modalidades de la identificación proyectiva. *Revista de Psicoanalisis* 22:263-278.

―――― (1966). The relationship between obsessive mechanisms and a state of self disturbance: depersonalization. *International journal of Psycho-Analysis* 47:177-183.

―――― (1976). *Teoria de la Identificacion*. Buenos Aires: Ed. Paidos.

Hora, T. (1957). Contribution to the phenomenology of the super-visory process. *American Journal of Psychotherapy* 11:769-773.

Klein, M. (1946). Notes on some schizoid mechanisms. *International Journal of Psycho-Analysis* 27:99-110.

Klein, M. (1955). On identification. In *New Directions in Psycho-Analysis,* ed. M. Klein, et al. London: Tavistock, 1955.

Racker, H. (1960). Estudios sobre Tecnica a Psicoanalitica. Buenos Aires: Ed. Paidos.

Searles, H. (1955). The informational value of the supervisor's emotional experience. *Psychiatry* 18:135-146.

Segal, H. (1956). Depression in the schizophrenic. *International Journal of Psychoanalysis.* 37:339-343.

Chapter 9

ANALYTICAL PSYCHOLOGY
AND COUNTERTRANSFERENCE

MICHAEL FORDHAM, M.D.

In this chapter I shall approach the subject of countertransference from the point of view of analytical (Jungian) psychology. Since this differs historically and conceptually from classical psychoanalysis I will first present Jung's position and then consider how his followers have criticized, modified, and developed his point of view. Jung conceived analytic practice to be a dialectical process between two involved persons. By implication he advocated what has lately been called an open systems viewpoint. A closed system is one with clearly defined limits or boundaries; two persons may stand in relation to each other yet function as distinct entities. In their conversation words have an agreed meaning or, if there are dysjunctions in their communications, these can be clarified by reference to the psychical system of one or the other. Open systems, on the other hand, are those in which boundaries are not fixed, with the result that the two systems — patient and analyst — interact and change in relation to each other. Difficulties or confusions therefore require a change in *both* psychical systems before validation is possible.

Developments in psychoanalysis appear to have led psycho-analysts close to conceptions being worked on by analytical psychologists, particularly in London. I have used the work of psychoanalysts extensively and recognize that many of my propositions were considered before I thought of them. However, since this article is about analytical psychology I shall not refer to their specific publications but will content myself with making a general acknowledgment to the following: Bion, Heimann, Klauber, Langs, Little, Meltzer, Money-Kyrle, Racker, Searles, and Winnicott (for a complete review, see Langs 1976).

Jung has laid great stress on the patient's individuality. He believed that each analysis differs in essential respects from every other. "Psychotherapy and analysis are as varied as are human individuals. I treat every patient as individually as possible, because the solution to the problem is always an individual one. . . . A solution which would be out of the question for me may be just the right one for somebody else" (Jung 1963, p. 130). He therefore placed less emphasis on method than on interaction. In later years he even adopted a sort of non-method: "Naturally a doctor must be familiar with so-called methods. But he must guard against falling into any specific routine approach. In general one must guard against theoretical assumptions. Today they may be valid, tomorrow it may be the turn of other assumptions. . . . In my analyses . . . I am unsystematic very much by intention. . . . We need a different language for every patient" (Jung 1963, p. 131).

These remarks were Jung's last statements on psychotherapy, but their spirit had for many years influenced the development of analytic psychotherapy, in my view to its detriment. I believe the study of the analytic situation was seriously delayed because there did not seem any point in describing what happened with one patient since in principle it would not apply to others. Thus Jung's statements lent themselves to an abhorrence of any general theory of technique, since any such theory could on this view only foster a misunderstanding and be used as an intellectualized defense against the patient as unique individual.

However, if Jung's expositions are studied in context, a different picture emerges. While Jung was consistently suspicious of theoretical abstractions, this did not prevent his developing a number of theories: e.g., the theory of types, of archetypes, and of the collective unconscious. He was, moreover, a master in their application, as a study of his analyses of dreams shows. The Tavistock seminars (Jung 1968) revealed his method of amplifying symbolic dream material. This procedure, which Jung used when studying alchemy, aims at elucidating symbols by placing them in their historical and cultural contexts. The method derives from the notion that there is always a penumbra of mystery around symbolic data and it is desirable to make that as explicit as possible while preserving the context of the imagery. In view of all this, Jung's final statements should be taken not as a denial of the value of theoretical guidelines for psychotherapy, but rather as a suggestion that the treatment of the patient is an art.

The development of Jung's conception of the analytic situation (see Fordham 1957, 1969, 1974, 1978), may be said to have started when he emphasized the need for the analysis of the analyst. He thought that it was the influence of the analyst as a person that was the decisive therapeutic factor, a conception that had been formulated in the deceptively obvious idea that no analyst can help his patient to progress farther than he has gotten himself (Freud 1910). In line with this position, Jung (1946) held that transference could often be the result of interaction between analyst and patient. He thought that transference, though ubiquitous in everyday life, is intensified in the analytic setting in reaction to the analyst's behavior. The real attitudes and personality of the analyst play a significant part in the form and intensity of transference. When the analyst is incapable of empathizing with his patient, an intense transferential reaction develops, representing the patient's effort to close the gap. Jung believed transference can also represent an effort by a patient to adapt to an analyst who, endowed with the qualities of a parent, can act as a bridge so the patient can move from his regressed state back to reality.

A conception more relevant to my thesis is that Jung recognized the analyst's capacity to introject his patient's psychopathology and become confused or disoriented.

> The doctor by voluntarily and consciously taking over the psychic sufferings of the patient, exposes himself to the overpowering contents of the unconscious and hence also to their inductive action. . . . The patient by bringing an activated unconscious content to bear upon the doctor, constellates the corresponding unconscious material in him. . . . Doctor and patient thus find themselves in a relationship founded on mutual unconsciousness. . . . [and] the unconscious infection

brings with it a therapeutic possibility — which should not be underestimated — of the illness being transferred to the doctor. [Jung 1946, pp. 175-176]

All these ideas are related to the theory of archetypes, which suggests that there is a substrate common to all human beings. It is conceivable that the archetypes are virtually the same for everybody. It is this archetypal activity that sensitizes analysts to their absorbing and taking over aspects of their patients.

In Jung's writings there are a number of other observations which imply his interactive approach:

1. He believed that a patient's resistances could be thought of not only as intrapsychic but also as related to the therapist's conflicts (Jung 1951, p. 115: see also Lambert 1976).

2. He implied that a patient might be ahead of the analyst in understanding and lead the therapist into appropriate functioning. During his lifetime he delivered (Jung 1937), but never published, a paper describing how he had become depressed at his inability to understand what was going on. With his patient becoming more and more ill, he offered to refer the patient to someone else. To his astonishment she said she thought everything was fine, and added that it did not matter at all if Jung did not understand her dreams. Jung continued the treatment.

3. He made it clear that in his relations with his patients he would from time to time express strong emotions openly, and that he did so because he thought they were needed by the patient (Jung 1937, p. 139).

In his writing Jung hardly mentioned countertransference, though he seemed to refer to it often in its current sense. In addition to his idea that the analyst absorbs the psychopathology of his patient, he thought of the analyst as just as much in analysis as the patient. If the patient was to change or transform himself, the analyst must be prepared to do so, too, and to have previously experienced the essential nature of this process in his own analysis.

Analytical psychologists, influenced by Jung's dialectical "method," have noted some of its inherent dangers. The open interactional approach, it is said, can lead to intrusiveness by the analyst. To them it seems weak in just the area in which classical psychoanalysis seems strongest: the development, analysis, and resolution of the transference neurosis. It is one thing for Jung to be "unsystematic by intention," but his open systems attitude is very difficult to apply satisfactorily. Furthermore, when divorced, as it often has been, from his statements on the necessity of method, it leads to undisciplined responses by analysts with insufficient knowledge and experience, especially with respect to the transference neurosis and countertransference.

It has further been argued that to develop a generalized description of how analysts behave need not mean that anything is necessarily imposed on the patient. The individual nature of the analytic situation can be preserved by attention to what a patient says; understanding by the analyst of the patient's participation can be facilitated by his own analysis. The concept of countertransference is useful in this regard since it relates to the apparent subjectiveness in Jung's ideas and helps in distinguishing between their valid and invalid aspects (Fordham 1957). Countertransference theory has been developed by classical psychoanalysts with assumptions about the analytic situation different from those proposed by Jung. The earliest classical view was that an analyst can develop illusions about the patient based on residues of the analyst's infantile neurosis or on disturbances in the analyst's personal life having no relevance to the patient. These data are to be treated by the analyst just as he might treat his patient's transference. That is, they must be analyzed and mastered intrapsychically. The difficulty with this viewpoint for analytical psychologists arises from the theoretical formulation about the data. To classical psychoanalysts, it is all related to the notion that transference and countertransference originate in the unconsciouses of separate persons with firm boundaries, that is, not as open systems interacting with each other.

Though it is convenient to think of transference and countertransference illusions emanating by projections or displacements from essentially closed systems, to Jungians there can be, at the same time, unconscious interactions. The contrast between the open and closed systems models, each of which has its relevance, does not necessarily mean they are antithetical. The differences can be related to stages in analysis or even to the requirements of different patients.

Analytical psychologists have worked extensively with borderline cases, as well as with a fair number of psychotics. Also, one of Jung's special contributions was his encouraging the treatment of persons in the second half of life. With older patients he engaged in a form of therapy which included considerable personal interaction and more or less frank education (Fordham 1978, Henderson 1975).

With the severe as well as with the less disturbed, the analyst's affective reactions to the patient may contain some validity. Elsewhere (Fordham 1957) I have suggested that as a result of some patients' effects on their analysts, the latter tended to introject their patients' unconscious fantasies or archaic objects. Consequently I surmised that the analyst is in a position to further study his patients within himself. This impact of patients on analysts I originally labeled *syntonic countertransference* (Fordham 1957). Unlike countertransference illusions, which should be mastered and resolved by the analyst, syntonic countertransference provides constructive information about patients. The concept of the syntonic countertransference was derived from Jung's observation that an analyst can introject his patient's psychopathology and the idea that this has therapeutic potential. Accordingly, an analyst might find himself behaving in ways out of line with what he knows of himself, but syntonic with what he knows of his patient. Among Jungians, Moody (1955) was the first to observe that this kind of response by an analyst might have a significant influence on the progress of analytic therapy. Plaut (1956) studied the influence a patient had upon him and showed that the analyst might, as he put it, "incarnate an archetypal image"; he then worked through that situation with the patient.

Later I came to think that something similar might be contained in countertransference illusions. This idea was developed in a paper by Kraemer (1958). He described the case of a depressed patient who was treated by a therapist who in turn came to him for analysis because the therapy was at an impasse. Kraemer's therapist patient had developed a countertransference love for her patient, whom she actually inhibited from doing the analytic work because she had dreamed about him in a positive light. She insisted on expressing her positive feelings to the patient despite his strong objections. Such behavior obviously needed analysis and the therapist knew it. Yet it soon was realized that some depressed patients tend to evoke loving feelings in their analysts, and it was conceivable that the therapist's feelings could have been used to advance the patient's treatment had the analyst's compulsion not stood in the way.

These two forms of countertransference are rooted in projective and/or introjective processes, although other defense systems also enter into their formation. For example, the analyst may identify with the content of his introjection and then inadvertently play out a role for his patient, which is actually a powerful way of perpetuating his patient's neurosis. Or the analyst will crudely or subtly force his patient to comply with his projection. These are deviations from the therapeutic process but are destructive only when they become inflexible, remain unconscious, and are not used as sources of information on which to build interpretations or interventions.

The question remains as to how countertransference data can be utilized, since "technique" has been criticized by analytical psychologists as a disguised defense which wards off the patient's natural effort at establishing a relationship with the analyst. Whether valid or not (I believe it is not), this criticism is tantamount to asserting that technique itself constitutes an impersonal and sustained countertransference. Jung himself never went so far (Fordham 1969). His criticisms of technique rested mainly on the need to preserve a patient's individuality. This must never be glossed over by those methods of interpretation that depend upon the analyst's authority. Jung rejected the assumption of irrational authority by analysts, asserting that the analyst should consider himself just as much in analysis as his patient. As an expression of this egalitarian attitude, he and the patient would sit in chairs facing each other. Of course, a person comes to another for help on the assumption that the other person has the expertise needed to be helpful. This inevitably gives the analyst authority, which is demonstrated by his capacity to understand the patient and provide conditions under which the patient can resolve or modify his conflicts. Thus authority in itself is inevitable, but it must be rationally based.

In this context a countertransference illusion may have one useful characteristic: it demonstrates the fallibility of the analyst. Though optimally the illusion does not last for long, it does seem to place the analyst on the same level as the patient. In addition it reminds the analyst of his tendencies to become irrationally involved. When countertransference does interfere with the analytic attitude and with technique, the analyst must struggle to find some resolution. These occurrences can be quite subtle. Minor manifestations of countertransference illusions may seem unimportant. Some may derive from the analyst's life outside the analysis, so that he will inevitably go through periods of stress which in turn influence his work. Overtly he may proceed consistently, but with an underlying mood change his participation will be colored. Sometimes this goes unnoticed. With others the effect is repressed. And with others it may be observed and reflected upon without being communicated.

It will, however, influence the course of patients' associations. I do not call this countertransference proper, in the sense that it is a reaction to a patient. However, if a patient consistently induces a specific mood in the analyst, then it is countertransference and must be understood, interpreted, and brought into consciousness. I mention this because they are human attributes. They are to be expected. Otherwise they can be the springboard for serious and pathological countertransference reactions.

Another criticism of technique centers around the tendency for it to become divorced from an analyst's affects, especially his love and hate (and their derivatives) for his patient. If an analyst believes that being loving, tolerant, kind, understanding, and long-suffering is enough for the relationship, he is mistaken. Yet this attitude can be supported by arguing that the patient's transference behavior is only to be expected because of his developmental history. Having understood the genesis of the transference, the analyst interprets and then waits for the working-through process to complete itself. Unfortunately, all this can conceal contempt for the patient. If, however, the patient is not cooperative, it may result in the analyst reinforcing the patient's detachment by increasingly splitting so that the patient becomes isolated and frustrated — in reality. This is liable to occur usually with the more severe character disorders, the narcissistic neuroses, and the borderline cases. These patients will attack the analytic frame as a whole (Fordham 1978) and try, in a delusional way, to engage in a "human" relationship. Since the analytic frame is threatened, the analyst may decide that the patient has developed a negative therapeutic reaction and conclude, erroneously, that the patient is untreatable. Then he either terminates the patient's treatment or clings to technical clichés long after they have proven fruitless. Such consequences do not, however, invalidate the need for a well-defined analytic method. They do suggest that descriptions of such a method are incomplete because they have yet to pay sufficient attention to the affective states that analysts go through during its use.

At one time the *syntonic countertransference* was seen as providing a clue to the patient in that it defined a condition from which an analyst could gain information about the patient without the patient's awareness, giving greater access to the patient's affective state. It was soon learned, however, that in order to accomplish this the introjection had to be reprojected, for only then could it be perceived as part of the patient. A *countertransference illusion* led to the converse conclusion. Before any positive content could be defined, the projection had to be withdrawn and assimilated. Thus, the concepts of projection and introjection came to be viewed in a different perspective. Could it not be then that in any analysis there is a sequence of projections, introjections, and identifications that provide affective information complementing the conscious use of the analyst's skills (Fordham 1969)?

Take the interview itself. When a patient comes into the room how does an analyst behave? Does he immediately know the state of his patient? I think not. He tends to wait till the patient tells him what is in his mind. But this does not answer the question What is the analyst's state of mind in the interim? While it will vary from patient to patient, it has occurred to me that a helpful attitude for the analyst is to empty his mind of what he has learned about the patient on other occasions. What happens if the analyst does this? The patient is approached by the analyst on each occasion as if they had never met before. Having emptied his mind, the analyst waits to see what happens. He lets his observations, thoughts, and fantasies develop in relation to his patient till they link up with material from past sessions which he recalls spontaneously and without effort, as well as with his own constructions, interpretations, etc.

CLINICAL EXAMPLE

A patient, over sixty years old, gets up from her chair when I come into the waiting room. She looks bright, with eyes sparkling like a little girl's. I feel annoyed at something hungry about her and think that she wants to be met with a hug and a kiss. It seems inappropriate and I don't want to do it. She lies down on the couch and says nothing. I feel a growing frustration and become aware that it is I who am hungry. She is not going to feed me with associations and I reach for my pipe. Then she starts talking and I put my pipe down. I am able to listen comfortably as the interview proceeds.

These incidents and reflections would not have become conscious had I not emptied my mind. This patient had been in analysis for some time and I actually knew quite well what this was about. I could have documented each of her actions. She was a somewhat narcissistic personality and easily felt angry if her virtues were not appreciated. I knew enough about her childhood to know why she had regressed when she came to her sessions and could have interpreted it without difficulty. But if I had done that none of the affective content of the meeting would have been felt and my underlying irritation would have been missed. Also, my projective identification, and the way it was withdrawn to discover my own hunger, would have been lost sight of. Finally, I might very well not have noted that she started to talk out of competition with my pipe. My technique had aims in addition to the ones considered here. These were (a) to individualize the meeting with my patient, and (b) to proceed in a sequence from unconsciousness to consciousness.

The details would have come through directly, I believe, in the timing of my interventions and small indications such as movements or tones of voice. I might even have made an interpretive reconstruction later on when an occasion arose, and done so tactlessly. In short, instead of resolving my own state of mind I would have developed a concealed countertransference.

THE ANALYST'S ERRORS

Many errors by an analyst are, with good reason, laid to countertransference. But in order to make judgments about errors it is necessary to know when an intervention is correct and when it is not. Indeed, to work with any degree of refinement on counter-transference requires some criteria for judgment.

Some criteria are derived from the patient's response and these are important (Wisdom 1967). But those stemming from the analyst are more relevant to the thesis of this paper. How is the analyst certain than an intervention is relevant and needs to be made? He listens and arrives at a hypothesis of the unconscious content of his patient's communications — the projective and introjective identifi-cations playing an essential part in stimulating it. Though the idea is tentative at this stage, it stimulates interest in what is going on. As the analyst continues to listen his idea may have to be discarded as faulty. If it is confirmed he reaches the conviction that it is relevant. Then he may communicate it to the patient. When the analyst has done so he listens again to what use, if any, the patient makes of this contribution. A useful interpretation will refer to what is uncon-scious in the patient. In that sense it may be relevant but incomplete. Therefore, it will not be accepted immediately. Indeed, it may be energetically rejected and only afterwards stimulate reflection or change in the patient's associations. Interventions are best thought of as a part of a dialectical interchange.

Flagrant errors of course indicate the presence of countertransference. But its presence is also suggested when the dialectical process is interfered with, especially (1) when the analyst experiences difficulty in listening dispassionately to his patient's response to an intervention so that he cannot estimate whether it is being digested, accepted, or rejected; (2) when he becomes aware that he is failing to pick up indications his patient may give that the intervention has been appropriate or not; and (3) when he misses what is happening (or discovers it too late) when the patient begins to guide him to a better formulation.

DEVIATIONS FROM THE ANALYTIC ATTITUDE

There are a good many instances in the literature where analysts have expressed their affects forcefully and I have discussed some of these elsewhere (Fordham 1978). They are all nonanalytic and, as responses to the patient's transference, may be classified as countertransference. They are usually aggressive and seem to be common with patients who are borderline, have psychotic traits, or are frankly psychotic. Often they take place when the patient threatens the analyst's posture and self-definition, either by consistently acting out or by frustrating the analytic process.

Some of these responses seem to be related to establishing the frame of analysis. Jung (1935) gave a dramatic example of an obsessional woman who had the habit of slapping her doctors in the face. He relates an instance when she threatened to hit him: " 'Very well, you are a lady. You hit first — ladies first! But then I hit back!' And I meant it. She fell back deflated before my eyes. 'No one has ever said that to me before!' she protested. From that moment on therapy began to succeed." An example given by Giovacchini (1977) illustrates this as well. His psychotic patient's delusions at first involved Giovacchini in protective actions, but to no effect, and his patient eventually ended up in jail. In the course of the subsequent treatment Giovacchini told his patient that he would absolutely "not get involved again and if he found himself in trouble, he would have to depend only on his own resources."

Little (1957) illustrated what she called "R" — the analyst's total response — in the case of a patient who told repetitive stories about children. Little told her that she was "as tired of them as [the patient] was of the children's behavior. The patient 'did not know' and went on into another story." Little then said, "I meant that; I'm not listening to any more of them."

No doubt many of these are states of the analyst which will not be repeated. Giovacchini (1977) infers as much when he describes another patient who made excessive demands upon him. He became furious and told him so. "I felt that I had over-reached.... But I did not become further distressed and the patient has not made any further demands of me. Undoubtedly he will, but I now believe I can reinforce the condition I set up without becoming upset" (p. 438).

PATIENT A.

Mrs. A. developed a delusional transference and did everything she could to break down my analytic posture. This was clearly expressed by her question, "Can't you stop being an analyst and become a person?" It was followed with great ingenuity and vigor. My reaction tended to be passive, to suspend my analytic efforts, and sometimes to retreat masochistically. Occasionally I found myself projectively identifying with my patient: the analytic method had no validity at all and I started looking at myself through her eyes.

In the face of her apparently negative therapeutic reaction, I reflected guiltily about what had gone wrong. Had my diagnosis been at fault, and should I never have taken on this patient? Had my technique been inadequate? Had my interpretations been wrong too often or badly directed? Had I failed to analyze defenses adequately? Had interpretations been too numerous so as to drive the patient to hopelessness and despair? And so on (Fordham 1974). During this period of self-scrutiny I felt very much more like a patient than an analyst. And the patient reinforced this by making attempts to analyze my state. Occasionally she was right. She believed, for instance, that my infantile traumata had emerged, but she consoled herself with the thought that I would eventually mature into a state in which I would be able to be of help to her. Despite what appeared to be a predominantly sterile, even destructive process, she showed no signs of wanting to terminate. The lengthy process that my patient and I went through did produce a satisfactory therapeutic result although I had to initiate its ending. The analysis was not as complete as I might have wished. During it I learned to sustain my analytic stance much better with such patients so that when comparable situations arise I am no longer inclined to react the same way.

PATIENT B.

Mrs. B. was concerned about her tendency to see penises everywhere. She apparently suffered from mild hallucinations, not to be thought of as clinically psychotic but making her concerned lest she be on the edge of psychosis. In this context she told me a dream in which there were long objects on a couch. She was uncertain as to whether they were feces or penises. The dream had occurred many years ago and she told me that she had taken it to her previous analyst and together they had agreed to call them "fecal penises." Some days later I had occasion to remind her of this incident. She adamantly asserted that she had told me nothing of the kind, that I had "gone mad" and that the incident was a figment of my "fertile mind." In various contexts similar situations had earlier arisen, when the patient, in addition to her denial, asserted that I had confused her with somebody else. On this occasion she inferred that I was in need of analysis, indicating that she would be ready and glad to undertake the necessary work. Like Mrs. A., she implied that only when that had been completed could her own analysis proceed.

On previous occasions I had bypassed this quandary, unable to find a way of resolving it. Here it presented itself again. This time I emphasized that there was a difference of opinion which, distressingly, did not seem possible to resolve, and I made no further attempt to do so. She made an attempt to object but the interview ground to a halt, giving me time for reflection. I did not give serious thought to the possibility that she was correct (as I had done at length with Mrs. A.). I was at a loss until I became convinced that an intervention was required. I told her that I thought the idea or feeling of a penis as fecal was relevant and I would tell her why I thought so, emphasizing the word "I" to indicate that it was offered to her as my idea and not necessarily one which she need agree to as relevant to her. It might, in short, be treated as part of my bit of "madness." There had been a number of times in her life from childhood onwards when she had been frightened or repelled by penises as disgusting or otherwise undesirable objects, and I summarized them at some length. After considerable reflection and further objection she came to agree that what I said felt true, but that her intellect kept producing arguments against such a mad proposition.

Which elements of this interchange are relevant to this discussion? There was the period after my patient's assertion that I was having an illusion about her which must have felt more to her like one of her "hallucinations." During this time I did not know what to do and was forced back on myself as with the countertransference to Mrs. A. Here was food for thought, but it was indigestible. Introjective identifications were contained in this and hence some uncertainty about whether she was correct. Looking back, it is clear that I had also identified with my patient's attitude in a projective way, and this made it possible for me to respect and empathize with her contention and to temporarily identify with it. Though these affective processes tended to make for a feeling of confusion, I was still able to reflect. The conviction that I had to intervene actively was not accompanied by the knowledge of what I was going to say. Indeed, I was still under the influence of my countertransference when I started to speak. When I began to talk, however, I found it surprisingly easy to develop my theme in such a way, as it turned out, that my patient could understand its sense so that a shift in her transference took place. If, as on previous occasions, I had not been able to respond adequately, then there would be no doubt that I had developed a countertransference which had interfered with the progress of the analysis. But what of the rest? The affects roused by my patient are the consequence of her attack and they counter it. There was introjection, temporary confusion, and after that the intervention came out of me, reflectively, but also as a spontaneous interaction. I had a certain feeling of surprise and satisfaction. It would be possible to consider all this part of a syntonic countertransference and to conceptualize it in terms of my reprojecting the introjected content with the intervention. This might even account for the spontaneity of my communication. But is the term *countertransference* necessary? It was an interaction in which projection, introjection, and identifications took part. Between these two clinical experiences I conducted a good deal of self-analysis. This paid off in my personal and social life. Since this occurred in relation to a patient it also facilitated the therapy. There were also other contributing activities: discussion with colleagues, writing papers (Fordham 1969, 1974), and reading the literature, thereby discovering that my experience was not unique. I ended up developing a new hypothesis about defenses of the self (Fordham 1974). I had apparently embarked, more or less under compulsion, on a research project. Such a project was to a large extent personal at first, and required significant changes in my affective states — a "transformation," as Jung would have put it. This seems to me an essential ingredient in all analytic research, and here countertransference entered into it. Once completed, I needed to discover whether it was a contribution to the body of psychoanalytic knowledge. Writing this paper is an attempt to find out.

Additional consequences of this research were that I reevaluated some patients' need for statements about the analyst's own affective states and also gained further insight into the notion of an analyst as a child.

A CONCLUDING STATEMENT

Looking back on the development of the concept of countertransference, one can see it as having gone through various phases. First it covered a set of undesirable data, arising from the analyst, to be controlled, analyzed, and resolved by him. It fitted in with the aspiration of analysts who hoped to achieve objectivity so as to know correctly what went on intrapsychically in their patients. Their own psychological states were to be thought of as essentially irrelevant. Not much attention was paid to Freud's view (1910) that the analyst uses his unconscious as an organ of perception, nor to Jung's emphasis on the importance of the analyst's personal influence. Next the term was expanded to cover the analyst's intrapsychic states. This had an important consequence: the analyst's personality, not only his psychopathology, could now be brought under review. In light of this approach, the analytic situation came under close scrutiny and thus led to a far more detailed description of what goes on between analyst and patient. There is the holding capacity of the analyst, as well as his capacity for projective and introjective identification with his patient. This is necessary for arriving at sufficient comprehension as to the processes going on in the patient, and between the analyst and his patient. A further study of how to validate the analyst's interventions led to understanding that a patient might work out mistakes, guide the analyst to a better formulation, and facilitate the analysis of the analyst.

It seems to me that these issues can all be brought under one heading, the analytic dialectic, and that they lead toward a view of the analytic situation as two open systems interacting. In the course of the development of the theory, the terms *transference* and *countertransference* have been expanded and generalized. Thus an analyst's appropriate feelings and affects about his patient have been included so that the original concepts to which the terms refer are in danger of losing meaning. Now the whole analytic situation is to be thought of as a mass of illusions, delusions, displacements, projections, and introjections. I would suggest that, apart from an analyst's appropriate reactions, his transitory projections and displacements cease to be called countertransferences since they represent the analyst acting on and reacting to his patient. These actions may contain false perceptions, fantasies, illusions, or even delusions, but these can be contained by the analyst till they are resolved; they can then be utilized to extract appropriate interventions. It is when the interacting systems become obstructed that a special label is needed and, to my mind, it is then that the term *countertransference* is appropriate.

I have suggested that rigidity be used as a criterion indicating countertransference, but I must qualify this. There are areas in analysis where there is rational rigidity: for example, the frame of analysis into which projections are made needs to remain stable till termination. In addition, there is a need for the analyst's stable style.

I believe the theory of countertransference has performed its main function. It has had the most desirable effect of taking analysts out of their ivory towers, making it possible for them to compare notes on what they really do during analytic psychotherapy. The pathological reactions of the analyst, comparable to the patient's transference, may be called *countertransference*. I would call the rest part of the interactional dialectic.

References

Fordham, M. (1957). Notes on the transference. In *Technique in Jungian Analysis*. London: Heinemann, 1974.

———(1969). Technique and countertransference. In *Technique in*

Jungian Analysis. London: Heinemann, 1974.

————(1974). Defences of the self. *Journal of Analytical Psychology* 19:192-199.

————(1978). *Jungian Psychotherapy.* Chichester: John Wiley.

Freud, S. (1910). The future prospects of psycho-analytic therapy. *Standard Edition* 11:139-152.

Giovacchini, P. L. (1977). The impact of delusion and the delusion of impact. *Contemporary Psychoanalysis* 13:429-441. See Chapter 11.

Henderson, J. (1975). C. G. Jung: a reminiscent picture of his method. *Journal of Analytical Psychology* 20:114-121.

Jung, C. G. (1946). The psychology of the transference. In *Collected Works of C. G. Jung.* Vol. 16. Princeton: Princeton University Press.

————(1963). *Memories, Dreams, Reflections.* New York: Pantheon, 1968.

————(1951). Fundamental questions of psychotherapy. In *Collected Works of C. G. Jung.* Vol. 16. Princeton: Princeton University Press.

————(1968). The Tavistock lectures. In *Collected Works of C. G. Jung.* Vol. 18. Princeton: Princeton University Press.

Kraemer, W. (1958). The dangers of unrecognised countertransference. In *Technique in Jungian Analysis.* London: Heinemann, 1974.

Langs, R. (1976). *The Therapeutic Interaction.* 2 vols. New York: Jason Aronson.

Lambert, K. (1976). Resistance and counter-resistance. *Journal of Analytical Psychology* 21:154-192.

Little, M. (1957). "R" — the analyst's total response to his patient's needs. *International Journal of Psycho-Analysis* 38:240-258.

Moody, R. L. (1955). On the function of countertransference. *Journal of Analytical Psychology* 1:49-58.

Plaut, A. (1956). The transference in analytical psychology. In *Technique in Jungian Analysis.* London: Heinemann, 1974.

Wisdom, J. O. (1967). Testing an interpretation within a session. *International Journal of Psycho-Analysis.* 48:44-52.

Part II

THE THERAPIST'S USE
OF COUNTERTRANSFERENCE

Chapter 10

THE THERAPEUTIC FUNCTION OF HATE IN THE COUNTERTRANSFERENCE

LAWRENCE EPSTEIN Ph.D.

Psychoanalysts would generally agree that the optimal treatment setting is one which would enable the patient to experience the full range of those intrapersonal conflicts which have stunted his development as a person and have impaired his capacity for coping with the problems of living.[1] There would also be general agreement that the analyst may be in the best position to help the patient resolve these conflicts when they are played out in the interpersonal field of the patient-analyst relationship so that the analyst becomes for the patient the primary object of his fantasies and the primary target of his feelings of love and hate. In short, concerning the therapeutic and maturational value of generating and resolving the patient's transferences and resistances toward the analyst, there is little argument.

Opinion varies, however, concerning the therapeutic and maturational value *for the patient* of those emotional reactions he typically induces in the analyst.

1. I wish to thank Drs. Jonas Cohler, Amnon Issacharoff, and Arthur H. Feiner, who critically evaluated this paper during its development.

EMOTIONAL COMMUNICATIONS AS A THERAPEUTIC TOOL

Positive feelings from the analyst are generally recommended as beneficial to the patient, sometimes with something like moral force: "compassion, interest, warmth, all within limits, are vital for the working alliance." (Greenson 1967, p. 379); "a certain amount of compassion, friendliness, warmth, and respect for the patient's rights is indispensable" (p. 391).

In such statements, it is strongly implied, but not explicitly stated, that it is therapeutically beneficial for the patient to experience positive feelings from the analyst. The subject of emotional communication as a therapeutic tool has always been an uncomfortable one for classical psychoanalysts, implying a departure from an objective analytic stance, acting out, dilution of the transference, etc. The communication of negative feelings is generally felt to be incorrect or is, at best, mistrusted. However, the following statement by Greenson seems contradictory: "Bearing the hostile and humiliating outbursts of his patients without retaliation is as important as remaining unperturbed by their sexual provocations. This does not mean that the analyst should not have feelings and fantasies in response to the patient, but their quantity ought to be within limits that enables him to control his responses *so that what comes into the open is only as much as the patient requires.*" (italics mine, Greenson, p. 394). It is implied here that the patient may have some therapeutic need for some of the negative feelings he induces in his analyst.

I intend to explore the vicissitudes of those transactions involving the induction of hate and anger in the analyst by those patients who these days would be diagnosed as borderline character disorders. Specifically I shall examine the following topics:

1. The problem analysts have with the hate that such patients may induce
2. The functional value that a hateful interpersonal matrix may have for such patients
3. The special problems which a hate-inducing patient encounters vis-a-vis a therapist
4. The damaging effects that may result from meeting the patient's hate with benign understanding or forbearance

5. The maturational gains that may result should the patient receive from the analyst communications of neutralized objective hate

There has been, in the thinking of some analysts, a marked shift away from an orientation to countertransference as "bad" and a hindrance, toward viewing the totality of the analyst's emotional reactions as having *value* for understanding the patient in the ongoing process of the treatment and for formulating interventions. Winnicott (1949), Racker (1968), Spotnitz (1976), Searles (1958), Levenson (1972), Kernberg (1975), Issacharoff (chapter 3, this volume), Wolstein (1976) and Feiner (chapter 2, this volume) all favor this view.

Communications of Induced Hatred

Winnicott, Spotnitz, and Searles have specifically indicated that the patient may have a therapeutic *need* for the analyst's hateful feelings when appropriate. In his paper, "Hate in the Countertransference" (1949), Winnicott was rather definite about this. After defining the subjective and idiosyncratic components of the countertransference, Winnicott writes: "From these . . . I distinguish the truly objective countertransference, or if this is difficult, the analyst's love and hate in reaction to the actual personality and behavior of the patient, based on objective observation." Following this, he writes:

I suggest that if an analyst is to analyse psychotics or antisocials he must be able to be so thoroughly aware of the countertransference that he can sort out and study his *objective* reactions to the patient. These will include hate. Countertransference phenomena will at times be the important things in the analysis.

Then:

If the analyst is going to have crude feelings imputed to him he is best forwarned and so forearmed, for he must tolerate being placed in that position. Above all he must not deny hate that really exists in himself. Hate *that is justified* in the present setting has to be sorted out and kept in storage and available for eventual interpretation.

And:

A main task of the analyst of any patient is to maintain objectivity in regard to all that the patient brings, and a special case of this is the analyst's need to be able to hate the patient objectively.

Later on he writes:

I want to add that in certain stages of certain analyses the analyst's hate is actually sought by the patient, and what is then needed is hate that is objective. If the patient seeks objective or justified hate he must be able to reach it, else he cannot feel he can reach objective love.

It is perhaps relevant here to cite the case of the child of the broken home, or the child without parents. Such a child spends his time unconsciously looking for his parents. It is notoriously inadequate to take such a child into one's home and to love him. What happens is that after a while a child so adopted gains hope, and then he starts to test out the environment he has found, and to seek proof of his guardians ability to hate objectively. It seems that he can believe in being loved only after reaching being hated.

Then he describes his treatment of a nine-year-old evacuated child during World War II whom he and his wife took into their home:

The important thing for the purpose of this paper is the way in which the evolution of the boy's personality engendered hate in me, and what I did about it.

Did I hit him? The answer is no, I never hit. But I should have had to have done so if I had not known all about my hate and if I had not let him know about it too. At crises, I would take him by bodily strength, without anger or blame, and put him outside the front door, whatever the weather or the time of day or night. There was a special bell he could ring, and he knew that if he rang it he would be readmitted and no word said about the past. He used this bell as soon as he had recovered from his maniacal attack.

The important thing is that each time, just as I put him outside the door, I told him something; I said that what had happened had made me hate him. This was easy because it was so true.

I think these words were important from the point of view of his progress, but they were mainly important in enabling me to tolerate the situation without letting out, without losing my temper and without every now and again murdering him.

Spotnitz (1976) has also been explicit on the issue of the patient's need for the analyst's countertransference reactions.

It is in the interest of patients that the analyst remain free of emotional involvement with them. ... But what if the patient has a maturational need to experience feelings from his partner in the relationship? His need challenges the attitude of emotional detachment. And observation of the therapeutic effectiveness of certain countertransference reactions strengthened the challenge [p. 48].

Spotnitz recommends that emotional confrontation be "carefully timed and graduated to prevent uncontrollable reactions."

He warns: "countertransference cannot be utilized with complete confidence unless it has been purged of its subjective element. These "foreign" influences have to be "analyzed out" of the objective countertransference before they contaminate the transference reaction."

Searles (1958) cites the example of a male patient who developed hallucinations of "contemptuous, taunting voices" which he would talk back to "in a furious, angry way." Searles came to view these hallucinations as a reflection of his own dissociated rage toward this particularly infuriating patient. He wrote that this dissociated rage was "presumably fostered by my labouring under so much discouragement and, still, threat of physical injury for so long. ... More than once I had felt lucky to get out of our sessions alive, but I had not realized that he could be looked upon as being fortunate in the same sense."

One way of describing what had happened is to say that my increasing recognition, and acceptance, of my own feelings of contempt and rage toward him served to arm me sufficiently for me to be able to step in and interact with him at the furiously vitriolic level at which he had often 'interacted' with his hallucinations, previously, while I had sat by, paralyzed with anxiety at the extraordinarily intense rage and contempt which his behavior was arousing in me at an unconscious level, I had come to realize that it actually relieved me greatly when he shunted the most intense portion of his rage, for example, off to one side, towards an hallucinatory figure, and disclaimed that he was having any such feeling toward me. But there came a certain memorable session in which I felt sufficiently furious about what was going on, and sure enough of my ability to meet both my own rage and his, to be able to step into the shoes, as it were, of the hallucinatory figure or figures at whom he was directing his greatest fury, and from that day on it was as though there were less and less 'need' for these hallucinatory figures in our interaction with one another. What I did, specifically, in that crucial session was to insist, with unyielding fury — despite his enraged threats to assault me — that these vitriolic tirades, such as he had just now been ventilating while denying repeatedly that they were meant for me, were really directed towards me [p. 204].

Problems Analysts Have With Their Own Hate

Despite Winnicott's widespread influence among analysts of different schools, the issue of the analyst's hate for his patient has received scant attention in the literature. Bird (1972) refers to the problem analysts have with the raw fact of human destructiveness:

Even our analytic language, which leans heavily on euphemisms, seems designed to ignore the reality of destruction. We tend to use words like "negative," "aggressive," and "hostile" in describing patient behavior that may have caused actual damage. Or we may speak of angry feelings, murder fantasies, castration wishes, and death wishes in respect to a patient's determined attempt to cause harm. To me, this language always seems at least once removed from what we are actually dealing with [p. 289].

Bird then raises the question: Why do analysts need to suppress the patient's destructive tendencies when they begin to emerge in the analysis? "Is it because we all sense the limited extent to which actual destructive tendencies can enter into the transference neurosis, and thus the limited extent of their analyzability?" (p. 289).

To my mind, this does not answer the question, raising instead, another question, namely, *why* do the destructive tendencies of the patient not enter into the transference neurosis? I would suggest that when such is the case the major reason is that the patient's hate and destructiveness as they emerge in the analysis, beget the analyst's hate and destructiveness and that for most analysts, it is their own hatred more than the patient's that is abhorrent.

For one thing, historically, analysts have shared a self idealization which includes such values as a high degree of rationality, objectivity, and a highly developed capacity for controlling impulses and detaching themselves from personal feelings and needs, in the service of the analytic task. In other words, such a self idealization requires them to be, vis-a-vis their immature and emotionally disturbed patients, something like a paragon of mature functioning.

Racker (1953 [1957]) believes such self idealizations to be narcissistically invested infantile ideals that are passed on, unanalyzed, from one generation of analysts to the next:

These deficiencies in the training analysis are in turn partly due to countertransference problems insufficiently resolved in the training analyst. ... Thus we are in a vicious circle: But we can see where the breach must be made. We must begin by revision of our feelings about our own countertransference and try to overcome our infantile ideals more thoroughly, accepting more fully the fact that we are still children and neurotics even when we are adults and analysts. Only in this way — by better overcoming our rejection of our countertransference — can we achieve the same results in candidates [p. 130].

Racker wrote this in 1953. Currently analysts may be considerably less narcissistically invested. We are generally much more accepting of aspects of our countertransference as valuable components in the therapy. I think, however, that our tolerance toward our own countertransference may desert us when that countertransference is dominated by intense hatred.

Leaving aside the issue of our narcissistically invested self-idealization, we may subscribe to certain assumptions concerning the nutriments a patient may require from the therapist. At the very least we believe that the patient requires our respect. We may also believe that the patient requires "warm concern," "unconditional positive regard," "compassion" etc. It is difficult to reconcile our hatred for another person with any intention to respect him, no less offer him nutriments.

So, to my mind, if an analyst unwittingly suppresses the actual destructive tendencies of his patient it is not, as Bird suggests, because he senses the limited extent to which they can enter the transference neurosis, but rather, because of their power to destroy the analyst's capacities of sustaining, or recovering, his therapeutic intention toward the patient. And hatred induced in us by the patient may cause us to become our own object of hatred and contempt, and for this we might have to hate the patient all the more.[2]

CLINICAL EXAMPLE: A HATE-INDUCING PATIENT

There are patients, however, whose destructive tendencies are blatant and immediately beget reciprocal emotions in the analyst. This would be the kind of patient described by Winnicott and Searles in the references cited earlier. I would like to present my own experience with such a patient, whom I treated many years ago. The therapy, though successful in many respects, was conducted largely in ignorance of any substantial rationale for treating a patient of such character structure. In fact, the steady and significant improvement in the patient's functioning did not make much sense to me at the time since, from the beginning to the end of the treatment, she denigrated me, and her persisting estimation of the therapy was that it was totally useless.

She had been referred to me by a colleague, who, after two sessions, found her impossibly obnoxious and decided he couldn't work with her. Thinking of me as being generally a more tolerant person than himself, he felt I might be better able to work with her, or at least, to abide her. I accepted the referral, thinking that anyone who wanted therapy couldn't be all that bad.

2. The intensification of our own destructiveness may issue not only from the assaults on our analytic self-idealization, but also from the awakening of a dormant cynicism (despair). (See Feiner, chapter 2.)

In fact, when I first met the patient, whom I shall call Marcia, I couldn't imagine what my colleague found to be so terrible about her. I was expecting some sort of demon. She seemed quite normal. She was conventionally dressed, in the style of an upper middle class sixteen-year-old. Actually, she was twenty-two. Her figure was good, and her face was moderately attractive. Her hair was drawn back in a bun, giving her a somewhat prim and shy look.

Initially, she gave brief answers to my questions. She lived with her father in a private house in the suburbs, he was a haberdasher. He treated her very badly. He was critical and mean, and they didn't get along. Her mother died of cancer when she was eight years old. She had an older brother in law school. They didn't get along. She dropped out of an art college after two years, and in the two years since that time, she did little more than stay at home, watching a great deal of television. She had no friends. She got along badly with almost everyone. She was anxious and generally unhappy about her life.

She was taken by surprise when Dr. P told her that he didn't want to work with her. She would have preferred to stay with him. She regretted having to come to me. She wanted to come to therapy twice a week. Her father would pay for treatment.

Soon I ran out of fact-oriented questions. She volunteered nothing. She sat stony-faced, never making eye contact with me. As the session wore on, I felt her growing disdain, and the tension between us increased. She would answer no questions as to what she wanted from therapy. Nor would she tell me anything of what she was thinking or feeling. I felt totally impotent. although she seemingly had agreed to be in therapy with me, I felt somewhat tentative about offering her a schedule of appointments. I more than half expected her to sneer at me for being foolish enough to presume that she would return for more sessions. She accepted the appointment schedule and left abruptly when I told her that the time was up.

In subsequent sessions, I attempted to deal with the impotence and frustration Marcia induced in me in the following way. I would remind myself that she was a woefully unhappy person, arrested in her emotional and psychosexual development, damaged and deprived by the early loss of her mother and by having been left with a cruel and insensitive father who preferred her high achieving brother. I would remind myself that her schizoid existence was barren of nutriments, and that her arrogant, queenly, rejecting behavior toward me was a narcissistic defense against feeling her own very poor self-esteem.

In other words, I attempted to counter the actual feelings induced by this patient by creating a more sympathetic image of her in my mind. This enabled me to affect a posture of forebearance vis-a-vis her withholding, rejecting and contemptuous treatment of me.

Her behavior toward me was mostly non-verbal, but she would, from time to time, tell me with considerable disgust that I didn't understand her at all. She reported that she was getting worse. She was becoming more withdrawn, and watched television day and night. Her relationship with her father was deteriorating even further. He hardly spoke to her except to say something nasty and critical. He said he thought the therapy was a complete waste of money, and that she was a hopeless case. Her brother agreed.

This was the situation after the first six months of therapy. At that time, I consulted one of my analytic supervisors, who responded to my presentation with a single sentence: "Why don't you use the voice of her father, but not his intention?" This statement was sufficient to dissipate the image I had created of my patient as a vulnerable, love-starved child. I now saw her as a nasty, withholding, contemptuous, uncooperative bitch, and I reacted to her accordingly. Having done with forebearance, what I now felt as anger and hate, I expressed as irritation. I challenged her stony silences, asking her how in hell she expected me to make any progress in therapy if she refused to talk and provide me with material to respond to. When she exuded contempt, I identified it and testily asked her what it was all about. When she would maintain her silence over long intervals, I informed her, with annoyance, that I would be making no further effort to engage her, but that I would respond when she would resume talking.

With this change in my behavior, Marcia's progress was rapid. Within the next six months, she sought and found a job, the first in her life, and one in which she could use her graphic skills. She found her own apartment. She never reported any of this as if she *felt* she was making progress, or that these changes amounted to anything that she truly wanted for herself. For instance, she never said she liked her job or having her own apartment. In fact, she didn't like either. She apparently got along better with her father and her brother: They helped her move into her apartment, and she no longer reported much in the way of friction with them, but didn't acknowledge any change in her relationship with them.

Within a year, she began socializing with other people her own age, and she entered into what was to become a long-term, intimate relationship with a man. As her life became richer, she was less often silent and withholding. She had more to talk about and when she needed help with some problem she was having in one interpersonal relationship or another, she would, for the moment, seem to forget how useless I was and consult me. The affective tone of those consultative transactions was more or less neutral. It was as if she had decided to declare a truce which was, however, abruptly ended, sooner or later, as if by a malevolent transformation. I again became the wrong therapist for her, being an insensitive person, incapable of understanding her, and hardly worth talking to.

Over the course of the therapy the hate-free intervals lengthened, and the intensity of her denigration diminished. Yet, its reappearance would revive my doubts as to whether the therapy had anything to do with her progress. At the time of my work with her, it made little sense to me that a patient could progress with a therapist whom she hated so much and who often hated her back with at least equal force.

I always took her complaints about me quite seriously, and on several occasions, when she made a good-enough case for my being totally useless, I would ask her if she wanted a referral to a therapist she might like better, possibly a woman. She never took me up on this. One day, after about two and one-half years of therapy, she surprised me by suggesting, herself, that since she had never liked me and never expected to like me, perhaps she would be better off with another therapist, possibly an older, maternal type of woman. I knew of such a therapist, and referred Marcia to her.

DISCUSSION

I would like to consider the functional value that a hateful interpersonal matrix may have for a person with a poorly integrated ego. Hateful transactions can provide a poorly integrated ego with a means of restoring its equilibrium. The feeling of hate can provide an ongoing sense of ego-identity. A person like Marcia can feel herself most definitely vis-a-vis a world of clear-cut enemies. Counterattacks from others may not penetrate to have emotionally disturbing effects. They seem often to have a relaxing effect. Induced counterattacks may relieve guilt and gratify omnipotent needs (because of the power felt in being able to control the behavior of others). More importantly, they reinforce the boundaries of the self vis-à-vis the other by establishing appropriate, necessary distance. Thus, whenever the sense of self weakens and becomes diffused, it can be most easily recovered by provoking others to attack. It is likely that most of Marcia's provocations came at moments when her ego-identity was becoming diffused through the danger of intimate merging.

Should she in unguarded moments engage in positive interpersonal transactions, her ego-equilibrium would become impaired. A person whose essential self-image is hateful, bad, and worthless requires a reciprocal hateful view of the world. Positive interchanges are likely to lead toward confusion and feelings of inauthenticity. They may stimulate violent internal attacks from deeply entrenched unconscious parental introjects. Perhaps her hate was a means of not betraying an unconscious irrevocable vow to her dead mother never to love, or be loved by another. Or if betrayal was not the issue, perhaps it was the risk of loving and the unbearable pain of losing another love object. Hate might serve here to keep dormant a more profound and dreadful cynicism and despair.

Since hate typically begets hate, by being hateful and rejecting, such a person as Marcia generally exerts sufficient control over other people's reactions to restore a failing sense of ego-identity. She is confronted with special problems, however, when she becomes a patient of a therapist.

Although surface cynicism may cause her to reject conventional viewpoints and expectations, she knows what they are. The conventional expectations of a therapist might include all or some of the following: that he is a person interested in other people, and that he is caring, loving, decent, reliable, skillful at healing others; that he is mature, intelligent and never wittingly destructive to others. The patient, then, who is by her own definition and the definition of others a hateful, bad and inferior person, is faced with the hideous prospect of a long-term relationship with a person who is defined as, and might actually turn out to be, something like a paragon of moral excellence. This is an interpersonal situation which might seriously threaten her sense of ego-identity. The contrast between her badness and the therapist's goodness is too great, and her feelings of inferiority and envy may become unbearably intensified. The first thing she must do is to reverse this imbalance, making the therapist a worse person than herself.

Her ego achieves this by a two-step process of splitting and projection, that is, by dissociating and disowning what she hates in herself and depositing it in the therapist. Hence, according to my patient's view of the two of us, I became the inferior and more worthless person; being stupid, insensitive, cold and unfeeling, and totally useless.

The success of the therapy, and the further maturational development of the patient will depend almost entirely on what the therapist does with the bad feelings and hateful impulses which the patient's ego-splitting and projective processes induce in him.

A Typical Analytic Error

An imbalance most damaging to the patient is created when the therapist persists in behaving *as if he were all good* in the face of the patient's relentless efforts to blacken him. This may be the error therapists are most inclined to make vis-a-vis their most frustrating and destructive patients.[3]

In order to maintain our sense of integrity as therapists with a hateful, hate-inducing person like Marcia, we might tend to *make believe* that she is not as bad as we experience her to be. However hateful she is, we are committed to the theory that the patient needs us to be a so-called object of her transference neurosis and, therefore, the target of all her feelings. To protect her from our counter-hate, we fall back on the knowledge we may have of such a person's unhappy history, and understanding that such hateful behavior is somehow based on security needs, we attempt to imagine the deprived, damaged, and vulnerable child-self behind the defensive facade.

By such means, then, we change the apparent reality into a construction of reality, and we no longer believe our sense data

3. A. Issacharoff has suggested in a personal communication that a person like Marcia may have a special aversion to hypocrisy and therefore, may be highly sensitized to *any* hostility which is covered over by the benign accepting attitude which is required by the psychoanalyst's ego-ideal. Searles' hallucinating patient (1958) is a case in point. For such people the other person's love simply cannot be trusted until his hostility is out in the open.

which informs us that we are confronted with a hateful, destructive and entirely frustrating person.

We shall be all the more moved to change our perception of our hate-inducing patient from "bad" to "good" if we also believe that *all* patients have a maturational need for our love and *never* for our "objective hate," as Winnicott has written. If such should be the case, our hate is likely to have been repressed, rather than suppressed, and once unconscious, may breed virulent, murderous wishes. It is at such times that the patient may become psychologically damaged because of his unconscious susceptibility to the therapist's unconscious hate, as Searles (1965) has pointed out.[4]

Damaging Effects of Benign Forebearance on Certain Patients

I would like to consider more fully the damaging effects that may result from meeting the patient's hate with benign understanding or forebearance.

Marcia, because of her ego-splitting processes and massive projective identifications, would be classified these days as a borderline character disorder. Had she reached a higher level of intrapsychic integration at the time she entered treatment, a benign response to her hatred might have confounded her essentially hostile view of the world, evoking some tolerable guilt, followed by remorse and positive feelings toward the therapist. She might recognize him to be a person having essentially decent intentions toward her. We would then have the beginnings of an emotionally corrective experience.

Alexander (1946) cites the example from Victor Hugo's novel *Les Miserables* of the conversion of the ex-convict Jean Valjean, in his encounter with the kindly Bishop. When the Bishop responded lovingly and charitably to Jean Valjean after the latter had returned his hospitality by robbing him, Jean Valjean was moved to give up his criminal, callous attitude toward the world and to become a loving person, a man of honor and integrity. Although this is an essentially literary fabrication, depicting a highly idealized, romanticized conversion from evil to virtue, such a conversion might actually be possible for a person who had reached what Melanie

4. In another paper, "The Informational Value of the Supervisor's Emotional Experiences," Searles (1955) observes that the therapist is likely to induce in his supervisor the unconscious frustration and aggression which his patient has induced in him.

Klein has called the depressive position and who had developed what Winnicott calls "the capacity for concern" (1965) *before* having been turned cold and hateful by the world's cruelty. The ego of such a person would have had to reach a high enough level of integration to enable him to tolerate the feelings of guilt and remorse that would be evoked by the loving treatment of the person he had injured. Prior to his unjust imprisonment Jean Valjean was depicted as a decent man.

In Marcia's case, should she receive love or tolerance in return for her hate, she would have to see the giver as either a fraud or a fool, as an object deserving of her contempt. Her capacity for loving either herself or others was either poorly developed or very deeply repressed. Therefore, there would be an insufficiency of good self-feelings to offset the guilt feeling that would follow upon her recognition that she was injuring a person who might be well intentioned *and* worthwhile. In other words, *the more benign the treatment she receives in response to her destructive behavior, the worse she would have to feel about herself if she were to believe in the goodness of such treatment.* To the extent that she may suspect that the treatment might be somewhat good and the giver not all bad, she is in danger of becoming an object of her own hate. She would then have to annihilate any intimations of the other's goodness and to vilify and denigrate him all the more so that he remains in her view a worthless, unloving, stone-cold thing.

Yet nothing can be successfully warded off by processes of splitting and projection. The persistent efforts of the therapist to return love for the patient's hate sets up the following vicious cycle with escalating destructive effects: The patient is destructive; the therapist is kind and forebearing; the patient is in danger of recognizing the therapist as good and himself as bad; fearing devastation by guilt and self hatred, he hates the therapist all the more for provoking this dangerous situation. Increments of contempt for the therapist are gained from the enhancement of cherished images of a self having great powers of destruction, an enhancement generated by the perception of the therapist's goodness as weakness or phonyness.

The effect on the borderline patient, then, of the therapist responding to hate and contempt with benign "understanding" is to stress and weaken the patient's ego; feelings of badness and guilt intensify with each succeeding desperate effort to get rid of them by depositing them in the other person. Suicidal impulses gain in strength; paranoid anxieties mount; manic and schizoid defenses are called into play.

Something on the order of this ego weakening process was induced during the first phase of the therapy with Marcia when I was *forging* the kindness and patience which I thought was owed to the vulnerable and love-starved child I imagined her to be.

Such treatment is likely to be felt by the patient as rejecting. In fact, it is. The therapist, in order to like his patient more, and to feel less hateful toward him, denies his "badness," and makes the patient a "better" person, thereby turning him into an object of the therapist's fantasy.[5] In this way, the therapist is being, to say the least, disrespectful to the self the patient feels himself to be. Behind such rejecting acceptance, there may even be unconscious murderous wishes.

At that phase of the therapy when my patient said that I didn't understand her, she was correct. My treatment clearly made her worse, causing her to be more withdrawn, to feel worse about herself, to become more anxious and depressed, all of which diminished her already limited capabilities for coping effectively with her problems of living.

Procedure for the Communication of Countertransference Feelings

There are some things I want to make clear at this point. I am in full agreement with the view that *all* of the analyst's affective reactions to his patient should be internally treated and neutralized so that they are fully under the control of his ego before any intervention is made. When hate is induced, the patient's interest is safeguarded if the analyst processes his feelings as follows; he should observe the full emotional impact the patient is having on him; be fully aware of counter-destructive impulses and wishes; reduce the intensity of his feelings without attempting to eliminate them lest they become dissociated and, therefore, virulent; discover whether the main source is subjective or objective; determine what the patient needs in the way of an intervention; and finally, observe carefully the effects of the intervention.

Not all patients are benefited by receiving some return of the hateful feelings they induce. Some are benefited more if the analyst

5. See Feiner (1970) for a discussion of various modes of inauthentic relatedness. The treatment I have been describing exemplifies "reification," an act whereby one negates the other's autonomy and turns him into a thing. Also see Laing (1960).

contains his feelings and conducts the analysis silently. Patients with masochistic aims are gratified, but not therapeutically benefited, if they are attacked with the hate they provoke.

I have found that hate can be safely communicated after I have succeeded in reducing its intensity to a level at which I am able to experience it as irritation or frustration.

When such communications of neutralized objective hate turn out to be therapeutically and maturationally beneficial for the patient, I think it might be due to some of the following reasons:

1. *The establishment of a credible emotional matrix.* When the analyst responds to hateful denigrating treatment in an emotionally appropriate way, the patient feels sufficiently at home to trust the reality of the interpersonal situation. It feels real because it makes emotional sense. This is what I inferred from my supervisor's suggestion that I use the voice of the patient's father but not his intention.

2. *The patient is reassured of his interpersonal impact.* By responding with feelings that the patient induces, the analyst reassures him of his power to have a reasonably predictable impact on significant figures in his life. This might relieve him of what could otherwise develop into an escalating desperation to make impact, leading to destructive behavior.

3. *It helps the patient achieve a more tolerable distribution of badness.* When the analyst responds to the patient's attacks with reciprocal emotion he rescues the patient from the maddening predicament of feeling himself to be an all-bad person vis-a-vis an all-good one. The analyst, in not behaving like a paragon of forebearance becomes somewhat bad in the patient's eyes. And this makes the patient feel more comfortable.[6]

4. *The patient is protected from the consequences of his destructiveness.* When he initially attacks the analyst, it may be out of a need to feel his interpersonal impact, or out of a need to maintain or restore a failing sense of ego-identity, to separate himself, to keep things in their place, or to achieve a more tolerable distribution of badness. If the attacks do not persist, the patient may need nothing more from the analyst than a feeling of acceptance and respect for the self-other boundaries that the patient needs to maintain.

6. Spotnitz explains this in terms of the narcissistic transference: "the patient is permitted to mold the transference object in his own image. He builds up a picture of his therapist as someone like himself — the kind of person whom he will eventually feel free to love and hate" (1976, p. 109).

The situation becomes dangerous for the patient when he is driven to penetrate the analyst's boundaries and attack his insides. This might be due to his ego's need to split off and project excessive portions of badness — possibly under the pressure of destructive envy. If such attacks persist and the outpouring of hate are intensified, it may signify that the patient is caught in a vicious cycle of destructive impulses, unconscious (unbearable) guilt, paranoid anxiety (fear of retaliation), more hate etc. It is as if he had struck his victim with an axe and hating and fearing the sight of the bleeding and the multilation, he hacks the dreaded object again and again.

If the patient's attacks are unanswered by the analyst, the patient may leave the session as if it were the scene of a crime, having no idea of how much damage he had done to the analyst's insides. At the level of his unconscious fantasy, he may have left the analyst with the analyst's insides fatally maimed or poisoned. In between the sessions, then, the patient might be highly vulnerable to the ravages of unconscious guilt and paranoid anxiety.

Since he is incapable of breaking such a vicious cycle by himself, he requires the analyst to do it for him. And it isn't any hating-back that he is in need of at such times so much as a strong enough response from the analyst to interfere with what is a self-perpetuating destructive and psychotic process.[7] The analyst, in standing up to the patient is, in effect, jarring him awake from a solipsistic nightmare. In presenting a surface hard enough for the patient to feel, he reestablishes the self-other boundaries which tend to be obliterated by the patient's attack, and reemerges separate, alive and well.

The following vignette portrays the relief a patient experienced when she was reassured by the object of her destructiveness (in this case, not the analyst) of his survival in good health.

A forty-year-old female patient, who feared nothing more than that she might destroy those she loved, became, over the course of the therapy, increasingly tolerant of the hateful wishes and impulses she sometimes had toward people she was close to and increasingly confident that she could contain and control them without destructive consequences. Previously self-attacking and somatizing and, in her interpersonal relationships, passive-aggressive and masochistic, she became asymp-

7. Again, see the example of Searles' hallucinating patient (1958).

tomatic and more spontneously self-assertive. On one occasion, her husband, through extreme provocation, enraged her to the point that she uncontrollably spewed forth intense hatred; and heaped obscenities on him, she ordered him out of the house, declaring she could no longer bear to live with such a vile, destructive person.

She reported, "I felt horrible immediately after I said all this because at the moment I said it, I truly meant every word. He ignored my command to leave, but took account of my feelings by staying out of the way, and by performing the chores he had agreed to do for me before provoking me. I felt so good, so relieved. I didn't understand this feeling until later when I realized I had done my worst to him, and I hadn't killed him. He helped me by not pulling his usual number on me. He didn't get that depressed, hang-dog look he used to get when I would displease him in the slightest way, making me feel like a terrible person. My parents used to get a look of pain on their faces when I was bad. When I used to see that look, I hated myself so much, I wanted to die."

The Progressive Humanization of the Therapeutic Relationship

I would like to consider the further course of the therapy with the hateful borderline patient and the eventual humanization of the therapeutic relationship.

Winnicott (1965) makes the point that the child needs his mother to perform two functions: "It is helpful to postulate the existence for the immature child of two mothers — shall I call them the object-mother and the environment-mother? . . . it is the object-mother who becomes the target for excited experience backed by crude instinct-tension . . . the object-mother has to be found to survive the instinct-driven episodes, which have now acquired the full-force of fantasies of oral-sadism and other results of fusion."

It is the environment-mother who "wards off the unpredictable and who actively provides care in handling and in general management. . . . Also the environment-mother has a special function, which is to continue to be herself, to be empathic toward her infant, to be there to receive the spontaneous gesture and to be pleased" (p. 75-75).

When the analyst responds to the patient's penetrating destructive attacks in a way that restores the integrity of the two-person situation, he is functioning as the object-mother. In being available for, and responsive to the patient's need to exercise his constructive tendencies he is functioning as the environment mother.

As the therapy progresses, the patient comes to rely on the analyst as something like a good-enough mother, as the best person with whom to work through hate-ridden internalized intrapersonal relationships. Consequently, hateful impulses come to be delayed until they can be released in the therapeutic setting. I would speculate that such transactions work something like a purgative, relieving the patient of hate and badness, allowing the ego to relax its security operations — especially splitting and projection — freeing appetites and energies for more constructive living. The patient can face the world more as a good-enough person to partake of its satisfactions and to risk interpersonal relationships, and with some greater sense of self worth caring for.

In the work with hateful borderline patients the bad and good intrapersonal relationships may be played out in a discontinuous way, as in the case of Marcia. For one or more sessions, we were a hateful couple. This would be followed by sessions in which we were neither loving nor hating; we were, I would say, in good-enough rapport to be able to address ourselves seriously to her problems in living. At a certain point in the hate-free session, or at the very outset of the next session, the hateful sector of her self would erupt without apparent provocation, and we were once again imbedded in a malevolent emotional matrix.

As the therapy progresses with such patients, the hateful transactions decrease in intensity and frequency, reflecting a diminution of malevolence in the internal relationships between self and other parts. The eruptions of hate then seem less capricious or generalized and more clearly connected with some reality deter- mined experience of feeling let down by the therapist. This suggests that the self and the object world are more integrated and no longer split between good and bad internalized self-other intrapersonal relationships: between bad-self parts and bad introjects on the one hand, and not-bad-self parts and not-bad introjects on the other. There is a more continuous experience of a good-and-bad self vis-à- vis a good-and-bad analyst. The relationship becomes progressively reality-oriented, humanized, and invested with more love than hate.

In the case of Marcia the integration of good and bad self- and other parts did not develop to the point that the relationship became humanized. I would speculate that when she said she saw no prospect of ever developing good feelings for me, it was a reflection of my own confusion concerning my role in her therapy. I did not fully understand that the intensely hateful emotional matrix that she established with me was necessary and desirable for the working through of intensely malevolent intrapersonal relationships. I suspected that her gains were in some way connected with my reacting to her in an emotionally appropriate way; but within myself I could not help agreeing with her persisting opinion that I was not the right therapist for her, and I was still doubtful that therapy could be accomplished in this atmosphere. I would not so readily accept her disqualification of me as a good-enough therapist were I treating her today.

My subsequent experience in working with, and in supervising the work of other therapists with hate-inducing borderline patients has led me to conclude that the humanization of the patient-therapist relationship — which is a function of the extent to which the patient's ego becomes integrated over the course of the therapy — will depend on the therapist's confidence in the potential therapeutic value of his countertransference hate and on his recognition of those instances when the patient needs to receive it.

References

Alexander, P., and French, T.M. (1946). *Psychoanalytic Therapy.* New York: The Ronald Press.

Bird, B. (1972). Notes on transference. *Journal of the American Psychoanalytic Association* 20:267-301.

Feiner, A.H. (1970). Toward an understanding of the experience of inauthenticity. *Contemporary Psychoanalysis,* 7:64-83.

Greenson, R.R. (1967). *The Technique and Practice of Psychoanalysis.* New York: International Universities Press.

Kernberg, O. (1975). *Borderline Conditions and Pathological Narcissism.* New York: Jason Aronson.

Laing, R.D. (1960). *The Divided Self.* London: Tavistock Publications.

Levenson, E. (1972). *The Fallacy of Understanding.* New York: Basic Books

Racker, N. (1953 [1957]). The meanings and uses of countertransference. In *Transference and Countertransference,* pp. 127-173. New York: International Universities Press, 1968.

Searles, H.F. (1955). The informational value of the supervisor's emotional experience. In *Collected Papers on Schizophrenia and Related Subjects,* pp. 157-176. New York: International Universities Press, 1965.

———— (1958). The schizophrenic's vulnerability to the therapist's unconscious processes. In *Collected Papers on Schizophrenia and Related Subjects,* pp. 192-215. New York: International Universities Press, 1965.

Spotnitz, H. (1976). *Psychotherapy of Preoedipal Conditions.* New York: Jason Aronson.

Winnicott, D.W. (1949). Hate in the countertransference. *International Journal of Psycho-Analysis* 30:69-75.

———— (1965). *The Maturational Processes and the Facilitating Environment.* New York: International Universities Press.

Wolstein, B. (1976). A presupposition of how I work. *Contemporary Psychoanalysis.* 12:186-202.

Chapter 11

COUNTERTRANSFERENCE WITH PRIMITIVE MENTAL STATES

PETER L. GIOVACCHINI, M.D.

DILEMMAS IN TREATING THE SEVERELY DISTURBED

This paper will demonstrate some of the dilemmas involved in the treatment of severely disturbed, psychotic patients. Furthermore, the resolution of such difficulties implies that some of these patients are potentially treatable.

The treatment of such patients also focuses upon early developmental phases. Therefore, I will direct my attention both to clinical and technical issues as well as to developmental disturbances that, I believe, are particularly significant for understanding some of the difficulties experienced in the treatment of delusional and deeply disturbed patients.

Some of the recent literature emphasizes that often our reasons for considering patients psychoanalytically treatable stem more from countertransference reactions than from diagnostic considerations (Giovacchini 1975).

Certainly, many analysts feel uncomfortable when dealing with psychotic patients. Bettelheim (1974) discusses how autistic children and schizophrenics can stimulate the emergence of disruptive impulses in the therapist which, if nondefensively experienced, he believes can lead to higher states of personality integration. But in some instances such feelings are so threatening that one has to erect rigid defenses against them. Bettelheim is considering the situation in a residential treatment center and his workers simply leave the institution when they feel too threatened. Analysts, by contrast, often convince themselves that such patients are untreatable and can collectively maintain such a defense by couching it in professional terms.

Sometimes, such opinions are correct. The patient may, in fact, be psychoanalytically untreatable. But that the patient is untreatable and that the analyst's judgment is chiefly determined by irrational countertransference attitudes are not mutually exclusive. Therefore, whatever one wishes to believe about treatability in general, it behooves us to learn all we can about countertransference attitudes. I agree with Bettelheim that such explorations can lead to higher states of ego integration for the therapist which, in turn, will enable him to be a more effective analyst with a wider range of patients. Thus, examination of our countertransference attitudes may, in itself, widen the scope of psychoanalysis.

In a certain sense, I am introducing a paradox. We begin with an untreatable case, a schizophrenic patient, for example, and then the patient, by helping to reveal our countertransference responses, teaches us how to treat him. We treat the untreatable in order to receive treatment ourselves so that our therapeutic armementarium and our knowledge of early developmental phases is enriched sufficiently to diminish the list of conditions that are considered to be contraindications to analysis. Searles (1975) writes of something similar, although not exactly so, when he writes of the patient as therapist to the analyst.

The judgment whether a patient is treatable, in this sense, depends more upon the analyst's psychic integration than the patient's psychopathology. This does not mean, however, that the analyst's psychic health is the sole determinant. Indeed, it is not; many technical factors which have to be learned and experienced are involved. Still, there is a reciprocal relationship between the analyst's receptivity which is a function of his integration and his ability to incorporate certain principles and procedures and make them inherent aspects of his analytic style. Moreover, the analyst's psychic health admits many variations and need not be considered from any moralistic position which would dictate that certain traits are good and others bad. Of course, there are certain fundamental prerequisites for all analysts, beyond which there is considerable variability which makes *absolute* judgments about the analytic interaction and indications for treatment superfluous.

I do not wish to make any elaborate formulations about countertransference. I include all of the analyst's more or less primitive reactions which are related to his infantile environment in this concept. Some responses may be conscious; however, I will pay particular attention to reactions that become disruptive to treatment. There are many types of countertransference responses, not just negative ones.

REALITY AND OBSERVATION

The patient brings his private world into the consultation room. The more psychotic the patient, the less his world, which includes object relationships, will be congruent or in resonance with the analyst's world, which presumably represents reality. The lack of correspondence between these two worlds not only defines the degree and severity of psychopathology but somehow determines whether the patient can relate in a psychoanalytic context.

The formation of transference, a specific type of object relationship, and the ability to make self-observations (Sterba 1934) are considered the essential ingredients required to conduct psychoanalytic therapy. It has been repeatedly stated, perhaps indirectly, that schizophrenics must be deficient in one or both of these qualities, and are therefore unlikely prospects for analysis. Usually such judgments stress their lack of contact with reality.

I believe that one should pause at this point in order to question whether a poor reality sense involves what analysts have taken for granted regarding criteria for treatment. That psychotic patients form transferences is now well known and need not be further belabored. It is sufficient to indicate that the use of projection as the predominant defense of severely disturbed patients facilitates the projection of hostile impulses and introjects into the analyst; this is transference. Whether the patient's delusional system or other manifestations of the reality distortion that characterize psychotic symptomatology diminish the patient's capacity for self-observation is another question which does not have a self-evident answer, although many analysts have concluded that it does. However, this question has seldom been explicitly raised. Usually one assumes that poor reality testing is a contraindication to analysis.

Freud (1914) considered the paranoid patient especially adept at making self-observations. He viewed the paranoid psychosis as including a regression of the ego-ideal (then synonomous with superego), that is, it is placed back into the external world from which it was derived. The patient then believes that others are observing him. His ideas of reference concentrate on his behavior, thoughts, impulses and other aspects of his psyche and soma. He is very much concerned with himself and his psychic productions.

Still, the paranoid patient's use of projection permits him to deny that these are self-observation. This, in turn, could interfere with the construction of an observational frame of reference where analyst and patient cooperate in creatively exploring how the patient's mind works. One can raise the further question whether even delusional self-observations cannot somehow be used in the service of analysis, rather than to simply assume they cannot.

Undoubtedly many other aspects of the patient's character structure have to be considered to determine whether the patient can participate in a productive analytic relationship. I believe that there are character traits in the analyst's personality that also have to be scrutinized and this brings us back to the question of countertransference.

Before proceeding with a discussion of such factors in specific clinical situations, I believe that the analyst's reality sense deserves some examination. The assumption that it is representative of the actual reality of the external world is neither warranted nor relevant.

For obviously, the analyst has certain unique viewpoints that are not necessarily shared by society in general. All analysts are familiar with attacks against psychoanalysis from segments of society which feel threatened by the analytic perspective. Indeed, the current culture with its emphasis on the group rather than the individual, on behavior rather than intrapsychic forces and on conformity (which is not usually acknowledged) rather than autonomy is at cross currents with our weltanschauung. Consequently, one must think of reality testing in a relative rather than an absolute sense.

In my experience, the reality sense of severely disturbed and many psychotic patients is not too different from that of the analyst. Society's sense of reality seems to be less similar to the analyst's than many patients. For example, I have seen a substantial number of patients who, without any instruction, spontaneously free associate and do not expect the analyst to respond to the content of their material. They tolerate analytic silence well and feel intruded upon if the therapist relates to their material outside its transference context. These patients may have been difficult to treat but this was not because they did not have the capacity for self-observation or the ability to understand the intrapsychic sources of their behavior and feelings.

I recall a particular patient who for a long period of time resisted becoming involved in analysis. He was delusionally paranoid and believed that his father was communicating with me in order to plot against and control him. At times, he insisted my office was bugged.

Nevertheless, we liked each other. Although I want my patients to lie down because I wish to establish an analytic frame of reference and I feel uncomfortable otherwise, this patient, for a number of reasons that need not be discussed here, did not disturb me when he insisted on sitting up. I decided to continue in this manner until I became uncomfortable and at that moment the patient could decide whether he would use the couch or see another analyst who would be better able to tolerate a face-to-face relationship. We never reached that point because the patient, after several months, lay down on the couch.

In spite of his fixed delusional system, he was able to blame me while he was sitting up because what we were doing was not analysis. If I made a transference interpretation, he would quickly chuckle a reply which usually amounted to a mandate to stop trying to analyze him. For example, he might smilingly retort, "Don't give me that psychoanalytic bullshit!" He would chide me because I was not "doing" analysis, but when I attempted it, he would benignly attack me. Throughout all of this, his paranoid delusions flourished.

It was particularly interesting how acutely sensitive he was to my maneuvers to create a psychoanalytic atmosphere. He could tolerate any kind of id-oriented interpretations outside the transference context. They did not bother him at all and he rather enjoyed discussing events from the viewpoint of unconscious motivation, symbolization, and so on, but as soon as I led him to considering the projection of his feelings toward me, he would admonish me. To me, this indicated that he had an excellent grasp of the essence of analysis; he simply did not choose at that time to become involved. Later, he changed and I do not know whether he sensed something within me that indicated that I was becoming uneasy with his avoidance of analysis. I was not aware of any such feelings, but I noticed that I enjoyed his cancelling appointments, and this must have been indicative of some ambivalence about continuing with the status quo.

To conclude, I wish to stress that some psychotic patients have a well-functioning self-observing ego which is quite capable of participating in the analytic process if they choose to do so.

PERCEPTION OF REALITY AND DEVELOPMENTAL VICISSITUDES

Such patients highlight the fact that the effects of early trauma are selective. Even though the sense of reality is sufficiently defective that the external world succumbs to delusional distortions, other aspects of the perceptual system, especially those directed to the inner psychic world, can be unusually sensitive and discriminating.

Severely disturbed patients reflect their psychopathology in object relationships and the lack of introjects that are later amalgamated in the ego's executive apparatus in order to construct both adaptations and defenses enabling them to cope with the demands of their environment.

Nevertheless, the comparative lack of ego structure may lead to what might be considered a fluidity enabling the patient to be in tune with both inner psychic elements and aspects of the external world that would ordinarily be unnoticed. The patient's need to introject rescuing experiences may make him particularly sensitive to selective attributes of object relationships which may be either consonant with or disruptive to his needs.

In some instances, the patient's self-representation may be so amorphous that he often has to believe that he has rescued himself, that is, he clings to the delusion that he is self-sufficient and needs no one. To admit dependence is to permit others to intrude upon his minimal autonomy, clearly a repetition of the assaultive infantile traumatic environment.

Insofar as psychopathology is based upon an intrusive traumatic infantile environment, the patient is exquisitely susceptible to any transaction which might impinge upon his precariously structured self-representation. The psychoanalytic process aims at preserving and promoting autonomy. Thus, regardless of how seriously disturbed such patients may be, many adapt quite well to analysis since it is designed not to impose values, not to manipulate and manage one's life. In other words, it is dedicated to releasing the patient's developmental potential.

DELUSION: PERVASIVENESS AND IMPACT

I do not want to give the impression that I believe that some psychotic patients who have an unusual grasp of analysis are easy to treat. Indeed, they are not. They present special difficulties which, if unrecognized, can be totally disruptive to analysis in the same way their early environment failed them. This does not mean, however, that there is something intrinsic in their psychopathology that would cause them to fail in analysis with every therapist. On the other hand, this does not require the analyst to have unique personality characteristics and sensitiveness beyond those usually found in analysts. Perhaps the only feature that deserves emphasis is the analyst's willingness to continue analyzing even though, because of countertransference difficulties, he has temporarily lost sight of his professional role. Furthermore, the type of countertransference difficulties to be described are almost ubiquitous and not necessarily indicative of specific psychopathology or an idiosyncratic orientation. I do not wish to dwell on the definition of countertransference except to indicate that I am referring to the stimulation of infantile elements in the analyst by the patients' transference projections. Infantile elements are not necessarily pathological.

I wish to discuss the disruptive effects of delusional material for analysis. Under what circumstances do analysts find themselves stymied by the patient's delusions and then decide that such patients are untreatable? I wish to present some clinical situations that include both schizophrenic and affective psychoses. I have presented this material elsewhere, but in a different context (Giovacchini 1979).

A scientist, in his late twenties, spent most of his interviews describing in tremendous detail his attempts at what he called soul traveling. By this he meant that some persons are able to separate their souls from their bodies and travel anywhere they wish, but their ultimate goal is to reach certain planes located at different heights according to some kind of spiritual hierarchy. I need not go into the intricacies of his system but its obvious goal was the attainment of total omnipotence. If one had a literary bent, this patient's material could be pulled together and undoubtedly fill several volumes of passable science fiction.

In addition to having complete control of the universe, the patient was also hypochondriacal and spent many hours talking about pathology, physiology, and endocrinology, especially at the beginning of his analysis. Even though the patient had practically no training in biology, he tended to be fairly accurate in his basic assumptions whereas when dealing with the physical universe, an area in which he had a Ph.D., he was appallingly naive and had suspended entirely his extensive knowledge of scientific methodology. I wish to concentrate upon the structure of the delusions here, rather than what were their fairly obvious psychodynamic antecedents, because the latter tended to make me forget about the former and this led to difficulties — my own — in treatment.

As stated, his construction of the universe was based upon some known principles so, to some measure, it was testable. He subdivided the universe into a spiritual and a material universe. For him, the spiritual replaced the material universe and since the essence of spiritual mastery was omnipotence, his achievements would include predicting the future. He, himself, had not yet achieved such omnipotent abilities but the various persons he talked to through telepathic communication had. I was surprised to learn that there are local and national organizations involved in soul traveling; the members achieve different degrees, in somewhat the same manner as Masons, based upon having reached various spiritual levels and "soul planes." In other words, his delusional system received considerable support from the external world and in that particular sector of the external world he would be considered eminently normal.

To repeat, the patient presented his universe as if it were testable in terms of my material universe. One of the masters telepathically told him that several different things would happen to him, about six in all, by the end of the year. All failed to materialize. My first inclination was to review the situation with him and to use this as evidence that he had made many unwarranted assumptions. I felt inclined to engage him in a discussion of scientific method and to help him regain some of his lost reality sense.

I was not able to suppress all of my feelings and I asked him, against my better judgment, what he felt about the reliability of all the assumptions of omnipotence he had assigned to various spiritual forces and deified persons in his soul traveling universe. I should have known better and been able to predict his obvious response. Of course, he was not the least abashed by the failure of the materialization of the predictions. The master that had made the predictions had negative karma toward him as a residue from a previous existence. I cannot tell you exactly what karma is, although he has repeatedly explained it to me. It has something to do with forces and feelings which can lead to positive or negative consequences for the person possessing it or for the person toward whom it is directed. I suspect it can be reduced to primal feelings of love and hate, but in any case the patient was using such concepts as karma and reincarnation to supply a retrospective explanation for the failure of his predictions. In fact, it seemed as if this failure served to strengthen further his belief in his system.

I was nonplused. I should not have been irked, except perhaps at myself, because, as we all know, one cannot deal directly with the content of a delusion. The paranoid patient is especially adept at using any kind of data, supporting, or, to us, nonsupporting, to reinforce his delusional beliefs. I believe that my irritation may have to some measure stemmed from certain specific characteristics of this patient that most patients do not have.

He was a scientist and truly an expert in scientific method. In any other area he would have been the first to emphasize that any hypothesis is meaningless unless it is phrased in such a fashion that it is capable of disproof.

The tremendous discrepancy between his scientific identity and the delusional system, and the degree to which I identified with his scientific identity, caused me to feel uncomfortably irritated with him. The fact that I had responded in a fashion that was contrary to my theoretical (scientific) orientation only served to increase my irritation because, in a sense, I was behaving in a way that was similar to the patient. I had flouted basic principles, principles which I hold in high esteem. I denied a part of myself as the patient had also done with his delusional system. He considered his system scientific and had forsaken conventional science. I will return to what amounts to an identification with the patient's psychosis later.

Although this patient spoke of many interesting things, for his was a colorful delusion, in an intelligent and engaging manner, there was very little entertainment value to his association and I often found them uninteresting. They were hard to listen to.

I was puzzled about this until I had a particularly significant glimpse of him one afternoon in my waiting room. He was sitting with a book in his hand, not reading it, just holding it by his side. His face had the most desolate, isolated look I have ever seen. He looked truly miserable in a quiet, desperate fashion. He seemed entirely alone. I then learned that his wife was very depressed. There was practically no relationship between the two of them because he was always "off" somewhere, reading the master's writings, doing his spiritual exercises, carefully noting his physical reactions in order to regulate his "cancer dissolving diet," and other activities involving his delusional system. He had even stopped working because he could not devote such a large block of time to a job. In fact, he was unable to work. He was completely blocked in his creativity, whereas prior to his delusions, he was quite productive.

The picture that emerged was of an empty, joyless life for him and his wife. This was a rare occasion when I felt sympathy for the spouse, whom I saw as a depressed woman whose whole life was directed toward keeping her eccentric "nutty" husband from doing something that would cause her humiliation or possibly endanger her financial security. She was afraid that he would irresponsibly donate or invest large sums of money.

I emphasize that his delusion was pervasive. It extended into all activities and it was this pervasiveness that made the atmosphere in the consultation room heavy and oppressive. More than anything, I felt the joylessness of his life, the total lack of anything in it that I could consider pleasurable. There were no frenzied feelings of depression or abject misery, only dull and colorless sermons. Consequently, I felt weighed down and, at times, I reacted to his associations as if he were pounding me, the blows becoming increasingly stronger.

I felt his impact and my natural inclination was to respond to him as his wife did, that is, to pull him out of his delusional system. She would constantly keep after him, calling him when he would start his spiritual exercises or when he would get a blank trancelike expression on his face indicative of a reverie in which he believed his soul had left his body. Of course, I could not use such methods. The only recourse I would have had would have been to argue with him.

The patient provoked his wife into treating him like a naughty little boy constantly getting into mischief. In analysis, he was becoming similarly provocative and this represented an important transference orientation. He was extremely ambivalent, clinging to his delusional system and, at the same time, pleading to be brought back into the world of material reality.

This picture of the patient and our relationship gradually emerged and my understanding made it easier for me to deal with him. Still, there were elements that continued to be disturbing and which I believe make the treatment of psychotic patients difficult. These are related to the all-embracing, pervasive quality of some delusions which tempt the analyst to abandon his therapeutic stance. Before discussing the various facets of the analytic interaction with such patients, I wish to present some material of another patient who had similar impact upon the therapeutic relationship, but it took a different form.

This patient, a middle-aged, lonely widower, was markedly paranoid. From time to time he heard persecutory voices and he was constantly getting himself in trouble because he attempted to fight his persecutors. For example, he would make innumerable telephone calls harrassing the administrative personnel of a hospital where he had once been hospitalized because of his psychosis. He felt mistreated and the calls were his method of "telling them off," and seeking revenge. He succeeded so well in antagonizing them that they threatened legal action and, indeed, on one occasion he was put in jail. With me, he continued blaming the world for all his troubles and would never spontaneously direct his attention to any possible intrapsychic sources for his reactions.

Our relationship was friendly. He wanted me to side with him, two against the world. He was an eloquent speaker and a very intelligent, sensitive, and perceptive person. So, in order to tempt me into being a conspirator, he would expound viewpoints, make analyses, and lecture about topics that I found extremely interesting. I found his expositions witty and informative and he was especially adept at expressing my views and convictions. It was very difficult not to get drawn into his discussions, so much so, that, on occasion, I participated. I was somewhat uneasy afterwards but not particularly uncomfortable.

All in all, I felt satisfied that I was able to maintain my analytic decorum and I continued viewing his persecutory delusions as manifestations of various projections. I interpreted the adaptive value of his projections but I was unable to bring such interpretations into a transference context. He was not at all paranoid about me and he listened to my explanations with considerable attention and respect. Clearly, he was dependent upon me and there may have been some hint of idealizing me, but this was so vague that it was difficult to bring it into focus so that one could make a

transference interpretation. However, my nontransference interpretations, although gratefully received and acknowledged, had no
effects whatsoever upon the flow of material.

One evening, the patient called me at home. He was in a state of
frenzy, bordering on panic. Apparently he had called a hospital
official and vented his anger on him to the point where his speech
became obscene. This official called the police and a policeman
paid him a visit. This time he was simply warned but the next time he
would be put in jail. I was not pleased about his calling me at home
but in view of his distraught condition and the obvious relief he
gained from sharing this traumatic experience with me, I decided
not to pursue the matter further.

As can be expected, matters became worse. Briefly, he made
more telephone calls and finally ended in jail. He would call me after
every escapade, not simply to ventilate, but to have me extricate him
from the dilemma he created for himself. A second time he called
the official, a therapist, who again threatened to call the police. The
patient became frightened but he somehow manipulated this
official into calling me so that I could explain the situation and
persuade him not to take legal action. This meant that I would
reassure him that there would be no further calls. I did not like this
situation but still I found myself talking to this person or, rather,
placating him. For a professional person working in a psychiatric
hospital, I was surprised at the intensity of his indignation and he
made no attempt nor was he interested in understanding the patient
from a psychodynamic viewpoint; he was just mad.

It was interesting to note how everyone became irritated with
him, not just the people he had been harrassing. The operators on
my telephone service were both amused and annoyed by him. My
wife and children resented his calls although he was always
courteous and respectful.

I reached my peak of annoyance when he was finally put in jail. I
had previously told him that I would absolutely not get involved
again and if he found himself in trouble, he would have to depend on
his own resources. Shortly after he was arrested, I received a
telephone call from the court psychiatrist, who happened to be one
of my former students. Before I could say anything beyond the usual
friendly amenities, he reassured me that he would do anything *I*
wanted concerning the patient. In contrast to others who dealt with
my patient, this psychiatrist, a big friendly warm type, liked him. On

one occasion, I had done something for this student which was more than would have been expected of me. I had, in fact, rescued him and now he felt impelled to return the favor. I explained the situation thoroughly to him, and although he accepted everything I said intellectually, I could still feel that he wanted to render some service beyond his official position. Therefore, he persuaded the judge that the patient was a worthy individual who would not repeat his mischievous behavior, since he could be controlled by psychotherapy. The judge released him with the provision that he make no more harrassing telephone calls and that he remain in treatment.

I began to feel as if the world were working against me, although I had not completely incorporated my patient's paranoia, since at times the situation struck me as comic. This soon turned to irritation when the patient tried to persuade me to call a former homosexual partner with whom he had had an altercation in order to effect a reconciliation. Not only would this have been therapeutically unfeasible; I simply did not want to intercede.

One might wonder why I found such situations so irksome. After all, I could do as I pleased; I was not going to be forced to do anything I did not want to do. True, I could not prevent others from calling me, but I could have presented the patient with an ultimatum, which eventually I did, rather than letting myself get upset. Apparently he had succeeded in stirring certain disruptive feelings in me, as had also the scientist patient, feelings which I believe many analysts share. Perhaps making them explicit may cause us to feel more charitable in our assessments of the treatability of psychotic patients.

I must emphasize that neither patient protested being in treatment. This was not their problem; they were never late, paid their bills promptly, and were disappointed when a session had to be cancelled. I was the one who was unwilling to continue analysis and it became clear that I was experiencing some countertransference difficulties, provoked by the patient's psychopathology, but insofar as these were my reactions, I had to question whether I was being fair in blaming the patients for the problems we were facing. Of course, blaming the patient or oneself leads nowhere. The best one can do is to try and understand what is going on between patient and analyst in these instances.

LOSS OF ANALYTIC STANCE

I concluded that I was disturbed because these patients had somehow succeeded in getting me to give up my analytic stance. This was painful because it was at variance with my ego-ideal.

The scientist patient created an atmosphere that was completely filled with his delusions. It infused all of his perceptions and activities in the outer world as well as completely filled the consultation room. It was omnipresent and pervasive. I could almost feel its heaviness and was burdened by its oppressiveness. Its joylessness only added to my distress.

Perhaps, I might have reacted differently if I had been permitted to do analytic work within this context, or at least what is considered analytic work, that is, interpretation of the transference. It seemed this was impossible to accomplish with this patient since he presented himself only in terms of the external world, one he himself had created but which kept everything outside of himself. Furthermore, he would constantly give the impression that nothing was wrong except the inability of others (specifically his wife and mother) to accept him as he was. Still, he willingly remained in treatment, but the manifestations of transference, insofar as it refers to past infantile orientations and fantasies, were usually imperceptible or eluded me for long periods of time. The patient had revealed many irrational elements in his material, but he either placed them outside of himself or saw them as an intrinsic aspect of the external world.

As stated, I felt impelled at times to shake some sense into him. The repetitive, monotonous recounting of the innumerable details and omnipotent aspects of his delusional system had a maddening effect. I was feeling the impact of this all-pervasive delusion and I had fantasies of being completely engulfed and inundated by his material. I was perhaps reacting with a *counter-delusion of impact*. I felt oppressed and weary as if I were carrying a heavy, inescapable burden.

The effect the second patient had was similar although he created somewhat different technical problems than the first. His material was as pervasive as that of the scientist but it was not dull and monotonous nor did I feel inclined to argue with him. I had no urge to impose my reality upon him; on the contrary, his sessions were interesting and, if anything, I ran the risk of becoming too involved. Still, within the context of his sessions, no matter how seductive his material may have been, it was not difficult to maintain an analytic orientation. The transference projections were easily discernible; he had idealized me by projecting omnipotent grandiose feelings and was trying to please me by presenting himself as a very interesting and sensitive person. He also wanted to effect a symbiotic fusion and then we could megalomanically control the universe. One could work with this material analytically.

Complications arose when the patient tried to *bring the analysis into the delusional outer world* he had constructed. The scientist, in contrast, brought the *delusional outer world into the analysis*. In either case I felt the impact of their attempts and reacted adversely.

Furthermore, even though the manifestations of projection were obvious in the second case, he involved so many people in his projections that it was difficult to keep the transference focused in the analysis. His transference was all-pervasive in the same fashion as the scientist's delusion. The latter proselytyzed but did not insist on others becoming involved in his system; he did not have any difficulty finding others to support him. The second patient was able to manipulate many persons, especially those close to me, such as telephone operators and my family into rejecting him. In turn, he continued to irritate me by demanding that I participate in his life outside the analysis. True, psychotic patients who relate to part objects split their transferences, projecting one aspect of their ambivalence into the analyst and the other into objects in the external world. This patient reacted similarly but more so. Everyone with whom he came in contact was immediately converted into an archaic infantile object and the persons involved readily assumed the role assigned to them.

My response with a delusion of impact is a somewhat dramatic and exaggerated expression of my reactions. I was not, of course, delusional in the traditional sense since I retained most of my faculties and at one level found all of this quite interesting. (I found it interesting and disturbing enough to be impelled to write this article, an activity which has mustered more secondary process and has enabled me to pull together what had been disparate observations.) Still, the fact that the label "delusion of impact" continues to be appealing must be, in itself, of some significance.

Myerson (1973) emphasizes how the patient's modus vivendi can lead to impasses in analysis which demand special, although not nonanalytic technical responses. Kernberg (1972) and Khan (1960) refer to particular aspects of patients suffering from severe psychopathology that create difficulties in treatment if they are not specifically understood and, even then, it may not be possible to transcend them. Milner (1969) presents a detailed account of the analysis of a severely disturbed schizoid woman who undoubtedly would have been considered too disruptive for analysis by many analysts. Milner was able to overcome certain technical difficulties by letting the patient bring drawings to her as equivalents to free associations and thus, was able to maintain the analytic setting. Winnicott (1954) discusses how patients tend to repeat in analysis the assaultive intrusions, the "impingements" of early object relationships, and the analyst may respond with disruptive discomfort to feeling impinged upon. In all of these articles, the authors directly or indirectly refer to maneuvers the analyst has to resort to in order to feel comfortable and to be able to function from an analytic perspective.

The discomforts emphasized here represent potentially disruptive countertransference reactions that are the outcome of the loss of the analytic stance. These patients threatened my analytic identity and I felt uncomfortable.

To threaten one's identity or to make the functional aspects of the identity sense inoperative must lead to an existential crisis. It may not exactly reach crisislike proportions but to some extent, one must feel confused and impotent (see Erikson 1959). My subjective reactions to these patient's attempts to paralyze my analytic activity was to feel submerged — the dominant manifestation of my delusion of impact. I felt submerged in much the same fashion as do patients who have identity problems because of an overwhelming, intrusive mother-imago (Giovacchini 1964). It is easy, under these circumstances, to view the treatment situation as impossible and to rationalize that the patient is untreatable. This may often be the case but this really means untreatable for a particular analyst, or even most analysts. The patient is unanalyzable only if *all* analysts react in the same fashion.

A professional identity contributes significantly to self esteem. It is a valued aspect of the ego-ideal. Analysts, generally, feel uncomfortable when, for whatever reasons, they are unable to continue functioning in their analytic capacity. In situations where the analyst's inner conflicts are not particularly operative in preventing him from functioning analytically, one must scrutinize particular aspects of the transference-countertransference interaction and focus upon the content of the patient's productions. The scientist patient, besides threatening my analytic identity, was also denigrating specific aspects of my ego-ideal. A scientist himself, proposing that his delusional system was scientific meant to me that he was attacking science, an area I hold in high esteem. Not recognizing what the patient is doing makes it easier to give in to the temptation to argue with the patient in order to protect and often to justify one's value systems (see Giovacchini 1972).

REGAINING THE ANALYTIC STANCE

In this section, I will be concerned with technical maneuvers or interactions which will help the analyst regain his analytic stance and hopefully for the analysis to progress or, at least, to be reestablished. Such maneuvers can be subdivided into two types: (1) those stemming from the patient, that is, the patient confronts the analyst in such a fashion that he is enabled to achieve again a calm analytic attitude, and (2) those that refer to demands made of the patient so that the analyst can continue functioning as an analyst. The two patients presented here, I believe, illustrate both maneuvers.

The scientist had to bring me back into the analytic frame of reference and thereby illustrate maneuvers that stem from the patients. Recall my reactions when he used the failure of predictions to materialize as further proof of validity of his delusion. As stated, I abandoned my analytic stance. He threatened my analytic identity by the continuing and unshakeable pervasiveness of his delusion and offended my ego-ideal by the obvious absurdity of his contention. I responded by emphasizing that he was clinging to omnipotence and his need for magic had apparently obscured his good judgment. Later, I realizd that my exaggerated reaction was also, in part, due to a tremendous letdown I experienced.

When he first told me about the predictions six months prior to their expected materialization, I had some trepidation. Some of them, such as moving his home and leaving analysis, could easily become self-fulfilling prophecies. Consequently, I was relieved when they did not come true. I must confess, I also felt somewhat smug and I saw myself sitting back in my chair like a mother hen clucking, "See, I told you so." Consequently, when he explained the lack of fulfillment of the predictions as the outcome of negative karma, I was suddenly deflated. My world could no longer be maintained as superior to his; it collapsed.

After my retort, which was in fact a rebuke, the patient's demeanor completely changed. His voice, in contrast to its usual monotonous quality, became emotional. With considerable affect, he agreed that he had a tremendous need for magic and that he, indeed, was clinging to omnipotence and magical salvation. He had to replace what he called the world of material reality by a world filled with karma. He emphasized how cruel and dangerous he found my world and how vulnerable, helpless, afraid, and devastatingly miserable he felt. He was justifying himself, but, interestingly enough, he was being solicitous toward me. He was indirectly telling me, "Come on, Doctor, wake up! Can't you see how weak I am? Can't you see through all this? Can't you see how desperately I need to cling to some type of salvation? You cannot take this away from me now. Be an analyst — help me not to need all of this and then I will determine whether I want to give up these beliefs. Now I have no choice." At least, that is the way I heard him, and I do not believe that I have particularly embellished what he was communicating, as one might out of guilt.

Initially, I felt foolish and somewhat ashamed of myself. Afterwards, however, I felt some exhiliration because I could now look at the patient once more from an analytic perspective. I had been properly reprimanded but both the patient and I survived the situation. I had, in addition, regained my analytic identity and could look at his delusion as an important adaptation which helped the patient maintain a defensive equilibrium. I also surmised that some time in the future I would once more transgress because I would again begin feeling the impact of the patient's material. He probably would need to remind me again that I am an analyst and this would, in a sense, refuel me for the analytic task.

Actually nothing dramatic happened. On occasion, I slipped into a mild debate about the validity of some of his assertions but my challenge usually brought some relevant material to the surface, material relating to anxiety about his vulnerable self-representation and a destructive maternal imago which threatened to devour him. Insofar as he could project the latter into me and then make me weak and impotent by his pervasive delusion, he felt relatively safe. Gradually, the elements of his delusion were traced to intrapsychic structures or superstructures to render frightening introjects harmless. The patient is still in treatment and this process is continuing.

The situation with the paranoid patient was quite different and required the second type of maneuver, that is, I rather than the patient, had to make a confrontation in order to preserve the analysis. Whereas the first patient helped me regain my analytic identity, I had to do something that would cause the patient to regain his *analysand identity*. Of course, this would help me to function comfortably as an analyst. This did not necessitate any difficult or subtle interventions; I simply told the patient that I would not continue to be involved with his life outside the consultation room. As far as I was concerned, for this patient there was no external world; everything he told me was a product of his imagination, something he had constructed such as a fantasy, dream, or delusion, or, at least, it would be considered in this way. The patient understood my reasons and agreed to abide by my wishes.

After several months of relatively serene analysis, he called me in order to put in a good word for him with a person he had once offended because he wanted to get reinstated in a dental clinic that had refused him further service. I was furious. I told him so and hung up. Later, I felt that I had overreacted and this was due to something personal that had been stirred up. But, I did not get further upset and the patient has not made any further demands of me. Undoubtedly he will, but now I believe I can reinforce the conditon I set without becoming upset. I have also learned that provoking me to feel angry was his method of defeating me, a need that is the product of his psychopathology and should not be mixed up with my personal feelings.

Borowitz (personal communication, 1974) had a similar experience with an adolescent patient. His patient, a nineteen-year-old male, could be very self-destructive, so much so that Borowitz feared for the patient's life. For months on end the patient would come to each session under the influence of drugs and extol the world of the drug addict and depreciate analysis. He viewed treatment as useless and made a great show of his scorn and indifference for the treatment. Borowitz was well aware of the adaptive and defensive nature of the patient's attitudes and behavior, and with this he could have been comfortable. However, the very definite possibility that the patient might seriously hurt himself, even kill himself, disturbed him, and he felt helpless and angry. Granted this may have been related to some personal idiosyncrasy, he nevertheless felt this way. One day he could no longer contain himself and he told the patient that since he was so little invested in treatment, it might be best if he were to discontinue.

He added that he did not like being a passive witness to someone destroying himself. This had a profound impact upon the patient and made him realize how much the analysis really meant to him. The patient revealed to Borowitz how dependent he was on the analysis and markedly changed his behavior. He stopped taking dangerous doses of drugs and could relate his scornful and depreciating attitudes about analysis to inner feelings of self-hatred and worthlessness.

Borowitz was demanding that the patient either be a patient or not be a patient. He also required a live patient. True, he was imposing restrictions upon the patient's autonomy but he had to be reassured that his functioning as an analyst was, if even in a small measure, being reciprocated. He needed that much reassurance in order to preserve the analytic setting.

Having the patient set us back on the analytic track or requiring the patient to change the manipulations of his psychopathology so that one can regain one's analytic identity brings into focus many subtle transference-countertransference reactions. Some analysts may object that what has been described are parameters of such magnitude that transcend analysis and others may feel that these interventions are obvious and self-evident.

These maneuvers differ from Eissler's (1953) parameters in a very important and essential respect. The purpose of the parameter is to relate to the patient in a nonanalytic fashion, so that later, analysis can be conducted. Presumably this is done in order to help the patient, to reassure and support him so his ego can become sufficiently integrated to withstand the analytic process. Such parameters are, in effect, a preparation for analysis.

By contrast, I have described interventions whose purpose is to preserve the analysis, and that are instituted so *the analyst rather than patient* achieves some degree of ego integration that he needs to function analytically. Of course, eventually it is in the patient's therapeutic interest, but such maneuvers are primarily for the analyst's comfort and designed to help him overcome the oppression stemming from the impact of the patient's delusion. The patient must cooperate sufficiently so the analyst feels secure enough to conduct analysis. The parameter, on the other hand, is designed so the patient can feel sufficient security so that he can become engaged in an analytic relationship.

The possibility that the magnitude of my intervention makes it impossible for the analysis to proceed, is contradicted by the subsequent course of events. Both my patients continued free associating in a relatively serene and productive fashion and I was able to work within the transference context. As stated, I expected that I would from time to time lose my analytic stance but this does not seem to have happened to any significant degree, at least, not yet.

As for the self-evident aspects of these maneuvers, I can once again refer to the reluctance of many analysts to become involved with psychotic patients because they believe that there is something intrinsic to the patient's psychopathology that is a contraindication to analysis. This attitude is antithetical to the one expressed here which emphasizes that the interaction between therapist and patient is the crucial factor which determines whether psychoanalytic treatment is possible and not the psychopathology per se.

Winnicott (1949) believed that experiencing hate in the counter-transference was necessary for the treatment of certain patients and he discussed this both from the analyst's and the patient's viewpoints. Here one can ask the question whether it is absolutely necessary for the analyst to react and respond as I did. Perhaps another analyst would not have felt any impact from the patient's delusion and therefore would not have needed to intervene. This would seem like a much more ideal situation.

Perhaps with sufficient knowledge and forebearance, it might not be necessary for the patient to remind the analyst that he should be an analyst. The scientist patient could have been uninterruptedly viewed from an analytic perspective and would not have been called upon to reestablish the therapeutic equilibrium. I believe this may be possible for some therapists; certainly, since that incident, I have found it considerably easier to relate to the patient's delusion. Still, such material may be inherently tedious and many analysts would feel its impact.

Regarding the paranoid patient. I do not believe it is possible to behave otherwise if one wants to continue the analysis. Possibly, one could remain uninvolved without explicitly making prohibitions but this is a matter of style. The prohibition is nevertheless there, and at best may be implicit and covert. I prefer stating it openly and not to deny my indignation and anger. Nor do I believe that one can remain calm under such circumstances, since one is being asked to do something that runs counter to one's inclinations and professional ego-ideal.

IMPACT OF AFFECTIVE PSYCHOSIS

The patients just described conducted themselves in a reserved, well-mannered fashion. Their overt behavior was not disruptive or threatening. By contrast, one sometimes encounters patients whose behavior is extremely agitated and perhaps borders on violence. Paradoxically, if analysis is attempted they prove to be less disturbing than the more subtle schizophrenic patients discussed here.

The patient I will now describe suffered from an agitated depression which led to total helplessness. She was so disturbed that she was considered psychotic, so much so that she had been given a course of electric shock therapy.

Such patients are commonly seen in hospitals and clinics but rarely in an analyst's office. Their behavior is so disruptive that they are summarily rejected for analytic treatment. The impact they create is so obvious that immediately the analyst is reluctant to become involved. Still, the fact that the impact they produce is so obvious and that from a developmental viewpoint they are considered further advanced than schizophrenics might cause us to wonder further whether the difficulties they create in treatment can be surmounted.

A psychiatrist referred a postmenopausal woman to me for "consultation." It was obvious that he could no longer stand her and was looking for a way out. Perhaps, he hoped that I would simply take her off his hands. I had no wish to see her but agreed to do so for reasons that are not relevant here. To my surprise, I learned that the only way I could relate to her was by strictly adhering to the analytic method.

The first time I saw the patient, a fifty-year-old woman, she was pacing back and forth in my waiting room with an anguished stare while her husband was sitting relatively calmly. Seeing me, she grabbed her husband's hand and started rushing into the consultation room. I let her pass but stood on the threshold of the door when her husband attempted to pass. I told him that I had to speak to his wife alone. She howled but he seemed to understand and stepped back.

She began by assailing me for not letting her husband in. She shouted that she was so confused that she could tell me nothing. She could not survive without her husband's support.

I replied that I wanted to understand her confusion. It would be especially confusing to me to deal with two minds, so I preferred dealing only with hers. She then screamed something about my having to help her and then in a rapid stacatto fashion poured out a tremendous amount of past history. I will not recount these details since they are not relevant to my thesis nor particularly meaningful for the understanding of the treatment process.

The patient stood throughout this narrative, or rather danced around, shifting her posture and going through the motions of walking, that is, marking time. I motioned her to the couch. She protested that she could not lie down as she was lying down. The upper part of her body seemed relaxed but she kept banging her feet together by alternately adducting and abducting her legs. She now screamed, "Aren't you going to give me drugs?" I answered, "Apparently you want me to fail you in the same way as my predecessors." She then calmly said, "I have been taking Marplan for fourteen years and now look at me." Her mood suddenly changed and she howled, "Tell me what to say." I chuckled, "It is really amazing how adept you are at asking me to do things I cannot do," and referred to her demands about seeing her husband, prescribing drugs, and now structuring the interview according to her preconceived notions. She made additional demands which ranged from telling her how to get to my office to how she would be able to pay my fees. I kept absolutely silent since I felt more comfortable saying nothing rather than attempting to make an obvious interpretation or asking an "analytic question," such as delving into her motives for asking such questions. She kept jumping up from the couch and staring at me and insisting that I answer her. I did not believe I was being silent simply to resist her demands; I felt that she was controlling me whether I replied or not, but it was easier for me not to reply and thereby I felt less controlled. I also felt it was in her best interest to let her express her need to control me.

The patient continued being demanding. Finally she absolutely insisted that I see her husband. I felt that I had to define the analytic situation incontrovertibly and assert my analytic identity even if I were to lose the patient. Consequently, I told her I would see her husband, but once he walked through the door, she would leave and could never return. I believe I said this in a nonchallenging fashion and perhaps with a tone of regret. She immediately relaxed and once again lay down. Our time was up however and as I was ushering her to the door she renewed her agitation. She clutched her chest and moaned that she was suffering from a terrible sharp pain. I replied that perhaps she was feeling the pain of separation. She whimpered that she has this pain all the time. I then said that she was trying to defeat and confuse me.

As I opened the door to the waiting room, the husband moved toward me and gently asked me for a report about his wife's condition. I stated that I could not talk to him about his wife's condition but she would be able to explain all that was necessary. She loudly protested that she was too confused and then proceeded to tell him that I wanted to analyze her, and that this would entail daily visits; she told him my fee and that I felt she was trying to drive everyone crazy. I thought I detected a pleased expression on the husband's face. He said nothing and started leading her out. She screamed that she could not go home and wanted to spend the rest of the day with me. He gently led her away.

During the next several sessions she continued protesting. She revealed that she had to construct an inordinately difficult — perhaps impossible — external world, one which caused her to feel completely helpless and totally inadequate. She would, for example, feel terror at the insurmountable task of getting to my office or returning home. Once on a cloudy day, the fog enveloping my building caused panic. Extraneous noises were chaotically intrusive. She constantly appealed to me to rescue her.

During the first session, she demanded to know why I did not take notes. I replied I was too busy listening to her. Several sessions later she repeated this question. I reminded her she had already asked that question. She did not remember. I was surprised because she had apparently remembered everything else I had said and then I repeated my response. In a calm, much deeper pitched voice, she said, "I can only take in the bad things."

It became easy to converse with two different aspects of the patient's character, one which I refer to as her "helpless vulnerable self" and the other as the "capable competent self." Prior to her depression she had been a highly competent business woman and even now she experienced this part of the self in her dreams, whose manifest content usually referred to successful accomplishment.

This patient continues in treatment and the course is stormy. I do not need to elaborate further because I wish to emphasize how her primitive orientation, that is, her infantile fixations threatened the establishment of an analytic relationship which many would have considered absurd even to consider. By contrast, even though the patient's demeanor produced a definite impact on me and threatened my analytic identity, I felt that the only way I could relate to her was in an analytic frame of reference.

The patient's behavior was incomparably more disruptive than that of the schizophrenic patient. She tried hard to make me experience her helplessness and misery and was often successful. Her maneuvering seemed to be directed toward making me relinquish my analytic stance and rescue her. Still, in spite of all her turmoil, it was not too difficult (although it was difficult) to maintain the analytic setting. This might have been made easier because I knew all else had failed — so what did I have to lose? I also believe that there are intrinsic aspects to her character that also account for the lesser impact she created than that of the schizophrenic patients.

She lamented that once she had been an effective functioning person and now she was just a "vegetable." Even this denoted some structure and organization because she said it with some humor. She referred to herself as a vegetable and then she made a comic gesture by shaking her head and said, "Not even a good vegetable." To me this meant that she had at one time constructed a well-established identity and I was seeing glimpses of it even now. Consequently, when she projected disruptive inner elements, that is, aspects of her self-representation, into me, I did not feel particularly threatened in my analytic identity.

The fact that the patient had once achieved an identity, regardless of how defensively constructed it might have been, could have made her less covetous of mine. Furthermore, patients suffering from severe characterological problems tend to project amorphous and destructive aspects of self-representation into the analyst. Insofar as patients suffering from affective disorders retain some aspects of a former identity, their projections, as they reflect the way they view themselves, are less pervasive and have less impact than those of some schizophrenic patients whose identity sense is more incoherently organized.

Depressed patients view objects ambivalently, that is, in terms of their loving or destructive potential. Schizophrenics relate in terms of total annihilation or omnipotent salvation, whereas in the analytic relationship, the depressed patient is able to perceive the analyst as a relatively well-structured person.

My depressed patient attacked discrete aspects of my identity, my analytic identity, by her demands which were very specifically nonanalytic. The schizophrenic patients, on the other hand, tended to inundate me totally, attacking the analytic and all other aspects of my identity.

DISCUSSION OF CLINICAL MATERIAL

Absence of constructive experiences during early childhood leads to lacunae, so to speak, in the ego's executive system. The lack of structure will determine how the patient perceives himself and will determine the nature of future psychopathology.

The schizophrenic patients demonstrated a total lack of confidence in their abilities to sustain themselves. The psychotic symptoms, manifested in the scientist by the construction of an omnipotent delusional world, and in the second patient by controlling the external world through paranoid projections represent overcompensatory defensive adaptations to the terrifying state of defenseless helplessness, inadequacy, and overwhelming vulnerability. Both patients were able to deny the absence of inner resources, and hostile destructive introjects through their delusions.

The extent of this denial was highlighted when the scientist patient, because of analysis, was no longer able to maintain his megalomanic delusional system. He then had to effect a massive withdrawal from a threatening and destructive world, one that he was completely unable to deal with. At first, he regressed to a state of extreme dependency and infantilism where he gave up all adult characteristics, remaining in bed and preoccupying himself exclusively with food. As this situation became intolerable to his family he had to be hospitalized. He then withdrew further into a catatonic stupor, sufficiently classical that he demonstrated the phenomenon of waxy flexibility. Gradually, he was able to relate gingerly to some of the safer aspects of his environment and after several weeks returned home and to analysis.

My depressed patient revealed her helplessness openly instead of constructing a delusionally elaborated superstructure. She also referred to a past which was characterized by initiative and confidence. The regressive elements of her psychosis were clearly evident.

Affective psychotics presumably have progressed further on the developmental scale than schizophrenics and, in spite of my patient's disruptive and unrealistic behavior, she seems to support this viewpoint. Her prepsychotic orientation was characterized by realistic achievement. Much of her successful activities had a frenetic compulsive quality which betrayed their defensive nature, but they were, nonetheless, reality-syntonic and not delusional.

Apparently, this woman had experienced infantile trauma of an intrusive, assaultive nature which caused her to establish an ambivalent introject of the nurturing modality. She maintained equilibrium by incorporating its positive aspects in her adaptations to the outer world and by virtue of her strength and competence was able to control destructive elements. To achieve this balance she hypercathected her adaptive capacities, which had been precariously and defensively established. Her good, "autonomous" adaption protected her from her destructive helpless inner core which was either repressed or split off.

With psychotic breakdown, this equilibrium disintegrated. Quite the reverse became conspicuously evident. Her good competent self was submerged and her behavior preponderantly, but not exclusively, reflected her destructive helpless aspects. It was curious that her dreams were pleasant, and depicted situations where she was admired and functioned effectively. Apparently she could reveal her good side only at night in her dreams.

Some patients project, along with hateful introjects, also valued parts of the self into the analyst (Giovacchini 1975). The patient credits the analyst with the ability to keep destructive and benign helpful introjects separate. My depressed patient, in contrast, had to hide her competent self. Whenever she revealed some element which referred to self-reliance and initiative, she would immediately withdraw and then moan, scream or otherwise emphasize her helplessness, what she referred to as her bad side. Basically, she was frightened that I would be envious and covetous and "steal" the valued aspects of the self-representation. Therefore, she had to hide them in order to protect them and this defensiveness had its genetic antecedents among her numerous siblings. I believe, however, that this concealment of positive aspects of the self is common among depressed patients.

In essence, this patient with an agitated depression revealed and projected very discrete feelings and parts of herself into me. The situation with the schizophrenic patients was somewhat different.

I wish briefly to describe two aspects of the transference situation that I have discussed in some detail elsewhere (Giovacchini 1975). First, I want to mention the projection of infantile feelings, internal objects and other parts of the psyche into the analyst, a conventional view of the transference. Next, the therapist has to consider the frame of reference in which these projections occur, the context, or, as I refer to it, the ambience. The patient attempts to construct an environment surrounding the analyst who has become the receptacle of his projections. Similarly, in order for a defense to be successful, it has to operate in a setting that supports it, one that is compatible with it.

I call the construction of such an ambience, in contrast to projection, externalization. As could be expected, there is considerable overlapping of these two mechanisms and they can be placed on a continuum. Still, each process has unique qualities. Principally, whereas in projection the patient is projecting infantile feelings and parts of the psyche, externalization involves the construction in the outside world of the traumatic infantile environment in which such feelings and introjects were formed. The patient attempts to externalize the background infantile ambience and make it part of the analytic relationship. He needs to surround the analyst, who has become the target of his projections, with such an atmosphere.

The analyst's task is to make himself available for the patient's projections, but not to become part of the infantile ambience. *The patient may try to externalize, but his externalizations and the analytic atmosphere are not compatible.*

The transference of schizophrenic patients is hard to keep in mind because they do not project principally into the analyst. I say principally, because no matter how focused the analysis, to some extent patients project into other persons besides the analyst. My schizophrenic patients put me in their delusional systems and assigned me a specific role. There were, however, many other persons in the same system and, as was especially true with the scientist, my role was no more important than anyone else's. Since his feelings were distributed in so many different directions, there was little that could be anchored in the analysis, and this was frustrating for me.

Schizophrenic patients make the work of analysis especially difficult because of the additional factor of the pervasive nature of their externalization. In many instances, it is impossible to distinguish between transference projections and externalization. *Because the boundaries between the self and the outer world are so poorly structured, the projections of parts of the psyche and the externalization of the infantile environment are no longer separate and discrete processes.* The analytic setting becomes submerged by the ambience the patient creates and the analyst becomes part of that ambience. The analyst finds himself immersed in the patient's delusional world and, as discussed, this causes problems as he struggles to remain an analyst.

SUMMARY

I have discussed the psychoanalytic treatment of some psychotic patients in terms of the impact their delusional material had upon me.

First, I examined reality testing and the self-observing function. One usually makes the assumption, perhaps implicitly, that there is an inverse relationship between the two. Examining clinical material with this particular point in mind challenges this assertion. Many patients who are quite delusional, and an example was presented here, show a remarkable capacity to perceive sensitively subtle nuances and other aspects of how their mind works.

Next, I focused on the oppressive nature of the patient's delusion, and found that the analyst's reaction with a delusion of his own, so to speak, creates special problems which interfere with the progress of analysis. I described an especially poignant episode where the patient helped me to continue functioning as an analyst.

By contrast, I described another episode which I believe is fairly common and potentially quite disruptive to treatment. In this situation, a patient demanded that I participate in his delusion, that is intercede for him in the external world. This patient, as did the first patient, also threatened my analytic stance. For analysis to continue, it became necessary to demand that the patient maintain analytic decorum and permit the analyst to analyze rather than participate. The first patient brought a pervasive delusion into the analysis whereas the second patient attempted to bring delusion and the analyst into the external world.

Finally, the discussion of a patient suffering from an affective psychosis referred to similar complications of treatment. However, in spite of agitated behavior, which at times seemed unmanageable, the patient's impact upon the therapist was less disruptive than that of the better behaved schizophrenic patient. By examining my countertransference, I was able to conclude that the patient was intruding upon a circumscribed facet of my identity, my professional identity, rather than encroaching upon all aspects of my self-representation.

In conclusion, the treatment of psychotic patients does not rely so much upon the content of the patient's psychopathology as it does upon the analyst's sensitivities, which are perhaps shared by a majority of analysts. The awareness of our sensitivities, usually referred to as countertransference reactions, can only lead to increased integration and forebearance for the analyst. In turn, the range of patients that we can treat is broadened and the benefits of analysis will become available to a larger number of persons who have, for the most part, known only suffering and misery.

References

Bettelheim, B. (1974). Countertransference problems in workers in a residential treatment center. In *Tactics and Techniques in Psychoanalytic Treatment, Volume II: Countertransference,* ed. P. Giovacchini. New York: Jason Aronson.

Eissler, K. (1953). The effect of the structure of the ego on psychoanalytic technique. *Journal of the American Psychoanalytic Association* 1:104-143.

Erikson, E.H. (1959). Identity and the life cycle. *Psychological Issues,* Monograph No. 1. New York: International Universities Press.

Freud, S. (1914). On narcissism: an introduction. *Standard Edition* 14:67-102.

Giovacchini, P. (1964). The submerged ego. *International Journal of Psycho-Analysis* 43:371-380.

———(1972). Countertransference problems. *International Journal of Psychoanalytic Psychotherapy.* 1:112-127.

———(ed.) (1975). *Tactics and Techniques in Psychoanalytic Treatment, Volume II: Countertransference.* New York: Jason Aronson.

———(1979). *Treatment of Primitive Mental States.* New York: Jason Aronson.

Kernberg, O. (1972). Treatment of borderline patients. In *Tactics and Techniques in Psychoanalytic Treatment,* ed. P. Giovacchini. New York: Jason Aronson.

Khan, M.M.R. (1960). Clinical aspects of the schizoid personality: affects and techniques. *International Journal of Psycho-Analysis* 41:430-437.

Milner, M. (1969). *The Hands of the Living God.* New York: International Universities Press.

Myerson, P. (1973). The establishment and the disruption of the psycho-analytic *modus vivendi. International Journal of Psycho-Analysis* 54:133-143.

Searles, H. (1975). The patient as therapist to his analyst. In *Tactics and Techniques in Psychoanalytic Treatment Volume II: Countertransference* ed. P. Giovacchini. New York: Jason Aronson.

Sterba, R. (1934). The fate of the ego in psychoanalytic treatment. *International Journal of Psycho-Analysis.* 15:117-126.

Winnicott, D. W. (1949). Hate in the countertransference. In *Through Paediatrics to Psycho-Analysis,* pp. 194-204. New York: Basic Books, 1958.

———(1954). Mind and its relation to the psyche-soma. In *Through Paediatrics to Psycho-Analysis,* op. cit., pp. 243-254.

Chapter 12

PRIMITIVE COMMUNICATION AND THE USE OF COUNTERTRANSFERENCE

JOYCE McDOUGALL, M.A., D.Ed.

> ... the analyst is prepared to wait till the patient becomes able to present environmental factors in terms which allow of their interpretation as projections. ... Sometimes the analyst needs to wait a very long time.
> — *D.W. Winnicott*

RECONSTRUCTION OF PREVERBAL TRAUMA THROUGH COUNTERTRANSFERENCE

Certain patients recount or reconstruct in analysis traumatic events which have occured in their childhood. The question has sometimes been raised as to whether we treat this type of material differently from other analytic associations furnished by the patient. And if so what are the differences? Ever since Freud's discovery that the traumatic sexual seductions of his hysterical patients revealed themselves to be fantasies based on infantile sexual wishes, analysts have been wary of mistaking fantasy for reality. Nevertheless there are many "real" events which leave a traumatic scar upon our patients — such as the early death of a father, a psychotic mother, or a childhood handicapped by illness. When these events are within

267

conscious recall they inevitably present us with specific problems because of the varied use the patient will make of them, and in particular because he will so frequently advance the argument that there is nothing to analyse in this material since the events "really happened." They have become, however, part of the patient's psychic reality also and must therefore be listened to with particular attention.

With regard to traumatic events stemming from even earlier periods before the acquisition of *verbal* communication the detection of their existence becomes considerably more complicated — to the point that we may only become aware of the traumatic dimension through the unconscious pressure it exerts upon the analysand's way of being and speaking, and thus eventually may only be accessible if captured through our *countertransference reactions*.

Definition of Trauma

Before proceeding further it is necessary to define what constitutes a psychic trauma for any given individual since it is evident that events which may have exercised a deleterious effect upon one patient appear to have left another unscathed. The appreciation of "traumatic" sequelae is further complicated by the need to distinguish these from the universal "traumas" which are inherent to the human psyche, namely the drama of separating oneself off from the Other, the traumatic implications of sexual difference with the interdictions and frustrations it engenders, and finally, the inexorable reality of death. Human beings must come to terms with each of these traumatic realities or they will fall psychically ill. My contention is that a catastrophic event may in general be considered traumatic to the extent that it has impeded the confrontation and resolution of these ineluctable catastrophes which structure man's psychic reality.

Before coming to the question of *early* psychic trauma in adult patients it is pertinent to the aim of this paper to consider briefly the role played in analysis by catastrophic events which have occurred after the acquisition of language and the capacity for verbal thought. Such events when recounted in the course of the analysis often present themselves as unshakeable facts, rather than as thoughts and free associations which can be explored psychically, and as such, serve the function of resistance to the unfolding of the analytic process.

Such was the case with a male patient whose mother had been killed in a road accident while driving her car, when he was only six years old. The father, warm-hearted and attentive to his little boy, was also represented as being somewhat alcoholic and at such times, irresponsible. In the early months of his analysis the analysand attributed the totality of his neurotic character problems to his mother's premature death, thus using the tragedy as an alibi which became a resistance to further questioning. Later his associations revealed the fantasy that the accident was in fact a suicide. In the mind of the bereaved child his father's drinking problem and irresponsibility (representing in the unconscious, a form of sadistic primal scene) had pushed his mother to this act of despair; the father was therefore responsible for his loss of his mother. However, under the impact of the ongoing analytic process yet another fantasy came to light: it was he himself who was responsible for this crime. He wished to take his mother's place with his father and be the only one to share in his warm sensuous way of relating. By dint of magical thinking he had caused the death of his mother. Whatever the facts of her accidental death, the only reality with which our analytic work was concerned was his inner reality, a childhood fantasy based upon a repressed homosexual wish and a repressed death wish toward the mother. These unconscious wishes weighed heavily upon the psychic functioning and the libidinal economy of the patient. An external event had accidentally become an accomplice to the little boy's imaginative life at a time when he was already struggling to resolve his homosexual and heterosexual oedipal desires, thus presenting him with a doubly traumatic experience which was to render the solution to his oedipal conflict more than usually difficult. In the process of the analysis it became possible to interpret the tragic happening *as though it were a projection,* the result of omnipotent childlike thinking. From this point onward the mourning and identification processes, blocked by the patient's infantile repressed fantasies, were able to resume their course. In place of a constant feeling of living fraudulently, of inner deadness, of terror in the face of any fantasy wishes, the patient was now able to construct an inner world peopled with living events and objects, and thus confront the world of others on a more adequate basis.

Modification of Traumatic Events

Although it is important to distinguish between real and fantasy events it is nevertheless true on the whole to state that psychoanalysis can do nothing to modify the effects of catastrophic events if they cannot also be experienced as omnipotent fantasies; only then can the analysand truly possess these events as an integral part of his *psychic captial,* a treasure trove that he alone can control and render fruitful. In other words, no one can be held responsible for the tragedies of traumatizing relationships that the external objects and the world have brought into the small child's ken, but each and every individual is uniquely responsible for his *internal objects and his inner world.* The important thing is to discover to what use he puts this inner treasury with its full quota of pain and loss.

It is admissible on this basis to hold that traumatic events often function as screen memories and as such may yield much valuable analytic material. Neurotic symptions may be conceived of in general as springing from parental words and attitudes, more precisely, from the child's *interpretation* of his parents' silent and verbal communications; they may likewise arise from his interpretation and psychic elaboration of traumatic happenings as in the case cited above. In the long run, the analyst's way of handling material stemming from traumatic events, although more complicated, is not markedly different from his way of dealing with neurotic intrapsychic conflict. From the point of view of countertransference he has only to be aware of the danger of complaisant confusion with the patient, since the tragic event, or crippling accident, did actually take place.

Can the same be held true for traumatizing experiences which have occured before the acquisition of verbal thought and communication through the symbolic use of speech? In the first years of life the small child communicates through signs, chiefly cries and gestures, rather than through language. And in fact he can only be said to *communicate* by means of these signs to the extent that they are understood by Another who treats them as communications. From this point of view it may be said that *a baby's earliest reality is his mother's unconscious.* The traces of this early relationship are not inscribed in the preconscious as are those elements which have become part of the symbolic verbal chain; thus they have a different psychic status from representations contained in the form of *repressed* fantasies, and thus have little chance of seeking partial expression through neurotic symptoms. The traumatic phenomena of infancy (*in-fans*: non-speaking) belong to the area of primal repression. When subjected to mental pain the baby can only reestablish his narcissistic equilibrium through primitive defences such as projection-introjection and splitting mechanisms, hallucination, and repudiation, and these are only effective to the extent that the relationship with the mother allows them to operate through her attempts to understand her infant and her capacity for introjective identification with him. It should be noted in passing, that psychic suffering at this presymbolic phase is indistinguishable from physical suffering, a fact that is evident in psychotic communications as well as in many psychosomatic manifestations. If the verbal child may be said to *interpret* his parents' communications in his own way, the infant makes, so to speak, a *simultaneous translation* of the parents' conscious and unconscious messages. Since the capacity to capture another's affect precedes the acquisition of language, the nursling cannot but *react* to his mother's emotional experience and her unconscious transmission of it in her way of relating to her baby. The mother's ability to capture and respond to her infant's needs will depend on her willingness *to give meaning* to his cries and movements, allowing him eventually to introject this meaning and be in communication with his own needs. Outside of what he represents for his mother the baby has no psychic existence. Not only is she the assurance of his biological and psychological continuity, she is also his *thinking apparatus*.

Fundamental Transference and Primitive Communication

This digression concerning the mother-baby relationship may serve to elucidate two of the main themes of this paper, namely the nature of our analytic approach to those analysands who would seem to be marked by a breakdown in communication with the mother in babyhood, and secondly the way in which such breakdown may express itself in the analytic relationship. The burden of this lack may fall to the analyst who will find himself in the position of the mother, obliged to decode or to give meaning to his patient's babylike, inarticulate messages. It is of course true that this primitive form of communication and archaic link is always present in the relation between analyst and analysand. We might call it the original, or *fundamental transference*. But this basic dimension does not require particular emphasis when the analytic discourse is freely associative, and when its manifest aim is to communicate thoughts and feeling-states to the analyst. We are then listening to a manifest communication which contains rich latent meaning to the analytic ear. The patients who I have in mind use speech in a way that has little in common with the language of free association. In listening to them the analyst may have a feeling that it is a meaningless communication at all levels, or he may be aware of being invaded with affect which does not seem directly attributable to the content of the patient's communication. The question is how to understand and use such countertransference affect. I hope to show in this article that these analysands frequently use language as an *act* rather than a symbolic means of communication of ideas or affect. At such times, unknown to analyst and patient alike, the latter is revealing the effect of a catastrophic failure in communication which has occurred at a time when he was unable to contain or to work through, psychically, what he was experiencing. The traces of these early failures are confined either to somatic expression which may be considered as an archaic mode of thought, or may give a hint of their presence by the incoherences and blanks they produce in the patient's way of thinking and feeling about what happens to him or concerns him. Such experiences may of course leave some verbal traces or find symbolic expression, but the attempt to elaborate or interpret these stops short. One may come to discover that with such analysands any feeling or fleeting thought which risks reanimating the originally catastrophic situation is immediately stifled, or ejected from the mind, with such force that the individual will suffer from authentic disturbance in his thinking processes or may appear to function like a robot. He is unable to allow sufficient psychic space or sufficient time for the unconscious remnants to become available to conscious processes. Once the nascent thought or feeling has been ejected, he will frequently plunge into action of some kind in an attempt to ward off the return of the unwelcome representation and mask the void left by the ejected material. Economically speaking, such action assures a certain discharge of tension, and might thus be termed an "action-symptom." In this way talking itself may be a symptomatic *act* and therefore an "anti-communication." The analyst might thus capture in negative, what has been up till then an inexpressible drama. The lost material behind such action-symptoms will often reach symbolic expression, for example, in dreams but then fail to stimulate associations or mobilize affect.

Here is an example of one such dream from a patient whose problems led one to suspect that his inner world contained many areas of desolation and destruction of meaning.

> I dreamed I was back in the town where I was born. It's a small village but in my dream it was vast. And empty. There wasn't a living soul. Empty houses, empty streets. Even the trees were dead. . . . I woke up suddenly. There was more to the dream but I can't remember what. And all because of my wife! We had a violent dispute at that moment over some silly thing. And I don't remember that either.

No associations were given, and the patient's interest in his dream seemed to vanish with the telling of it. The dream theme, which awakened in the analyst a feeling of desolation and of something uncanny, gave rise to no such sentiments in the analysand. On the other hand his quarrel with his wife, a familiar theme with this patient, continued to fill him with rage, even though he had forgotten what the quarrel was about. His intensity over the incident was in marked contrast to the deadness of the dream theme and mood. An unconscious link between the two "forgotten" items clearly provides a clue as to the dynamics of the patient's psychic situation. We had already discovered that he only felt "fully alive" when he was engaged in hostile exchanges with those around him. The quarrel was a form of "manic defense" against dead or depressing inner experiences, the latter having failed to find representation in either thought or feeling. There was little doubt in my mind and indeed in the mind of this patient that he had suffered early psychic catastrophe in his relation to those who cared for him, but there were no memory traces, and such remnants as were able to arise from unconscious sources led to no further associative processes. They appeared to seek expression uniquely in action. The repressed elements from which we might hope to reconstruct the infantile past are nonexistent here. The "catastrophe" has affected the patient's capacity to think about himself and to contain painful affect, and can thus only be guessed at through his acts — which are not yet capable of translation into communicable thought.

For certain analysands, *speech itself becomes this act* in the analytic relationship. Rather than seeking to communicate ideas, moods, and free associations, the patient would seem to aim at making the analyst *feel* something, or stimulating him to *do* something: this "something" is incapable of being named and the patient himself is totally unaware of this aim. Such an analysand will often put questions to his analyst or say things like: "Well, after all the things I've told you, isn't it time you said something? Can't you tell me what's wrong with my life?" Or: "How do I know there's someone there if you don't speak? I might as well talk to a wall!" Obviously all patients are apt to express such feelings, but the usual neurotic patient will accept that his turning to the analyst and addressing him in this way has some meaning, and will try to cooperate with the analyst when he seeks to interpret the feelings which prompt such remarks. With luck he will recognize readily that a childlike part of him demands reassurance or feels frustrated by the rigors of the analytic relationship, and he may then use this insight to further his understanding of his personal history and his forgotten past. But the patients I have in mind are not able to maintain sufficient distance to observe these phenomena in themselves and so are unable to examine the underlying significance of their transference relationship. They feel constantly angry or depressed with the analysis and yet desperate about the feeling of stagnation. The demand that the analyst interpret in a context in which there is no apparent interpretable material is a sign that the analysand is in the throes of an experience which cannot be expressed, giving way instead to a feeling of uneasiness. This in turn makes him want to call upon the analyst to show signs of his existence in order to stifle the rising tide of emotion, or to put a stop to the continuation of the analytic process. One discovers later, that at such moments the patient is submerged by feelings of rage, or anxiety, to a degree that prevents him from *thinking further* in this context. In his distress he is no longer sure that he is accompanied by a live individual who is listening, and following him, in his difficult analytic adventure.

The analyst, who tends to feel constantly questioned, or pushed to take action, will at the same time find himself blocked whenever he attempts to interpret. That is he will become aware *that he is no longer functioning adequately as an analyst.* In fact he is receiving what I am calling a *primitive communication* — in the same way in which we may conceive of an infant who is gesticulating wildly, or screaming, as *communicating* something to someone.

I am making here two propositions:
1. In these cases it is permissible to deduce the existence of

sequelae to early psychic trauma which will require specific handling in the analytic situation.

2. This "screen-discourse," impregnated with messages that have never been elaborated verbally, can in the first instance only be captured by the arousal of countertransference affect.

CLINICAL EXAMPLE

To better illustrate what I am describing I shall take a clinical example. This analytic fragment, which dates from fifteen years ago, is not one of the most incisive to throw light upon this type of analytic problem, but it is the only fragment on which I took lengthy notes at the time, and indeed was prompted to do so because I did not understand what was happening between my patient and myself. Since that time I have often been able to capture such oblique communications and this has enabled me to establish better contact with an archaic dimension of the patient's psychic structure — thanks to what I was able to learn from the analysand about whom I am going to tell you.

Annabelle Borne was forty four years old and had eleven years of analysis behind her when she was first sent to me by a male colleague. After one single interview with this colleague she asked him for the name of a woman analyst. In our initial interview she told me she had already had three analysts. The first analysis had been terminated on her own initiative because the analyst became pregnant during the third year of the analysis and this fact was intolerable to her. She continued for five more years with a male analyst, a valuable experience in her opinion since she was able for the first time in her life to have a sexual relationship, after many years of painful solitude, and to get married at the age of forty to a man with whom she shared many intellectual interests. Although not frigid, she was uninterested in the sexual side of their relationship. Partly because of this loss of sexual interest, but also because of a persisting feeling of dissatisfaction with all her relationships, a feeling of not understanding people, of being an outsider, badly treated by others, she decided to continue with a third analyst. The latter, after three years, advised her to discontinue on the grounds that she was "unanalyzable."

Perhaps because I showed surprise at this apparently forthright prognosis, Mrs. Borne asked the analyst to write to me, which he did, saying that he did not advocate analysis but that the patient might benefit from a modified form of psychotherapy. In spite of this gloomy verdict, Annabelle Borne wanted to continue with analysis. Life seemed so hard and she had already been greatly helped by her former analytic experience. At our second meeting she told me something of her initial reasons for seeking help. She did not feel "real" and had little contact with people of her own sex and none whatever with men. At the age of nine she had been sexually attacked by a brother six years older than she. For many years she believed that this event had permanently damaged her and was responsible for most of the painful aspects of her life. She no longer felt this to be a sufficient explanation of her difficulties; that the answer to her problems probably lay within herself although she could not see why. She added that she had little hope of finding an analyst who would suit her. She had not cared for Dr. X who sent her to me and she didn't care for me much either. Nevertheless she had decided to ask me to accept her as a patient in spite of this mistrust. I, on the other hand, found her likeable. Her story intrigued me and her frankness also. Several months later we began our work together and this continued for four years.

Our first year together was trying for both of us. Nothing about me suited my patient. My silence exasperated her and my interpretations even more so. My consulting room, my clothes, my furniture, my flowers incited constant criticism. As for her life outside analysis, it seemed that everyone in her entourage lacked tact, thoughtfulness, and understanding in their dealings with her. At the nursery school attended by her little boy, no one gave her the cooperation she expected. We searched in vain for some insight into this endless repetition both within and without the analytic situation. Interpretations which one day seemed fruitful proved the day after to be sterile, or would give rise to a flood of denigrating remarks from my unhappy analysand. She considered me indifferent to her painful experiences, or if not, incompetent to understand and help her. When, one day, I remarked that she felt me to be a disastrous mother who would not, or could not, help her child to understand what life and living was all about, she replied that I was exactly like one of Harlowe's cloth monkeys — a reference to H. Harlowe's famous research experiments on infant rhesus monkeys brought up by a surrogate cloth mother. (These monkeys, incidentally, were noted for their incapacity for contact with other monkeys, and for their inappropriate expressions of rage.)

Annabelle also accused me of ridiculous optimism in continuing my persistent efforts to understand her distress. I myself began to feel that I was about as useful as a cloth monkey for all the good she was able to get out of our analytic work together. A couple of days later this pessimistic opinion became a certitude. On this occasion Annabelle Borne found yet another metaphor apt for expressing her discontent and irritation with her analyst. She had recently read of Konrad Lorenz's experiments with ducklings who have lost their mother in the first days of life. If presented with an old boot, they will follow it just as readily, and will show to this grotesque maternal substitute the same attachment as they would have shown towards a real mother. I was this old boot — and she, presumably, was the bereaved duckling. I suggested she was waiting for me to become a *real* mother towards her. "Not at all" she replied. "I've never expected anything from anybody. But you're worse than nothing! This analysis is making no progress ... if anything, my problems are getting worse ... it costs money so that all the family must suffer because of you. Otherwise we could have long holidays in the sun. But I keep coming here, no matter how bad the weather. ... Impossible to park my car in this wretched Latin Quarter. I'm sick of analysts ... sick of you ... your blond hair, your consulting room, your flowers! You don't care about me — and you haven't the guts to tell me that this analysis is a waste of time!" And so on, till the end of the session. As she was leaving, Annabelle cast a withering glance at a pot of flowers on my desk and spat out one last furious remark: "People who like flowers should be florists — not analysts!"

This session was not markedly different from many which had preceded it, yet on this occasion I felt discouraged and depressed. Up to this point my patient's negativism, although fatiguing, had given me food for thought and led me to question the efficacy of a classical analytic approach with an analysand so devoid of insight and of willingness to examine anything at all. Yet she obviously suffered greatly, so I was prepared to carry on in the hope that one day we would discover the true object of her immense rage and frustration. But it now seemed to me that what little therapeutic alliance existed had finally fallen apart. She was clearly unwilling to continue in analysis so why should I bother to encourage her in such a fruitless endeavour. The more I thought about it, the more I became convinced she was right, though I was aware of stifling an uneasy feeling that I was simply slipping out of a disagreeable task, and letting down a patient in distress. To get rid of this uneasiness I decided to take notes on the session, and to make a summary of our year's work together — a final attempt to see more clearly into her impalpable psychic world.

Her parents as she presented them were a typical middle-class couple: father, much admired, but very involved with his professional activities, mother represented as somewhat vague, artistic, narcissistic. Then there was the brother at whose hands she had suffered sexual assault when she was nine. She had never dared tell her mother about it since he was the mother's favorite child; nor could she tell her father because she felt too guilty about the whole incident. Her many years of analysis had led her to understand that she had experienced the sexual relation as an incestuous one with her father. In spite of its traumatizing quality it had also represented the fulfillment of an infantile oedipal desire. From her earlier analyses there had been many interpretations relating to penis envy as the basic reason for her bitterness and dissatisfaction with life. She had complained often of her mother's preference for the older brother, and of the supposed facility of his life as compared with her "hard" existence, but other than this had furnished little material that warranted further interpretations of her envious attitude to her brother or his penis. Her associations tended to be centered on the feeling that her mother was more gifted, more feminine, more loved by the father and that she herself could never equal her mother. There was a recurring screen memory relating to her mother which dated from the time when she was four or five years old. She had a clear vision of gazing at her mother's breasts which were overflowing with "green sap." This phantasy-memory filled her with anguish. My attempts to link this green sap — sap of life? cadaverous death? with other associations such as her feelings about the analysis and all she hoped or feared from her mother, or from me as an analytic nursing mother, had led us nowhere. My attempts to uncover the underlying significance of her manifest thoughts and feelings were rebuffed as a refusal to admit the daily injustices from which she suffered.

Apart from the vivid screen memory there was little other evidence of fantasy activity, and a paucity of dreams. My interventions had failed to set in motion that interplay of primary and secondary processes which is the hallmark of a functioning analysis. As for the transference relationship, all attempts to find meaning in it were given short shrift. I had little doubt that she experienced me as a bad, almost a dead mother, and that I, and the whole environment which treated her so badly, also occupied today the place of the envied brother, nourished with the green sap of maternal love — and of which Annabelle so clearly felt herself deprived. But a year's work had shown me that Annabelle wanted nothing of this, rather as though she clung to feeling angry and ill-treated and wanted to prove that nothing could be done about it.

Having thus collated and reflected upon the many harassing questions this analysis raised in me, I took the decision — not without a twinge of guilt — to tell Annabelle that she was right to wish to terminate her analysis with me. After all, I said to myself, I would not be the first analyst to find her "unanalyzable".

Right on time as always, Annabelle arrived with an expression almost of gaiety on her face. She began speaking the moment she stretched out on the divan.

"I don't remember a thing about yesterday's session — I only know it was a *good* one. I did lots of things afterwards."

I heard myself reply "You don't remember anything about yesterday's session?"

"Absolutely nothing!"

"What makes you feel it was a 'good' session?"

"Well ... I remember that I was humming a song as I went down the stairs, straight after I left here. And goodness knows I don't often feel that happy!"

Still acutely aware of my distinctly *unhappy* feeling, and anxious searching, after this same session, I asked her, thinking it might provide a clue, if she remembered the song she was humming.

"Let's see ... um ... oh yes, that children's song 'Auprés de ma blonde, qu'il fait bon, fait bon ... dormir'." (How good it is to sleep beside my blonde girl.)

Her angry vituperation of the previous day in marked contrast with the euphoric aftermath, her irritated reference to my blond hair, in equally marked contrast with the revelation of a libidinal wish in the song, and other incongruities, decided me to tell her that I remembered yesterday's session very clearly; she had expressed strong feelings of anger, disappointment and irritation with me and the analysis. There had been no trace of a feeling that it could be "good to sleep" beside a blond analyst. Annabelle was very struck by this recall of the material of her session and began to wonder herself what all these contradictory expressions might mean. I suggested — following my own countertransference affect of the day before — that perhaps she went off so light-heartedly with the hope that *I* would feel disappointed, irritated, and angry in her place.

"How strange! I think you're right. I've often thought to myself that I'd like to see you cry."

"Would they be *your* tears that I am to weep?"

For the rest of this session Annabelle gave much thought to this new idea — in striking contrast to her familiar attitude of disdain or dissatisfaction. At the same time I began to realize that she rarely ever expressed any *depressive affect*. Indeed in thinking back I was also aware, for the first time, that in spite of the virulent content of her analytic discourse I had the impression that much of what she said was *devoid* of affect. Her apparent anger was perhaps hiding inexpressible sadness.

The following session she brought a dream: "They were taking me to a police station in a sort of tumbril. A huge poster announced that 'Mrs. Moon was wanted for murder.' I am wheeled down a long corridor, like a big hospital. I'm very small and the tumbril has turned into a cot. As we go along I throw pieces of cotton-wool in a furious way onto the floor."

In her associations to the dream, "Mrs. Moon" suggests the analyst "who is supposed to throw light on what is dark and murky." Then she went on to realize that this dream-name was also an anagram of her own mother's name. The cotton-wool recalled something she had been told about her babyhood. She was a baby who "never cried"; her mother, who was often occupied for long periods of time, would give the baby pieces of cotton-wool in her cot, and she would suck these frenetically until her mother returned. "But where was she?" cried Anabelle. "I never had a mother!" And she began to sob. The little "child who never cried" was to cry in her analysis for many months to come.

DISCUSSION

> To survive is easy. The hard thing is to know how to live.
>
> — *Annabelle Borne*

I shall leave aside all the associative links, forgotten images and fantasies, which enabled us to reveal in Annabelle the small abandoned baby-self, catastrophically searching for an omnipotent yet absent mother. All she could find was a surrogate cloth-mother with cotton-wool breasts, and for which, apparently, no true transitional object had ever been created. Any introjection of, or identification with a loving, caretaking mother, stopped at this point, depriving Annabelle of any possibility of being in contact with her own needs, or in any way fulfilling a maternal role towards herself. As in the analytic situation, she made magic, megalomanic demands upon people at the same time treating them like cloth monkeys and punishing them accordingly. In moments of tension she could neither contain, nor psychically elaborate upon her distress.

The next three years were spent in recognizing this dilemma and in studying the moments when the lonely, rage-filled baby occupied the whole of her inner psychic world; then, in putting this traumatized infant into communication with Annabelle Borne the adult.

Although these two sessions allowed me considerable insight into the way in which my patient thought about herself and her relation to the world — or rather the way in which she *prevented* herself from being able to think and feel about her involvement with internal or external objects — she found no immediate relief in our analytic work. Later she was able to tell me that the two years which followed this phase of the analysis had brought her more suffering than she had ever known. Nevertheless the working through of this psychic pain wrought a profound change in her which she herself called her "rebirth." I should add that she did not suffer alone. My own countertransference was sorely tried, but I was better able to put it to use. I had constantly to be on the lookout for her tendency to pulverize any nascent thoughts or feeling-states of which she became aware; and she would frequently evacuate these by trying (unconsciously) to get me to feel them instead. Further, I was in no way free from feelings of exasperation when she would systematically decry or destroy the meaning of any interpretation which promised to modify her stony feeling of anger and incomprehensible solitude. It was through analyzing my own perplexity that I discovered she felt *humiliated* by each discovery and each new turning in her analytic adventure. My compensation was that I no longer felt lost with her on this difficult journey. Even though my words often angered her I knew that she needed to hear them. For without my realizing it, my somewhat silent and expectant attitude during our first year of work together, had reproduced the original situation which she carried inside her, of an evanescent maternal imago which was both out of reach and persecutory at the same time. Thus Annabelle did not treat me like a real person. She accorded me as much individual status as a voracious nursling might do; she could not conceive of my having any independent thoughts or wishes which were not controlled by her; nor could she accept that I be occupied with any other person or thing than herself without feeling that this would be damaging to her. The painstaking exploration of her struggle allowed us to analyze her constant use of projective identification, and the inhibiting effect this exercised upon her constantly painful existence. Instead of immediately getting rid of any hurtful thoughts or depressed feelings which came to consciousness during the sessions, she would now try to hold on to them, and to put into words the unexpressed, at times inexpressible, fantasy and affect they aroused in her. Three years of patient work allowed us to (re-)construct and explore the contours of the empty desert of baby Annabelle's psychic world. The old-boot-analyst that one was unwillingly but compulsively bound to follow, the cloth-monkey-analyst with cotton-wool breasts that one was obliged to accept as nourishment, slowly became a *transference object* whose existence was recognized, and towards whom infantile needs and primitive wishes could now be attached, and talked about. Every object in my waiting room or consulting room, the slightest sign of the existence of any other people in my life (particularly other analysands), any change of clothing, furniture, my pots of flowers, all brought forth torrents of anger which seemed to Annabelle, not only painful, but impossible to contain, and to reflect upon. We needed many sessions to plumb the wells of hatred and despair which lay behind her earlier provocations. "You will never be able to imagine how much I hate you and envy you; how much I want to tear you apart and make you suffer."

Despite the fact that my existence as a separate individual, having needs, wishes, and rights which did not necessarily coincide with hers, was a source of constant pain, and in spite of the fact that the idealized object she projected upon me engendered a continuing narcissistic wound, at least I was also now part of her analytic process, and no longer a simple receptacle destined to contain all that was too heavy for her to carry alone; no longer a mummified mask for all the objects who had failed her in the past. We came to understand that she felt constantly persecuted by me, as she did by everyone in her entourage, but neither she nor I had been aware of this. Her despair, so long a part of her, had become virtually painless.

Role of Destructive Envy

The most important conflictual material at this stage of her analysis could be summed up under all that is included in the Kleinian concept of *envy*. Instead of being caught in the toils of jealousy and in conflict with the desire to triumph over the rivals for her mother's or father's love, she sought total *destruction* of any object belonging to the Other. In the light of this understanding, her sexually traumatic relationship with her brother took on a new significance. Through the sexual act she now possessed her mother's adored object — and in her fantasy she possessed it *in order to destroy it*. She had created an illusory solution which was not a psychotic but an erotic one, and thus could feel she had triumphed over the traumatic event. She was able for the first time to reveal the elements of her erotic scene, and this enabled us eventually to be able to analyze its significance. Her childhood and adult masturbation fantasies all turned around her brother. She would imagine him immobilized against a wall, while different kinds of "tortures" were carried out upon his sex; these were fantasied as being orgastically satisfying to the brother, and were highly exciting to herself. Thus she controlled in imagination her brother's sexual response. Under the guise of giving him pleasure his image was also protected against feelings of destructive hatred. As with many sexual deviations, her sexual game served several contradictory purposes (McDougall 1974): she as able to show and deny at the same time her incestuous wish; and more important, she was able to master actively what she had passively experienced, for she was now both author and actor of her fantasy-film, and no longer the victim of the rape which had been lived as a castration. It was now she, the all-powerful castrator. The disavowals included in her erotic fantasy also allowed her to triumph over the primal scene — by inventing a new one; and provided her with fantasy revenge upon the mother-son relationship. But it gave her no adequate resolution of her oedipal conflicts and also left her with a damaged image of her own body and sexuality. One part of her had never assumed her feminine sexual reality. When for example adolescent classmates talked about waiting to get their periods, she would mock them in her mind "because I was convinced that this would never happen to me. I was somehow different from all other girls in my imagination. When I finally discovered my own menstrual blood I didn't recognize it. I thought it was something due to masturbation. I kept it a secret for two months."

With regard to this nexus of sexual fantasy as well as the torture game upon her brother's penis, it is evident that "penis envy" is not an adequate explanation of its significance. The destructive elements of the fantasy went far beyond the traumatic experience, and also had primitive roots which were concerned with more archaic sexuality than the discovery and understanding of sexual differences. These roots led us back to the green sap of the mother's inaccessible breasts. The manifest "game" of her brother's castration, rendered ego-syntonic through erotization, hid a deeper fantasy, namely of controlling and destroying the breast-mother in order to possess for herself the magical green sap. Father and brother, symbolically represented as phallic appendages of the omnipotent mother, were regressively fantasied as being the contents of her breasts.

Without sex, without sap, without knowledge about how to live, Annabelle lived out defensively an unelaborated depression, poorly compensated by her particular form of relationship to others, more an act than an exchange, contact rather than communication, but nevertheless a living link.

Dissolution of the Idealizing Projection

In an effort to transmit her continuing experience that each day presented her with insurmountable problems, Annabelle would often talk of the "hardness" of life. The word recurred incessantly, attached at one time or another to each relationship, to all the part objects... the mother's stony breast, the brother's dangerous penis, the analyst's rigorous timetable, etc., etc. "I have come to realize that I have never for one minute felt comfortable — neither in my body nor in the presence of others. It's so hard, hard to feel good, hard to do the simplest things. Eating, walking, defecating, making love. So hard, so complicated. Why do I not have the secret? Why don't you give it to me, you mean, hard creature!" The analyst-breast, omnipotent idealized image had survived as an inner object in spite of the three years of "hard" blows dealt out to it by the suffering analysand-child, who occupied most of Annabelle's inner psychic space. There was no doubt that I now existed as a separate individual and also as an analyst, so that she could "use" me effectively to understand different aspects of the intersystemic war within her. (Winnicott 1971) But she refused all approach to the idealized, hard, omnipotent being who was supposed to contain the secret of life, as well as of *her* life; and I had to be patient while waiting for the possibility of interpreting this idealization. I was able eventually to make an intervention born in part out of my exasperation at not being able to get further on this question. "Why are you so hard? Who do you not tell me *how to live?* You stand there mocking me, waiting for me to discover everything all by myself." I replied that she asked me for a secret to which she alone held the key; that I did not know the answer, nor why she stopped the sap of life from running through her veins. I understood how much she was suffering but I too was discouraged by my own failure to be able to interpret better what she was experiencing. "I know you are trying to communicate this hard and terrible feeling," I said, "and it is a failure on my part somewhere to catch your message; I do realize that we are both going through a hard moment, and I feel I have let you down." This intervention produced an unexpected and explosive reaction — of joy. Could it be possible that an *analyst* did not understand? That an *analyst* could feel baffled, discouraged? That analysts were not *omniscient* had never once crossed Annabelle's mind in fifteen years of analysis. I was eventually able to show here that she needed to believe in this fetish like magical "knowledge" in order that she too, at the end of her analysis, might come into possession of it. Her discovery that no one was endowed with this ineffable quality inaugurated the final phase of her analysis with me. The exploration of her idealizing projection enabled her to mourn for its loss and to relinquish her own omnipotent demands: which included the demand to be spared every frustration, to triumph effortlessly over every "hard" reality, whether internal or external.

Annabelle was at last able to take care of the confused and desperate child within her, and to understand that there were other solutions than destructive elimination whenever she was faced with envious rage and voracious wishes. Construction began to replace destruction in ways which she alone could discover. For the first time she began to care genuinely about her body, her health, her appearance, her love life, her work life, all of which had been left untended, as though growth and change were impossible. She confided these changes shyly to me. In one of our final sessions she confided, significantly, that she had sown flower seeds in the spring, without telling anyone, in case they died. To her astonishment they had all borne flowers.

Some years later Annabelle sent me a beautiful book dealing with the artistic domain she had made her own, and of which she was the author. In a handwritten dedication she attributed to analysis the discovery of the essence of creativity — that *living was creating*.

PRIMITIVE COMMUNICATION

I have given the name of primitive communication to this kind of analytic discourse in order to emphasize its positive aspects, since in general we are much more aware of its negative effects. Patients who tell us many things as a way of not saying anything, of not revealing, even to themselves, what lies behind their communication, or who talk in order to keep the analyst at a distance, are of course maintaining strong resistance to the analytic relationship and mustering powerful forces against the analytic process itself. And they may even be quite conscious that this way of communicating with the analyst (and often with their whole entourage) is defensive, and in some way is eluding what they really would like to say. Nevertheless, to the extent that the analyst reacts to the patient's words, some form of communication is taking place. This latent communication is not a truly symbolic one and cannot be compared with the repressed thoughts which lie behind normal-neurotic analytic associations. Here instead we find words being used in place of action — as weapons, as camouflage, as a desperate cry for help, a cry of rage or of any other intense emotional state of which the patient is but dimly aware. These feeling states may have no connection with what the patient is recounting.

This kind of analytic material raises a number of questions. We might question the function of such "communication" and then compare it with the free-associative analytic monologue which ordinary neurotic patients produce in response to our invitation to do just that. We might also ask why certain patients are more apt to use verbal channels in this way and what may be inferred from such language "symptoms" with regard to traumatic childhood history and its ensuing effects upon ego structure and defenses. Although I shall deal briefly with these questions my main interest is the exploration of the way in which the analyst receives this kind of analytic communication, and how he may best use it to further the analytic process. This process depends to a high degree on language communication, and the particular mode of communication which we call free association allows us to explore the interpenetration of primary and secondary processes. The "basic rule" relies on the verbal expression of thoughts and feelings. And it is hoped that to the extent that the analysand can eventually allow ideas, fantasies, and emotional states free expression in ways in which he would not normally permit himself to function verbally this interpenetration of conscious and unconscious knowledge of himself will set the analytic process in motion. The invitation to "say everything" — along with its implicit counterpart, "and do nothing" — not only opens the way to transference affect but also enables the analysand in hearing his own words, to get to know his thoughts and feelings in an entirely new way. However, this expectation becomes questionable with individuals who use language in ways which alter its essential function, and more particularly in the analytic situation with its intimate dependence on language and communication.

What indeed are the aims of what I am calling primitive communication, and in what major ways does it differ from other verbal communications? What role does it play in psychic economy? To what system of internal object relationships is it entailed?

The Unconscious Aim of Primitive Communication

Although the efficacy of *words* in the communication of thoughts and emotions is considerably more limited than we like to admit, nevertheless the primary aim of verbal exchange among adults is the desire to communicate information to those to whom one chooses to address oneself. But this is far from being its only aim. *Communicate* — from the Latin communicare: to render common, to be in relationship with, to be connected — reveals its underlying etymological and affective meaning. All people in certain situations, and some people much of the time, use verbal communication literally as a way of maintaining a contact, being in relation with, or even being part of, "common to," another person. This vital link with the Other may override in importance the symbolic function which consists of the desire to *inform* someone of something. From such a viewpoint verbal communications might be considered an approximation to crying, calling out, screaming, growling, rather than to *telling* something. To this extent such communication would be a means not only of remaining in intimate connection but also a way of conveying and discharging emotion in direct fashion, with the intent to affect and arouse reactions in the Other.

The analytic situation, since it dispenses with the usual conventions of verbal exchange, is particularly apt to reveal unusual features in verbalization which might pass unnoticed in everyday conversation. (Rosen 1967) The austerity of the analytic protocol tends to highlight such differences. In Annabele Borne's analytic associations it was noted that her words had partially lost their communicative aim. In addition, this use of verbalization impeded the free association of ideas. The fact that we were able to discover together the wide gap between what she *said* and what she *felt*, between the content and its accompanying affect, finally allowed her discourse to become meaningful to both of us, and the patient to recover many lost feelings. At the same time we were able to understand that she frequently spoke with the main intention of arousing feeling in the *analyst* without knowing why this was so important, nor what this feeling represented to her. Her need to induce feeling-states in others was in fact connected with early traumatic situations in which she had been unable to deal with intense emotion and did not know how to communicate her need for help; instead of containing and elaborating her emotional pain and using it to think further, she had effaced all knowledge of its existence or meaning. Thus past events and affective experience had been simply ejected from consciousness as though they had never existed. For the first time many of these emotional states were able to achieve psychical representation. Communications like those of Annabelle Borne differ in an essential way from those found in an ordinary neurotic associative process, even when these are directed towards arousing feeling in the analyst. In the latter, the attempt to let one's thought and fantasy roam freely tends to reveal, behind the patent communication, a latent theme to which the analyst is "listening." The individual unknown to himself is communicating another story, revealing himself an actor upon another stage, but for which the script, once conscious, has been forgotten. Such secret scripts and dissimulated scenes are of course present in patients who use language to penetrate the listener and provoke reaction from him, but from the standpoint of analytic work vitiate the aim of laying bare this latent underlying mean and render the capturing of repressed ideas and memories peculiarly difficult. Meanwhile, the analyst is likely to feel bewildered and invaded by affects which hinder his analytic functioning — *unless he pays attention to them*.

The depressive and frustrating feelings which Annabelle Borne aroused in me had little to do with repressed ideas in her analytic material. The primary aim of her words might well have been described as an attempt to discharge, through the very act of talking, pent-up and painful tension, whose content and causes were unknown to her. The secret aim of which she was able to become conscious was to *share* a pain which could not yet be expressed through the medium of language and was not capable of being thought about. It was a demand to be *heard rather than listened to;* a need for communion rather than communication. In the months to come we were able to pinpoint the moments at which such communication became imperative. Faced with the slightest hint of a painful thought or feeling, Annabelle would immediately manage to pulverize its psychic representation. As a consequence she had no true awareness of the existence of the idea or affect in question. But the debris of this psychic elimination had the effect of altering her perception of others, and in consequence her manner of feeling about them and communicating with them. And the same thing occurred in the analytic transference.

Of course, the various themes that Annabelle Borne used to fill up the essential silence left in the wake of all that had been repudiated from consciousness were not devoid of significance in themselves, nor of any reference to repressed material. It was, for example, patent that, lurking behind the persecutory images and ideas, the problem of *envy* loomed large, but it remained out of interpretable reach as long as the ejected feelings of depression, abandonment, and deprivation — along with their inevitable corollary, intense feelings of hatred — remained blocked from access to psychic expression, blocked therefore to verbal reflection and expression. In a sense many of Annabelle's remarks and observations were devoid of interest for her; she was relatively unaware that they might have a potential effect upon her analyst or her friends and family, or any others with whom she maintained communicative links. The unconscious benefit thus procured was the protection of her inner object world from destruction due to her envious rage and narcissistic mortification. At the same time it permitted her to maintain contact with the external object world in spite of the continual feeling of dissatisfaction which her relationships afforded her. Perhaps too, her aggressive contact strengthened her feeling of identity. But all this was obtained at a high price. Not only did she feel overwhelmed by the "hardness" of existence in all its aspects, she suffered a veritable impairment of her capacity to *think*, in particular with regard to the causes of her mental suffering. With her defensive, almost brutal elimination of awareness of affective pain she was in fact hampered in dealing with her genuine *needs* and not only with the fulfillment of wishes. At the beginning of our analytic work together she was relatively unaware of possessing any personal desires other than the wish to be "comfortable," and was equally unaware of what she demanded and expected from others.

The Demand to be Understood Without Words

This way of experiencing raises the question of the space occupied in psychic life by the external objects. Implicitly the Other is called upon to capture and deal with an inexpressible appeal. In a sense it is a demand to be understood without passing by the normal verbal channels, to be understood by mere signs. *Infans*, the infant unable as yet to talk, must have his needs heard and dealt with in this way, since he has no other means of communication. When he is capable of *asking* it is no longer a question of vital need, but until this time he is totally dependent upon his mother's interpretation of his cries and gestures. To the extent that an infant can conceive of Another who will respond to his cry he may be said to be "communicating" in this primitive way. At this point he has already reached a certain stage of psychic growth in regard to the object; he no longer feels that the Other is a hallucinatory part of himself (which might be equated with a psychotic form of object relation) but instead believes the Other to be *all-powerful*, in which case the response of the object to the signs emitted is interpreted as positive because the object wants the infant to be gratified, or in the case of a negative response, as a refusal because he wants the infant to suffer. That is to say, this type of relationship is under the sway of primary process thinking: if good things or bad things occur, in either case they are felt to derive from the omnipotent desire of the all-powerful Other. This Other automatically understands and responds as he wishes! (This type of thinking prevails in what we might call narcissistic character pathology). With regard to this projected idealization and expectation of the external world, we are sometimes inclined, as Bion (1970) has pointed out, to overlook the fact that, in spite of the satisfaction which symbolic communication eventually brings to the growing individual, to be *obliged* to speak in order to be understood, and to have wishes granted, is a continuing narcissistic wound in everyone's unconscious. For certain individuals, fusion and communion, rather than separateness and communication, are the only authentic means of relating to another person. (One patient who regarded separateness as a calamity used to say that if she had to *tell* her husband what she needed or wished for in any field then his complying with her wish no longer had any significance. It was indeed a proof that he did not love her.)

Fusional communion, that archaic form of loving which is the nursling's right, is still implicitly awaited by certain adults. Any threat of separation, or reminder of subjective difference such as having to convey one's wishes through verbalization, can only spell punishment and rejection. We are dealing here with the small "infant" inside the adult, who has never truly understood the role of verbal communication as a symbolic means of making one's desires known. No doubt these are the babies who were not sensitively "listened to" and "interpreted" by those who brought them up. My own clinical experience with patients who live out this inarticulate drama leads me to believe that their childhoods were marked by incoherent relationships with the earliest objects, and in a context in which the inevitable frustrations of human growing and development were not tempered with sufficient gratification to make them bearable, so that the supreme reward of individuation and subjective identity was not acquired with pleasure, but instead continues to be lived as a rejection and an insult. The fact that one's wishes can be both communicated and responded to is scarcely believed to be true. Such was the case with Annabelle.

One further factor: the demand to be understood without words implies also a terror of facing disappointment or refusal of any kind. This is felt not only as a narcissistic wound but as an unbearable pain which cannot be contained and psychically elaborated, and which may destroy one. Thus the ineluctable factors which structure human reality — otherness, sexual difference, the impossibility of magic fulfillment of wishes, the inevitability of death — have not become meaningful. Otherness with its reward of personal identity and privacy; sexual difference with the reward of sexual desire; the refinding of magic fulfillments in creativity; the acceptance of death itself as the inevitable end which gives urgent and important significance to life — all may be lacking for these patients. Life then runs the risk of being "meaningless" and "hard." Other people tend to be seen as vehicles for *externalizing* this painful inner drama of living. It is in fact the creation of a system of *survival*. At least contact with others is assured and something is communicated. Many people with this way of relating find themselves pushed to manipulate others, although unaware that this is what they are doing, in order to bring about the catastrophes they already anticipate. Thus relationships are often directed towards proving the inevitability of preconceived conclusions concerning them. This is another way of "communicating" one's distress and of combatting one's feeling of utter impotence in the face of overwhelming forces. There are many ways in which such a system of interpersonal relations may be expressed theoretically: in terms of persecutory anxiety and projective identification (Klein, Grinberg); of the need of the subject to use others as containers (Bion); of the urgent necessity to recover lost parts of oneself, the "self-objects" (Kohut); the tendency to deny the independent existence of others as a defense against pathological forms of object-relating (Kernberg); the "false-self" concept (Winnicott); the use of others as "transitional objects" (Modell).

The Inability to Tolerate the Separate Existence of Others

Out of touch with important aspects of themselves, these patients have difficulty in accepting that others are equally prone to anxiety, depression, frustration and irritation. Thus the struggle against archaic fantasies and emotions is reinforced by the struggle against outer reality and the pain of others. Like nurslings forced to become autonomous before their time, they must be prepared to stave off all sources of conflict and psychic suffering, whether these come from inner or outer psychic space. Unknown to themselves, they are working with a model of human relations in which separate identity must be vigorously denied since absence and difference have not been compensated by a well-constructed inner object world; thus the patients' own feeling of identity is unstable. Nor is it easy then to grasp what others are trying to communicate, and assumptions about human motives run the risk of being erroneous. Separateness is rejected as a postulate and in its stead we find the constant externalization of conflict in an attempt to keep everything in its place, and in this way exercise an illusory control over other people's reactions. These are the "wise babies" described by Ferenczi, who must control everything with the babylike means at their disposal. We must of course admit that such an imperious nursling slumbers inside all of us, but he is usually confined to the omnipotent world of dreams. Neurotic patients discover this megalomanic child within themselves, with astonishment; others, like Annabelle, discover that throughout their lives they have been striving to reinstate the rights of this demanding infant, and most of all, his right to be heard and his need to be in meaningful communication with others. Although the adult ego is unaware of his existence, the angry and desperate child is screaming to be allowed to breathe. Only thus is there any hope that this inarticulate infant may have access to a more elaborated form of self-expression.

It is evident that the analyst who receives such communications in analysis finds himself listening to a discourse which will not make sense if he consistently treats it as a normal-neurotic transmission of ideas and affects under the sway of free association. He will seek in vain for repressed ideas pushing their way into consciousness, and will be forced to realize that he is observing a part of the personality dominated by primitive mechanisms of defense: disavowal, splitting, foreclosure, all of which serve to exclude a number of psychic events from the symbolic chain, particularly those that are apt to produce psychic pain. We might well ask ourselves to what extent it is possible to penetrate the barriers of primal repression and explore the basic layers of the personality structure. Can we hope to "hear" that which has never been formulated in ways in which it might form part of preconscious ideas, that which has never been encoded as thought and thus not preserved in a form accessible to recall and to symbolic elaboration? Here the limits of the analytic process must be called into question.

I would suggest, however, that to the extent that areas of experience have been repudiated from the psychic world to be projected into the external world, these ejected fragments of experiencing are expressed in behavior, or constantly enacted in the form of primitive exchange described in this paper. In certain privileged situations and moments we can "hear" at least the distress signals; we come to know that these signs are an indication of profound pain which cannot yet be fully recognized by the individual as personal suffering. He feels blocked, hampered, hamstrung, and furious with the world. This is the basic message.

THE ROLE OF COUNTERTRANSFERENCE

How does this message strike the analyst? In the first place the analytic ear may be rapidly alerted by the particular *use of words*. In the case of Annabelle Borne there was a notable discordance between content and affect, so that much angry and discontented feeling was in fact hiding inexpressible depression; with other patients in a similar inner drama, we find ourselves listening to an interminable monologue recounting daily facts which seem to have no further echo beyond the mere words, either for the analysand or the analyst. Others again use words in ways which make us feel confused, that is to say, the ordinary associative links such as we find in everyday conversation and everyday analytic communications may be lacking. In Rosen's illuminating article *Disorders of Communication* (1967) he speaks of subtle disturbances in the encoding of thought processes which emerge in the analytic situation, and of the fact that the analyst must sometimes become aware of the latent content through media other than words — signal systems such as gestures, posture, facial expression, intonation, pictograms etc. I think that we are often attuned to such subliminal messages well in advance of our being able ourselves to encode and verbalize what we have understood. Arnold Modell (1973), in an important article on affects in the analytic situation, suggests that the capturing of affect may well preceed the acquisition of language. On the basis of personal experience with very young babies (who often react in striking fashion to the affective states of those who are looking after them) and also deductions drawn from my analytic observations I would go further and say that the transmission of affect is unquestionably earlier than symbolic communication. Modell's further observation that an analytic discourse which lacks affect is a sign that the analytic process has come to a halt, seems to me highly pertinent to analytic research into the nature of communication.

A further observation concerning "primitive communication" is that veritable "free association" (with all the limitations and filtering systems that normally accompany it) is lacking. There is no *einfall* (which means literally a sudden upsurge or breakthrough of a thought, fantasy, or image from some inner but hitherto unrecognized source). This interpenetration of primary and secondary processes, hallmark of a functioning psychoanalytic process, is not taking place, and thus tends to give a featureless aspect to the analytic monologue. Although it may seem like an "empty" communication it will often produce a feeling of "fullness" in the analyst, a frustrating feeling to which he must turn his attention. In the analysand's desire to be intimately "linked" with the analyst through his verbalization, he may take little heed of the fact that the analyst is apt to respond emotionally to the content especially if it is depressive, aggressive, or anxiety arousing, and there is correspondingly little questioning of the supposition that the analyst will be equally pleased to be linked through this verbal stream — even though it be, for example, a vituperative monologue which takes the analyst as its target, or a confused discourse which takes no account of the difficulty in seizing its meaning. Thus in their efforts to remain plugged in, as it were, to the analyst's mind, these patients are both appealing for help and pushing the analyst away at the same time. The patient may be said to be under the sway of a condensation, not of thought, but of aim. He seeks to obtain love and attention which will reassure him that he is being heard and being held, that he exists, and at the same time must punish the Other for all the bad and hard things he has had to endure in his existence. It could be conceived of as a demand upon an idealized breast, of maternal function, such as a nursling might experience it were he able to express it.

If these patients do not talk about what really concerns them — their contradictory seeking, their pain in living, their difficulty in feeling understood or truly alive — it is because *they do not know it*. Unaware of the impact of their words they are equally unaware that they too occupy a psychic space in the minds of others. The others are considered to be alive, existent, and therefore need little else, whereas the subject of this distress is screaming out his right to become alive too, with the underlying assumption that the world owes him this. Thus for many patients the discovery of this dilemma may be an inaugural experience encountered in the analytic situation. The analysand may for the first time make a conscious distinction between himself and Another, with the recognition that both exist, each with his individual and separate psychic reality. People with no clear representation of their own psychic space and their own identity tend otherwise to relate to others in ways which elude *their* psychic reality too; that is to say, they tend to perceive only what accords with their preconceived notion of the Other, and of the world in general, and to eliminate perceptions and observations which do not fit with the existing idea.

This way of relating has a marked effect upon the transference relationship. Much of the force of transference comes from the interplay between the analyst as a figure of imagination and projection, and the analyst as a real being. As an imaginary object he becomes the eventual target for all the investments attached to the original inner objects, whereas his qualities as a real person remain largely unknown to the analysand. Patients who operate within the relational framework described in this paper maintain only a minimal distance between the imaginary and the real analyst, so that transference projections are rarely perceived as such. Neither partner to the analytic tandem will be endowed with any clearly delineated identity status. This sort of analytic relationship might be included in the concept of an idealized narcissistic transference as described by Kohut, or as an attempt at fusional denial of separateness, or again as an attempt to establish a pathological form of archaic object relations as envisaged in Kernberg's papers.

Such patients will tend to use a model of human relationships based on the postulates which belong to primary process thinking — that is to say that all things bad or good which happen to the subject are due to another person's wish, and indeed his good or bad will towards the individual. There is thus little questioning of the important events in his life as far as his own participation is concerned. In analysis if the patient feels badly he is quite likely to believe that the analyst is indifferent because deep down he *wishes his analysand to suffer*. If and when these analysands become conscious of their own projected aggressive and destructive wishes they are more than likely to stifle such feelings and rapidly eject their associated ideas from consciousness. Thus they often do not know when they are angry, frightened, or unhappy.

As already emphasized we are not dealing with mechanisms of repression or isolation but of repudiation from the psychic world, splitting and projective identification. In consequence the principal anxieties to be faced are more concerned with the self and the maintenance of identity than with sexuality and the fulfillment of desire; "psychotic" anxiety mobilized by fear of disintegration and dedifferentiation takes a larger place than "neurotic" anxiety attached to all that is included in the classical concept of the castration complex. If the latter runs the risk of producing sexual and work inhibitions or symptoms, the former disturbs the whole pattern of relationship with others. There will be a tendency to use others as parts of oneself, or in the place of transitional objects where they are destined to play a protective role and to be used to filter hostile impulses. Within the analytic relationship this tends to create the type of fundamental transference which Stone (1967) referred to in his classic paper on the analytic situation, that is, transference affect which is more concerned with otherness and the fear of (wish for) fusion than with the transferences typical of the neurotic structure.

The symptomatic kind of analytic discourse which ensues may be a manifestation of a number of psychic ills. In a sense the "signs" discerned here as being the unformulated but true communication, might be regarded as minimal elements of psychotic thought and expression; nevertheless there is no contamination of thought, nor do we find the surrealistic use of words so markedly present in psychotic verbalization. Annabelle Borne had not created a personal grammar; there was no confusion between the signifier and the thing signified. But she had a similar fragility in her idea of herself and her relationship to others, in which the limits were ill-defined, suggesting a lack of early structurization of a stable self-image, and consequently an unclear picture of others. This form of relationship may well give rise to a form of personal esperanto whose communicative aim might have psychotic overtones. The idiosyncratic use of language which may pass unnoticed as such in the every day world since it respects syntax and symbolic reference, seeks nevertheless, in the way that psychotic communications do, to restore the primary mother-child unity, to be understood, through and in spite of one's way of communicating. The distinction may be said to lie here: patients like Annabelle Borne do not use words in accordance with primary process functioning, but their way of relating to others follows the primary process model, namely, total dependence upon the omnipotent will of the Other — thus is language used in the service of this form of relationship. Perhaps in this way psychotic disorganization is prevented, for these patients are not detached from outer reality; they do not dream up situations, causes, and perceptions which exist only in their inner world. Instead they utilize others, in accordance with what they find, who are apt to take in and give back to the subject something that is offered and something else that is demanded. Nevertheless the patient may be said to be "creating" the meaning that the other person has for him without taking too much account of the Other's reality, while at the same time submitting himself to this Other, and suffering accordingly. I would add that such relationships are by no means rare in the world at large, and that relatively few such people seek analytic help.

My contention is that when we find this way of communicating, and relating reproduced in the analytic setting, we have indications of early psychic suffering, presumably rooted in that period of time in which the small child tries to use the mother as a subsidiary part of himself and so deals with vital needs and conflicts through the "language" at his disposal. We might say that part of the patient is "outside himself," in analysis as in everyday life, and he therefore treats others, or the analyst, as vagrant segments of himself, which he naturally attempts to control.

It is evident that this will give rise to countertransference phenomena which are different from those that arise with the normal-neurotic analysand. For the latter, equipped as he is with the familiar neurotic forms of defense against psychic pain and conflict, the analyst becomes a figure of projection for his own inner objects, since his mental conflict stems in large part from intrapsychic struggles. Such a patient introjects a representation of the analyst who thus becomes an object of the analysand's ego, although constituted differently from the genuine inhabitants of his inner universe. The analyst is, so to speak, an immigrant with a temporary visa who draws upon himself forbidden desires, idealized representations, threats, fear, anger, etc., belonging to the original objects. The analyst's unique position in this psychic world provides the transference relationship with considerable force, and as already emphasized, permits the patient to measure and explore the distance that separates the analyst as an imaginary person from the analyst as a real being with an individual identity. It is in this space between the visions of the analyst that the most fruitful interpretative and reconstructive work is accomplished. Countertransference interference, if present, stems mainly from unresolved personal problems of the analyst — and it is not an uncommon occurrence for a "good neurotic analysand" to become aware of these, see clearly that they are not a matter of his own projections, and point them out!

But in the case where the distinction between transference projection and reality observation is blurred the way in which the analyst receives the patient's transference expression is likely to differ. Hidden in the shape of "pseudocommunication" that seeks less to inform (literally: to give form to) the analyst of his thoughts and feelings than to get rid of painful intrapsychic conflict and arouse reaction in the analyst, we must wonder how the latter may best capture and interpret this "language." In the beginning he does not "hear" the message nor does he immediately become aware of its emotional impact. It is difficult to detect that which is missing, particularly since its ejection leaves no unconscious trace, and no neoreality has been invented to take its place as with psychotic patients. Gradually affect is mobilized and indeed accumulates in the analyst; while the analysand flattens or distorts his affective experience the analyst becomes literally "affected." The patient's associations have a penetrating or impregnating effect which is missing in the usual neurotic transference relationship and analytic monologue. What has been foreclosed from the world of psychic representation cannot be "heard" as a latent communication. It is the emotional infiltration which contains the seeds of future interpretations, but in order to be able to formulate these the analyst must first understand why his patient's discourse affects him in the way it does. I would agree fully with Giovacchini (1977) when he points out with regard to delusional patients that to view them as unanalyzable on the basis of an insufficiently self-observing ego is too glib a dismissal of a complex problem. With the kind of patients I am describing the analyst is apt to feel in the first instance that he has somewhere along the line *ceased functioning adequately as an analyst* with this particular analysand.

Although the analogy cannot be carried too far, the analyst is at these moments in the situation of the mother who is trying to understand why her baby is crying in some angry or distressed fashion. At this stage it is evident that the baby can have no identity over and beyond what he represents for his mother, and it is she who must *interpret* his signs and give them meaning — that is, tender them into communication. In Bion's terminology she must fulfill the role of being her child's thinking apparatus until such time as he is able to think for himself. The analyst of course has more modest aims than those which would imply becoming his patient's thinking apparatus! It is not his role to teach his analysand how to perceive the world and how to react to it. At most he hopes to lead his patient to discover who he is — and for whom. But to do so he must be prepared to decode the sounds of distress which lie behind the angry or confused associations.

One is tempted to surmise that these analysands had mothers who for various reasons were unable to "listen" to their infants and to give meaning to their primitive communications. Perhaps the mother herself reacted with resentment and rejection to her baby's unformulated demands, as though they were a personal attack upon her, or reflected a narcissistic failure on her own part; in such cases she would fail in her role of "interpreter" who must teach her baby to express his needs, to discover his desires, finally to be able to *think* for himself. But then this also requires a mother who grants her child the *right to independent thoughts* even if these run counter to her own at many points. We have here another seed to the creating of communication disorders.

Whatever the reasons may have been, the analyst who inherits this psychic puzzle will feel himself "manipulated" by his analysand in the latter's attempt to protect himself from psychic pain, and avoid, for ever after, becoming the plaything of another's desire. By writing the script in advance he lays out the scene in such a way that little is left to chance — other than the capacity of the chosen actors to fulfill their roles. Traumatic thoughts and feelings are in this manner controlled through immediate evacuation from the subject's own psyche, to be played out in the external world, an attempt at magic fulfillment and narcissistic reparation.

The analyst must be prepared to capture the patient's difficulty in thinking about himself through the block the analyst experiences in his own thinking, in order eventually to recover the expelled representations and the stifled affects. These may then be rendered into archaic fantasy, capable of being expressed verbally, and the associated feelings may then be contained, and explored, within the analytic relationship. The durability of this relationship functions as a guarantee that such powerful affects may be safely experienced and expressed without damage to either analyst or patient. I think this is what Winnicott means when he says that "the reliability of the analyst is the most important factor (or more important than the interpretations) because the patient did not experience such reliability in the maternal care of infancy, and if the patient is to make use of such reliability he will need to find it for the first time in the analyst's behaviour" (Winnicott 1960).

It is probable that what has been submitted to primal repression cannot be communicated except through "signs" such as those described here; and that these signs will in the first place be registered through countertransference feelings. The inadequate functioning of the analyst at these times will manifest itself in many subtle ways. In addition to feeling manipulated he may find himself reacting to the sessions with boredom or irritation, or catch himself giving aggressive interpretations, maintaining a stubborn silence, or wandering in his mind along paths which have no relationship to the patient's associations. In spite of all the well-known pitfalls of countertransference affect, I am obliged to suppose here that these "signs" in the analyst are more than the unique reflection of his own inner emotional state, or his unconscious reactions to the patient's monologue, and that we are dealing, not with a repressed, but with a primitive communication, not decodable in the usual way. If at such times the analyst persists in seeking repressed content, in giving interpretations as though to neurotic material, in replying aggressively, or turning away in silence, then the *analyst is acting out.* He is now obstructing the analytic process by his *countertransference resistance.* Like all other human beings we, as analysts, have difficulty in hearing or perceiving what does not fit into our preestablished codes. Our own unresolved transference feelings here play a role, since the garnering of analytic knowledge has been accomplished and deeply impregnated with transference affect and thus tends to carry an inbuilt resistance of its own, making it difficult for us to "hear" all that is being transmitted. We tend to resent the patient who does not progress in accordance with our expectations, or who reacts to our efforts to understand as though they were hostile attacks upon him. These problems, added to our personal weaknesses, provide us with a delicate task.

Thus Annabelle Borne's analysis had come to a standstill due to my own inability to catch the meaning, and to examine my countertransference expectations and irritations — up until the moment when I told her she sought not so much to communicate her ideas and emotions as to make me feel sad and helpless. When she was, so to speak, able to take back and possess her own tears, we could then listen together to the paralyzed, unhappy child entrapped within her. From that time forward we could permit this child to grow and to express herself for the first time.

The way in which we normally listen to our analysands, a free-floating attention similar to that asked of them, might better be described as free-floating theorization, and it is notable that with the patients under consideration here, it is difficult to utilize our various "floating theories" about the patient and the nature of his analytic tie to us. Such floating hypotheses take much longer to organize themselves. This is due in part to the analysand's particular way of communicating and in part to the difficult roles he implicity needs us to assume on his behalf. The attitude of "expectant silence" which to the neurotic spells hope, and opens a psychic space wherein long-buried desires may once more come to light, offers little but desolation and death to patients like Annabelle. Their need to feel that they exist in other people's eyes, to feel truly alive, to a large degree dominates all other wishes, and invades almost totally the territory of desire. The unsure limits between one and the other makes the analysis of the relationship between the two partners hazardous, and the mourning for lost objects difficult. It is impossible to mourn the loss of an object one has never possessed, or whose existence has never been truly recognized as distinct from one's own, or as an integral part of one's inner world. On this shifting sand "transference" interpretations are not constructive, and indeed run the risk of perpetuating the misunderstandings and mutual distortions of the first communications between mother and child. Thus silence, or the so-called "good analytic interpretation," instead of creating a potentially vital space for feelings and thoughts to come into being, or stimulating further associations and memories through which a new way of experiencing may come to life, runs the risk of opening instead on to the silence of the primal unconscious, psychic death, nothingness.

Nevertheless, all that has been stifled by the force of primal repression remains potentially active, and indeed actual, since it is inevitably ejected into the outer world. All that has been silenced becomes a message-in-action, and it is this action-communication, language used as an act, which may install itself within the analytic situation, there to express itself through signs and secret codes. It is then possible for the analyst to aid his patients to stop the psychic hemorrhage created through the continual acting-out and direct discharge of tension, pain and confusion; to render the action-symptoms apt for expression through language, and the patient apt to undertake his analytic adventure.

References

Bion, W. (1970). *Attention and Interpretation*. London: Tavistock. Reprinted in *Seven Servants*. New York: Jason Aronson, 1977.

Giovacchini, P. (1977). The impact of delusion and the delusion of impact. *Contemporary Psychoanalysis* 13:429-441. See Chapter 11.

McDougall, J. (1974). The anonymous spectator. *Contemporary Psychoanalysis* 10:289-310.

Modell, A. (1973). Affects and psychoanalytic knowledge. In *Annual of Psychoanalysis* 1:112-124.

Stone, L. (1967). The psychoanalytic situation and transference. Postscript to an earlier communication. *Journal of the American Psychoanalytic Association* 15:3-58.

Rosen, V. (1967). Disorders of communication. *Journal of the American Psychoanalytic Association* 15:467-490.

Winnicott, D. (1960). The theory of the parent-infant relationship. In *The Maturational Processes and the Facilitating Environment*. New York: International Universities Press, 1965.

———(1971). The uses of an object and relating through identifications. In *Playing and Reality*. New York: Basic Books.

Chapter 13

THE ANALYST'S EXPERIENCE WITH JEALOUSY

HAROLD F. SEARLES, M.D.

PRIMITIVE JEALOUSY PHENOMENA

In a recent paper entitled "Jealousy Involving An Internal Object" (1979) I stated in summary that —

Jealousy which is related to an internal object within either oneself or the other person in an ostensibly two-person situation is at the heart of much severe and pervasive psychopathology and accounts, in psychoanalytic treatment, for much of the unconscious resistance, on the part of both patient and analyst, to the analytic process. These jealousy phenomena, derived basically from inordinately powerful ego-splitting processes in the original infant-mother relationship wherein the infant's earliest ego-formation was taking place, constitute a much more powerful source of severe psychopathology than do those jealousy phenomena referable to the oedipal phase of development.

These primitive jealousy phenomena are among the most powerful determinants of, for example, ego-fragmentation, depersonalization, castration anxiety and, in the transference relationship, negative therapeutic reaction. These phenomena, being referable to the earliest infantile phases of ego development when no clear differentiation between human and nonhuman, or between animate and inanimate, ingredients of the experienced self-and-world had yet been achieved, often are found in the transference-relationship to involve nonhuman objects which have the jealousy-engendering connotation of actual human beings.

Such jealousy phenomena may become detectable only after prolonged analytic work has occurred, by which time the analyst and patient have come to possess a degree of emotional significance for one another approximately equal to that which the internal object — or ego fragment — in question has for its possessor.

Melanie Klein's concepts [1957] concerning the infant's primary envy of the mother's breast, his resultant feeling that a good and a bad breast exist, and the consequences of these experiences for his later ego development, are of fundamental relevance for the formulations which I have presented here. [pp. 399-400]

That paper contains a relatively detailed theoretical discussion as well as a review of the relevant literature. The present paper is made up largely of descriptions of my psychoanalytic therapy with two chronically schizophrenic patients; these descriptions highlight the role of such "internal object jealousy." The countertransference aspects of my work with these patients will be described time and again, although not focused upon exclusively.

These two clinical narratives were written in 1974, as part of an intended monograph concerning internal-object jealousy. In the interim, each of these patients has continued in psychoanalytic therapy with me, and each has continued to improve. The first of them, Miss Herman (pseudonym), had to be rehospitalized at Chestnut Lodge for about six months, but has resumed recently her full outpatient status, and is now better integrated than I have ever seen her. The second of these patients, Mrs. Douglas (also a pseudonym), continues as an inpatient at Chestnut Lodge, but shows during her sessions with me a degree of ego functioning which is appreciably better than was characteristic of her in 1974. She will soon be allowed to visit her relatives, who live at some distance. There is considerable reason to hope that she will be able to move to outpatient status within a couple of years.

At the present writing, Miss Herman and I have been working together twenty-six years ago last month; Mrs. Douglas and I shall have been working together for twenty-six years within another six months. Both in psychoanalytic therapy, Mrs. Douglas's treatment has been at a frequency of four hours per week throughout, and Miss Herman's on a basis of four hours per week until a year and a half ago, when we agreed to reduce the number of hours to three per week. Neither of these patients has had drug therapy in all this time, beyond occasional nighttime sedation. A detailed history of Mrs. Douglas's illness, and of some other aspects of the earlier years of my work with her, is included in another of my published papers (1972). For more than twelve years I have sound-recorded (with her knowledge) all her sessions, and have preserved these tapes for research purposes. This communication is presented in the belief that not only the jealousy phenomena, but also the more general countertransference experience with such staggeringly long-range treatment endeavors as these two, are of inherent interest to my colleagues.

THE CASE OF MISS HERMAN

Miss Esther Herman, a forty-one-year-old woman with paranoid schizophrenia, was transferred to Chestnut Lodge after a year of unsuccessful treatment at another hospital. After many years of living an increasingly reclusive life, as a kind of maid-and-companion to her elderly widowed mother, she had become acutely psychotic; by the time of her arrival at the Lodge, her psychosis had settled into chronicity. Our work together brought to light a very severe impoverishment of her personal identity as a human being, and a corresponding predominance of identity-kinship with various nonhuman ingredients of her surroundings. Having become, evidently, troubled about the depth of her emotional involvement with her pet cat, she had said — among those personally uncharacteristic philosophical utterances that emerged from her in her acute psychosis, as reported by her older siblings — "People should love people, not cats." In my work with her — a small, slight woman — I found her to express anxiety lest the wind blow her away like a piece of tissue paper; it required a number of years of treatment before her feeling of corporeal insubstantiality gave way to the delighted and relieved realization that "I have weight!"

Meanwhile, she often circled despondently on the lawn of the hospital, like a bird with a broken wing, or sat crumpled for long periods on the grass there. A private patient of mine in that period came to my office looking shaken, and reported that he had just passed, on the lawn, what he had thought to be a pile of clothing, and had seen a woman uncannily materialize, moving slowly but unmistakably, from it.

During the earlier years of treatment, this woman's few friends and acquaintances had been overtly pitying and condescending toward her because of the constricted life she was leading; but there developed much evidence that behind their pity lay much envy of her apartness from the many frustrations of their more ordinary human lives—their marital problems, career concerns, and so on. In my own work with her, her underlying fears lest she be exposed to envy caused her to cling tenaciously to images of herself as being far more impoverished than, overall, she actually was. For example, before very long she had improved sufficiently to be allowed various "privileges" which many of her fellow-patients, even more incapacitated than she, had not attained; but she clung tenaciously to a view of herself as having nothing, and chronically expressed bitter envy and resentment of people around her, whose lives in general she perceived as relatively trouble-free.

Her mother, who died of a coronary occlusion about two years after Miss Herman's admission to Chestnut Lodge, had held, according to the social worker who interviewed her, a remarkably rigid and constricted image of the daughter as essentially a nice little girl. The older siblings were much concerned to protect the mother from the impact of the daughter's illness, and the mother clearly could not imagine that once out of the hospital her daughter would be anyone at all different from the nice little girl the mother had always known her to be. During the first several months of my work with the patient, I heard on endless occasions, during the otherwise predominantly silent sessions: "I was always a nice little girl—I went to the corner grocery store"—repeated such a maddeningly great number of times as to indicate that this was all the life she had been allowed to have, either in her own eyes or in those of her mother. The two had functioned without any overt dissension over the years, and I thought accurate the social worker's impression that "Esther had lived as just the dim shadow of her mother."

Miss Herman showed, from the beginning of her stay at the Lodge, a severe splitting in the Kleinian sense, as regards her introjects, and a corresponding power in fostering splits in her interpersonal milieu. The members of her family were in her view, for literally several years, totally good and blameless, and her loyalty to them was unbroken; while the staff of the hospital, especially me, were blamed by her for all her difficulties. During our sessions she clearly strove to maintain an angelic, "nice little girl" self-image—a self-image which could not at all accommodate any sexual or aggressive feelings; this involved her reacting to me, much of the time, as correspondingly diabolical and malevolent.

In a context of her paranoid berating me as the principal cause of her illness and incarceration, and therefore of her separation from her family, she would say, "My family want me well." But this statement of hers acquired, as the months and years went on, an increasingly woeful tone, an increasingly strong hint of her dawning realization that her family wanted no part of her unless she were "well"—unless she were able to become again the constricted caricature of a person she had long been, prior to her acute psychosis.

After the first several months, her psychotherapeutic sessions came very much to life in a setting of having stormy and venomous arguments with one another—probably linked genetically with the recurrent "squabbling," as the family called it, between herself and her older sister, who had shared the same room until the patient was in her twenties. I knew at the time that our arguments had a sexual component, for we would go into a kind of orgastic ecstasy of self-righteous vituperation at one another. I now realize, in retrospect, that there was a jealous component in them also; it was very much as though there were one angel in the room, and each of us was self-righteously and vindictively demonstrating that he (or she) was that angel, the other being exposed as a devil. In this dimension of the transference situation, the jealous competition evidently was for the role of Mother's Angel.

She was enormously formidable in her power to mobilize ordinarily unconscious guilt in the other person. She is the only patient I have ever found so upsetting that I had to prematurely terminate the treatment session. This happened twice in my work with her. Once, I recall, was on an occasion when the session was held in her room on a locked ward, and she confronted me with some imperfectly laundered item which had come back from the hosptial laundry. I felt so stung, so infuriated, by her treating me entirely as though I were the hospital laundress who had done the item, that I stormed out of the room. I can now believe, in retrospect, that I was at the time unconsciously jealous of the hospital laundress, as having, despite her "failure," a far simpler job than my task as this difficult woman's would-be psychotherapist.

Pitting Superego Figures in Jealous Competition

Only after many years of therapy did it become clear that, on her side, she felt so highly vulnerable to being utterly overwhelmed, crushed, by various superego figures in her environment, such as me, that the only way she could survive any one of them was by playing them off against one another—pitting them in destructively jealous competition with one another in relation to her.

These dynamics became clearest in a relatively recent session. She has been living on an outpatient basis for some years now, in her own apartment, handling her own finances, and she received word from the Internal Revenue Service that her tax return for the previous year was being audited. She seemed to me to be responding to this information in a relatively mature and capable manner; but it was evident that for her the problem was enormously complicated by her feeling—as she had phrased it bitterly and helplessly for years—"under analysis." This feeling she had experienced not only during her sessions with me, but also in relation to the many superego figures which abounded in her daily life. Some of these were real, but many, particularly figures from the past, were largely figments of her paranoid-delusional projections. She was feeling in this instance under *very* critical scrutiny—a meticulously critical evaluation as to how she was setting about meeting this practical problem—not only from me, but also from her older sister, her administrative psychiatrist, her social worker, and a number of other people in her life. It was very striking to me to see that she reacted to all of these people (including myself), which she might realistically turn to for help, not as potential helpers but rather as, collectively, a vast additional hindrance and burden to her in her already burdened life-situation. She had attributed to us a destructively critical orientation, but behind this paranoid defense the repression of her dependency needs was quite apparent.

In the first five minutes of the particular session in question, it became evident to me that she tended to feel overwhelmingly criticized and condemned, in this regard, by her social worker (whom the patient sees regularly once each week, and who in my opinion actually gives the patient relatively little cause for feeling so threatened), and clearly was invoking her sister's support against the social worker. The sister herself was a social worker, and it was apparent to me that the patient was playing very skillfully (although apparently largely unconsciously and certainly not in a consciously powerful, dominant position) upon the latently jealous rivalries between the two women in regard to her. She evidently gave each of them to feel protective of her, and was angry at the supposed bullying callousness and condemnation on the part of the other woman in the threesome. Never before had she functioned, during the session, in such a manner as to enable me to empathize so fully with her—to see that, from her view, such Machiavellian behavior on her part was her only means of staving off being crushed by these superego behemoths (which included, as was clear enough, myself during the session in question). It was clear to me, but still not to her after all these years, to what a degree her feeling "under analysis" involved projecting her own repressed feelings of a perfectionisti- cally critical, inhumanly condemnatory sort—feelings which she has vented upon me, with disturbing and unrelenting harshness, innumerable times.

The projectional aspect of her feeling scrutinized in so critically evaluative a manner reminded me of my reaction to my fellow staff members at Chestnut Lodge, twenty years ago, after learning of the death of my training analyst, with whom my analysis had ended about a year or two before. For perhaps two or three days thereafter, I felt an uneasy self-consciousness among my colleagues at staff conferences and elsewhere, feeling that they were watching me with a critical eye as to what, if any, feelings I was experiencing in this setting. My uneasiness on this score vanished with my realization that, in actuality, *I* had been evaluating *them*, critically, as to how *they* were responding to me—whether, for example, in an over- or under-sympathetic manner.

Jealousy Phenomena Permeate the Treatment

I have mentioned a few of the manifestations of Miss Herman's incomplete differentiation between human and nonhuman realms. This was a factor in the jealousy-phenomena which, from very early in the work with her, permeated her treatment. She formed such intense and intimate and "personal" attachments to various nonhuman things as to give one to feel jealously left out, as from a relationship between two other persons. In equipping her apartment for out patient living she came to say, for instance, "I love my little vacuum cleaner," with all the adoration a woman usually reserves for a husband or a child. In one of her sessions, for instance, she spoke in such a tone, "My darling vacuum cleaner ... that vacuum cleaner is just wonderful...." She said that she had told her sister this (about the vacuum cleaner) also, on the telephone. It seemed clear to me that she was making a formidable effort to evoke jealousy, toward her vacuum cleaner, in both her sister and in me. During this session she expressed dissatisfaction toward me, for the nth time, for not "turning off" the hallucinatory voices which continued to plague her—for not, as it were, cleaning them up, as her vacuum cleaner so beautifully cleaned up her apartment. Later in the same session, she reported, "The voices just say, 'How come everybody's so sweet and nice to ya?'" I suggested, "The voices sound a bid jealous of you?"—at which she promptly said, "*Yes,*" in empathic confirmation.

There was a prolongued period in our work—coinciding approximately with that time during which she very slowly, almost imperceptibly, in fact, over years, ventured bit by bit into outpatient living and then became more and more firmly established in it— during which I (having left the Chestnut Lodge staff and established a fulltime private practice in Washington) felt jealously pitted against Chestnut Lodge as to whom, or which, were more important to her. Here was involved, again, her incomplete differentiation from the nonhuman realm, for "Chestnut Lodge" evidently meant something different from, or certainly far more than, a collection of persons (a large collection indeed) who had been significant to her during the many years of her treatment there. To my mind, she spoke of it in such a way as to conjure up more the grounds of the sanitarium, the physical settings of the successive units in which she had lived, and so on. I had been off the Lodge staff for several years, and she evidently felt in the middle of a tug-of-war to cling to, gravitate further back into, her old ways of living at Chestnut Lodge, or to increasingly relinquish them and gravitate more toward the extrainstitutional life which I personified.

For me, this phase of her treatment involved on occasion experiences of jealousy which made me feel a peculiarly painful sense of division within myself. I had my own separation reactions to deal with, in consequence of having left the staff of Chestnut Lodge, and it felt to me strange indeed—having worked there so many years and feeling myself to be still part of the institution as regards her treatment—to now find myself pitted, in the work with her, in jealous competition with Chestnut Lodge. I know that, working alone with her in the earlier years—without the aid of the vast number of personnel (and fellow patients) which improvement to her present level of functioning had required—I could not possibly have met with this, even partial, success. I felt a deep sense of respect of what "Chestnut Lodge" had done, and was continuing to do, for her and, here again—as in my work with other patients in other contexts—I felt a sense of awe at the prospect of becoming sufficiently acknowledged by her, in terms of her dependency upon me, so that she and I would be able to continue the psychotherapeutic work without her needing to resort at all to the help of any administrator, social worker, nurse, or aide at Chestnut Lodge. This weaning process (obviously on both our parts vis-a-vis the Lodge) is not yet complete, if it ever will be. But it is progressing steadily, to the extent that she and I can deal with, among other matters, the kind of jealousy-phenomena upon which this paper focuses.

Any full-length book comprised of my reporting a necessarily tiny sample of the events during this woman's astronomically long treatment would inevitably pursue, as major among many themes, the analytic exploration of her hallucinatory phenomena, for it is that theme which gives greatest continuity and coherence to her treatment and to the ego-growth she has manifested during her treatment.

In the early months of our work she made clear that she was subject to hearing voices, and later on made clear that she had also experienced these at the previous hospital, from which she had been transferred to the Lodge. During perhaps the first year or two of my work with her, whenever she spoke of these she indicated that she found them to be a weird, uncanny, nonhuman phenomenon—an "electric voice," as she called them. But increasingly, after that first year or two, she made clear that the voices were more human in quality; they spoke to her much as a companionable other human being would, saying to her teasing things, witty things, amusing things, consoling and reassuring and explanatory things, and even, on at least one occasion, telling her accurately and helpfully where she had left her glasses which she had misplaced absent-mindedly. She continued to reproach me for not "turning off" the voices; she is, to this day, predominantly sure that they are caused by some sort of electronic device which, she is more than half-sure, I could turn off if

I only would. But it is clear, nonetheless, that they represent nothing like the weirdly nonhuman threat they once did, for otherwise she could by no means have moved at the Lodge into units occupied by patients less and less ill, and by now into relatively firm outpatient living. Parenthetically, after about three years of our work together, her parental family members conveyed to the Lodge staff that they found her (at what proved to be this relatively early stage of the treatment) already far healthier than they had ever known her to be. She came to be, as the years of her treatment went on, still far stronger in her ego functioning than she had been at that early juncture.

I well remember the time, several years along in our work when, for the first time, as she was reporting some between-sessions hallucinatory experience, I found myself feeling jealous of the described relatedness between herself and the hallucinatory voice. Specifically, she described having heard, while in a local drug store, a man's voice saying something to her of a sort that was intimate and clearly sexually interested. The jealousy I experienced on hearing this was reminiscent to me of that I had come to feel, years before, in working with a hebephrenic man who was much involved, during our sessions, with hallucinatory presences; my experience with him is detailed in my earlier paper on this subject (1979).

Although Miss Herman reports hearing voices on innumerable occasions during our sessions, it is rare for me to experience jealousy in this regard, for usually I can see clearly that the folksy comfort (or advice, or whatnot) with which the voices provide her are a poor second best, in terms of her unconscious yearnings, to wished-for identical words in my voice. Generally, she hears them at times when I have been silent, and when I do speak, rarely if ever do I express the kind of companionable, or supportive-psychothera-peutic, sentiments which the voices generally convey to her.

In one session, she reported, "The voices just said, 'You're about to find out the truth: you've won.'" the voices' tone, as quoted by her, was such as to imply that they were surrendering to her, although I felt sure, from innumerable previous attempts, that she would disclaim any such connotation. She went on, "I don't like it," with a tone of relatively decisive disapproval, but which became uncon-vincing when she said, with intended emphasis, "I didn't come all the way out here to hear the *voices*; I came to see my *doctor*." I felt that, in the tone in which it was said, she was introducing, unconsciously, the possibility that she comes to sessions primarily to hear the voices. "My doctor" was said with softness, fondness, in contrast to a note of relative dislike in saying, "the voices." Her statement clearly tended, in essence, to portray "the voices" and "my doctor" as rivals for her interest. Later in the session—at a time when, again, I had been silent—she said, ". . . the voices say, 'Why are you so nervous?'" The voices' tone, as quoted, was polite and solicitous.

Jealousy of the Other's Image of One's Self

My jealousy of the hallucinated male voice she reported having heard in the drug store, which I mentioned a bit earlier, is similar to another unusual jealousy experience I had in another session with her, also after she had been in treatment for many years. In this instance, I was shortly to go on a modest summer vacation. She said, looking at me, "You'll get tanned, won't you, Dr. Searles?. . . attractive . . . bronzed. . ." I felt, as she talked, that she was clearly visualizing my looking this way in her mind's eye, and this definitely tended to make me feel jealous of the attractively bronzed image of me.

This occurence, which lasted possibly a minute, remined me of her having said innumerable times, in the early years of her treatment, "My family wants me well," and, "My family want to see me well." In retrospect, I saw that in all likelihood her illness had served as a necessary defense against the family-inspired jealousy, in Miss Herman, of their image of her as "well." I remembered, too, the shock I had felt, very early indeed in the work, upon hearing from her that her "family" (probably more specifically her mother—her perceptions of her family were those more of an undifferentiated unit than of clearly delineated individuals) used to caution her not to lean her face on her hand too long, for instance, lest she supposedly permanently disturb the contours of her precious little face. She had presented this, in passing, as one more bit of evidence how cherished she had always been in her family. In essence, one sensed how careful she had had to be not to disturb their images of her (one recalls her mother's "nice little girl" image of her) by her allowing a flesh-and-blood human being, with sexual and aggressive feelings and all the rest, to emerge from within her—as indeed did emerge when she finally became overtly psychotic.

In all my long work with her, perhaps the most frustrating, oftentimes maddening aspect of the work is that she gives me clearly to visualize a much more capably functioning person than she is presently in her daily life or her treatment sessions. But when I endeavor to help her to become cognizant of these larger capacities, she manifests increased fearfulness and paranoid suspicion. I can well believe, from my above-mentioned isolated experience of feeling jealous of the attractively bronzed man she was evidently visualizing as she looked at my face, that similar jealousy is mobilized within her on occasions when she senses that I am visualizing her as a person capable, for instance, of driving a car, being married, and so on.

THE CASE OF MRS. JOAN DOUGLAS

Mrs. Joan Douglas is a chronically schizophrenic woman whose illness has been, in the main, much more severe even than that of Miss Herman. The work with her has shown that jealousy (and related envy) has been among the major emotions against which her awesomely severe psychosis has been serving as an unconscious defense. I by no means wish to imply that this is all that her tremedously severe and complex illness is about; but it is among the several most prominent aspects of her illness.

When I became her therapist, she was thirty-seven years of age, and had been psychotic for some four years. She was functioning in a paranoid-schizophrenic manner, extremely resistant to psychotherapy, and manifesting an ever-changing, endless series of delusions. After the first few years of my work with her, she became much less dangerously homicidal than she had been initially and much more collaborative in many ways, not only with me but with others about her in the sanitarium. But then she began manifesting predominantly an enormous confusion about her personal identity. For many years now, she has steadfastly disavowed her real name, reacting to her whole prepsychotic life experience as thoroughly alien and unacceptable to her. Her sense of identity, in its stead, has consisted over the past approximately fifteen years in an endless series of identity components. Any one component may persist for a few weeks; but, much more often, it is replaced by another within days or even hours. Many times during psychotherapy sessions she has experienced herself as now being a totally different person from the one who had been there a moment before. Her perceptions of me, as well as her experiences of her own body-image, are incredibly distorted. She perceives me more often than not as multiple, and frequently changing totally. She is convinced that she has been murdered many times (each shift in her identity seems to be felt by her as her having been killed), and often feels and perceives me as being dead, always with great concreteness and literalness.

Psychosis as a Defense Against Envy and Jealousy

When I began working with her, it quickly became evident that her profuse delusions were serving to defend her against being conscious of feelings of envy and jealousy (although there were many other determinants of her delusions, which are beyond the scope of this paper). For example, she would describe ballet dancers she had seen in a concert hall in Washington, or one or another prominent and successful and widely envied person (such as in a movie or on television), and would describe the horrible tortures or deaths they had suffered, unbeknownst to them. She was delusionally convinced, in other words, that they were not really to be envied—far from it—despite their superficial appearance of success, and so forth.

Throughout my experience with her, she has had only "splashes of memory"—disconnected fragments of memories—of her pre-psychotic past. These memory fragments, taken with historical data provided by her siblings, have made clear, from very early in our work, that her upbringing was permeated with intense envy and jealousy from a variety of sources. The sibling rivalry in her large and outstandingly accomplished parental family was evidently fierce. She seems to have been for many years an adored favorite of her father, to a degree that evidently greatly complicated her positive oedipal complex. Our work together, over the years, has made abundantly clear that, behind this, has been a much more tenacious and powerful, unresolved negative oedipal complex. From the very beginning it was clear that she was manifesting enormous penis envy, and her castrativeness toward males, including myself, has seemed at times limitless, although in actuality she is, in this regard as in various other ways, now a much more kindly person than she once was.

All these envy- and jealously-phenomena seem to represent not unusual clinical findings, except for their unusual intensity. But there are several additional findings, having to do with envy- and jealously-phenomena involving introjects, which indicate that psychotically defended against jealousy is among the major determinants of her remarkably severe indentity disturbance.

The Analyst's Envy and Jealousy

It is not irrelevent, I am sure, that over the years I have experienced envious and jealous feelings toward her to a more personally troublesome degree than with any other patient. I have been long accustomed to such feelings in my work with any of my patients, at one time or another. But never before have I found cause to feel so troubled, literally for years, lest the tenacity of this woman's severe illness be due more than anything else to my envy and jealousy of various of her attributes, and of various of her relationships with "others"—no matter to what degree these "others" be projected aspects of herself. This countertransference problem is now sufficiently noninterfering in my work with her so that I feel reasonably sure, in retrospect, that this envy and jealousy, and the attendant guilt over such feelings, have been predominantly in the nature of experiencing within myself such feelings which were being psychotically defended against in her, as by projection upon me. There is certainly every reason to believe, from both her prepsychotic history as well as her course in treatment, that such feelings in her are enormously intense, and vastly less admissible to awareness than are such feelings in me.

At any rate, to detail some of the ways in which I have envied her in the past: being a woman, able to sexually possess a man, as a woman does; having had for many years a husband; having borne four children, at least some of whom seem to be more successful and accomplished than my own three children; possessing a fabulously creative imagination (even though it is more accurate to say that she is possessed by it), a rare wit, and a kind of indomitable strength which I could well use in my life; having come (as I have not) from a socially prominent and wealthy family in which various of the members are individuals of outstanding accomplishment. And so on.

The Patient's Fear of Her Projected Jealousy

Now, as for the jealousy-phenomena she has manifested, I want first to mention that, after several years, I began seeing that the Mrs. Joan Douglas component of her identity was so alien to her that it could best be dealt with as being in the nature of a paranoid projection, with respect to her conscious ego functioning. She said, for example, "That Joan Douglas! Why, if I were a cat, the hairs on my back would rise!" Moreover, and more specifically relevant to this paper, I came later to see that she clearly reacted with jealousy to this Mrs. Joan Douglas whom everyone—the ward-staff as well as myself—kept trying, whether gently and indirectly, or bluntly and furiously, to help her to realize, or make her realize, is herself. In her view, everyone kept bringing up this Mrs. Joan Douglas, who was evidently so important to them and who she was firmly convinced was not at all even related to herself. She seemed to be so much less important, to the person talking with her, than was this Mrs. Joan Douglas.

Furthermore, as the years passed it became evident that prominent among the determinants of her endlessly changing series of personal identity components was a fear of her projected jealousy. She felt unfree to inhabit any one identity component more than a matter of hours or days or weeks, because of a feeling that she must vacate it and relinquish it to the "real" possessor of that identity, who was experienced as murderously jealous of the patient for having stolen it, as it were. Parenthetically, most of these identity components were given names, by her, which I have not been able to link up with any real persons, present or past.

Thus, she will come into a session feeling only the most tenuous, if any, sense of relatedness with the person who was present in the preceding session—with, that is, the different identity component which had held sway in her during that previous session. Moreover, when I remind her of some of the things she said during that previous session (a day or two before, usually), she quickly manifests jealousy of that supposedly other person, evidently feeling that that person—whom she feels to be not at all herself, and only most distantly, if at all, related to her—means more to me than she does, sitting before me.

The "Group-Relatedness" Atmosphere of the Sessions

Although she is verbal more often than not, there have been many predominantly silent sessions, and more than a few in which she has been mute throughout. It is commonplace for her to hallucinate auditorially, to all appearances (she has many times reported visual and olfactory hallucinations as well), and to show every evidence of responding obediently to an hallucinatory prompter, often identified as her mother. Particularly during the sessions when she has been either mute, or verbally highly oppositional to me, I have felt jealousy on many occasions in response to the so much more intimate relationship which is prevailing between her and the hallucinatory figure in whose communications she is attentively and obediently immersed. She often nods obediently and understandingly, as she listens.

After many years, the sessions developed at times a distincly *group* interpersonal atmosphere (a phenomenon which I have experienced with other highly ego fragmented patients). This came about through her responding to various nonhuman items in my office—the several plants, the lamps, the wicker basket in which I keep napkins for the couch pillow, and a modernistic wooden sculpture, and so on—as persons. This had far more of interpersonal impact than a child's play would have upon a bystander, and was an indubitably real experience to her. For many months she was convinced that the wicker basket was her sister, with whom she was clearly on far more lovingly intimate terms than she ever was with me; and she indicated on many occasions that she was experiencing more of a sense of human kinship with one or another of the plants, for example, than she ever felt with me. In this setting, I many times experienced jealousy in response to her relatedness with one or another of these items—which, remember was to her quite evidently a person. She often pled to me the cause of this or that innocent person who had been turned (as by Circe), she was sure, into this form (the plant, or the wooden sculpture, or whatnot), and was yearning to be restored to her or his rightful human form.

Her own jealousy of what she perceives as my relatedness with one or another item in the office, actually nonhuman but perceived by her as essentially human, has emerged on many occasions. After many sessions in which I found her to be reprimanding me, in one way or another, for being so informal and unprofessional as to be leaning casually against my nearby desk as we talked, it dawned on me that she was speaking in an identifiably jealous way of my desk. She evidently was jealous of the intimate casually-touching relationship it enjoyed with me. She has many distorted perceptions of my tape recorder (which is in full view); throughout several years of using it in our sessions, she has been convinced—and remains so—

that it contains whole but miniaturized people; she often reminds me, in this regard, of the way an aborigine might react to a photograph of a person, as being the person himself. For the purpose of this paper, however, I want to mention particularly her referring a number of times to the recorder as "your daughter," in a jealous tone. After several such incidents it dawned on me that I do indeed treat my tape recorder in a loving, attentive, cherishing manner—very much as, for a time at least, her father treated her, and as her former husband had treated their daughter.

The "group-relatedness" atmosphere of the session first became apparent to me during the seventeenth year of the work, about four years ago and lasted, as I recall, not more than a few months.

Clinical Examples

With some temerity—because the material from the sessions is so multideterminedly psychotic and confusing—I shall now present a few passages from sample sessions to show the raw material of the kind of envy and jealously manifestations, in the work with her, about which I have been writing.

In the session on March 16, 1972 emerged a highly typical example of her daily life experience of another person (in actuality a hallucinatory figure) "who" has suffered violence as a result of the patient's own unconscious, murderous jealousy:

> one of my baby daughters, who was a *perfect* little lady, and *never* did anything wrong, who was just an exquisite little character [her tone is effusively saccharine throughout] ... I don't see how my perfect gem should die at the Lodge [as she was convinced this baby had]—the baby—she's never done anything wrong! [Tone of wonderment and protest.]

Mrs. Douglas has had in reality one daughter and three sons, all now adults. But she is delusionally convinced that she has had innumerable babies, many of whom, she is anguishedly sure, have suffered all imaginable forms of destruction or torture. She has told me many times of hearing them crying at night in the walls of the building where she lives. Her unconscious sadism and murderous hatred toward babies is clearly enormous.

In the session of December 12, 1972, she was mute for about the first twenty-five minutes, appearing to be immersed in listening obediently to an hallucinatory voice. I spoke only seldom and briefly during this time. After about fifteen minutes of her silence, I suggested (guessing on the basis of past experiences which, however, had been so varied that I felt far from sure), "Your mother won't let you talk, huh?—to me?" She nodded in convincing confirmation of the accuracy of this surmise, but remained silent.

Then, about ten minutes later she suddenly broke her silence by announcing, decisively, "Barbara Batchelder murdered at Chestnut Lodge forty-eight times." That name I had seldom, if ever, heard before (she utters almost innumerable names in our sessions). She said "murdered" in a tone such that I assumed she meant "committed murder," rather than "was murdered"; but in listening to the playback of the session, I was unsure. In any event, her communication had a faintly shocking effect upon me; I have heard, however, innumerable, far more shocking communications from this woman.

In response to what she had said, I replied, "Rather shocking thing to hear, or not?" She said bitterly and caustically, "Well, not for a *psychiatrist* that was the psychiatrist during the time when nine hundred and ninety-seven quaduary trillion women from Europe *died* at Chestnut Lodge." I said, "I — psychiatrist at Chestnut Lodge?" She agreed, "Yeah." I went on, "So that a little thing like *that* wouldn't shock *me*? She agreed, "No."

She was being unusually realistic in speaking of me as having been a psychiatrist at Chestnut Lodge; much more often in our work over the years, she has identified herself as being the doctor, or the psychiatrist. Later in this same session, she asserted that she is the psychiatrist. This particular distortion in her sense of identity clearly is linked to an intense and unresolved power struggle in her relationship with her mother, beginning very early indeed in the patient's childhood, as to who had the status of mother, and who the child.

About fifteen minutes later in the session she began to explain, using one of her many odd vernaculars, "See, uh, Queen of Egypt, she come to Chestnut Lodge; she fix all women so they in contact with *nothing*, for the rest of their lives." I responded, in a kind of semiplayful tone, "Really? Why would she hate women that much?" She said, "I don't know. She jealous, stupid—" I interjected, "Sounds jealous, yeah, she sounds jealous," agreeing with her. She went on "—and, anyway, there's some confusion there about, uh, a man named, uh, Ken Wainwright [a name I'd never heard before] and the

Shebas [she had spoken for years of Sheba, in apparent reference to certain of my own qualities, and God only knows to what, or who else]. He was supposed to be her electricity [meaning, so I gathered, her sexual stimulus, her inspiration, her *raison d'etre*]. 'Steada being *her* electricity, he went running around *raping all* the *women* he *contacted* everywhere and turning them into radium, daylight, so forth —." I suggested, "*She* felt ignored by him or abandoned by him?" She agreed, "I guess *so*. so then she preceeded to destroy all women. ..."

There is abundant data, from my work with her over the years, to indicate that such a murderous, possessive, jealous woman was an aspect of her mother's personality, and an aspect of her own personality during the dozen or so years of her own married life, and later on in this session there were clear hints that she was seeing such a woman in me. She usually perceives me as comprised of more than one person, and many of the constituent persons she has perceived in me, over the years, have been women—not infrequently homicidally-inclined women, as she herself has been many times in reality. I assume that it had been such a possessive, jealous hallucinatory mother-figure who had made her afraid, during much of the session, to share verbally with me anything of what she was experiencing.

What was unusual, and encouraging, to me about this session was that she was proving able to explore, with me, the meaning of someone's murderous jealousy. she had acted out such jealousy innumerable times, from the very beginning of our work; but we had been able, before, to work together in exploring it as a dimension of the psychotherapeutic investigation.

Some ten or fifteen minutes along in the session of June 7, 1973, I responded to something she had said a moment before, in my usual attempt to facilitate her developing this further. She responded, in a rather self-effacing tone, "I—I think Mrs. Brooks [(a pseudonym for) her older sister, toward whom the patient had accepted, long since, the status of a kind of feeble-minded one, unworthy of being considered really a sister] is in here and *she* was talking to you." I inquired, "You think she was in—that head?"— referring to her head. Since very early in our work she had experienced both her head and mine as being replaced unpredictably by an endless series of heads. I was long accustomed to her referring, for example, to her own head as being an alien object. She replied, in a confirming tone, "Mm." I went on, "That would, I think, make you feel rather left out,

if you thought that a conversation was going on between Mrs.
Brooks in your—in that head, and me, or us." ["Us" because she
usually perceived me as multiple; so I not infrequently referred to
myself as "us."] This she did not confirm, but I believe it to be a valid
surmise. I believe, that is, that her sense of identity shifts so very
frequently, oftentimes during our sessions, that at many junctures
she feels she is not at all the person, in her chair, who was conversing
with me a moment before. And this, I find much reason to believe,
fosters jealousy in her toward that previous aspect of herself, that
previous "person." She had pointed out to me quite explicitly, by
way of reminder—on some occasion when I was trying to help her
remember something which had occurred during the most recent
session—that millions of persons "have sat in this chair during these
sessions," clearly referring not to other actual patients of mine, but to
the innumerable components of her fragmented self.

After some five minutes of conversation about other matters she
was saying, "Well, if ya died, you're a chameleon; if you didn't die,
you'd be a plant." She then paused for several seconds; I was long
used to her frequently experiencing either herself, or me, or both, as
being literally dead. I responded, in an ironically polite tone, "You of
course have no way of knowing whether I have died?" She was
again silent for several seconds, and then said, "Yeah, there's
evidence on your face." I replied, in a calmly inquiring, unastonished
manner, "Evidence on my face, of my having died?" She nodded
confirmation. I asked, directly and factually, "What's the evidence?"
After several seconds of silence from her I persisted, "Can you
describe the evidence?" To this she retorted in a loud, harshly
rejecting tone, "I don't have to *tell* you those things; I'm not a teacher
any more." Parenthetically, she has never been a teacher in any
conventional sense, although surely she has been a teacher in many
unofficial ways, both within and without her psychotherapeutic
work.

I replied, "No, you don't; that's true. You don't have to. To the
extent that you want to remain *largely incomprehensible* to your
fellow human beings, it would be fine *not* to tell me. See, that way
even I, who have spent so many *years trying* to fathom your way of
experiencing yourself, and the world you live in, *even I* wouldn't be
able to fathom it. So that to the *extent* that you wish to be
unfathomable, don't bother teaching me." I said all this in a kind of
gently sarcastic tone, with a kind of ironic patience, until the last four

words, at which my tone switched suddenly to a rapid, brutally rejecting one.

After this she was silent again for several seconds, and then explained, "Well, the teachers would only come over to me and murder me *again*, so —" I interjected, "If you taught me?" She said, confirmingly, "Mm." I went on, "The jealous teachers would only come over and murder you again?" She replied, "Yeah.... When *she* [apparently referring to a momentarily dominant one among the hallucinatory "teachers"] wants you to know something, she'll *tell* you." I suggested, "They're so jealous of their prerogatives, are they?" She said, in emphatic confirmation, "Yeah."

In the session of June 30, 1973, within the first few minutes we had spoken, in the course of a lively back-and-forth discussion, of many persons, many of whom she herself had introduced into the conversation. Then, after I had been trying vainly to help her to remember one of her sons, to whom I felt she had alluded indirectly, she said, in a kind of rejected, left-out demeanor, "Well, he's over there in the circle anyway. [Said very concretely, as usual, as if referring to a circle of people a few feet away, in the very room.] She told me in a session a month later that she has to share her room at Chestnut Lodge with twenty-seven other people; actually only one other person, her roommate, lives there, and these twenty-seven people proved, on further inquiry, to be shadowy hallucinatory presences. "So you have forty-seven persons over there, and I guess they're all your family." I suggested, "So you don't see why *I* don't go *over* there." She said, "Yeah." I went on, "— Particularly as I do seem discontent here? — do I?" She replied, "Yeah." I long ago had started to realize something of how easily wounded she was at any indication of my being other than contentedly immersed in being with her, without thought of anyone else. It was evident that she had found reason to feel once again rejected, not part of my intimate family circle of forty-seven persons. I cannot say that in this instance she appeared jealous; rather, I surmise, she felt too insignificant to me to be able to hope, even, to be in such a competition.

Less than five minutes later, however, she was in the midst of one of her long-familiar upbraidings of me for not bestirring myself to the constructive activities which, she felt, urgently needed doing: "You've had a lot of opportunity around here to tell people what to do; but you never seem to think too much about it. You just kinda feel sorry for yourself all the time. ... You coulda gotten my body started being made, and my mother's, and a few things like that; but you haven't done it." I suggested, "I've let you down, thus far?" She agreed, "Yeah. So I got Victor Immanuel [a fantasy-figure of whom I have long heard. Of course I realize that this is the name of the last king of Italy; but I do not know what more personal significances the name has for her], because he's a real worker, and knows what to do, and knows how to go about it. [I distinctly felt that she was trying — with little if any success — to make me jealous of Victor Immanuel]. Maybe he'll help you — let you help *him*, something like that. But I *asked* you to put up an ice skating rink, and you didn't do *that*, and you — you just let things drift. Day after day, nothing gets done; nobody builds up the gyms anywhere; they all need to be *fixed*. And everything of ours has to be made *giant* size; but you haven't done it yet. We've got big giants standing around all the buldings, and you haven't — you know, raised the ceilings, or *any*thing." She spoke in a tone which varied from exhortation, to disgust, to scorn. Here she was perceiving me entirely as she had often perceived her husband, and as, in her childhood, her mother had often perceived the patient's father.

I replied, "Puzzles you that I could be so — inert?" She readily agreed, "Yeah." I went on, not harshly but persistently, "Yet if I ever seem anything *but* inert, you feel that I'm discontent, and restless, and wanting to be elsewhere?" She said emphatically, "Yeah." Although she did not seem to feel any personal responsibility for modifying these conflicting demands, she had here acknowledged, more clearly and simply than ever before, the fact of her making opposing demands upon me.

Some ten minutes later, minutes filled with verbal communications about many matters, I commented that "I get the impression that whenever I speak of someone other than yourself, you assume that I like that person better than I like you?" She replied, in a tone implying that she had not thought of it this way before, but decisively confirmatory of it, "I guess *so*." By now, I felt that I had gained a memorable series of glimpses into the detailed and pervasive manner in which the heretofore unseen jealousy among her various identity components, or introjects, was contributing to the enormous and long persisting fragmentation of her ego functioning.

References

Klein, M. (1957). *Envy and Gratitude*. New York: Basic Books. Reprinted as *Envy and Gratitude & Other Works 1946-1963*. New York: Delacorte Press/Seymour Lawrence

Searles, H. F. (1972). The function of the patient's realistic perceptions of the analyst in delusional transference. *British Journal of Mededical Psychology* 45:1-18.

———(1979). Jealousy involving an internal object. In *Advances in Psychotherapy of the Borderline Patient*, ed. J. LeBoit and A. Cappponi pp. 345-403. New York: Jason Aronson.

Chapter 14

NARCISSISTIC COUNTERTRANSFERENCE

HYMAN SPOTNITZ, M.D., Med. Sc.D.

Psychoanalytic literature of the last quarter century reflects two evolutionary developments in the operational concept of counter-transference. One is the tempering of the wholly negative attitude it originally evoked, which was so succinctly expressed by Fliess: "undesirable and a hindrance. ... Ideally, therefore countertrans-ference should not occur. But it does. ... always resistance, must always be analyzed" (1953, p. 286). Without disputing the ubiquity of countertransference or dismissing its resistance potential, the theoretical formulations of all psychoanalytic schools currently accord some measure of respect to the phenomenon. In this process of detoxification, outright proscription has given way to thoughtful assessment and specific recommendations for the constructive use of countertransference.

Growing Recognition of Primitive Transference States and Reciprocal Countertransference Reactions

A parallel development, more implicitly suggested in the literature since mid-century, has been the gradual dissolution of the initially monolithic concepts of transference and countertrans-ference . The simultaneity of the so-called widening scope of indications for psychoanalysis and reports of essentially different transference states observed in patients with the more severe emotional disorders was more than coincidental. The existence of narcissistic transference and its implications for the treatment of schizophrenic (Spotnitz 1969) and nonpsychotic patients (Kohut 1971) were comprehensively explored. Formulations on a continuum transference states, ranging from the familiar oedipal-type transference to psychotic transference, were followed by impression characteristic emotional reactions to each state. Thus Kernberg postulated a "continuum of countertransference reactions ranging from that related to the symptomatic neuroses on one extreme to psychotic reactions at the other" (1975, p. 54).

This ongoing refining process enhances understanding of the interpersonal dynamics of the analytic relationship, especially in cases that encompass the evolution of primitive transference states into object (oedipal-type) transference, which permits the therapist to exert a decisive influence on the patient. In addition to their general diagnostic values and clinical implications, these distinctions , may be usefully applied in the course of a case to determine whether progress is being achieved. Moreover, intellectual understanding of the transference-countertransference continua prepares the analyst to recognize and deal appropriately with those significant changes in his affective reactions that usually accompany fluctuations in the patient's transference state.

THEORETICAL APPROACH:
THE PERSPECTIVE OF MODERN PSYCHOANALYSIS

In the present chapter, these transference-countertransference vicissitudes are viewed in the perspective of "modern psychoanalysis." The term is applied here to a specific operational theory that was initially formulated for the treatment of schizophrenic patients (Spotnitz 1969). Modern psychoanalysis adheres to the Freudian framework in recognizing and investigating transference and resistance phenomena but differs from classical psychoanalysis in sanctioning an extensive range of interventions, including symbolic, emotional, and ego-reinforcing communications, rather than relying entirely on interpretive procedures. The basic model technique is amplified to reflect the technical implications of oscillating transference states. Recent findings on the role of aggressive forces in the early evolution of the mind figure in the operational theory, and these forces are dealt with first.

Contractual arrangements reflect the degree of purposeful participation the patient is capable of at the emotional level at which he enters treatment. The analyst accepts responsibility for results until the patient has progressed sufficiently to share it, and works systematically to transform the relationship into a full-fledged working alliance.

Although it was formulated primarily for patients who do not respond sufficiently to the classical approach, modern psychoanalysis appears to be developing into a broad psychotherapeutic science applicable in all psychologically reversible conditions.

In modern psychoanalysis, countertransference is defined as the therapist's unconscious reactions to the patient's transference attitudes and behavior. (Excluded from this conceptualization are transferences that the therapist may develop to the patient as a neutral object before the patient attaches feelings to the therapist.)

Subjective Countertransference, Objective Countertransference, and Countertransference Resistance

Two groups of countertransference reactions are identified: (1) subjective countertransference, that is, atypical feeling-responses which are attributable to insufficiently analyzed adjustment patterns in the therapist and are usually rooted in distortions created by memory processes; and (2) objective countertransference, the feelings that are realistically induced by the patient's transference feelings and attitudes.

The terms "countertransference" and "countertransference resistance" are used as reciprocals of "transference" and "transference resistance." The working concept itself is thus purged of any value judgment. Subjective countertransference is the source of most countertransference resistance, but it is recognized that the objective countertransference may also give rise to antitherapeutic interventions.

The importance of "analyzing out" the subjective countertransference is emphasized. On the other hand, while the resistance potential of the objective countertransference is recognized, the student analyst is trained to sustain it and use it as a source of therapeutic leverage as well as for understanding the patient. It is recommended that the induced feelings be experienced freely and fully in order to help the therapist maximize his empathic understanding of the patient. The induced feelings are communicated selectively, according to the specific therapeutic requirements of the situation. These feeling-responses are utilized, in principle, for the specific purpose of resolving an immediate resistance of the patient. Therapeutic leverage resides in their impact on the patient. This, as the trainee learns, is directly proportionate to their genuineness.

Narcissistic Countertransference

The focus in this chapter is on the phenomenology and technical implications of the therapist's affective reactions to a patient functioning in a state of narcissistic transference. To distinguish these feeling-responses from those evoked by the patient in a state of object (oedipal-type) transference, they are classified as "narcissistic countertransference."

Of historical interest is the early use of this term in a strictly pejorative sense by Ferenczi and Rank (1925). They state that the "narcissism of the analyst seems suited to create a particularly fruitful source of mistakes: the development of a kind of narcissistic counter transference which provokes the person being analyzed into making flattering remarks about the analyst and suppressing unpleasant remarks about him" (p. 41). Obviously this statement refers to the analyst's transference to the patient as a neutral object or to his subjective reactions to the patient's transference attitudes, that is, narcissistic countertransference of the subjective type.

But I am exclusively concerned here with the analyst's realistic affective reactions to a patient in a state of narcissistic transference — the *objective* type of narcissistic countertransference. Without conceptualizing it as such, many authors have implicitly referred to it or highlighted its characteristics (for example, Boyer 1977, Eigen 1977, Giovacchini 1977, Modell 1976, Moeller 1977, Searles 1965).

THE RECIPROCAL INTERCHANGE OF NARCISSISTIC TRANSFERENCE AND COUNTERTRANSFERENCE REACTIONS

The primitive attitudes manifested by a patient in a state of narcissistic transference suggest a symbolic revival of clusters of experience during the preoedipal period. These attitudes may also be viewed as the patient's unconscious attempts to reveal basic maturational needs that were not met by the primary object during the undifferentiated period. Kernberg (1976) refers to the activation of "units of early self and object images and the primitive affects linking them" (p. 400).

A severely disturbed patient may appear to be totally unaware of the therapist's presence and totally preoccupied with himself. The therapist may then tend to focus on himself and become totally unaware of the patient.

The patient may experience the therapist as part of the self or like the self. The therapist may feel that he is in the presence of a kindred spirit or experience a strange sense of harmony. Meadow, working with a young woman in a "pre-ego state... found herself experiencing the same feelings of objectlessness" (Spotnitz and Meadow 1976, p. 193).

The patient may attribute his own feelings to the therapist or the therapist's feelings to himself. When, for example, the patient feels tired, he may think that the therapist is tired. In that situation, the therapist may become aware of feelings of fatigue in himself. At times when the therapist is in a cheerful frame of mind, he may have the impression that the patient is in a similar state of mind.

When a very depressed patient talks repetitively about committing suicide, I suddenly experience strong anger. I become aware of urges to get out of the office for the day, or get rid of the case.

Schizophrenic patients early in treatment characteristically verbalize feelings of emptiness, strangeness, confusion, and hopelessness. The therapist may then be assailed by feelings of helplessness and hopelessness. At the height of the narcissistic countertransference (objective), he tends to oscillate between states of self-preoccupation and anxiety. The patient's delusions and other psychotic productions may alarm the therapist and he may become aware of desires to "tranquilize" the patient. The therapist tends to feel more and more removed from the patient.

Many years ago, for example, I treated a psychotic woman who told me, "I talk to you one hour a week in this office, and the rest of the week in my mind." I tried to understand the gibberish she talked during the first year of the relationship, and made a great effort to talk to her, but I felt totally withdrawn. I attributed this emotional withdrawal to some problem in myself but subsequent analysis helped me recognize that the patient was inducing that state in me.

By and large, the analyst uses many conscious and unconscious mechanisms not to experience and not to be controlled by the realistically induced feelings. Until the patient's problem is fully understood, however, the "truly objective countertransference" (Winnicott 1949) may give rise to countertransference resistance.

CLINICAL EXAMPLES

Countertransference resistance originating in the objective type of narcissistic countertransference is delineated below in clinical material drawn from two cases. In the first, the prompt recognition and resolution of such resistance facilitated the treatment of a borderline patient. The second case illustrates how narcissistic countertransference resistance led to temporary regressions in a schizophrenic patient.

The Case of Mrs. C.[1]

A bright and attractive woman in her late thirties, Mrs. C. voiced fears of falling apart and paranoid ideas when she entered treatment with me. There was a strong element of depression in her personality; she had contemplated suicide on several occasions.

The wife of an attorney and mother of two adolescent girls, she edited children's books for a well-known publishing house. She described her husband as an overbearing bully who forced her to comply with his sexual demands. Quarrels about the upbringing of their daughters and financial matters were other sources of conflict. She felt that her marriage was destroying her.

An only child, she characterized continuous combat with a domineering mother as the primary event of her childhood. In the initial interview, she scarcely mentioned her father, a retiring and submissive figure in the household. Periods of withdrawal alternating with periods in which she felt intact and capable had marked her college years.

She expressed a desperate need to understand her current difficulties and her conflicting feelings about divorcing her husband. Making up her own mind about how to resolve them, she

---

1. This borderline case is more fully reported elsewhere (Spotnitz 1979). The nature of the narcissistic countertransference and its role in the case is focused on here.

felt, would enable her to accomplish something for herself. She said, "My main concern now is my own survival."

During the first two years of the therapy, Mrs. C. related to me primarily as the "influencing" part of her mind. In discussing this period of evolving narcissistic transference later, she said, "My ego boundaries wavered continually. Sometimes you were part of my ego, sometimes outside it." Often she said she knew precisely what was on my mind. Although she was usually wrong about this early in the relationship, there were instances later on when she accurately described my immediate thoughts and feelings.

For several months, Mrs. C. was totally absorbed in what she was thinking and saying. She did not interrupt her ruminations to ask questions or elicit comments. As she rambled on without manifesting any interest in my presence, I would become self-absorbed, drowsy, or aware that my mind was wandering. I resented the state of disinterest that often swept over me.

To alleviate her suffering and eliminate the danger of destructive acting out, I asked her four or five factual questions in each session on subjects of mutual interest. She experienced these brief verbal feedings as attempts to influence her. Since whatever I said was interpreted in a hostile way, I experienced pressure to maintain silence. At times I felt completely shut out.

Her insinuations that I was trying to influence her to remain with her husband were rankling, because I fully respected her wish to make up her own mind. Vague hints that I would mastermind her into a reconciliation evoked strong urges to prove to her how wrong she was.

You are like my preoedipal mother; you either stuff me with food I don't want or you starve me. This dominant theme of the narcissistic transference was communicated in various ways. For example: You are trying to manipulate and control me. You are not telling me what I want to hear. You don't talk because you don't like me. You have hostile wishes for me. You treat me as your prisoner.

Silent analysis of her defensive reactions to my sparse interventions made me aware that she was inducing desires to put her under pressure to accept my ideas. Recognition and understanding of this narcissistic countertransference resistance was greatly facilitated by the dream material she reported.

Early in the relationship, she reported dreams of being overpowered and then choked or raped. For many years she had dreamed of these and other terrifying situations. Great importance was attached to these dreams because of their frequent recurrence. She responded to my interest in these dreams by reporting dreams at frequent intervals.

Changes in her conscious attitudes and clinical symptoms paralleled changes in the character of her dreams. For example, the waning of her fears of being overpowered in the relationship dovetailed with dreams of being able to defend herself. Eventually, when she experienced me as a cooperative object, she dreamed of nonthreatening encounters. Mrs. C.'s dreams thus served as a barometer of her progress in the treatment relationship and in her life.

The early dreams, pointing to an unconscious wish to be dominated, made it clear that acting on my urges to put pressure on Mrs. C. would be antitherapeutic. Inclinations to do so were resolved by permitting her to direct me.

This approach was implemented at a moment when she was accusing me of trying to influence her to do what I thought would be best for her. I replied, "I'm not playing that game. I won't impose my will on you in any way. I will talk to you only when you want me to, and tell you only what you want to know" (self-demand feeding).

This paradigm, which quickly resolved the countertransference resistance, also initiated one of the major battles of the analysis. When I responded to her signal to talk, she complained that I was trying to influence her; when she did not signal me, she complained that my silence made her miserable.

These two patterns of narcissistic transference resistance were resolved by demonstrating to her that she could get me to talk when and how she wanted me to. Moving out of both patterns, she began to relate to me as a separate person. Later the idea of controlling me became as distasteful to her as the idea of being controlled. She began to crave a mutually cooperative relationship. She would not try to control me and I would not try to control her. In this partnership, she wanted me to be spontaneously cooperative — to talk when I wanted to and to say what I wanted to say.

Early in the treatment, I was often preoccupied with identifying and clarifying the induced feelings, and decisions on how to respond to them usually required much thought. In contrast to the elusive quality of the narcissistic countertransference, my affective reactions to Mrs. C. after the narcissistic transference had evolved into object transference were immediate givens. I became much more aware of the emotional interchange and responded to it more rapidly.

The Case of Mr. M.

At the advent of his senior year, following a breakdown precipitated by an unhappy love affair with a classmate, Mr. M. dropped out of a Midwestern art school on the recommendation of the school psychologist. He was twenty-one at the time.

He was the only child of divorced parents. His mother, a legal secretary and amateur artist whose paintings had been exhibited in a local museum, was a cold and reclusive woman with a family history of severe mental illness. She did not coddle her baby or pick him up from his crib when he cried. (Neighbors living on the floor below the family reported often hearing him rock himself to sleep in his crib.) She felt that the child was being spoiled by his father and paternal grandparents, who demonstrated much affection for him.

The father, a salesman, was often away from home during the child's early years and during the span of World War II, the little boy rarely saw him. When the father returned home from military service in Europe, the mother requested a divorce. A few years later, she became overtly psychotic and was eventually committed to a state hospital where her sister had spent many years. The boy, then eleven years old, was remanded to the custody of his father, who had recently remarried and moved to New York City.

From then on, until he completed high school, the youngster lived with his father and the father's second wife. Bright and personable, he appeared to be well-adjusted in adolescence and was popular with his schoolmates. With the encouragement of a high school art teacher, he decided to pursue a career in art.

He worked hard at art school with no let-up for vacations during his three years there. The necessity of interrupting his studies was a shattering blow to him.

The psychiatrist he consulted on his return home found him withdrawn and depressed. He was told that he was suffering from the effects of severe emotional deprivation in his early years. During the consultation, he expressed great eagerness to resume his studies in a local art school. His father, now a successful sales executive, agreed to finance whatever treatment the youth required and to continue to support him until he was fully capable of supporting himself.

Mr. M.'s first therapist was a female psychologist who had worked successfully with many severely disturbed children and adolescents. He developed a cooperative relationship with her, in the course of which he worked through many of his problems with his mother. His self-attacking tendencies were focused on but not resolved. Nevertheless, he appeared to be improving. He completed his undergraduate studies and earned a master's degree. The therapist was impressed by his determination to strike out for himself as soon as possible. With her encouragement he moved out of the parental home into a studio of his own, secured an appointment as an art teacher in a private school, and some freelance assignments as an illustrator of children's books.

All seemed to be going well with Mr. M. when he suddenly collapsed the day before he was to open an exhibit of the work done by his art class during the school year. The cancellation of his teaching contract precipitated a psychotic episode. Overwhelmed by suicidal and homicidal impulses and auditory hallucinations, he was unable to do any work. He wrote many notes to himself dominated by the themes, "Try harder," and "You are not your mother." Then he entered a state hospital. On his discharge seven months later, he resumed treatment with the same therapist. Later developments revealed a significant error in the treatment; she gave him many interpretations which he apparently experienced as an attack. The crux of his problem, in her view, was his tendency to drive himself to keep working.

About a year and a half later, when he was making an effort to socialize, he fell in love with a girl he met at a dance and proclaimed his intention of marrying her; but the girl, frightened by his bizarre behavior, broke off the relationship. Another psychotic episode followed and he spent the next year in another psychiatric hospital.

On his discharge from the second hospital, the psychiatrist he consulted told Mr. M. that he had failed with the first therapist because she had not recognized the nature of his problem. Mr. M. then resumed treatment with another therapist, a man who apparently employed a more directive approach than the first therapist. The second therapist liked Mr. M. and wanted to help hm. But each time the patient was on the verge of significant progress in his career, he fell apart again. He formed a pattern of signing himself into a mental hospital until he was able to resume his work. A few weeks later, he would return to private treatment even more determined to resolve his problems. There were many brief hospitalizations during this four-year period.

Mr. M was in his mid-thirties when he entered treatment with me. Initially, he impressed me as being an individual with a strong drive for accomplishment. He spoke about his desire to make a name for himself, to marry, and have children. If I would help him, he said that he would accept his present dependency situation and cooperate to the best of his ability.

I felt challenged to accomplish results in this case. I was also interested in ascertaining why he had failed with his previous therapists. Nevertheless, the precise nature of the therapeutic problem eluded me for some time. Since his breakdowns had coincided with an impending improvement in his life situation, I tended to operate on the theory that an inability to tolerate success was implicated. Meanwhile, to my great chagrin, he had two more relapses into psychosis, each followed by a brief hospitalization.

Mr. M. was a difficult person to understand. He reported no dreams, and withheld important information about himself. He tended to verbalize what he thought I wanted to hear.

He was generally immersed in feelings of helplessness and hopelessness. He repeatedly castigated himself for getting nowhere. He demonstrated little awareness of my presence. Occasionally he established contact with me, asking whether I thought there was any hope for him, and similar questions.

In response, I tended to feel withdrawn and disinterested. When he was totally self-absorbed and ignored my presence, I was not disposed to pay attention to his repetitive communications. In reaction to these feelings, I experienced urges to shake him up and help him get going.

Acting on these urges, it eventually became clear, was the countertransference resistance that had repeatedly stalemated the case. In other words, what had precipitated each of Mr. M.'s retreats into psychosis was not inability to tolerate success but encouragement to achieve his stated goals. Encouragement put him under intolerable pressure to accomplish. Then, instead of blaming the therapist for encouraging him, he attacked himself. The frustration-aggression turned inward had produced regression.

While the rewards of success appealed to him, his behavior demonstrated that he did not really want to make the effort to achieve it. The unconscious message, so long undetected behind his misleading communications, finally came through: I'm an infant. I don't want to do anything.

His anger at himself for not wanting to work had been exacerbated by the encouragement he had been given. Not only did he hate to work, but he hated himself for not wanting to work. And he had a remarkable facility for escaping from an intolerable situation into psychosis.

Two brief retreats into psychosis after he had been encouraged by me to accomplish were the essential clue to the presence of countertransference resistance. These regressions indicated that I, like his first two therapists, had been sucked into acting on the feelings he induced.

This understanding dictated a radical change in strategy. At the present stage of the relationship, when Mr. M. attacks himself for not accomplishing anything, he is given no reinforcement in this attitude. He is being educated to the idea that he broke down because he was put under too much stress, and that he needs a long period of recuperation. Forget about going to work, he is told. Just take it easy. Let your father support you. Live off the fat of the land. Baby yourself.

It is much easier to tell a schizophrenic patient that you like him and want to help him get well than to tell him to live like a vegetable. The second position is, in fact, rather frightening to take, and I have had a lot of resistance to taking it. While communicating to the unconscious ego so that it feels understood (loved), one has to try to minimize the narcissistic injury to the conscious ego.

Mr. M. no longer has to please me into thinking that he really wants to work. In response to the negative joining of this powerful transference resistance, instead of hating himself for not wanting to accomplish anything, he now hates me for directing him to do nothing. And for the first time since he entered treatment, he has shifted from attributing his lack of progress to his own inadequacies to blaming me for it.

In the therapy of a patient with Mr. M.'s personality structure, this shift is a sign of forward movement. It testifies to two concomitant developments: His tendency to internalize aggressive impulses in an ego-damaging way is weakening and he is forming a pattern of attacking the object. The establishment of this pattern will enable him to choose between attacking himself or somebody else, as the situation warrants. The choice is one that he has not previously been capable of making.

The symbolic "replay" of Mr. M.'s preoedipal relationship with his mother, in which he felt responsible for her difficulties in raising him, mobilized his self-attacking tendencies. These were a strong source of narcissistic transference resistance. In the process of dealing with it — specifically to deflect aggressive impulses from his ego and help him discharge them in words — I presented myself as a target for verbal hostility (Spotnitz 1969). (Nonpunitive acceptance of the patient's criticism is viewed by some practitioners as a strategy for modifying an overly harsh superego; usually it serves this purpose.) This formidable pattern of transference resistance is in the process of being resolved, and Mr. M. is moving into a state of object transference.

DISCUSSION

Narcissistic transference reflects a stage of development in which the boundaries between ego and object in the patient's mind are indistinct. The impression this creates on the analyst is also indistinct, and it is often difficult for him to determine his immediate influence on the patient. The more resistant the patient is to communicating what he really thinks and feels, the easier it is for the analyst to be fogged in boredom, drowsiness, gloom, and the like and to attribute his lack of understanding of what is going on to blind spots in himself. He does not realize that the patient has succeeded in confusing him.

The successful analysis and resolution of this objective type of narcissistic countertransference resistance is the key to the effective treatment of the preoedipal patient.

It is generally recognized that narcissistic transference encompasses different degrees of indistinctness in ego boundaries. The counter phenomenon also has different gradations and qualities, as illustrated by the two cases presented above. This becomes clear when one compares the interplay between narcissistic transference and narcissistic countertransference in the case of Mrs. C. with that in the case of Mr. M.

Mrs. C., a borderline patient, was relatively easy to work with. The degree of separation between ego and object in her mind was clearer, despite her oscillating transference states. She was more communicative and more direct in attacking the transference object. Her early dreams of being overpowered alerted me to the presence of narcissistic countertransference resistance, as I have indicated, and changes in the character of the dreams reported later told me whether the therapist was moving in the proper direction. The feelings Mrs. C. induced facilitated my recognition of the therapeutic problem and guided my interventions.

Mr. M. operated on a primitive level of narcissistic transference. He was a much more difficult person to analyze. His material was sparse and, as I stated above, he did not report dreams. Demonstrating the ego-sacrificing attitudes characteristically observed in schizophrenic patients, he was usually passive and indirect in his reproaches. The sole clue to his immediate emotional state was the degree of regression demonstrated by his behavior. When he maintained the status quo or was making progress, I assumed that I was conducting the therapy properly. The presence of narcissistic countertransference resistance eluded me until it had precipitated two psychotic episodes.

In reviewing the situation, I became aware of my inclination to convey approval of one or another grandiose plan he reported for the advancement of his career. His attitude that he could accomplish whatever he had a mind to do, given my encouragement and support, had misled me. A brief expression of approval — for example, "That's a great idea" — had seemed to be appropriate when he contemplated an exhibition of his drawings or entering a national competition for a prestigious art fellowship. But rather than being experienced as supportive, such interjections put him under intolerable pressure to realize his ambitions. Either maintaining silence or a neutral attitude, which would have led him to consider his ability to succeed in the project, would have been the therapeutic response to Mr. M. at that time. Thus it eventually became clear to me that, instead of analyzing the situation thoroughly, I had been intervening in harmony with his expectations. The destructive impact of these interventions made me aware that I had been operating in a state of narcissistic countertransference resistance.

By and large, in working with schizophrenic patients, it is difficult to detect the presence of countertransference resistance because they induce feelings in the analyst that he tends to identify as his own. One is inclined to operate by trial and error in these long-term cases until the patient's transference resistance is fully understood.

The general attitude that schizophrenia is incurable is almost invariably an expression of narcissistic countertransference resistance. The patient feels incurable and he induces that feeling in the analyst. If the analyst accepts that feeling as his own, and acts on it, the therapy fails. If, on the other hand, he recognizes the source of the feeling and also becomes aware of his affective responses to it, the constructive use of these counter feelings dramatically brightens the prognosis for the patient.

References

Boyer, L.B. (1977). Working with a borderline patient. *Psychoanalytic Quarterly* 46:386-424.

Eigen, M. (1977). On working with "unwanted" patients. *International Journal of Psychoanalysis* 58:109-121.

Ferenczi, S. and Rank, O. (1925). *The Development of Psycho-Analysis*. New York: Nervous and Mental Disease Publishing Co.

Fliess, R. (1953). Countertansference and counter-identification. *Journal of the American Psychoanalytic Association* 1:268-284.

Giovacchini, P.L. (1977). The impact of delusion and the delusion of impact. *Contemporary Psychoanalysis* 13:429-441.

Kernberg, O.F. (1975). *Borderline Conditions and Pathological Narcissism*. New York: Jason Aronson.

———(1976). Technical considerations in the treatment of borderline personality organization. *Journal of the American Psychoanalytic Association* 24:795-829.

Kohut, H. (1971). *The Analysis of the Self*. New York: International Universities Press.

Modell, A.H. (1976). The "holding environment" and the therapeutic action of psychoanalysis. *Journal of the American Psychoanalytic Association* 24:285-307.

Moeller, M.L. (1977). Self and object in countertransference. *International Journal of Psychoanalysis* 58:365-374.

Searles, H.F. (1965). *Collected Papers on Schizophrenia and Related Subjects*. New York: International Universities Press.

Spotnitz, H. (1969). *Modern Psychoanalysis of the Schizophrenic Patient*. New York: Grune & Stratton.

———(1979. Psychoanalytic technique with the borderline patient. In *Advances in Psychotherapy of the Borderline Patient*, ed. J. Le Boit and A. Capponi, pp. 207-226. New York: Jason Aronson.

Spotnitz, H. and Meadow, P.W. (1976). *Treatment of the Narcissistic Neuroses*. New York: Manhattan Center for Advanced Psychoanalytic Studies.

Winnicott, D.W. (1949). Hate in the countertransference. In *Through Paediatrics to Psychoanalysis*. New York: Basic Books, 1958.

Part III

COUNTERTRANSFERENCE WITH PARTICULAR TYPES OF PATIENTS

Chapter 15

COUNTERTRANSFERENCE WITH SEVERELY REGRESSED PATIENTS

L. BRYCE BOYER, M.D.

FROM OBSTACLE TO INSTRUMENT

The burgeoning literature on countertransference includes several reviews (Glover 1955, Orr 1954, A. Reich 1960), the most recent and comprehensive of which is that of Langs (1976), although it restricts itself to writings which are available in English. As is consonant with the earlier view that psychoanalytic therapy is applicable only to neurotics, the vast majority of relevant material pertains to their treatment.

Freud (1910) introduced the term countertransference a few years before he wrote the bulk of his papers on technique, although he never devoted a special study to it. It was considered roughly the obverse of transference, the repetition of the analyst's irrational, previously acquired attitudes, now directed toward the patient, and was assumed to be absent except in situations in which the therapist was inadequately analyzed. Freud deemed it to be the obligation of the analyst to eliminate such unconscious reactions as obstacles to treatment. Earlier, he had described how Breuer reacted to Anna O.'s erotic transference with anxiety and took a hurried vacation with his wife (Breuer and Freud 1893-1895).

Today the definition of countertransference remains unsettled. Most analysts see Freud's original use of the term to define counteransference neuroses. Many, in agreement with Alexander (1948) and Little (1957), view countertransference to consist of all of the therapist's emotional responses to the patient but perhaps more see it as representing the whole of the analyst's unconscious reactions to the individual analysand and particularly to the analysand's own transference. In any event, the majority of the literature stresses the role of countertransference as an interference with treatment (cf. bibliography of Langs 1976, Benedetti 1964, Gruhle 1915, Rank 1931, Sauguet 1959, Stekel 1934). Hann-Kende (1933) appears to have been the first to suggest that the therapist's emotional reactions can be turned to uses which enhance treatment, a position which has been emphasized subsequently with increasing frequency (Beres 1968, Chessick 1965, Giovacchini and Boyer 1975, Langs 1975a, 1975b, Pokorny 1959, Racker 1948a, 1953, 1958).

During the past thirty-odd years, increasing attention has been paid to the signal role of countertransference reactions in the treatment of seriously regressed patients, both from the standpoint of their constituting interferences in the pathway of treatment and that of their use as a potential source of therapeutic enhancement (Arieti 1955, Bion 1955, 1956, 1957, Boyer 1971, Fromm-Reichmann 1950, Giovacchini 1975, chapter 8 this volume, Hill 1955, Milner 1969, Searles 1965, 1975, Volkan 1976). Boyer (1961), while not denying the importance of the role of the characteriological structure of the patient in the development of serious analytic impasses, suggested that unresolved countertransference reactions may constitute the major obstacle to the successful treatment of some patients with serious characterological or schizophrenic disorders.

An increasing number of analysts now consider the introduction of the concept of projective identification to be important in understanding countertransference, particularly in the treatment of severely regressed patients (Carpinacci et al. 1963, Cesio 1963, Grinberg 1957, 1958, 1962, chapter 18 this volume, Kernberg 1975, Langer 1957, Nadelson 1977, Pinto-Ribeiro and Zimmermann 1968, Rosenfeld 1952a, 1952b, 1954, Searles 1963, Siguier de Failla 1963).

It is difficult to define and delineate one's inner experiences while working with regressed patients and the effects of those experiences on one's technical and tactical maneuvers; few analysts beyond

Searles and to a lesser degree Giovacchini have sought to do so. In this communication, I shall present three vignettes taken from the psychoanalytic therapy of two such patients. They illustrate my inner experiences when confronted with selected trying treatment situations, including the manner in which I defended myself and used my understanding of my reactions in the service of turning threatened or actual impasses into steps forward in treatment. It is possible to present the material in unusual detail with confidence because I record rather extensively during interviews. During the past fifteen years, those notes have included a recording of many of my own reactions and fantasises. The data which are thus accumulated permit subsequent review and reconstruction of what most probably transpired during the session. Searles' (1975) clinical vignettes are so poignantly convincing because he makes periodic lengthy notes after interviews, which include his emotional responses and fantasies in response to the patients' communications and, with some patients, systematically tape-records lengthy partial or entire treatments.

For over a quarter of a century, I have been treating borderline and psychotic patients in a manner which Searles (1963, p. 700) noted "apparently conforms more clearly to classical psychoanalysis than does any other reported approach by anyone treating such patients." In the discussion, I shall make selected general remarks pertaining to my style, and the attitudes I have developed during those years, in my efforts to avert development of untoward countertransference involvements, as well as therapeutic measures which I have come to employ.

CLINICAL MATERIAL

The Case of Robert

When first seen, Robert was seventeen years old. He was the older of identical twins who were succeeded by brothers ages fifteen and twelve. During the previous two years he had received electroconvulsive, drug, and supportive therapy for a hebephrenic condition, with but transient effects (Boyer 1976). His father, who suffered from a severe obsessive-compulsive characterological disorder, read a previous publication (Boyer and Giovacchini 1967) while Robert was hospitalized at sixteen and then called me, requesting that I allow Robert to undergo psychoanalytic therapy after his discharge. I heard nothing further for many months. His mother, a borderline schizophrenic, had insisted that he have drug, vitamin, and supportive therapy from another psychiatrist. Robert accurately perceived his family role to be that of the assigned psychotic who was to be disturbed in order that his mother maintain her capacity to function psychologically as if she were normal, and to keep the family intact. He improved greatly during several years of analytic therapy but when he became convinced that his mother's condition worsened as his bettered, he eventually decided to stop treatment in order to enable her to improve once again and maintain the household for his father and two younger brothers.

Prior to the interview which will be presented below in detail, only gross data pertaining to his past and current behavior and experiences were available to me. I was able to elicit more detailed information only after letting him know in secondary process language that I understood something of his communications, which were often dominated by primary process thinking except for brief periods when he was responding to a timely, accurate interpretation (Giovacchini 1969).

While his latest therapist was on vacation, Robert called for an appointment. He was vague, somewhat silly and evasive. Over the years I have learned that dealing interpretatively and calmly with the vicissitudes of aggression frequently reduces the anxiety of the regressed patient and helps in the early establishment of rapport (Boyer 1961, 1971). Accordingly, I suggested that his silliness and vagueness were efforts to disguise information which he feared I might use against him. He became briefly lucid, was relieved and intrigued. In a second interview following another call, his speech was more strongly dominated by primary process thinking. He was preoccupied with listening to the voices of God and Satan, which gave him contradictory advice. I indicated that his regression was being used in the service of defending himself against anxiety. He then revealed that he had been accustomed to anxious responses on the parts of his parents and therapists when he spoke incoherently and alluded to hallucinatory experiences. I spoke then of his use of such material in the service of secondary gain. When he observed that their function and content were deemed by me to be interesting data for investigation, he visibly relaxed and delightedly said he wanted to become a psychologist, like me. He had never previously considered any adulthood role but that of becoming a religious mystic. I silently understood his reaction to indicate that he had begun to introject my calm and objectivity.

Two months later, the father asked me to see his son on an interim basis. Robert knew that his therapist had been hospitalized because of an acute, severe eye disorder and might not resume his practice.

During the third interview, Robert stated as an aside that the eye was the window to the soul and I understood his apparently disconnected remark to mean that he had perceived anxiety and anger in his mother's and therapist's glances. Accordingly, I suggested that he feared that unvoiced anger at his psychiatrist had caused his eye disorder. He responded by saying that he had asked his father whether feeling anger was ever justified and had been forcefully told *no*. Later I was to learn that angry outbursts on the part of a younger brother were tolerated and even passively encouraged by his mother and father and that each of the parents, while usually rigidly controlled emotionally, was given at times to angry outbursts. I was to learn also that many contradictory messages of all sorts had been consistent in his socialization experiences. Following his father's answer, Robert had reverted immediately to believing in the reality of his continuing hallucinations of the voices of God and Satan, and felt hopeless. He also voiced the fear that if he were to tell his still hospitalized therapist that he wished to transfer to my care, that doctor would be blinded permanently. That he at some level equated blindness and castration was indicated by his casually and apparently disconnectedly mentioning the word Oedipus. Later I was to learn that one reason he had turned to deep involvement with Eastern religions had resulted from his having heard from a Zen leader that Freud had misinterpreted the Oedipus myth.

The fourth time we met, I indicated that he feared not only intense negative feelings, but intense positive ones as well. He replied that when he returned from trips and sought to hug his mother, she pushed him away. When I inquired whether he feared that I would be unwilling to accept him as my patient, he agreed with relief and said he could now take a fortnight's vacation driving with his twin, then enter college and reside in a dormitory to live away from home for the first time.

When Robert returned from his driving trip and learned that his therapist was still hospitalized, he was both frightened and relieved. While on the journey, he had read the book by Giovacchini and me (1975), an action I understood to mean that he sought to keep me with him during our separation. Despairing of improvement from convulsive, drug, and supportive therapy, he wanted to undertake psychoanalysis. I told him I would be willing to begin such treatment when time was available only if his parents agreed. Accordingly, I had an interview with his mother and father.

During that interview, I learned that his mother had been a virgin until her marriage at thirty-six and that the parents were sexually incompatible. They had been in conjoint therapy for many years, treatment which had been kept secret from their sons. Although their communications to me were guarded, I surmised that Robert's mother was a domineering and grossly exhibitionistic woman who stimulated their sons sexually but thwarted their efforts to be physically affectionate with her. It was my impression that she more or less passively encouraged them to watch her toilette and bathroom activities and was only uneasy when partially clad in front of them after they reached puberty.

The fifth interview followed his having moved to the dormitory. He entered the office silently, inspecting it in its entirety and looking bewildered. He sat rigidly on the edge of a chair alongside a wooden desk and regarded me with what I perceived to be suspicion and apprehension, in contrast to his previous predominantly shy and friendly attitude. I silently recalled his disappointment and regression when his father told him that angry feelings and thoughts were unjustified.

Translating the Countertransference Experience into Data

Over the years, I have come to credit with increasing conviction the roles of projective identification and counteridentification in the interactions between regressed patients and their therapists. Accordingly, it is my opinion that when I think or fantasize about some person who is important to the patient, I may be responding to his or her need to have me assume some role or attribute of that person. I suspected the presence of an acute transference psychosis. I unwittingly moved forward in my chair and softly and calmly asked whether he might be thinking of his father. He nodded in agreement, gradually relaxed and settled back into the chair. He sat in silence for some minutes during which his gaze seemed to be focused on the upper part of my face, reminding me of the watching behavior of a nursing baby.

Then he began to rhythmically rub the wooden arms of the chair with his palms. I had the sensation that my own arms were being caressed and briefly recalled that wood is a frequent symbol for a woman in dreams and folklore. I asked whether he were now wondering whether I might be his mother. He quickly agreed with a nod and became overtly frightened. I found myself feeling somewhat confused and fearful. Upon reflection after the interview, it appeared to me that during that period I had vaguely feared loss of my own identity and was afraid of fusion with him, experiencing concordant identification (Racker 1957). In the interview my uneasiness went on until I soon thought that he had begun to confuse himself with his mother and was worried lest he become lost in her, but I remained silent and continued to view him with sympathetic interest.

He suddenly began to hit the desk with his palms, asking whether it were a table. Soon, each time he slapped the desk, he said the word table. Then he seemed to enter a dissociated state, or at least I concluded that that might be so since I felt I had lost contact with him. He became progressively more frightened and repetitively shouted the word table although he ceased slapping the desk. I then remembered that the table too is often used in dreams and folklore to symbolize the mother and I no longer felt strange. I thought also of the last section of Freud's (1915) article "The Unconscious," in which he commented (p. 199) that "in schizophrenia *words* are subjected to the same process as that which makes the dream-images out of latent dream-thoughts." Then it occurred to me that Robert had ceased using the word table as a symbol but instead was now concerned only with the word as an object. Soon he ceased using the word table but instead repetitively said its syllables separately: tay-bul, ta-bul. Eventually he said "tay-tay-tay" and then "bul-bul-bul' over and over and I understood that the word itself had now become fragmented and only the syllables were being used as concrete objects.

Regaining the Analytic Stance

I found myself again feeling unreal and once more turned to the use of active thinking and knowledge recall in the service of regaining my personal sense of integrity. I remembered that the growing child, before he begins to speak words, becomes actively interested in his vocal utterances as discrete phenomena which he can control and attend and that when he learns to speak, he likes to play with his newly acquired words by using their sound qualities. Noy (1969, p. 168) noted, "This first encounter with the object is not to be confused with the later approach to an object as part of reality, because in this first stage, all percepts have meaning only in terms of their relation to inner states of drives, needs, tensions and affects."

I considered the possibility that his regression was being used in the service of defense and that he had begun to use the word-fragmentation as a primitive representation of body or world destruction, a statement that he felt himself to have no personal identity, and to have become lost in imagined fusion with his mother. Concurrently, I felt somewhat fragmented, but when I remembered that I could test the validity of my thoughts by investigative questions and interpretations, I once again felt calm. I remembered that he had told me earlier that when he returned from trips and tried to hug his mother, she pushed him away. I recalled, too, my impression that she was a frustrating exhibitionist, and that when the boys reached puberty she was uneasy in their presence while nude or partially undressed. I wondered whether she had projected incestuous wishes onto them and feared overt sexual advances by them.

By this time, I was able to formulate what seemed to be a rational approach to the investigation of the validity of my assumptions. I asked whether on his vacation with his brother he had been lonely for his mother. He immediately regained contact with me, nodded agreement and began to cry. After a time he said, "She pushed me away." I inquired whether he meant that she had done so when he sought to hug her on his return from the trip. He agreed and then began to speak of his loneliness in the coeducational dormitory.

On the preceding Saturday he had been frightened by observing interactions between male and female students which he understood to mean that they were going to have sexual relations. He had thought one girl had indicated that she wanted to be involved sexually with him. He then heard God's voice say, "Thou shalt not commit adultery." As he had told me earlier, both of his parents but particularly his mother demanded premarital sexual abstinence on the parts of their sons. When he was unable to get superego support from a faculty member, he drove home where he was greeted with what he took to be displeasure by his parents. When he sought to hug his mother, she had been unresponsive. He had been unable to tell his parents why he had to come home, feeling the need for some demonstration of affection before he could confide in them. Later, when his mother was undressing in her bedroom with the door open, he went toward her, seeking an understanding word or some physical caress. She reacted to his approach with terror, screaming for his father and claiming Robert wanted to rape her. His father then furiously reproached him for disturbing his mother and also accused him of incestuous desires.

By the end of the interview, he was calm, shy, and friendly and eagerly sought reassurance that our next appointment would be held at its regularly scheduled time.

In subsequent interviews, we retraced the events of this dramatic session in detail and it was possible to reaffirm that my various conjectures had been accurate. Concurrently, it was possible to review for the first time the onset of his initial overt psychosis at the age of fifteen and to understand that the essential elements which led to that regression were all recapitulated during the experience which preceded the interview in which he made concrete objects of the words and syllables.

The Case of Mrs. X.

Fifty-three years old when first seen, Mrs. X. was Caucasian, twice-divorced, a filing clerk, friendless, living alone, and almost totally impulse-dominated (Boyer 1977). Under almost constant psychiatric treatment of myriad forms for emotional aloofness and chronic alcoholism for almost twenty years, she had been hospitalized frequently, often diagnosed as schizophrenic. She had also been jailed many times and while in the "drunk tank" had masturbated openly, smeared feces and menstrual effluvia and screamed endlessly. She had lived dangerously, having on various occasions provoked sexual assault by gangs of black men in ghettos. When she came for treatment, she quite literally believed she had never had angry impulses and that any behavior which might have been interpreted so was motivated by altruistic motives. Her principal stated reason for seeking analytic treatment was that she had been told by the therapist of her psychotic son that her interactions with him contributed to the continuation of his disturbance; she eagerly sought a form of treatment which she knew would be very painful for herself, in the service of helping him to improve.

Mrs. X. was the child of a self-centered, vain, impulsive, and hypochondriacal mother and a depressed, exhibitionistic, profligate father who committed suicide during her adulthood. His chronic alcoholism had led to the loss of the family fortune. In her preschool years, she had read and done arithmetic precociously but after the first year of school, she became effectively barely literate and lost her mathematical abilities. Her failure to pass any examination in all her school years after the first grade did not concern her parents, whose goal for their daughters, of whom she was the second, was that they use their beauty and social graces to acquire rich husbands who were to lavishly support the family. She stated during an early interview that she had had a secret sexual liaison of some sort with a swarthy chauffeur who wore black gloves, for a period during her grammar school years.

She had a severe obsessive-compulsive neurosis with strong altruistic features from the age of seven or eight until she was sent from home at about twelve years of age to a girls' finishing school where she felt loved by an admired classmate. At sixteen, she felt deserted by her idol and withdrew to the degree that she functioned essentially as a robot for almost six years. She had no boyfriends and behaved mechanically at obligatory social functions, including her own debut. When she was twenty-one, her older sister seemed to have "hooked" a rich medical student from an elite social level which paralleled her own. Mrs. X. was galvanized into action, apparently by her need to be the financial family savior, and got the man to marry her instead.

Her sexual passivity and frigidity infuriated her selfcentered and unfeeling husband who had many affairs which he flaunted before her. While he was in medical school in another city, she lived with his parents near her nuclear family. Following his graduation, he entered the military and moved her to a distant area. He was soon sent overseas. Her shyness and passivity led to her being almost constantly alone. She began to drink in solitude and while drunk had autoerotic and vengeful fantasies which were repressed when she sobered up. She bore three children, none of whom she could believe to be her own for varying periods after their births. She feared touching them and various nursemaids were hired to take care of them and her. She began to frequent bars where she picked up men and had affairs which she forgot.

Her third child was an autistic and exceedingly hyperactive boy who was hospitalized when less than two years old. Her husband divorced her and thenceforth had the rarest of contacts with her or the children. She then selected only black men whom she encouraged to use her sexually but she repressed the actual sexual experiences. When her son was with her on occasional weekends during the next few years, she brought men home with her and submitted to fellatio and sodomy before him, subjecting him to primal scene traumata which, as became manifest later, repeated experiences to which she had been subjected during her early years. As she had repressed them, she also repressed the behavior to which she exposed her son, learning of her actions only because they were recounted to her by nursemaids. Her children were all removed from her and sent to various institutions. It was then that her behavior became increasingly irrational, resulting in her being hospitalized and jailed.

During one of her hospitalizations, she met a man who was a chronic alcoholic. They began to live together and eventually married. He was so like her physically that she often wore his clothes. Sometimes they got drunk together and spent days in bed, performing polymorphous perverse sexual activities to the point of exhaustion while lying in their own excreta. For her, they were at times psychological continua and she often experienced bliss, consciously believing they had achieved a symbiotic physical union. They lived on grudging charity from her relatives, and on welfare. A psychiatrist suggested that she would have more self-value if she were to become employed and stop living on family and governmental dole. She managed to complete a course in practical nursing and had some success in state hospitals, caring for psychotics and senile patients with empathetic tenderness. She was fired repeatedly because of drunkenness. Eventually her husband tired of her and left her, an action she had great difficulty in comprehending since she perceived that he also depended on their fantasized physical and psychological continuity, and because she supported him financially. A couple of years before she undertook treatment with me, she had obtained a job as a filing clerk in a place where her inefficiency and instability were tolerated. Her low-cost therapy was financed by a small allotment from a deceased family friend.

Resolving Impasses through Processing the Transference

I turn now to two examples of how my coming to understand my emotional responses to treatment-setting constellations enabled me to change what seemed to be impasses into therapeutically beneficial steps.

Following an early interview to which she came drunk, seeking through bizarre behavior to test my anxiety tolerance, to seduce me, and to establish a symbiotic union, she decided not to come to the office intoxicated. Soon thereafter, she vowed also to cease going to bars, picking up men and submitting to their sexual demands, or, as she expressed it, "to be a good girl." Nevertheless, during the first four or five months of her treatment, on Friday or Saturday night she drank a little wine or beer, rationalizing her behavior as attributable to her need for nourishment, since her diet was skimpy. The following mornings, she then found herself either alone in her rumpled bed or in the company of some man whom she often could not recall having met. She had no memory of their activities. After a time, she was able to remember an intervening step, of having gone to a series of bars until she found some man who was willing to be picked up. I understood her acting out or, more accurately, reenactment behavior to have a symbolic communicative role in which she unconsciously sought to inform me of the meanings of past activities (Ekstein 1976, Robertiello 1976). My initial trial interpretations of her activities in transference terms as my being a father surrogate were rejected; she symbolically informed me that my transference role was that of a phallic mother surrogate.

On Mondays she often presented dreams or fantasies in which a young animal or child had been abused or unjustly punished. I assumed there was a connection between them and her weekend activities but was unable to locate it. I found myself silently annoyed with her, believing that her claim of having forgotten her actions with the man to be a lie. During one interview, my silent accusation was followed by becoming sleepy (McLaughlin 1975). While dozing I pictured myself as a young child whose contradictory wishes to be good and bad controlled me without my will. With a start, I became alert and thought it had been necessary for her to subject me to her emotional experience or that my own emotional needs were being satisfied by an empathic response. I briefly recalled Searles' oft-repeated statement that working with regressed people requires mutual emotional growth of both patient and therapist. I then consciously put myself in her place and supposed that she was experiencing similar helplessness in the face of contradictory wishes. I further assumed that she sensed my repeated questions as to whether she might have recalled some further detail to constitute accusations, that my actions had given support to her externalization of a self-punitive need, and also that she had expected a reward for her vow to be a good girl but felt that she had received none.

When I questioned her about the validity of my assumptions, she became aware that they were true and also that she had been disappointed that I had not previously understood what she was experiencing. That awareness was followed by her recalling going to a bar and being disappointed when a man refused her advances, saying she was "too old a pussy" for him. Soon she subsequently dreamed that a boy poured kerosene onto and lit the tail of a kitten which ran away terrified, while wanting to bite and claw her tormentor, symbolizing actions which had taken place in the early dramatic interview when I repulsed her overt attempt to seduce me. That material was followed by a change of attitude in which she became aware that she was both angry with the men who rejected her and also with the men who acceded to her seduction to get them to misuse her, although the actual sexual interactions remained repressed. She did not, however, yet learn that her various disappointments with me also screened angry feelings toward me.

When her treatment was first undertaken, I had informed her that after six months, I would be leaving for a period of several weeks. Periodically during that time she recalled vividly that during her childhood her mother customarily went alone to Europe on the Grand Tour, that she had been bitterly disappointed and lonely and that she feared her mother's failure to return, either because mother would prefer to be unburdened by her children and despised husband or because she would die. She also told of having assumed that mother left because of the malfeasances of Mrs. X. with the chauffeur and because of her envy of her sisters, at least two of whom got more of mother's attention than she, via temper tantrums and other forms of disturbing behavior. Mrs. X. had assumed the role of family martyr in part to assuage her guilt. When I left, I felt secure that her separation anxiety had been dealt with adequately.

Upon my return, I was completely surprised to learn that immediately after I left she had attempted to commit suicide by taking sedatives which I had not known she had saved from previous periods of therapy and that her effort had been thwarted quite accidentally. Her attempt at self-murder had been determined by several unconscious motivations. As a child, she had believed that her parents had a limited quantity of love to distribute among their daughters. She had blamed her existence for the emotional upsets of her sisters, which she deemed to be the result of receiving too little parental love. She had often contemplated altruisitic suicide for their welfare. She had also equated mother's absence with death and thought that, were mother to die, Mrs. X. could reestablish symbiotic union with her. But a new element gradually emerged from repression.

In very early childhood, when she had been frightened on shipboard and her mother had ignored her distress, a black waiter had solaced her. There had been a consistently dependable love object during her preschool years, her mother's father, who had held her on his lap, read and told fairy tales to her, and admired her reading them to him and her mathematical precocity. He had died during her first school year but she had not been allowed to view his corpse and unconsciously retained the belief that he still lived. He had once promised her a white elephant and she had thought he meant one that was living. From Kipling stories which he had read or told to her, she knew that white elephants might be found in India. In later life, she became seriously involved in Eastern religions, unconsciously believing that they would lead to her finding a white elephant and rejoining her grandfather, who must be in India. She also knew him to be dead and retained the notion that if she were to die, she could join him in heaven and reestablish the gratifying relationship she had experienced before. We discovered also that her attempted suicide had been designed to keep me alive, as a parent surrogate who would provide love for her still disturbed sisters, now represented by my other patients. Another motive was clear, namely, that she was at some level angry with me and had hoped that her self-murder would destroy me professionally. Though she came to this conclusion intellectually, her anger at me was not experienced consciously. We found that the loss of her capacity to learn, that is, to read and to do mathematics, was based in part on her attempt to deny what she had learned, namely, that her grandfather had died.

After much of this material had been worked through, another impasse developed which was resolved through my coming to understand my emotional responses to her behavior during interviews. It will be recalled that she had subjected her son during his home visits from the hospital to seeing her drunken sexual behavior with men. Sometimes, when she was unwittingly angry with me she would return to her shameful memories of being confronted by the nursemaids with those actions. There came a period of some weeks during which her interviews were dominated by ruminations pertaining to this issue. I gradually noted that I began to respond to such recitations by irritation and sleepiness. She reverted to her seduction of men whom she picked up in bars and our rapport all but disappeared. I then regretted for the first time having accepted her in treatment and wondered why I had done so. I found myself in a dreamy state during an interview and when I became alert, forgot the content of my fantasy. But that night I had a dream which reminded me of my own past. I had learned in prior periods of analysis that I had become an analyst with the unconscious motivation of curing an important love object of my childhood who had suffered from a borderline psychotic disorder. Analysis of my dream made me aware that another reason for my becoming an analyst was that I had sought to protect a younger sib from the effect of that adult's personality disorder. I knew then that I had accepted Mrs. X. in treatment not only to effect changes in her, but in her psychotic son as well.

I then became aware that underlying my conscious identification of her with the disturbed love object of my past lay an unconscious identification of her abused son with my sib and myself as a child, and I was expressing my anger by withdrawal and refusal to recognize her, as her autistic child had done during several of the first years of his life. Such knowledge permitted me to regain my objectivity. Finally, I could interpret to her her wish to provoke me to abuse her and she responded by remembering dreams and hypnopompic fantasies in which she was forced to watch women being raped anally and of having huge phalluses shoved into their mouths. This lead to the recovery of memories of what had transpired between her and the black-gloved, swarthy chauffeur. She had equated him with the kind black waiter and, following her grandfather's death, had sat on his lap, seeking to make him a grandfather surrogate. However, after initially telling her fairy tales, he had held her head and forced his phallus into her mouth.

The themes of her interactions with the chauffeur, and of her behavior before her own son, disappeared in the analysis. For about three years after the recovery of this memory, when they did reappear, they could be interpreted as attempts to master by action her terror and feelings of dissolution when she had watched theretofore repressed parental sexual activities.

DISCUSSION

It is axiomatic that the analyst does whatever he can to avoid discussion, I shall comment on some of the means I use in my efforts to achieve this difficult task.

Speaking of the training analysis in a simplified way, Isakower (1957) stated that its goal is to facilitate the development of an analyzing instrument. It is held to be self-evident that the analyst's primary tool is his own unconscious, his intuition, which is made more available to consciousness and intellectual controls by his training analysis and becomes, thereby, more cognitive and readily accessible to the secondary process (Heimann 1968). The emphasis in this training analysis is to free the analyst's ego functions from libidinal and aggressive conflicts to the degree that they can be used with a minimum of neurotic distortion in the analytic process with which the analysand will identify in the successful analysis.

Freud (1912) perceived an outcome of the successful training analysis to have resulted when the analyst is able to listen to his patient while in a state of "evenly-suspended attention," a period of altered consciousness which has been compared to the dream state (Lewin 1955, Stein 1965). As Fliess (1942) and others have indicated, the comparison is useful but not completely accurate since the analyst places himself in the position of being ready to dream without actually dreaming or without permitting himself the luxury of uninhibited fantasy. The analyst tries to maintain a state of being able to dream while still awake and controls, to a degree, both fantasy and dream. The analyst listens in a position of passivity in which his processes of identification and empathy remain intact and without surrendering his capacity for attention. While he listens without a particular focus, his attention remains selective since he preconsciously or consciously chooses those cues and clues which can lead him to the unconscious content in a patient's verbal and nonverbal communications. The successfully analyzed analyst should be able to scan his empathic and intellectual responses to the patient's productions and eventually discern with a high degree of accuracy the extent to which those responses have been determined by his idosyncratic past and unresolved conflicts (Calef and Weinshel 1977).

While the development of threatened or actual impasses appears to be inevitable in all analyses (Giovacchini and Boyer 1975, Glover 1955, Langs 1975a), they are more frequent and often more severe in the treatment of those patients whose personality structures lie nearer the psychotic end of the continuum of psychopathological conditions. So long as the analysis proceeds smoothly, the therapist's scanning of his response to the patient's communications is more apt to be preconscious. When, to the contrary, impasses threaten or are obvious, his examination of his reactions is more apt to be consciously goal-directed, as was illustrated most graphically in the first case fragment.

It is my impression that some training facilities expect satis-factorily analyzed therapists to retain the state of "evenly-suspended attention" during much of each session. I believe this to be an unreasonable expectation and subject to a high degree of individual variation. I find myself in that altered ego state but a small percentage of the time. Instead, I am more frequently engaged in the process of active thinking, with or without impending or extant impasses. This is particularly true when I am working with regressed patients and especially so during periods of crises. While this mode of operation is a product of my early development of intellectualiza-tion as a major personal defense, I believe that same intellectuali-ation to have come to serve sublimated purposes in work with patients.

Importance of Understanding the Patient's Cultural Heritage

Over the years I have developed the impression that my work proceeds more evenly when I periodically consciously place myself in the place of my patient. To this end, I learn all I can about the actual facts of the patient's cultural heritage as well as his personal socialization experiences. As a result of some twenty years of field investigations with anthropologists of North American Indians of different Athabascan tribes and a single field trip among Alaskan Eskimos, I have learned from personal experience how misleading unvalidated assumptions about the personal meanings of nonverbal behavior and language usage can be. There is a vast literature pertaining to the influence of cultural background, whether frankly exotic or less foreign, that is, determined by the patient's socioeconomic, religious, or other subgroup of Western culture. I am among those therapists who seriously heed that literature and extrapolate from its implications the emotional and intellectual set of the individual patient. Many analysts hold that their work with patients who stem from sociocultural backgrounds similar to their own is more effective than that done with patients from different backgrounds. I am of the opinion that more thorough analyses may result from the treatment of people from the second group, because of the presence of fewer mutually accepted givens, the defensive and symbolic meanings of which may go uninvestigated.

When I am working with patients from cultural backgrounds with which I am unfamiliar, I consult the relevant anthropological, sociological, and cross-disciplinary literature pertaining to their heritage and glean what I can about statistically expectable meanings of the patients' various types of communications, personality configurations, conflicts, and expectations. Given this background of knowledge, I find it easier to imagine myself in the position of the patient at various periods of his life and to have more confidence in my judgment of what is important to investigate at any given time during his analysis. This orientation has led Freeman (personal communication, 1976) to an awareness of and the capacity to treat syndromes among immigrants from southern Italy and their offspring which have confused other therapists; he found their origins in native *mal occhio* practices and beliefs. Freeman was similarly able to diagnose and treat derivatives of the Puerto Rican *ataque* syndrome.

In my judgment, my field work and my acquaintance with such literature enables me to more easily simultaneously identify with the patient's conflicts and expectations and to remain relatively objective, thus diminishing the risk of impasses resultant from countertransference distortions (Boyer and Boyer 1977).

Importance of Identifying with the Patient's Nonverbal Expressive Behavior

From the inception of our profession, psychoanalysts have considered the analysis of the patient's symbolic behavior to be important. Over the years, increasing attention has been paid to the need to include the study of less obvious forms of nonverbal communication, such as the patient's customary posture, facial expressions, gestures, muscular tensions, moods, idiosyncratic sounds and the like, as well as transient variations from such habitual behavior. Some analysts, such as Bruch (1963) and Sperling (1960, 1963), have stressed the advisability of viewing psychosomatic disorders as nonverbal communications and noted that a close link may exist between those disorders and the borderline and psychotic disorders. Searles (1975) opines that for the analyst to help the autistic patient to become able to participate in a therapeutic symbiosis, the analyst must first have become able to immerse himself in the patient's autistic world.

What I wish to stress here is that I seek to remain alert to all of these forms of nonverbal communication and that I have learned that when I consciously place myself in the position of the patient who expresses himself in such manners, my comprehension of his messages, conflicts, and expectations is enhanced.

A brief clinical example follows. It pertains to a woman who suffered from a pathological narcissistic disorder who had been in psychiatric and psychoanalytic treatment for several years with various therapists, without improvement in her interpersonal relationships or her depression. She had been able to remember practically nothing of her prelatency life. As she dealt with self-damaging aspects of her passive expression of aggression, this rather muscular, right-handed woman whose only remembered athletic activity consisted of noncompetitive swimming, occasionally tensed her right forearm and sometimes moved it in a clockwise direction. She became aware of her action and the fact that her arm hurt near the elbow only after I inquired concerning her thoughts about the action, and her associated sensations. While she was intrigued, her direct and indirect associations gave us no useful clues. Eventually, I imitated her movement and on the basis of personal experience thought it might have represented a tennis service. I then asked her whether there might have been a period during which she was engaged in competitive athletic pursuits. She responded with a series of dreams manifestly unlike any previously reported in that they involved more and more overtly depicted war scenes. Then she recalled that she had played tennis during early adolescence with a consciously idealized older sister and on one occasion had intentionally aimed an overhand smash so that it hit her sister in the face. The recovery of that memory led directly to the recollection of repressed problems pertaining to early sibling rivalry and her cathectedly remembering much significant preoedipal data. My technical device appeared to have led to significant turning point in her analysis.

Prevalence of Early Sexual Abuses Among Psychotic and Borderline Patients

Freud was initially convinced that his patients' remembrances of early sexual abuses by parents or their surrogates were to be understood as actual experiences and pointed to the tremendous importance of the childhood environment in shaping character formation. In this view, Freud was strongly supported by the neofreudians and anthropologists who developed the *tabula rasa* formulation of character formation (Boyer 1977a). For a time, Freud (1896, 1954) seriously considered the likelihood that perversion on the part of the parent leads to hysteria in the child. In recent years Freud's early diagnoses of hysteria and serious obsessive-compulsive personality disorders have been questioned and many of his so-diagnosed patients would now be called borderline personality disorders or some equivalent term (Boyer and Giovacchini 1967). And we remember Freud's dilemma when he discovered that such recitations often represented the child's fantasies rather than actual memories (Jones 1953).

I have come to believe that in the case of the psychotic or the sufferer of a borderline personality disorder, Freud's early viewpoint was often accurate. There is ample evidence that the development of such disorders results from continuous minor psychological assaults and we know that the presence of actual sexual traumatizations has been reported only rarely. Yet I have found with startling regularity that in borderline and schizophrenic patients, actual dramatic psychological or physical sexual assaults have been commonplace rather than exceptional, a finding which might have been anticipated from the high incidence of psychological disturbance which has been found to be prevalent in the parents of schizophrenic patients (Lidz 1973). I did not come to this realization from clinical work alone, but also from socialization studies of Apache Indians, who as small children are often subjected to actual primal scene experiences in which the frequently drunken parents' sexual activities are accompanied by grossly hostile behavior, thus affirming the child's oral- and anal-sadistic fantasies (Boyer and Boyer 1972). This has fortified my persistence in aiming at the recovery in treatment of factual early childhood memories.

Clearly, my increasing conviction has influenced my technical approach and made me view the phenomenon of reenacting in the transference as the patient's attempt to remember through actions, rather than as something to be discouraged, provided I do not deem such reenactment to be potentially quite dangerous to the patient or to others. Ekstein (1976a, p. 386) noted "that the psychotic acting out may become the royal road toward the strengthening of reality testing and the secondary process rather than be the primrose path to disaster."

Conscious examination of my emotional reactions in response to the patient's communications and transference state has become a significant component of my therapeutic method, particularly in the treatment of regressed patients. Such examination is more apt to occur during the individual interview in times of emergency, as demonstrated in the first clinical example. I have come to assume that in general my emotional responses constitute valid clinical data, although I routinely seek to evaluate whether those reactions are determined to a hindering degree by my idiosyncratic problems. In the examples cited from the case of Mrs. X., I believe the treatment impasses which developed resulted from my incapacity to objectively examine my emotional reactions. I was unable to understand her identification of me as her autistic son because I had unwittingly accepted that project for personal reasons.

Function of Projective Identification in the Analytic Situation

I have come to understand the operational functions of projective identification in rather simple terms. I agree with Kernberg's view (personal communication, 1976) that that which is projected remains to a degree unrepressed and that the patient maintains some level of continuing to feel what he seeks to project into the therapist, thereby continuing to be preconsciously aware of what he imagines the therapist to experience. His initial aim when he projects hostile wishes into the therapist is to control their ascribed omnipotence by defending himself from the imagined hostility of the analyst and controlling the latter's actions. In the long run, the therapist is used as a repository for projected internalized objects and attitudes which make him feel uncomfortable, and the patient believes he has succeeded in locating them within the analyst. One of the countertransferential problems in the treatment of such patients arises when the therapist unwittingly accepts the projects. The general view is that those elements stem solely from the patient's fear that his hostile wishes or thoughts may result in the destruction of the therapist or retributive damage to himself. Once he believes that such hostility is a part of the analyst, he then more or less continuously scans the analyst's behavior. Over time, the effectiveness of interpretations combined with the patient's observation that the projects' alleged presence within the therapist has not resulted in deleterious effects enables the patient to gradually reintroject them in detoxified form to be integrated into his evolving personality, the nature of which has been discussed cogently by Loewald (1960). Some patients fear that their love is destructive (Searles 1958) and project it "into" the therapist for safekeeping; they similarly cognitively come to view love not to be dangerous (Giovacchini 1975).

There are, of course, other reasons why the patient seeks to project his emotional experiences into the therapist, not the least of which is to make the analyst share and understand them. Frequently, such an attempt is made on the basis of the idea that were the therapist to suffer as does the patient, he will then use his ascribed omnipotence to relieve the patient of his distress. However, I have also come to view such behavior as an attempt to recreate in the therapeutic milieu actual early childhood situations with the ultimate goal of recovering memories and thereby enable reconstruction of the traumatic childhood in an effort to make it "come out right this time."

SUMMARY

Three vignettes taken from the psychoanalytic treatment of two seriously regressed patients illustrate my inner emotional experiences when confronted with selected trying treatment situations and how my use of them resolved a serious crisis in one case and therapeutic impasses in the other two. All three examples illustrate the usefulness of seeking to understand countertransference phenomena in terms of projective identification; the first shows how conscious thinking and knowledge recall can assist the therapist in regaining his objectivity when he feels personally threatened when confronted with acute psychotic transference regressions. Elements of my personal style are presented in the context of aspects of my idiosyncratic past.

In the discussion, attention is drawn to selected means of preparing oneself to avoid the development of untoward countertransference reactions and technical approaches which can be used to resolve them.

References

Alexander, F. (1948). *Fundamentals of Psychoanalysis*. New York: W.W. Norton.

Arieti, S. (1955). *Interpretation of Schizophrenia*. New York: Robert Brunner.

Benedetti, G. (1964). *La Psicoterapia delle psicosi schizofreniche*. Milan: Centro di Studii di Psicoterapia Clinica.

Beres, D. (1968). The role of empathy in psychotherapy and psychoanalysis. *Journal of the Hillside Hospital* 117:362-369.

Bion, W.R. (1955). Language and the schizophrenic. In *New Directions in Psychoanalysis*, eds. M. Klein, P. Heimann, and R. Money-Kyrle, pp. 220-239. London: Hogarth Press.

———(1956). Development of schizophrenic thought. *International Journal of Psycho-Analysis* 37:344-346.

———(1957). Differentiation of the psychotic from the non-psychotic personalities. *International Journal of Psycho-Analysis* 38:266-275.

Boyer, L. B. (1961). Provisional evaluation of psycho-analysis with few parameters employed in the treatment of schizophrenia. *International Journal of Psycho-Analysis* 42:389-403.

———(1971). Psychoanalytic technique in the treatment of certain characterological and schizophrenic disorders. *International Journal of Psycho-Analysis* 52:67-86.

———(1976). Meanings of a bizarre suicidal attempt by an adolescent. In *Adolescent Psychiatry* 4:371-381.

——— (1977a). Working with a borderline patient. *Psychoanalytic Quarterly* 46:386-424.

——— (1977b). Anthropology and psychoanalysis. In *International Encyclopedia of Psychiatry, Psychology, Psychoanalysis and Neurology*, vol. 2, ed. B. Wolman, pp. 56-62. New York: Aesculapius Publishers and Van Nostrand Reinhold.

Boyer, L.B., and Boyer, R.M. (1972). Effects of acculturation on the vicissitudes of the aggressive drive among the Apaches of the Mescalero indian reservation. *Psychoanalytic Study of Society* 5:40-82.

———— (1977). Understanding the patient through folklore. *Contemporary Psychoanalysis* 13:30-51.

Boyer, L.B., and Giovacchini, P.L. (1967). *Psychoanalytic Treatment of Schizophrenic and Characterological Disorders*. New York: Jason Aronson.

Breuer, J. and Freud, S. (1893-1895). Studies on Hysteria. *Standard Edition* 2.

Bruch, H. (1963). Disturbed communication in eating disorders. *American Journal of Orthopsychiatry* 33:99-104.

Calef, V., and Weinshel, E.M. (1977). The analyst as the conscience of the analysis. Paper presented before the San Francisco Society, March 1977.

Carpinacci, J.A., Liberman, D., and Schlossberg, N. (1963). Perturbaciones de la comunicacion y neurosis de contratransferencia. *Revista de Psicoanalisis* 20:63-69.

Cesio, F.R. (1963). La comunicacion extraverbal en psicoanalisis: Transferencia, contratransferencia e interpretaction. *Revista de Psicoanalisis* 20:124-127.

Chessick, R.D. (1965). Empathy and love in psychotherapy. *American Journal of Psychotherapy* 19:205-219.

Ekstein, R. (1976). General treatment philosophy of acting out. In *Acting Out*, eds. L. Abt, and S. Weissman, pp. 162-171. New York: Jason Aronson.

Fliess, R. (1942). The metapsychology of the analyst. *Psychoanalytic Quarterly* 11:211-277.

Freud, S. (1896). The Aetiology of Hysteria. *Standard Edition* 3:191-221.

———— (1910). The future prospects for psycho-analytic therapy. *Standard Edition* 11:141-151.

———— (1912). Recommendations to physicians practising psycho-analysis. *Standard Edition* 12:109-120.

———— (1915). The unconscious. *Standard Edition* 14:156-216.

———— (1954). *The Origins of Psychoanalysis Letters to Wilhelm Fliess, Drafts and Notes. 1887-1902*. New York: Basic Books.

Fromm-Reichmann, F. (1950). *Principles of Intensive Psychotherapy*. Chicago: University of Chicago Press.

Giovacchini, P.L. (1969). The influence of interpretation upon schizophrenic patients. In *Psychoanalysis of Character Disorders*, pp. 279-291. New York: Jason Aronson, 1975.

———— (1975). Self-projections in the narcissistic transference. *International Journal of Psychoanalytic Psychotherapy* 4:142-166.

Giovacchini, P.L., and Boyer L.B. (1975). The psychoanalytic impasse. *International Journal of Psychoanalytic Psychotherapy* 4:25-47.

Glover, E. (1955). *The Technique of Psychoanalysis*. New York: International Universities Press.

Grinberg, L. (1957). Perturbaciones en la interpretacion por la contraidentificacion. *Revista de Psicoanalisis* 14:23-28.

———— (1958). Aspectos magicos en la transferencia y en la contratransferencia. *Revista de Psicoanalisis* 15:15-26.

———— (1962). On a specific aspect of countertransference due to the patient's projective identification. *International Journal of Psycho-Analysis* 43:436-440.

Gruhle, H.W. (1915). Selbstschilderung und Einfuhlung; zugleich ein Versuch der Analyse des Falles Banting. *Zeitschrift fur die Gesamte Neurologie und Psychiatrie* 28:148-231.

Hann-Kende, E. (1933). On the role of transference and countertransference in psychoanalysis. In *Psychoanalysis and the Occult*, ed. G. Devereux, pp. 158-167. New York: International Universities Press, 1953.

Heimann, P. (1968). The evaluation of applicants for psychoanalytic training. *International Journal of Psycho-Analysis* 49:527-539.

Hill, L.B. (1955). *Psychotherapeutic Intervention in Schizophrenia*. Chicago: University of Chicago Press.

Isakower, O. (1957). Problems of supervision. Report to the Curriculum Committee of the New York Psychoanalytic Institute. Unpublished manuscript.

Jones, E. (1953). *The Life and Work of Sigmund Freud*, vol. 1. New York: Basic Books.

Kernberg, O. (1975). *Borderline Conditions and Pathological Narcissism*. New York: Jason Aronson.

Langer, M. (1957). la interpretacion basada en la vivencia contratransferencial de conexion o desconexion con el analizado. *Revista de Psicoanalisis* 14:31-38.

Langs, R. (1975a). Therapeutic misalliances. *International Journal of Psychoanalytic Psychotherapy* 4:77-105.

———— (1975b). The patient's unconscious perception of the therapist's errors. In *Tactics and Techniques in Psychoanalytic Therapy, Volume II: Countertransference*, ed. P. Giovacchini, pp. 230-250. New York: Jason Aronson.

_____ (1976). *The Therapeutic Interaction, 2.* New York: Jason Aronson.

Lewin, B.D. (1955). Dream psychology and the analytic situation. *Psychoanalytic Quarterly* 24:169-199.

Lidz, T. (1973). *The Origin and Treatment of Schizophrenic Disorders.* New York: Basic Books.

Little, M. (1957). "R" — the analyst's total response to his patient's needs. *International Journal of Psycho-Analysis* 38:240-254.

Loewald, H. (1960). On the therapeutic action of psychoanalysis. *International Journal of Psycho-Analysis* 41:16-33.

McLaughlin, J.T. (1975). The sleepy analyst: some observations on states of consciousness in the analyst at work. *Journal of the American Psychoanalytic Association* 23:363-382.

Milner, M. (1969). *The Hands of the Living God: An Account of a Psychoanalytic Treatment.* New York: International Universities Press.

Nadelson, T. (1977). Borderline rage and the therapist's response. *American Journal of Psychiatry* 134:748-751.

Noy, P. (1969). A revision of the psychoanalytic theory of the primary process. *International Journal of Psycho-Analysis* 50:155-178.

Orr, D. (1954). Transference and countertransference: a historical survey. *Journal of the American Psychoanalytic Association* 2:621-670.

Pinto-Ribeiro, R., and Zimmermann, D. (1968). Notas sobre la contratransferencia. *Revista de Psicoanalisis* 25:847-862.

Pokorny, M. (1959). Uber die "Einfuhlung." *Schweitzerische Zeitschrift fur Psychologie und Ihre Anwendungen* 18:112-132.

Racker, H. (1948 [1953]). The countertransference neurosis. *International Journal of Psycho-Analysis* 34:313-324. Reprinted in *Transference and Countertransference.* New York: International Universities Press, 1968.

_____ (1953 [1957]). The meaning and uses of countertransference. *Psychoanalytic Quarterly* 26:303-357. Reprinted in *Transference and Countertransference,* op. cit.

_____ (1958). Counterresistance and interpretation. *Journal of the American Psychoanalytic Association* 6:215-221. Reprinted in *Transference and Countertransference,* op cit.

Rank, O. (1931). *Die Technik der Psychoanalyse,* vol. III. Leipzig, Vienna: Dueticke.

Reich, A. (1960). Further remarks on countertransference. *International Journal of Psycho-Analysis* 41:389-395.

Robertiello, R.C. (1976). "Acting Out" or "Working Through." In *Acting Out*, eds. L. Abt, and S. Weissman, pp. 40-47. New York: Jason Aronson.

Rosenfeld, H.A. (1952a). Notes on the super-ego conflict of an acute schizophrenic patient. *International Journal of Psycho-Analysis* 33:111-131.

———— (1952b). Transference-phenomena and transference analysis in an acute catatonic patient. *International Journal of Psycho-Analysis* 33:457-464.

———— (1954). Considerations regarding the psycho-analytic approach to acute and chronic schizophrenia. *International Journal of Psycho-Analysis* 35:135-140.

Sauguet, H. (1959). Notes pour une introduction a un colloque sur le contretransfert. *Revue Francaise de Psychoanalyse* 23:393-408.

Searles, H.F. (1958). Positive feelings in the relationship between the schizophrenic and his mother. In *Collected Papers on Schizophrenia and Related Subjects*, pp. 216-253. New York: International Universities Press.

————(1963). Transference psychosis in the psychotherapy of chronic schizophrenia. In *Collected Papers*, op. cit., pp. 654-716.

————(1965). Feelings of guilt in the psychoanalyst. *Psychiatry* 29:319-323.

————(1975). The patient as therapist to his analyst. In *Tactics and Techniques in Psychoanalytic Therapy, Volume II: Countertransference*, ed. P. Giovacchini, pp. 95-151. New York: Jason Aronson.

Siquier de Failla, M. (1963). Transferencia y contratransferencia en el proceso analítico. *Revista de Psicoanálisis* 23:450-470.

Sperling, M. (1960). Symposium on disturbances of the digestive tract. II. Unconscious phantasy life and object-relationships in ulcerative colitis. *International Journal of Psycho-Analysis* 41:450-455.

————(1963). A psychoanalytic study of bronchial asthma in children. In *The Asthmatic Child*, ed. H. Schneer, pp. 138-165. New York: Harper and Row.

Stein, M.H. (1965). States of consciousness in the analytic situation, including a note on the traumatic dream. In *Drives, Affects, and Behavior*, vol. 2, ed. R. Loewenstein, pp. 60-86. New York: International Universities Press.

Stekel, W. (1934). Das Phánomen der Gegenúbertragung. *Psycho therapeutische Praxis* 1:64-72.

Volkan, V. (1976). *Primitive Internalized Object Relations*. New York: International Universities Press.

Chapter 16

COUNTERTRANSFERENCE WITH
BORDERLINE PATIENTS

LAWRENCE EPSTEIN, Ph.D.

This paper[1] has developed out of a study I have been making of my own analytic work and the work of supervisees with some difficult patients, most of whom would be diagnosed as borderline character disorders, in order to gain a more articulated understanding of how one might do more effective therapy with such patients.

The paper is divided into two sections. Part I was first presented in August 1977 at the Sixth International Forum in Berlin. The major focus is on the therapeutic use of countertransference data in working with borderline patients. I was prompted to write Part II in response to questions which were raised by colleagues concerning the exclusive use of noninterpretative interventions in the case material presented. In Part II the major focus is on the possibly damaging effects of interpretations which aim to convey insight to the borderline patient. Alternative interventions and strategies, which have proven in practice to be more effective in facilitating ego-maturational processes will be discussed.

1. I want to thank Drs. J. Cohler, H. Field, and A. Issacharoff who critically evaluated this paper during the course of its development.

I

I have been especially interested in the therapeutic leverage that might be gained from understanding the relationship between the patient's transference projections and that component of the analyst's countertransference which is generated by such projections. I am referring to what Winnicott has identified as the objective component of the countertransference. He has defined this as "the analyst's love and hate in reaction to the actual personality and behaviour of the patient" (Winnicott 1949).

Following Winnicott again I would say that the goal of analysis would be the facilitation of those maturational processes which would allow for "the gradual growth of ego organization and strength" (Winnicott 1965, p. 116). In a functional sense I would take this to mean that the person becomes increasingly his own master.

Primary and Secondary Maturational Failures

As the patient's presenting ego pathology varies from the more benign to the more severe levels, I find the analysis to become increasingly (but not exclusively) focused on deeply embedded persisting disturbances in the relations that obtain between the patient's self and its internal objects. This is especially so in the case of those patients who might be diagnosed as borderline character disorders. I would assume that the patient's pathological intrapersonal relationships developed out of his ego's attempts at coping with chronic parental failures to meet his *particular* constellation of maturational needs during the periods of infancy and early childhood.

Such conflicted intrapersonal relationships stress and weaken the ego; they prevent the development of a unified self that is felt to be good enough vis-a-vis representations of parent images which are also valued as good enough. Instead the self may be divided into various good and bad child-self images which are fused with various good and bad images of significant others.[2]

While such split-self and split-object relationships may be derived from the early conflicted interpersonal relationships between the

2. The influence of Melanie Klein (1946) and Kernberg (1975) will be recognized here.

child and his parents, they are not identical with such relationships. They are, rather, subjective transformations of such relationships.

I would term the inadequate parenting, in response to which the basic intrapsychic warping was laid down, the *primary maturational failure.*

Deeply embedded pathological intrapersonal relationships are superimposed on interpersonal relationships throughout the patient's life by means of primitive defensive processes of ego-splitting and projection. They are reenacted in ways that tend to be repetitive and predictable. Other persons with whom the patient becomes engaged are unlikely to make maturationally corrective responses. They typically react to the patient on the basis of feelings and impulses rooted in their own pathological intrapersonal relationships. If this is not the case, they may react on the basis of feelings and impulses which are induced in them by the patient's projective and ego splitting processes. Another way of stating this is that transference projections, as they are expressed in interpersonal relationships, typically beget responses which are under the sway of raw countertransference reactions.

Thus, the human environment may repeatedly fail to respond in ways that might be structurally corrective for the persisting internal pathological self and object relationships which were laid down in response to the *primary maturational failure.* I would term these repeated occurrences the *secondary maturational failure.*

The Essential Task of the Analyst

Typically the analyst becomes the target of the borderline patient's transference projections early in the analysis. In the heat of such interactions, powerful reciprocal conscious and unconscious affects, impulses, and defensive reactions will be induced in us. Such internal reactions are typical of those which his projective processes have aroused in other emotionally significant persons over the course of his lifetime and which continue to be aroused in persons in his current life. *When we are in this emotional position vis-a-vis the patient, I consider that our main task will be to learn how to function with the patient in such a way as to correct or reverse the secondary maturational failure.* We need to discover, in other words, those interventions which facilitate his ego-maturational processes.

Countertransference as Data

Our countertransference reactions to the borderline patient provide valuable data which, when studied and properly understood, can guide us in our task of developing therapeutically effective interventions and strategies. For one thing, the induced feelings and impulses suggest how other people might be impelled to react. This provides us with a rough index of a *wrong* response, that is, an untreated countertransference reaction. Such a response is likely to perpetuate the pathological organization of the patient's self and his internal object world. For another, the countertransference data, when related to other data we have accumulated in our study of the patient, may enable us to understand the particular internalized self-other relationship that he may be reenacting at the moment.

We can then formulate alternative interventions aimed at breaking the vicious cycle of the patient's internally programmed transactions. In our role as participant observer we can then assess the adequacy of our hypothesis and our strategy by studying the effects on the patient's functioning.

CLINICAL EXAMPLE

I have chosen a segment of a beginning psychoanalytic psychotherapy process, under my supervision, to which the theory of projective identification was applied to formulate a hypothesis about the ongoing transference and countertransference and a strategy for working it through.

The patient is an attractive, very intelligent young woman of college age, the only child of a professional couple. She recently dropped out of a highly competitive college after two years because her emotional problems were interfering with her academic functioning. She was overly anxious concerning her ability to perform brilliantly, and she was constantly examining the contents of her mind and testing her memory and always finding both deficient. Since leaving college, she has been living at home with her parents and working at a part-time job in an academic setting. Although she performs her duties to the satisaction of her supervisor, she feels like a fraud and in constant danger of being found out to be the very deficient person she believes herself to be. Work, therefore, exhausts her. She feels physically weak, suffers headaches, dizzy spells, and in order to recover, she takes to her bed, sometimes for twenty-four or more hours. She has a minimal social life. She does not enjoy the company of other people because she becomes intensely self-conscious and self-critical of her own behavior and her mental processes. She is again insufficiently brilliant and witty. She is depressed much of the time and takes poor care of herself. Life and living feel valueless, and she thinks a great deal about suicide. She feels herself to be a morally weak person for having such problems and feels she must be self-indulgent to come to therapy.

She opened her first session with her therapist, a female, by making the following comment: "I find this a degrading impossible situation. I object in principle to therapy because it can never be a relationship between friends, and one should only talk about meaningful things to friends." The therapist responded by asking such questions as what did she mean by degrading? Could she describe what it felt like to be degraded? Why should one only talk about meaningful things with friends?

The patient responded by denigrating the therapist for asking such stupid questions since any intelligent person would find the answers self-evident. The therapist inquired what her objections were to answering stupid questions. This frustrated and exasperated the patient further and caused her to complain about having to spend her time and money talking about such ridiculous matters.

The patient came to therapy three times a week. Over the first three months, in many sessions she was frustrated and complained about the therapist and the way she was conducting the therapy. It made no sense. What was the point of all her questions? The therapist seemed to be indulging herself.

The therapist informed her that according to her conception of analysis, the patient's task was to talk, to say what was on her mind at the moment, and the therapist's task was to facilitate her talking. That was why she asked questions. The patient complained that these questions prevented her from talking about anything meaningful. Up to that point in the therapy, what she considered meaningful were general cynical pronouncements concerning the emptiness and the futility of life, and the insensitivity and the stupidity of people. She would never give details and always resented being asked for any, yet when the therapist was quiet and listening she accused her of being disinterested and emotionally disengaged.

She said that she continued with the therapy mainly because she didn't want to begin with a new therapist and because the therapist had been recommended by a person whom she and her parents held in high esteem. She had expected that a therapist recommended by such a person would have many brilliant and illuminating things to say and she was still hopeful that this might happen. She thought, however, for the time being, because the sessions were so bad, that it might be a good idea to reduce the sessions to once a week.

Countertransference Data Illuminates Ongoing Intrapsychic and Interpersonal Relations

At this point the therapist brought the case to supervision. She reported that she felt like a bad therapist for this patient and that she was doing bad therapy with her. She had no understanding of the therapeutic process at this point or of its value to the patient. She shared the patient's wish that she would say something illuminating and brilliant and shared her disappointment in her inability to do so. Apparently the patient's relentless denigration had eroded her confidence and destroyed her capacity for objective participant-observation.

In supervision, the therapist was first asked whether, apart from the patient's persisting *subjective* dissatisfaction, there was *objective* evidence that the therapy was having bad effects on the patient? She reported that, as a matter of fact, she had the impression that the patient was markedly less depressed, was functioning better at work, seemed free of psychosomatic reactions, and had more contact with friends. Her worst feelings were centered on the therapy and therapist.

It seemed reasonable, then, to conclude that the ongoing interpersonal transactions — in which the patient complained to the therapist about the therapist's faults and the therapist responded by asking questions which the patient found frustrating — were having progressive therapeutic effects. The therapist, while being consistently perceived as a bad therapist, was apparently functioning like a good one.

On examining the faults the patient found with the therapist, it becomes clear that they paralleled her own. As she was intellectually deficient and self-indulgent, so was the therapist. She found the therapist, as she found herself, persistently unsatisfying and frustrating, and they were, the both of them, disappointments to her high expectations. She had so little to offer to other people that she couldn't bear spending much time with them. The therapist was such poor company that the patient wanted to reduce the amount of time spent in her presence by two thirds.

For her, the therapist seemed to be, then, in that phase of the therapy, the externalization of her own deficient, hated and unwanted child-self. *Vis-a-vis* her own bad-self-in-the-therapist she was functioning as her own internal sadistic parent.[3]

Countertransference reactions and the analyst's internal self and object relationships. The countertransference reactions which are induced by a patient's efforts to blacken the therapist will depend on the therapist's internal self and object relationships. A therapist with a good-enough self and a good-enough internal parent would be in a favorable position to understand the patient's denigration as projection and would have minimal difficulty in functioning therapeutically. A therapist who has the residuals of a grandiose omnipotent child-self — developed in response to a persecutory internal parent — might feel impelled to retaliate viciously when criticized.

The internal relationship of this therapist's parent and child paralleled that of the patient. At the time she brought the case for supervision, her own sadistic internal parent had joined forces with that of the patient in attacking her own inadequate child-self. Because of this she had lost her capacity for rational participant-observation and felt in full agreement with the patient that neither she nor her therapy was any good.

Possible effects of acting on induced feelings. The therapist brought the case to supervision at a critical moment. Had she reduced the frequency of the sessions, acting on the low opinion she shared with the patient concerning the treatment, it might have had bad effects on the patient's ego and irreversibly destructive effects on the therapy. It would have substantiated the power of the patient's aggressive impulses to penetrate the therapist's insides and destroy her goodness and replace it with her badness. As a

3. This transference-countertransference matrix parallels what Racker (1953 [1957]) has described as "a 'manic transference situation' (of the type called 'mania for reproaching')" and a corresponding complementary "'depressive-paranoid' countertransference situation." (pp. 140-141).

consequence, the patient would be vulnerable to the ravages of unconscious guilt and paranoid anxiety. The therapist, at the level of the patient's unconscious fantasy, would become a bad object, infected with her poisons, and a potentially dangerous, vengeful persecutor.

Up to the point that she brought the case to supervision, the therapist had not functioned with the patient in such a way as to confirm the patient's power to be destructive. While being perceived as the patient's bad self and evoking her denigration, the therapist continued to function as a separate person, steadily giving evidence of her capacity to survive in good health.

Progression of Therapy

The supervision having restored her capacity for objective participant-observation, the therapist responded to the patient's idea that the number of therapy sessions be reduced by suggesting further discussion of the matter. She asked the patient to elaborate on her complaints about the way the therapy was being conducted and asked for her ideas about how she might become a better therapist. She asked such questions of the patient as, what was the value to her of good sessions? Why did she so strongly object to bad sessions? How did they make her feel? Why did she object so strongly to talking to a banal therapist? etc. The therapist, in effect, was responding to the patient's projections by taking them seriously, investigating them, and getting the patient to discuss them.

Over the next three months, the patient found the therapist's questions less and less frustrating, and she would answer them seriously. It gradually emerged that she wanted to cut down the frequency of the sessions because things were going well in her life, and she had no significant problems to bring to the sessions. She dreaded that her mind would become at times, a total blank or at best, produce banalities and trivia. She was becoming afraid that the therapist would find her so dull and ordinary that she would lose interest in working with her. Gradually, she became less concerned with the quality of either her own performance or the therapist's and entered another phase of the therapy, talking tentatively of her babylike dependency needs. All the while her functioning outside of the therapy sessions, with some ups and downs, progressively improved.

Strategy of Mutative Interpersonal Transactions

I would like now to attempt some explanation of the maturationally facilitating effects of the therapist's interactions with this patient.

The therapist's technique of responding nondefensively to the patient's complaints, questioning her further concerning her objections to the therapist's defects induced frustration and further expressions of denigration. I would understand the frustration to be essentially with the therapist's puzzling persistence in maintaining her own integrity and in *not* reacting as she is expected to on the basis of the patient's internal programming. According to this programming, the therapist would be expected either to defend herself, counterattack, reject the patient, or appease her. Such reactions, at the moment, might reassure the patient of her power to dominate and control both the other person's insides and behavior. In the long run, her ego would be either unaffected or weakened. In any case, the pathological organization of her self and internal object world would be perpetuated.

The therapist's technique continuously drew out the patient's projections of her own insufficiencies until her ego was ready to take them back. In the process, the therapist said nothing to challenge the accuracy of the patient's perception of her as banal, self-indulgent, mentally deficient etc., nor did she say anything that might invalidate such negative feelings and judgments. To have done so might have induced the premature return of the patient's badness to her ego.

Nor did the therapist make what I think would be the error that analytically trained therapists would be most inclined to make in working with this patient: namely, communicate an accurate understanding of the situation to the patient by making such an interpretation as, "I think you must be so intolerant of your own deficiencies that you are putting them into me and attacking them." During a phase of overt negative transference, when the analyst is perceived as a bad object, such interpretations are likely either to be rejected or to have the effect of prematurely disqualifying the patient's need to project her badness.

I shall elaborate further the possible psychonoxious effects of interpreting to the patient her ego-splitting and projective processes in the second part of this paper.

The Borderline Patient's Intolerance of the Two-Person Situation

I would speculate that the analyst's persisting study of the patient, and his persisting attention over the full course of the therapy to the effects of his interventions contributes per se to the strengthening of the patient's ego boundaries and to his developing a sense of himself as a separate and significant person.

For much of the analysis, those patients whose internal self-and-object-world is divided into good and bad self-other bondings find the analyst's objective interest alien, puzzling, frustrating, and anxiety arousing. The patient is not internally organized as a full and separate person, and it unsettles him to be treated as such. The analyst's autonomous objective functioning may constitute a threat to the patient's omnipotent aims and causes him to feel a loss of control. In order to nullify the analyst's separateness and his frustrating objectivity and to reconstitute an interpersonal emotional matrix that feels familiar and under his control, the patient's primitive ego-splitting and projective processes become intensified. He attempts to force the analyst into the role and function of some part of his self or of some internalized other.

These are the times that our egos may be especially stressed by countertransference disturbances.[4] Destructive impulses may be aroused in us and may be turned either against the patient or ourselves. This will depend on our own internal self-object relationships. Our impulses to act out may be heightened, such as to appease the patient or to blame or to attack him. Or they may be unconsciously neutralized by the formation of symptoms, such as depressive reactions, somnolent detachment, fatigue, feelings of tedium, psychosomatic reactions, etc. Our capacity for rational objective judgement may break down for greater or lesser periods of time.

In my opinion, these transactions in which the patient is unwittingly driven to penetrate and dominate our insides and in which one's ego is struggling to survive and maintain its integrity have the greatest potential value for producing positive mutative effects on the patient's ego. The success of such transactions will depend on whether we are able during the process to sustain or regain our capacity for rational judgment and observation and

4. The transference and countertransference situation which is created by the patient's ego-splitting and projective processes will be discussed in greater detail in Part II below.

intervene in a way which is based on a comprehension of the intrapersonal meaning of the ongoing interpersonal matrix.

I would summarize my speculations concerning the reasons for such changes in the case I have been discussing as follows:

1. The patient's destructiveness is drawn out by the analyst, deflected away from the patient's ego and is diffused in the process.

2. The analyst by accepting the patient's view of her as defective and imperfect gradually enables the patient's internal parent to become more tolerant of its child's deficiencies.

3. The analyst's resistance to the patient's efforts to nullify her separate existence causes the patient's ego to come up against the boundaries of the analyst's ego repeatedly. In the process, the boundaries of the patient's ego become strengthened. Her ego becomes increasingly capable of tolerating frustration, and of tolerating and containing her own bad feelings, without having to project them, turn them against herself or convert them into symptoms. She becomes more accepting of the reality of the two-person situation. In brief, such transactions provide a kind of calisthenics for the ego.

In conclusion: in the patient's internal self-and-object-world, the persecutory parent's treatment of the inadequate child-self does not go unanswered. The persecuted child seeks vengeance and retaliates by frustrating the parent, going on strike for protracted periods of time, becoming passive, helpless, too infirm to perform—thereby inducing further attacks from the frustrated parent. Such was the case, I believe, with the patient under discussion.

When the patient projects his or her bad self into the therapist, she provides him with an opportunity to break an internal vicious cycle. In this case, the therapist's interactions with the patient, which were shaped and sustained by her understanding of the countertrans-ference data, ultimately subdued the hatred and suffering of the patient's internal parent and gained its acceptance of her deficient, needy child, contributing thereby to the gradual growth of ego organization and strength.

II

Therapeutic strategies evolve according to the requirements of a particular treatment situation. That the strategy which emerged in response to the patient's resistances in the case discussed was transactional rather than interpretative raises a controversial question: namely, how thoroughgoing are changes in a patient's functioning which are brought about by interpersonal interactions, unaccompanied by conscious insight? Are such changes phenotypic, having only the superficial value psychoanalysts would typically ascribe to such results as are brought about by behavior modification techniques, or can they reflect true and enduring changes in the patient's psychic structure? Such questions ramify, raising others, such as, what are the criteria for deep and enduring psychic change? What is the function of interpretation and insight? What interventions are considered appropriately "psychoanalytic"? I am not prepared to elaborate on such issues in this paper.

I have, however, for some time been interested in ascertaining, on an empirical basis, which interventions and strategies prove to be effective in working with borderline patients and which interventions prove either to be ineffective or actually damaging to therapeutic progress. My main purpose in this essay will be to develop the implications of the following clinical observations: (1) that up to a certain point in the analysis of many patients, communications from the analyst which aim to convey insight via interpretation are either ineffective or are followed by psychonoxious effects; (2) that such is not the case regarding insights which the patient comes to on his own; and (3) that at some later point in the therapy the patient increasingly assimilates the analyst's interpretations with therapeutic effects.

Specifically I shall discuss the following issues:

1. The damaging effects that interpretations which aim to convey insight may have on borderline patients whose psychological survival depends mainly on primitve ego-splitting and projective defense mechanisms, and particularly, on patients with split-off destructive envy.
2. How the unconscious counter-destructive impulses which are typically induced in the analyst by the borderline patient's ego-splitting and projective processes may cause the analyst to attack the patient unwittingly with interpretations.
3. Alternative strategies and interventions which take account of the patient's resistances and ego-maturational needs.
4. The problems generated by the development of the *pseudo* working alliance between the borderline patient and the analyst.

5. Why it is usually necessary to work with the transferences of the borderline patient in the here-and-now.
6. Factors that may interfere with the analyst's capability of recognizing that his interpretative activity may be contributing to a deteriorating treatment situation and with his capability of developing alternative strategies and interventions.

Kernberg has, to my mind, contributed a comprehensive understanding of the borderline personality organization and of the vicissitudes of both the transference and the countertransference in the treatment of such patients (Kernberg 1975). I fully agree with his recommendation that the treatment of the borderline patient be conducted in such a way as to foster the "systematic elaboration of the manifest and latent negative transference without attempting to achieve full genetic reconstruction on the basis of it ..." (p. 72). I would also agree that "a consistent undoing of the manifest and latent negative transference is an important, probably indispensable prerequisite for a broadening of the observing ego and for solidifying a therapeutic alliance" (p. 82).

Based on my observations of the effects of various interventions in my own work and in the work of supervisees with borderline patients, I would have to disagree with Kernberg's major technical recommendation for dealing with the patient's negative transference, namely, "confrontation with the interpretation of those pathological defensive operations which characterize borderline patients, as they enter the negative transference" (p. 72). He concludes that "the observing ego and interpretation of projective-introjective cycles mutually reenforce each other" (p. 83).

Currently, my choice of the optimal intervention in any given clinical situation will depend on my grasp of the patient's ongoing resistances and on my best understanding of how to resolve them in such a way as to facilitate maturational processes. In this I have been influenced by the work of Spotnitz (1969, 1976) with patients suffering from preoedipal disorders. The deficiences in the ego organization and strength of such patients usually requires that resistances be resolved indirectly and slowly over time.[5] Spotnitz has observed that the standard psychoanalytic intervention of interpretation is usually ineffective.

5. See Spotnitz (1969) for a discussion of techniques for resolving resistances.

The Special Place of Interpretation in Psychoanalysis

According to Sandler, Dare, and Holder (1973)

Interpretation occupies a special place in the the literature on psychoanalytic technique. Thus Bibring (1954) has remarked that '*interpretation* is the supreme agent in the hierarchy of therapeutic principles characteristic of analysis....' The central role of interpretation is equally stressed by M. Gill (1954) who asserts that 'psychoanalysis is that technique which, employed by a neutral analyst, results in the development of a regressive transference neurosis and the ultimate resolution of this neurosis by techniques of interpretation alone' [p. 104].

Concerning interpretation, Greenson writes,

This is the procedure which distinguishes psychoanalysis from all other psychotherapies because in psychoanalysis interpretation is the ultimate and decisive instrument. Every other procedure prepares for interpretation or amplifies an interpretation and may itself have to be interpreted. To interpret means to make an unconscious phenomenon conscious. More precisely, it means to make conscious the unconscious meaning, source, history, mode, or cause of a given psychic event [Greenson 1967, p. 39].

I think it would be valid to state that interpretation remains the intervention most widely and traditionally favored by almost all schools of psychoanalysis. The purpose of interpretation is to convey or stimulate insight. Disagreements among schools center mainly around the nature of the particular contents or the particular psychological or interpersonal process to be included in the interpretation, in other words, what it is valuable for the patient to have insight about. An exception to this is the work of Sullivan as explicated by Leston Havens in his study of Sullivan's technique, *Participant Observation:*

The difficulty the resistances offer both Freudian analysis and Reich's character analysis—that the analyst may not be able to gain a conscious acceptance of his interpretation—is not a difficulty of the same degree for interpersonal method. Interpersonal method does not seek consciousness or aware- ness so much as learning. The patient need have little insight— indeed insight may cause trouble—so long as the projections and responses to them are worn away [Havens 1976, p. 46].

Negative Effects of Interpretation on the Borderline Ego-State

I want to elaborate here on the possible negative effects of interpretative interventions which aim to convey insight on patients whose psychological survival seems to depend largely on their ego's use of primitive splitting and projective mechanisms. Such patients require an external depository for one or another of their internal embattled and polarized parts. When we as analysts become the depository of such projections, we also become for the patient a potentially dangerous persecutor. This potential emerges from two sources: (1) within the patient, as a consequence of his ego-splitting and projective processes; and (2) from the countertransference reactions aroused in the analyst by these processes.

Kernberg (1965) has described the consequences of ego-splitting and projective identification as follows:

In terms of structural aspects of the ego projective identifica- tion differs from projection in that the impulse projected onto an external object does not appear as something alien and distant from the ego because the connection of the ego with that projected impulse still continues, and thus the ego "empathizes" with the object. The anxiety which provoked the projection of the impulse onto an object in the first place now becomes fear of that object, accompanied by the need to control the object in order to prevent it from attacking the ego when under the influence of that impulse [p. 45].

I would put this somewhat differently, that is, in terms of the patient's possible unconscious understanding that he is doing the analyst harm: powered by powerful unconscious aggressive impulses, he has ejected something from within himself and forcibly injected it into the analyst, thereby violating the analyst's boundaries and vitiating his personhood, making of him an object of use. This created within the patient's ego a state of paranoid expectation to receive some counter assault against his own insides. Therefore, what we say to the patient at such a moment, and how we say it, may be critical.

Should the patient receive from us an interpretation of the transference—*which would be some statement directed at his ego*—informing him about what he is making of us or doing to us and why (in terms of his internal processes and dynamics) his ready-to-be-persecuted ego is likely to perceive such a communication as the expected and deserved counter assault. The interpretation, in other words, is unlikely to be appreciated as a therapeutically meaningful statement offered in good faith, because such things are not expected from one's most immediate enemy. It is rather something to be defended against, and the first order of defense is likely to be nullification. At best, then, the interpretation is rendered ineffective. At worst, depending on how attacked the patient's ego feels, the interpretation may cause the ego to intensify its defensive and ego-splitting and projective processes, resulting in an even higher level of paranoid anxiety and the possible escalation of what may have started out as a simple negative transference into a negative therapeutic reaction and possibly into a treatment-destructive resistance.[6]

The patient's ego-state might be aggravated considerably if our interpretations are powered by unconscious counter-transference reactions which arise under the pressure of the patient's transference projections. Kernberg describes the analyst's counter-transference situation as follows:

> The therapist is now faced by several dangers from within: (i) the reappearance of anxiety connected with early impulses, especially those of an aggressive nature which now are directed toward the patient; (ii) a certain loss of his ego boundaries in the interaction with that particular patient; and (iii) the strong

6. Freud (1923) introduced the term "negative therapeutic reactions" to describe those reversals of therapeutic progress which he observed to follow the patient's awareness of improvement or the analyst's expression that improvement had taken place. He ascribed the negative therapeutic reaction to the arousal of the patient's unconscious guilt.

I am not using the term, negative therapeutic reaction, in this specific sense. I mean it to apply generally to reversals of therapeutic progress, the causes of which may vary from situation to situation. "Treatment-destructive resistance" refers to a more lethal and malignant process and implies an *intention* to destroy the treatment.

temptation to control his patient in consonance with an identification of him with an object of the analyst's own past [Kernberg 1965, p. 45].

Put more simply, we may feel vitiated, controlled, and threatened and our own survival needs may impel us to rid ourselves of the patient's projections so that we can experience the relief of feeling ourselves again. And this is true whether the patient makes of us a devil or an angel.[7]

The act of interpreting at such moments, then, may be an *unwitting acting out* of our need both to rid ourselves of the unwanted projections and to attack the patient for what he is doing to us. If such should be the case, interpretations which are freely and fairly given by the analyst from the conscious, task-oriented sector of his ego would be powered as well by his unconscious hostility, the effects of which are likely to be far more noxious for the patient than if he were confronted by the analyst's open aggression.

A Safe Strategy: Containing, Reflecting and Investigating the Projections

As illustrated in the clinical vignette presented earlier in the paper, a safe course for the analyst to follow when he is the depository of the patient's projections is, first, to contain the projections and then, to restrict his comments and questions to those which are directed away from the patient's ego and toward his own ego. If the patient, for instance, finds fault with the analyst or impugns his motives or intentions, the patient's perceptions and ideas should not be challenged. They should either be reflected, for example, "you mean, I am such-and-such a kind of person, or I'm really out to get you;" or they should be objectively investigated: the patient can be asked, for example to describe the analyst's faults more fully and asked for his ideas on how they should be corrected. He can be asked to elaborate on his ideas concerning the analyst's motives and whether he thinks they are conscious or unconscious, and asked in a

7. Erwin Singer's (1970) comment is worth noting here. "To transfer ... is to generalize in relatively unquestioning terms. To do this requires a more or less prominent disregard of the therapist as he actually is, pressing him into a mold no matter how much it violates his reality. To distort another person by ascribing angelic qualities is by no means less disrespectful than to invest him with diabolic tendencies. In either case his personality is disregarded and attacked" [p. 276-277].

nonchallenging way if he can describe any of the evidence upon which he is basing his conclusions.

In this approach the question of how much of that which the patient attributes to the analyst is distorted or reality-based is treated as irrelevant. *All* of the patient's ideas and perceptions are taken seriously. This approach reduces paranoid anxiety because it steadily conveys the reassurance that the analyst has been unharmed by the patient's projections and is more interested in understanding him and in investigating his projections than in counterattacking and punishing.

In such interpersonal transactions, the analyst's objective nonrejecting attitude toward all that the patient projects on him, I would speculate, is of crucial importance in facilitating within the patient an integration of his own good and bad parts, that is, a greater tolerance for his own faults and weaknesses together with a reduction of self-hatred, destructiveness, and compensatory omnipotent strivings.

The technique I have been discussing would apply mainly to patients whose destructiveness is reactive rather than malevolent; that is, to patients who do not enter treatment primed with a strong unconscious intension to destroy it. Should their destructiveness be aroused in the course of the analysis, it is likely to be in response to the therapist's errors. Such patients enter therapy with a need to externalize an intrapersonal conflict so that it can be played out in an interpersonal interaction with the analyst. What they mainly require of the analyst is that he function as a "good container" of projections and that he intervene in ways that do not unduly threaten the ego and provoke it to generate negative therapeutic reactions or treatment-destructive resistances.

Counteraggressive Confrontations

There are special situations, however, which I have taken up at length in, "The Therapeutic Function of Hate in the Countertransference" (chapter 13, this volume), in which the patient may need to be confronted with the analyst's aggression in order to interfere with a vicious cycle of psychotic proportions. Such a malignant process may be set in motion by massive outpourings of abusive hate, or by a more insidious penetration of the analyst's boundaries with the aim of destroying, maiming, poisoning or otherwise damaging his insides. In such instances, the patient needs an openly aggressive response from the analyst of sufficient strength to reestablish the self-other boundaries which tend to become obliterated by such attacks, and to reassure him of the analyst's survival in good health.

Confrontations which convey the analyst's aggression openly and directly against an intensely negativistic borderline patient's frustrating and stalemating tactics often have the effect of engaging his reasonable ego and of resolving his resistance to progressive communication. Bird (1972) has made a similar observation concerning resistances which are used to attack the analyst. He recommends "confronting the patient with what he is doing."

> I choose the word "confront" in place of "interpret" for the same reason that I prefer "destructive" and "harmful" to "hostile" and "negative," viz., to move from the concept of wish to the concept of deed, from hostile feelings to hostile acts. In my experience, resolving this destructive situation depends upon speaking of it directly, even assertively, in terms of action.
>
> The patient's initial reaction to this confrontation depends upon many variables. A common reaction is a verbal attack in return, an attack which, perhaps for the first time, contains an injurious intent that is unmistakable to both patient and analyst. Sometimes the reaction is dramatic. One patient responded by telling me with some wonderment in his voice, that for several weeks he had been carrying a gun in his car. Whatever the response, it will no doubt be a welcome relief, for the patient as well as for the analyst, from what has probably been a monotonous, many-months-long stalemate [p. 292].

The aggression in such direct confrontations will more likely than not be received by the patient as an emotionally appropriate expression of the frustration aroused by his provocative behavior. Having received the expected and deserved counterattack, he is reassured concerning the analyst's survival in good health, his paranoid anxieties are laid to rest, and he may be free to say many things that he had been concealing behind his negativistic behavior.

In any case, a direct communication of counteraggression which is under the control of the analyst's ego is far less dangerous and less emotionally confusing to the patient than interpretations which are *consciously* aimed at informing him about his "projective-introjective cycles" but *unconsciously* loaded with muted hate and counterdestructive impulses. The analyst's indirect and underground hostility, in such a case would be likely to induce an intensification of the patient's indirect, underground destructive reactions.[8]

Noxious Effects of Interpretations on Patients with Split-Off Envy

There may be additional difficulties generated by the analyst's interpretative activity in the analysis of those borderline patients who have intense destructive envy. Among Melanie Klein's most important contributions is her penetrating insight into the insidiously destructive effects of the split-off (unconscious) envy which may be aroused in some patients by the analyst's interpretative activity (Klein 1957).[9]

For those patients with impoverished and embattled selves, each interpretation given by the analyst may be a painful reminder of the analyst's superior creative powers, which are made to seem perpetually regenerative by the flow of interpretations. If the patient's ego is not strong enough to bear the emotional pain that might follow on his becoming aware of his impoverishment and inferiority vis-a-vis the analyst, such awareness must in some way be dissociated along with intense quantities of envy and hate. Unconsciously the patient acts to reestablish a more tolerable balance of goodness, badness and power by nullifying the effectiveness of the interpretations. As the intensity and the virulence of the unconscious envy and hate increase, the patient's unconscious attacks become directed at the analyst and the analysis itelf, which means that he *acts* to destroy both. Typically such attacks take some form of psychological self-destruction, including an exacerbation of symptoms, somatization, or antitherapeutic acting out.

The virulence of such antitherapeutic reactions depends, I believe, on the interaction of two factors: (1) the patient's predisposition to destruction envy, and (2) the amount of stimulation of it which is given by the analyst. Klein and those analysts who have been strongly influenced by her theories (Racker 1968, Segal

8. See Searles's paper, "The Schizophrenic's Vulnerability to the Therapist's Unconscious Processes" (in Searles 1965).

9. Racker (1968) has elaborated this in his chapter, "Analysis of Transference Through the Patient's Relations with the Interpretation."

1964), follow the standard analytic practice of interpreting resistances; therefore, they interpret to the patient all manifestations of his split-off envy. I have observed that this practice may exacerbate the situation, causing an escalation of negative thera-peutic reactions into treatment-destructive resistances. I believe this is because the split-off destructive envy, which is aroused to begin with by the analyst's interpretative activity, is intensified rather than relieved by additional interpretations directed at the envy, itself. His silent destruction of the treatment may constitute the patient's only possible defense against becoming conscious of unbearable emo-tional pain—feelings of abysmal inferiority and utter hopelessness— and possibly against the arousal of dangerously insistent suicidal urges.[10]

In general, it would be well to assume, until we can find out otherwise, that the exacerbation of negative therapeutic reactions is an indication that the patient may be desperately trying to survive the noxious effects of the interventions which are being used at the time. When interpretations are having such destructive effects, some alternative approach is needed if the vicious cycle is to be broken.

As Klein has pointed out, destructive envy and hate which "forms part of the negative therapeutic reaction" may be masked in certain patients by cooperative behavior in the analysis. (Klein 1957, p. 14)

CLINICAL EXAMPLE

I had a rather unnerving experience with such a patient, a businessman in his mid-fififtes, who suffered from severe depressive reactions. In the early stage of the analysis, he would produce a flow of rich materal, including early memories and dreams, and he was quite receptive to exploring these data for the meanings and implications they had for his current life. He was interested in my interpretations and would respond with associations which led to further clarifications. He seemed to be so free of resistances that I

10. This would be consistent with Klein's theory of the schizoid-paranoid position, according to which, ego-splitting and projective identification in the infant originate as the rudimentary ego's first survival defense against self-destruction by the excessive quantities of its own rage (which Klein calls the death instinct) aroused by its frustrating and helpless dependence on the maternal environment (the breast) (Klein 1946).

lost contact with what I knew about his psychopathology; that he
was severely psychosomatic and accident prone, that he was very
dependent on marihuana and, in addition, drank a great deal of
alcohol; that he was extremely self-conscious and insecure in the
company of males, especially authority figures, often to the point of
developing paranoid obsessions of persecution.

After some weeks of such productive and apparently collaborative activity, the patient reported, without any particular sense of
alarm, that for some time now, after leaving the sessions, he found
himself engaged in "self-destructive behavior." Before driving
home, he had been going into a working class bar, drinking heavily
and provoking heated political arguments with the men in the bar,
sometimes almost coming to blows. With his mind still foggy from
alcohol he would then drive the twenty-five miles to his home
recklessly and at high speeds.

I noticed a faint smile on his face as he reported all this. He agreed
with my observation that he might be smiling and that he didn't
seems to be as concerned as one might expect him to be about his
behavior. He could make no connection between any of his feelings
and thoughts during the sessions and the way he reacted after
leaving. He did notice, however, that he sometimes found himself
thinking with admiration of my competence as an analyst and of the
self-confidence that I seemed to exhude, and that he thought that he
was a long way from having such good feelings about himself.

I said that I wondered whether in addition to feeling admiration
for me, he might also be feeling something more disturbing, like
envy, and whether this might be spilling over into destructive and
self-destructive behavior. The patient said that for some reason this
struck him as being correct, and he asked if I had any further
thoughts as to why he would be acting out in this way. I said that I
thought it might be his way of equalizing things, that if he got hurt or
killed it would be sad commentary on my analytic competence. He
accepted this interpretation and said, with some expression of awe,
that he was struck with the lengths to which his unconscious was
willing to go in order to defeat me.

At the next session, the patient reported that after leaving me,
became drunk in the bar and provoked a fight with a much larger
man and was knocked unconscious. He said that it was a miracle that
he was able to drive home in his condition. He had, in fact, a minor
accident, sideswiping a divider railing on the highway. At this point

I felt myself a helpless victim of the deadly game he was playing with me.

I asked him for his thoughts on whether it would be ethically correct for me to continue working with him if my therapy continued to make him worse. This seemed to alarm the patient somewhat, bringing forth his first overt expression of anger at what appeared to him to be an attempt to blackmail him. I said that I could see how he might think I was blackmailing him, but that as far as I know I didn't have blackmail in mind. In any case, what about my question. Did he think it ethical, etc? After some discussion he said that he could see that it might not be ethical for a therapist to continue to treat a patient if the treatment was clearly having destructive effects and that he was afraid that I might decide to discharge him.

I believe my acknowledgement of my impotence in the face of his superior destructive power and my willingness to accept a total defeat of my analytic competence served both to quell his raging split-off envy and to awaken some concern for his own well-being. In any case, from this point on, the patient made good progress in the analysis. For a long time, however, until he became fully conscious of his hate and envy toward me, I was very careful to keep a low profile, making no interpretations, and turning all of his questions back to him (e.g., "What are your own thoughts about that?"). Almost all my interventions were confined either to reflections of his own thoughts and feelings or to simple questions asking for clarification or for more information.

Keeping a Low Profile: A Safe Strategy for Unconscious Envy

When I have determined that split-off destructive envy and hate may be causing a deterioration of the treatment situation, I attempt to find some way of reducing any impact I might be having on the patient that would continue to excite these unconscious processes. To begin with, I stop communicating any of my understandings and insights to the patient. I conduct my interpretative work silently and confine most of my communications to brief reflective comments or questions which are aimed at getting him to produce his own understanding and insight. I also aim to give the patient the feeling that I am attempting to understand him as well as he understands himself, but no better, and I find that it sometimes helps matters if the patient has the feeling that I may not be having the easiest time in understanding him.[11] Instead of envying me the patient may begin to experience some frustration with me and begin to find fault with me in a way that he can easily verbalize. What this does is create a more favorable distribution of good and bad parts and of power. All badness and inferiority is no longer all within the patient; nor is all goodness and superiority within me. He feels more comfortable with me as a person who is more like himself.[12] He no longer is driven to destroy the analysis or himself as a means of surviving or getting back at me.

Detoxification of Split-Off Envy and Its Assimilation by the Ego

It might be argued that if the analyst blocks or dampens the arousal of split-off envy by stopping his interpretative activity, he simply ceases to do analysis and is conducting supportive therapy. This argument, however, would not be consistent with a view of analysis as being essentially an ego-maturational process. It fails to take account of the patient's ego deficiencies and of the defenses his ego must employ in behalf of its own survival.[13]

There remains, however, the legitimate question of when and

11. Amnon Issacharoff, in a personal communication, has suggested that from an interpersonal point of view interpretations may have the following effect: the patient who is already in a down position, is being put further down by the all-knowing, analyst-parent who is, in effect, telling the patient-child what is wrong with him. Jonas Cohler, also in a personal communication, has pointed out that premature interpretations may cause the patient to experience himself as being robbed of his superiority and omnipotence which he still needs as part of his defensive system. This is in line with the views of Kohut (1971) and Spotnitz (1976).

12. This is similar to Spotnitz's description of the narcissistic transference: "the patient is permitted to mold the transference object in his own image. He builds up a picture of his therapist as someone like himself — the kind of person whom he will eventually feel free to love and hate" (1976, p. 109).

13. In what is to my mind an excellent paper, Pine (1976) has challenged the counterposing of insight and supportive therapies as being in opposition to each other. In psychoanalytically oriented work with ego-deficient patients he points out that supportive and insight approaches must be "counter*poised, i.e.*, in some *balance* with one another." He also states that the psychoanalytically oriented supportive therapies, which are based on psychoanalytic developmental theory "are complex affairs, intellectually taxing, including many moments of interpretative work" (p. 554).

how the patient's unconscious destructive envy will be dealt with in the analysis and ultimately detoxified. I think this might come about in roughly the following way. With the split-off envy and hate in a more dormant state the patient's ego is relieved of having to exert itself to fend off the conscious experience of unbearable emotional pain. In addition, the ego is no longer weakened by silent, insidious turning-in-on-itself its own destructiveness. As the patient's resistances are progressively resolved in the course of the analysis, his ego becomes increasingly capable of tolerating and containing a wider range and greater intensity of bad feelings and destructive impulses. These will eventully include feelings of inferiority vis-a-vis the analyst along with hate and envy. The patient's destructive impulses are now available to be discharged verbally and in the process lose their power to be insidiously and silently destructive. The patient knows now that he has wishes and impulses and the means to destroy the analyst and the analysis, but he is also less able to deny the cost to himself of doing so. In addition, as the therapy progresses there will become established within the patient a more integrated image of the analyst as someone he loves as well as hates, a person who is not simply his persecutor and who, therefore, is that much more difficult to destroy.

The Pseudo Working Alliance

This leads me to say something about the establishment of the working alliance in the treatment of the borderline patient. Greenson (1967) defines the working alliance as follows:

The reliable core of the working alliance is formed by the patient's motivation to overcome his illness, his sense of helplessness, his conscious and rational willingness to cooperate, and his ability to follow the instructions and insights of the analyst. The actual alliance is formed essentially between the patient's reasonable ego and the analyst's analyzing ego.

With those patients who are capable of a genuine working alliance, it is generally unnecessary for the analyst to be especially deliberate and cautious in his choice of interventions. The patient is more, rather than less, open to knowing and understanding himself, and he assimilates interpretations with therapeutic effects. Under such conditions, it is appropriate for the analyst to communicate his understanding to the patient of whichever ongoing conflict, transference, or resistance may be salient at the moment.

I would agree with the following statement made by Kernberg (1975) concérning patients with a borderline character organization:

> To establish a therapeutic alliance with the therapist becomes equal to submission to him as a dangerous, powerful enemy, and this further reduces the capacity for the activation of the observing ego (p. 82).

Yet all, of the elements that Greenson has included in what he calls "the reliable core of the working alliance" are sufficiently present in many borderline patients to mislead the therapist to believe that a true working allance is in operation from the very outset of the treatment. When such is the case he is likely to engage in routine interpretative work, and the patient may respond overtly to such interventions as if he found them acceptable and useful—as did the male patient I presented with the split-off envy. Covertly, however, insidiously destructive processes may be set in motion which attack both the interpretation and the analyst for having given it. In many cases, by the time the patient returns for the next session, his memory of what was said to him may be grossly distorted and his grievance against the therapist may seem totally unjustified when measured against the therapist's memory of his actual communication to the patient. The analyst is now in the position of the patient's persecutor, and it will generally make matters worse if he offers further interpretation or clarification of reality.

More importantly, however, such an occurrence is a clear indication to the analyst that he has been misled into believing the patient capable of a working alliance.

It would seem that the capacity for a true working alliance will depend on the stability of the patient's perception of the therapist as good enough and that this, in turn, would depend on the stability of a matching internal good-enough whole object representation. Whenever such primitive defensive operations as ego-splittling or projective identification prove to predominate in the patient's interpersonal transactions with the therapist, it is a strong diagnostic sign that the patient's internal self and object world is divided and dominated by partial self and object relationships. Under such conditions, the patient is mainly capable of what Spotnitz (1969, chapter 5) has termed "rudimentary" cooperation, and the therapist's interventions should be delimited to those that aim at the facilitation of ego-maturational processes. As the pathology of the patient's internal self and object relationships diminishes, and as an enduring capacity for a true working alliance develops, the range of therapeutically effective interventions would increase accordingly.

There may be many moments in working with borderline patients that the analyst, in an unwitting effort to escape the intense countertransference feelings which are typically aroused, may attempt to engage the patient's rational ego *before* an adequate foundation for an authentic working alliance has been established. A form in which this error is frequently cast—because it has the appearance of a psychoanalytically appropriate intervention—is to shift the patient's attention from the heat of the here-and-now to the past. Although this strategy may succeed in quieting things down for the moment, it generally retards the working through of the transference.

Necessity of Working with Transference Projections in the Here-and-Now

I would like to consider more fully why the transferences of the borderline patient ususally requires us to work with them in the here and now.

Greenson makes a distinction between transference displacements and transference projections. He states that the essential mechanism in the neurotic transference is the displacement onto the analyst of reactions to *whole* significant persons or *whole* object representations from the patient's past. There is, then, a close correspondence between the memory of such whole significant persons and such whole object representations. In transference projection the patient is "ejecting something from within his *self representation* onto or into another person" (Greenson 1967, p. 175.) In the transference of patients with multiple good and bad self-other fusions, the projection of self and other *parts* is likely to predominate over displacements of *whole* object representations. *Transference projections*, then, rather than transference displacements, are characteristic of the borderline patient.

In the analysis of transference displacements, the patient's recall of the past helps him to differentiate internal from external reality. His memories of experiences with earlier significant figures serves to reduce the correspondence between internal imagos and the real person of the analyst. He becomes increasingly aware that he is reenacting an unresolved emotional situation from his past. In this way the transference displacements are dissolved.

The function of the transference projection is different and more urgent. Its function is to preserve a weak ego against the toxic, possibly disorganizing effects of highly charged primitive internal conflicts. By ejecting one of the conflicting elements, together with its attendant affects and impulses, and depositing it in the other person, the ego externalizes the conflict, thereby creating an adversary situation. We are reminded, then, that the mechanism of transference projection is essentially a paranoid solution; as such it is unlikely to be *directly* influenced either by memory or other rational processes of the ego. The analyst may not, by simply stepping out of the adversary position, reduce the borderline patient's need to have him there.

Should the patient cooperate with the analyst in shifting the focus of attention to the past, it may be because he unconsciously senses the analyst's inability to tolerate the adversary position. This is likely to result in what Langs has termed a "therapeutic misalliance" (Langs 1975). I have observed that when misalliances develop in response to the analyst's inability to tolerate the patient's projections, there is a corresponding increase in pathological reactions, for example, a deterioration in the patient's outside interpersonal relationships or exacerbation of symptoms.

Leston Havens makes an interesting and sophisticated argument in favor of what he calls Sullivan's "counterprojective method." This technique would shift the patient's attention from the analyst as a transference object to other persons in the patient's past or present life. "The goal is not to reduce or eliminate projection [in patients] but to move them" (Havens 1976, p. 101). The immediate purpose is to prevent their escalation into unmanageable transference psychoses. The therapist allies himself with the patient's ego against his hostile introjects (now pro-jects). The rationale is that "sharing the feelings and, above all, acknowledging any reality at their root opens the way to their acceptance and then disavowal or reduction" (p. 103).

I would favor "joining" the patient in this way at certain times that he expresses paranoid reactions toward other persons in his life. When I myself have been the target of his projections, I have found it possible to maintain the patient's paranoid reactions within manageable bounds by investigating them as if they had some sound basis in fact, or by the judicious use of counter-aggression when indicated.

When the working through of the transference projections has been carried far enough to yield an enduring improvement in ego organization and strength, the patient generally becomes more tolerant of insight and of gaining a true understanding of how his past experiences may have contributed to his present difficulties.

Up to this point many borderline patients dwell on static childhood memories of deprivation and persecution, using them as secondary gain resistances; they serve as a means of inducing guilt, pity or sympathy in others, as a plea for special exemptions, and as a justification for not getting on with one's life. As the patient's memory function is released from its bondage in the service of illness, it becomes free to contribute to the enlargement and the enrichment of the self.

The Compulsion to Interpret

In conclusion I would like to comment on some unconscious countertransference reactions that might interfere with an analyst's ability to adopt alternative strategies to interpretation when faced with a deteriorating treatment situation.

If, in response to what we have been educated to believe is correct analystic procedure, the patient persists in developing negative therapeutic reactions and treatment-destructive resistances, at best we encounter frustration and confusion. At worst, we are in danger of hating the patient or ourselves or both because of all the implications of suffering an analytic failure. Narcissistic defenses may be called into play to shield us from depressive anxieties, and we may be impelled to increase our interpretative activity as a manic defense, in order to reassure ourselves of our analytic potency. And as I have said earlier, the interpretations may be driven as well by unconscious impulses to attack and punish the patient. Our difficulty in disengaging ourselves from what has now become a *compulsion* to interpret will be compounded to the extent that we are identified with a "psychoanalytic group-ego" that *requires* us to interpret in order to feel ourselves a proper analyst. Should we become, in this way stuck in our interpretative activity, the treatment situation will deteriorate accordingly.

References

Bird, B, (1972). Notes on transference. *Journal of the American Psychoanalytic Association* 20:267-301.

Freud, S. (1923). The ego and the id. Standard Edition 19:3-66.

Greenson, R. (1967). *The Technique and Practice of Psychoanalysis.* New York: International Universities Press.

Havens, L. (1976). *Participant Observation,* New York: Jason Aronson.

Kernberg, O. (1975). *Borderline Conditions and Pathological Narcissism.* New York: Jason Aronson.

Klein, M. (1946). Notes on some schizoid mechanisms. *International Journal of Psychoanalysis* 33:433-438.

———(1957). *Envy and Gratitude.* New York: Basic Books.

Kohut, H. (1971). *The Analysis of the Self.* New York: International Universities Press.

Langs, R. (1975). Therapeutic misalliances. *International Journal of Psychoanalytic Psychotherapy* 4:77-105.

Pine, F. (1976). On therapeutic change: perspectives from a parent-child model. In *Psychoanalysis and Contemporary Science* 5:537-569.

Racker, H. (1953 [1957]). The meanings and uses of countertransference. In *Transference and Countertransference.* New York: International Universities Press, 1968.

———(1968). *Tranfserence and Countertransference.* New York: International Universities Press.

Sandler, J., Dare, C., and Holder, D. (1973). *The Patient and the Analyst.* New York: International Universities Press.

Searles, H.F. (1965). *Collected papers on Schizophrenia and Related Subjects.* New York: International Universities Press.

Segal, H. (1964). *Introduction to the Work of Melanie Klein.* New York: Basic Books.

Singer, E. (1970). *Key Concepts in Psychotherapy,* New York: Basic Books.

Spotnitz, H. (1976). *Psychotherapy of Preoedipal Conditions.* New York: Jason Aronson.

———(1969). *Modern Psychoanalysis of the Schizophrenic Patient.* New York: Grune & Stratton.

Winnicott, D.W. (1949). Hate in the countertransference. *International Journal of Psychoanalysis* 30:69-75.

_____ (1965). *Maturational Processes and the Facilitating Environment*. New York: International Universities Press.

Chapter 17

COUNTERTRANSFERENCE WITH CHILDREN AND ADOLESCENTS

ROBERT J. MARSHALL, Ph.D.

I: ANALYSIS OF THE LITERATURE

The Dearth of Literature

This chapter[1] proposes to: (1) review and analyze the literature in the field of child and adolescent psychotherapy and psychoanalysis with the especial goal of understanding the reasons for the limited attention to the area of countertransference; (2) define four types of countertransference; (3) provide clinical cases demonstrating how certain countertransference reactions which threatened to impede progress were used to facilitate treatment; and (4) delineate some of the complications of, yet values in, countertransference reactions toward parents.

A most significant feature in the area of countertransference towards children and adolescents is the limited literature. Of 217 references on countertransference provided by an American Psychological Association Abstract Search covering 1967 to 1976,

1. The author would like to acknowledge the assistance of the staff of the Northern Westchester Center for Psychotherapy and the clarifications provided by Jacqueline Foley and Cynthia Plumpton.

only 19 references — 6 of which were foreign sources — pertained to children or adolescents. *The Bibliography for Training in Child Psychiatry* (Berlin 1976) has no references. The venerable *Psychoanalytic Study of the Child* provides ten index entries in twenty-five years. The three editions of the *Index of Psychoanalytic Writings* cite only seventeen references from 1900 to 1969. A scan of subject indexes in child therapy books reveals only nominal attention to countertransference.

Several authors have also noted the relative lack of attention to countertransference. Maurice Green (1972) speaks of the "neglect," Christ (1964) observes the "virtual silence" while Akaret and Stockhamer (1965) note the "dearth" of literature in respect to late adolescents.

Similarly, in case conferences and reports, attention has traditionally been on topics other than the therapist's feelings.

The Neglect as a Reflection of Countertransference Problems

The early educator-psychoanalysts. Kohrman et al. (1971) also recognize that "we don't talk about such things," but provide an excellent analysis of the lacuna. Taking an historical and cultural tack, Kohrman et al. argue that the first child analysts had been educators who dealt with children from the lower echelons of society. Functioning out of an educational mode, the educator-analysts emphasized needs for growth through learning, sheltering, protecting, and transmitting of cultural values. The therapists' backgrounds oriented them to function as real objects, to develop a positive transference and provide a "giving" relationship. Aichhorn (1935, 1964) is a good example of an early worker who functioned as educator and psychoanalyst. Berta Bornstein had worked as *Fursorgerin* (combining some duties of social worker and welfare worker) according to Blos (1974).

The transference controversy — the influence of A. Freud and M. Klein. Another factor which may have deflected the early child therapists from developing the concept of countertransference was Anna Freud's (1955) declaration in 1926 that "transference neurosis" could not be established with children although she allowed that "transference reactions" could occur. Forty years later Anna Freud (1965) revised her position by recognizing that "transference neuroses" could occur, but not equal to the adult variety in every respect. Abbate (1964), Van Dam (1966), and Casuso (1965) provide panel reports on this issue.

Anna Freud (1955) also indicated: "negative impulses toward the analyst ... are essentially inconvenient, and should be dealt with as soon as possible. The really fruitful work always takes place with a positive attachment." This pronouncement perhaps led to an inculcation of guilt and anxiety in therapists who found their charges to hold less than a "positive attachment."

Then, too, the curious disregard of countertransference phenomena by Anna Freud and by Melanie Klein probably deterred less courageous therapists from formal exploration of countertransference.

Obstacle or instrument? In the realm of adult psychoanalysis, the change from viewing countertransference as an obstacle, to using it as a formidable vehicle has been traced by Feiner (chapter 5), Issacharoff (chapter 1), and Epstein (chapter 10). In general, the field of child therapy has not shown the same steady course toward a studied use of countertransference. Among the child analysts, Berta Bornstein (1948) appears to be the first to have delineated some of the emotional factors which *limit* a therapist's effectiveness. She cited the child's unpredictability, his highly charged affects, his narcissism, and the closeness of his productions to the unconscious. S. Lebovici (1951, 1959, 1970) was an early and continuing contributor to the understanding of the *pitfalls* of countertransference not only to the child, but to the parents. Slavson (1952) tended to see countertransference problems in terms of personality types of the therapist. For example, he depicted the "negative" therapist being angry and disapproving as a function of the therapist's identification with his own parents' attitudes toward him and a rejection of his childhood.

Szurek (1950) saw identification with the child as promoting acting out. Rubenstein and Levitt (1957) *warned* of the therapist's feelings toward the father of the child. Corday (1967) spells out the *dangers* of the countertransference as a male therapist while treating pubertal girls. More recent authors such as Pearson (1968), Friend (1972), and Masterson (1972) recognize the importance of the countertransference, but tend to portray it as an *obstacle* to be surmounted by supervision or personal analysis. Marshall (1978) finds the countertransference to be the central *problem* in the treatment of delinquents, especially since contacts with family, school, and court may be necessary.

Viewing countertransference in a more positive vein, Colm (1955) appears to be the first to advocate the countertransference not as a "fault," but as a necessary means of investigating the interpersonal field. Winnicott (1949), in his discussion of hate and appropriate handling of it by the therapist, opened wider the range of affects which could be talked about in a detailed and personal manner. Proctor (1959), in clinically rich descriptions, spelled out both the pitfalls and the uses of countertransference reactions in the treatment of juveniles with character disorders.

Holmes (1964) sensitively discussed the active use of induced feelings in the treatment of adolescents, while Christ (1964) openly discussed his sexual transference-countertransference with a psychotic girl. He emphasized the private and personal nature of his feelings rather than the pathological. Kohrman et al. (1971) provide a well-balanced discussion of the active use and dangers of countertransference phenomena. Articles in Strean's (1970) anthology also provide a more positive view of countertransference. Marshall (1976) suggests that countertransference feelings provide clues to the analysis of the resistance of children and adolescents. Giovacchini (1974), noting that recovery of infantile memories and traumatic childhood events are rare today, believes "that these transference-countertransference reactions, if properly handled, become an event that is equivalent to lifting infantile amnesia" (p. 282).

"There's too much of it." Many authors subscribe to the "there's too much of it" theory, which provides a paradoxical explanation for the neglect of countertransference. It appears that overwhelming feelings of guilt, inadequacy, and anxiety underlie many therapists' attitudes toward their child and adolescent patients, particularly those therapists whose analyses and supervision have not fully encompassed the personal and technical problems of conducting therapy with troubled youth. King (1976) cites rejection, the wish to punish, and appeasement-identification as three significant countertransference reactions of child care workers to violent youth. Giovacchini (1975) cites procrastination of adolescents as being particularly trying. Pichon-Riviere (1952) discusses the following feelings: competition with the mother, stealing the child from the mother, and pregnancy envy. Frequently, in institutional settings the child workers are extremely reticent in revealing not only their feelings toward their charges, but are loath to comment on their

methods. For example, in one setting known to the author, only after some trust was established were those workers able to reveal their bewilderment and deep despair in handling their patients and to allude to the guilt about their feelings and practices. In one instance, a highly popular group worker, who was being promoted, did not attend the farewell meeting of his group because he could not even handle their positive feelings. More frequently, fear and anger were the dominant, confusing feelings. Ekstein, Wallerstein, and Mandelbaum (1959) discuss not only the therapist's countertransference to an institutionalized child, but emphasize the staff's countertransference as a compounding disturbing factor. Marshall (1978a) provides a clinical portrait of a milieu therapy program wherein a team of child workers tended to use reality problems as a defense against examining countertransference issues. He offers the hypothesis that the ability to discuss countertransference represented the acme of the functioning of the total program.

Berta Bornstein (1948) illustrates the threat and fear that grips the therapist because of the child's emotional lability and easy availability of libidinal and aggressive material. She cites the seductiveness and provocativeness of children which facilitates the acting out of the therapist, and warned of the danger of regression, which "no one in continuous contact with children can escape." Kabcenell (1974) in a memorial note amplifies Bornstein's position. Ester Bick (1962) believes that the stresses and strains produced in the child analyst "are more severe than those on the analyst of adults. The intensity of the child's dependence of his positive and negative transference, the primitive nature of his fantasies, tend to arouse the analyst's own unconscious anxieties. The violent and concrete projections of the child into the analyst may be difficult to contain. Also, the child's suffering tends to evoke the analyst's parental feelings, which have to be controlled so that the proper analytic role can be maintained. All these problems tend to obscure the analyst's understanding and to increase in turn his anxiety and guilt about his work."

Friend (1972) views the countertransference as evidence of residual pathology, "opportunities to defend against the incompletely analyzed infantile-parental problems of the analyst, the omnipotent need to maintain a nurturing feminine identification or a powerful, authoritative masculine identification with the adolescent as a figure for projective identification. There may be unconscious seductive erotic determinants of unresolved infantile components and a desire for leadership or omnipotence that extends the analyst into areas of interaction that he himself would never individually narcissistically enjoy. The painfulness of an individaul's adolescent reactions may temper the unconscious aspects of one's own reactions and substitute for unresolved aspects of this developmental phase" (p. 325). Friend also cites the "complexity, strain and communication problem" in exclusively treating children "just as a mother might have too many children to take care of personally."

The more formidable defenses are erected against destructive thoughts, impulses, and feelings toward children. One of our core cultural values is that of helping and loving children, while child abuse is considered an abomination. Certainly, respect and care for children are a mark of the highest form of civilized life. Nonetheless, the recorded history of the child offender (Sanders 1970) and of children in general (DeMause 1974) indicates that children have been treated with incredible savagery. Reingold (1967) believes that impulses toward infanticide are more widespread than is commonly accepted. Virtually every mother who has been in treatment with me has guiltily expressed a wish to be rid of her children in one way or another. Moreover, patients frequently report that their parents wanted to be rid of them. Winnicott (1949) gives eighteen reasons why a mother may hate her baby, even though it is a boy. Although the treatment of violent children has been described frequently, virtually nothing has been written about the feelings of the therapist. Marshall (1974, 1978) has outlined a theory and technique of handling the delinquent and aggressive child through a utilization of the therapist's feelings. Masterson (1972) tangentially refers to this area. The quiet in this countertransferential area certainly suggests that "there is too much of it" and that the violent feelings of the therapist perhaps are not being used constructively.

Closely associated with the firm taboos against aggression toward children and infanticide are the strictures against sexuality. De Mause (1974) presents some startling reports of child sexual abuse and adds that historical reports about sexual abuse of children are still locked in library vaults. As this is being written, the news reports declare that special civil and police actions will be taken against persons using children in producing pornography.

The Homuncular Theory

Another factor which may be termed the "homuncular" or "little adult" theory was suggested by a young therapist who, when asked about his reasons for wanting to treat children, jokingly replied, *"Kleineh kinder, kleineh tsores; groesseh kinder, groesseh tsores"* (little children — little problems; big children — big problems). The primitive, fallacious, and lulling assumption is that the type and intensity of countertransference problems with children are more diminutive than with adults. This "little adult" theory is likely to be an especial defense against the contrary — "there's too much of it."

Contribution of Client-centered Therapy

Another source of neglect of countertransference may stem from the client-centered approach to psychotherapy. Basing their work primarily on Carl Rogers's philosophy, child therapists such as Axline and Moustakas emphasized the need for nonconditional acceptance of their client's feelings. This acceptance and the correlative permissiveness seeped into the sphere of behavior. Moustakas (1953), for example, advocated telling his children "In here you are free to do what you want." The notion of "setting limits" certainly had to be evolved in order to contain intolerable behavior. Dorfman (1951) indicated that in order to remain emotionally accepting, client-centered therapists set limits including terminating the session and putting the child out of the playroom. Truax and Carkhuff (1967) in their monumental series provide evidence that successful therapists had accurate empathic understanding, nonpossessive warmth, and genuineness. One gets the impression that feelings other than those prescribed by the above triad are not permissible, lead to negative therapeutic consequences, are indicative of an unsuccessful therapist, and must be eliminated. "Counselors or therapists who are low in communicated accurate empathy, nonpossessive warmth and genuineness are ineffective and produce negative or deteriorative change in the patient because they are noxious stimuli who serve primarily as aversive reinforcers *and* also because they elicit negative affect in the patient (which increases the level of the patient's negative self-reinforcement, increases the level of negative affect communicated to others, and thus increases reciprocally the negative affect and negative reinforcement received from others" (pp. 161-162).

Jourard (1971) has suggested that disclosing the therapist's feelings to the patient and working the feelings into the relationship are valid options.

The Parental Trap

Still another source of avoidance of countertransferential feelings may be rooted in the fact that most therapists are parents themselves and tend to see their own children in their patients. The feelings, both positive and negative, which ordinarily should stay at home, filter into the consultation and playroom so that transferences and countertransferences are evolved but not explored.

The Nature of the Conceptual Model

A medical model of disease seems to be a major conceptual view of countertransference. Preventively, it is as if one must go through an elaborate process of immunization in order not to experience any of the dread symptoms. And if one should discover any of its symptoms, one should go for treatment. A less threatening medical model might view the countertransference as normal growth and development which the patient induces in the therapist. This accretion would represent a regeneration of pathology from the patient's past in order for the therapist to help improve the patient's future. Colm (1955) uses a field-theory interpersonal model which conceptualizes countertransference as a necessary dynamic part of the interpersonal field. Less anxiety evoking would be a communications model as suggested by Searles (1975) and Langs (1975) wherein the feelings of the therapist may reflect unconsciously transmitted messages of the patient.

The Contribution of Behavior Therapy

Historically, the last resistance to exploring countertransference evolves from the behavior therapy movement. Although there has been much research on "therapist variables," there appears to be little interest in investigating feeling states of the therapist. There have been important exceptions such as Bandura (1956) who found a positive correlation between therapist anxiety and competence. Bandura, Lipsher, and Miller (1960) examined the therapist's "approach-avoidance" reactions to patient hostility. Conceptually, there appears to be little room for such a subjective variable as countertransference. When therapist attitudes do seem to interfere with patient progress, the behavior therapists seem to take a "rise above it" stance and recommend further training — which brings us to Freud's original position.

II: THE DEFINITIONS

While the term can be used generically to describe all of the reactions of the therapist to his patient, countertransference, in this sense, is too vague and general to be of much scientific help. A. Reich (1960) pointed out that this "totalistic" definition, preferred by many authors, is of limited value — just as useless as defining transference as the total reaction of the patient to the therapist. A "totalistic" definition, however, has had the virtue of removing some of the stigma from "being in countertransference." Perhaps the "totalistic" definition has deterred researchers from considering that there are different types of countertransferences thus obscuring some of their results (Fiedler 1953, Cutler 1958, Horwitz 1974). Hopefully, the following distinctions will assist in clarifying the semantic morass characterizing the area of countertransference.

To be more precise and operational, two broad groupings of countertransference can be discerned. One group's main characteristic depends on the source of the countertransference: therapist or patient. That is, one type of countertransference is a response of the therapist which is *induced primarily by external (patient) behavior*. It is a response which most therapists would experience in a given situation. Another type of countertransference is a response of the therapist which is *induced primarily by the internal promptings of the therapist*. The former type of countertransference is similar to Winnicott's (1949) "objective countertransference": "the analyst's love and hate in reaction to the actual personality and behavior of the patient." The latter type of countertransference, akin to a true transference neurosis, has been termed "subjective countertransference" by Spotnitz (1969).

There is also another definitional dimension — the degree of consciousness. On one side of this continuum there is no recognition of a reaction to the patient. On the opposite pole the therapist is fully aware of his reactions and can determine from where the main stimulus derives. This two-dimensional or factor model yields four types of countertransference as illustrated in Figure 1.

FIGURE 1

TYPES OF COUNTERTRANSFERENCES

	Unconscious	Counscious
Therapist Induced	I	II
Patient Induced	III	IV

Traditionally, the unconscious-therapist induced response (Type I) has been the major and most feared type of countertransference, and is a true transferential response to the patient — a whole response (Gitelson 1952), posing a symbiotic problem (Tower 1956). The resolution of a Type I countertransference appears to be via additional analysis or analytically oriented supervision. The major problem is that the therapist, because of the unconscious nature of the conflict, is unaware of the real situation. The therapist is acting out in concert with his patient, and can be alerted only through recognition signs such as those spelled out by Menninger (1958, p. 88) and Spotnitz (1969, p. 170). Other clues, applicable to children and adolescents, are:

1. Excessive play with diminuation of talk
2. Quick yielding to requests
3. Gratification of child, particularly feeding and gift-giving
4. Any strong feeling, especially accompanied by guilt or anxiety
5. "Lulling" (Sarnoff 1976, pp. 243-246): "The process of altering attention ... when a child plays out similar fantasies repetitively."
6. Impulsive talk or action
7. Physical contact

8. Allowing parents to use child's time
9. Consultation with parents or others without child's involvement or agreement
10. Strong, unresolved feelings toward parents
11. Inability to involve parents appropriately
12. Preoccupation with changing behavior, especially as desired by parents or school.

Some of the above factors, when under deliberate conscious control, may be used as parameters.

In the treatment of children where the situation is more labile and where the child will tolerate errors, Type I countertransference may occur for longer periods than with adults. A reflection of Type I countertransference can be found sometimes in the quality of the relationship with the youth's parents. That is, if the therapist has too little or too much contact with the parents, or if the therapist/counselor of the parents is experiencing difficulty, the therapist may search for Type I countertransference.

The Type II countertransference (counscious-therapist derived) is less pernicious, but may prove to be troublesome to resolve. In this situation the therapist "knows" the problem, but cannot surmount it. Analytically oriented supervision seems indicated.

Type III countertransference usually stagnates or obscures the therapeutic situation. Although much may seem to go on in the session, no real movement occurs because the patient is in control of the treatment. Given a cooperative patient and a reasonably alert therapist, progress can resume as soon as the therapist recognizes that there is a problem. Strean (1970), Langs (1975), and Searles (1975) address themselves to this area. Supervision of any kind, including peer discussion, can be helpful. Frequently, Type III resolves into Type IV countertransference.

Type IV countertransference, which is the focus of the clinical material in this chapter, denotes that the patient is primarily responsible for inducing thoughts and feelings (but no action) in the therapist which are fully within the therapist's awareness.

The therapist's main task is to study the interactional field and devise proper interventions. There is considerable support to the idea that Type IV countertransference is not only unavoidable, but is a prerequisite for successful therapy especially with those patients who function primarily at a preverbal level. For example, Spitz (1956) speaks of three steps by which the analyst understands the patient. (1) The therapist becoming aware of the derivatives of his own unconscious response to the patient's unconscious; (2) inferring of the underlying processes in himself; (3) creating a transitory identification with the patient. Ackerman (1959) believes that avoidance of countertransference may protect the therapist but will not heal the patient. A. Reich (1951) declares, "Countertransference is a necessary prerequisite of analysis. If it does not exist, the necessary talent and interest is lacking."

The Communication of Countertransference

The issue always arises — should the countertransference be communicated to the patient? Clinicians such as Tauber (1954) and Little (1951), and child therapists Colm (1955), Proctor (1959), and Greene (1972) believe that it is therapeutic to the patient (and therapist) to reveal dreams and feelings. Most authors are circumspect about this issue and generally imply that the counter-transference should not be shared with the patient. Gitelson's (1952) statement seems to strike the middle ground: "You can reveal as much of oneself as is needed to foster and support the patient's discovery of the actual inter-personal situation as contrasted with the transference-countertransference situation." Freud's statement, in a 1913 letter to Binswanger (1957), is salient. "It is one of the most difficult ones technically in psychoanalysis. I regard it as more easily solvable on the theoretical level. What is given to the patient should indeed never be a spontaneous affect but always consciously allotted and then more or less of it as the need may arise. Occasionally a great deal, but never from one's unconscious. This I regard as a formula. In other words, one must always recognize one's counter-transference and rise above it, only then is one free oneself. To give someone too little because one loves him too much is being unjust to the patient and a technical error. All this is not easy and perhaps possible only if one is older."

My own experience has led me to believe that no gratuituous revelation of countertransference is indicated and that countertrans-ference material be given only when the information will be predictably helpful. When the youth does guess my feeling state, I validate his perception in accord with the principle of reinforcing his reality testing. One delinquent youngster, who was provocative and destructive in my office asked whether I was mad at him. While affirming his perception, I asked him how that information would be helpful to him. He replied, "It makes me feel good to know what people are really thinking about me and it helps me control myself when I know people are mad at me."

In another situation, an obsessional seven-year-old boy quizzed me incessantly after each of his quasi-provocative moves, "Are you mad at me, doctor?" Interpretations seemed to have no impact on him. Aware of my own growing annoyance, recalling his mother's murderous rage toward him, and mindful of his own internal fury, I quipped half playfully, half seriously, "I'm so mad, I could kill you." Startled, but pleased, he enthused, "You are?" Reaching for some guns, he said, "Now we can play killing each other."

III: CLINICAL STUDIES

Several clinical studies are offered in order to illustrate how Type IV countertransference can be utilized to understand and resolve patient resistances. In effect, a countertransference reflects the presence of and leads to a counter-resistance. The counter-resistance must be studied, understood, and dissolved by the therapist before he is in a position to resolve the resistances of the patient. The analysis of the counter-resistance can frequently lead to an understanding and a derivation of an effective resolution of the resistance.

In many of the interventions made in the following examples, classical means of handling resistances are not typically used. The reasons for this have been spelled out by many authors. Lorand (1961) cites many difficulties in treating adolescents. Strean (1970) outlines the vulnerability of the adolescent and suggests methods of treatment usually reserved for the borderline or schizophrenic adult. Sarnoff (1976), in discussing the latency child, advocates flexibility according to the cognitive, dynamic structural and developmental aspects of the child. He speaks of inducing those defenses and structures which will lead to the "calm, pliability and educability" of the latency state. Bornstein (1951) sees the latency child in "precarious equilibrium." Her therapeutic approach is as follows. "Because the child battles against his impulses and needs to keep up his defenses, we must be particularly careful to respect his resistance and to work through his defenses before we approach the material which is warded off." "Defense analysis is more complicated in the analysis of children than in that of an adult." "The utmost care has to be exercised in the analysis of latency to strengthen weak structures and to modify those which interfere with normal development." Geleerd (1957) advocates the need to use different techniques in the approach to adolescents, reminding us that "consistent and systematic analysis of all defense mechanisms is not possible," and that a major goal is to increase the tolerance of the ego to pathological conflicts. In the treatment of resistant children, Gardner (1975) describes many different techniques. In respect to delinquent youth Aichhorn (1935), Eissler (1949), and Marshall (1978b) have outlined some of the parameters necessary to evolve a viable treatment situation.

In the following examples many of the techniques are oriented toward supporting rather than actively analyzing the ego defenses. When the defenses are supported and not attacked, the child or adolescent tends to give them up as resistances and tends to "grow out" of them, especially as the ego experiences less anxiety and develops more adaptive defenses. With children and adolescents whose conflicts are intense or stem largely from preverbal stages of development, joining and mirroring techniques are used in order to help evolve the narcissistic transference. From that vantage point, the therapist works to resolve the narcissistic transference into an object transference which, in the context of a healthy ego, can be analyzed with more traditional methods.

It may be noted that the therapists described tend to foster the narcissistic transference in contrast to Kohut (1977) who tends to allow the narcissistic transference to evolve more slowly. The narcissistic transference is conceptualized as a reflection of the symbiotic relationship (akin to Kohut's mirror relationship) with the maternal figure. In those children or adolescents whose sense of self has not been well differentiated, it appears essential to the treatment relationship to (re)establish those early relationships which had not been negotiated successfully. Similarly, other relationships (akin to Kohut's idealizing transference) must be established and worked through to object relationships.

The question of whether to actively re-create a transference relationship with children and adolescents is highly controversial and in need of considerable exploration. Regardless of one's persuasion in the matter, it appears that Type IV countertransferences can be helpful in conceptualizing and reconstructing early relationships.

"Rip Van Winkle"

A ten-year-old boy, Gary, was referred because of limited school performance in spite of sound potential, poor peer relations, particularly his tendency to assume the position of the scapegoat, and an annoying, teasing manner in respect to his family. Gary generally tended to project blame onto teachers and peers and otherwise did not seem to involve himself in exploring himself and his own contributions to his difficulties. The therapy sessions tended to drift unproductively with little emotional contact. As therapy wore on, it became increasingly clear that the therapist began to dread and be annoyed with the boredom, lack of contact, and unproductivity of the sessions. In particular, the therapist was subject to feelings of fatigue and drowsiness during the sessions. The therapist was alert and functioning normally with the patients scheduled before and after Gary. Gary, too, reported feelings of sleepiness and in fact would close his eyes and nap for short periods. It became clear that Gary was "acting in" and that the therapist was being induced to "act in" as well. Gary would rationalize his tiredness in terms of a long and arduous school and unhappy peer experiences. At the same time, Gary would persistently quiz the therapist about the need for therapy and nag about its worth. In similar cases where the child or adolescent complains about sleepiness, the resistance usually can be resolved by the therapist's asking, "Why don't you take a nap?" The patient will usually respond by saying that he wasn't in therapy to sleep and go on with his report. Gary, however, interpreted the therapist's question as sanctioning sleep. As Gary would begin to doze off, the therapist asked him, "What should I be doing while you sleep?" In other cases, this question would be startling enough to rouse the patient into further communication. But Gary said he didn't care — that the therapist could also take a nap. The therapist felt that he was "up the creek" which he associated to being up the Hudson River sleeping as Rip Van Winkle. There was also a curious emotional admixture of frustration, annoyance, anger, and not caring about the treatment situation. The therapist then asked Gary, "How come you'd let me get away with sleeping during your session?" Gary replied casually, "Everybody sleeps a lot in my family." A few more questions revealed that Gary's father, upon returning from his work, would promptly take a nap. Again, after supper, he would sleep until he went to bed. This depressive pattern of the father apparently was more or less accepted by Gary as being "normal." Gary did admit that he wished his father would play with him rather than sleep, but had abandoned any hope that the father would change. I told Gary the story of Rip Van Winkle and asked him if he would like my help in waking up his father. To this idea, Gary offered an inordinate amount of resistance, which was not clearly understood. Slowly but surely we worked out ways and means of waking the father and getting more attention from him. Gary's caution became clear about waking the father too abruptly, for Gary intuitively understood that the father's depression masked considerable rage. Gary also came to recognize that some of the anger he fantasized in the father was a projection. Gary agreed that the best and most conservative approach to the whole problem was to demonstrate an interest in the father — that Gary try to get the father to tell the story of his own life. Gary soon found out that his father, when seven years old, had lost his own father. Gary then was able to see that his father had lost interest in him when Gary was about seven years old. As Gary put it, "His father went to sleep on him when he was seven too." From that point on, Gary seemed to "come to life." However, it appeared that Gary's interest in the father had so deeply touched him that the father, in turn (registering the fatherly interest of Gary), became more alive. Gary then was able to recognize his identification with his depressed, uncaring father and to see that his annoying and teasing of others represented the only ways he had known to stay in contact with his father.

Discussion. This case is prototypical of many therapeutic situations wherein both the patient and therapist are drawn into a therapeutic impasse characterized by mutual "lulling," ennui, and stagnation. The disinterested, uncaring, bored, sleepy, uninvolved patient is easily identified and is well known to us. But the other side of the transference — literally the counter-reaction to the transference — is not so easily discerned and not so easily resolved. Who among us likes to stay with and study our own feelings of boredom, lack of care and interest, especially in respect to a child? It is clear that many of these "Rip Van Winkle" children act out the parental feelings to them and induce in the therapist their own feelings of being neglected (Racker's [1953] "concordant identification") and the parental feelings of neglect ("complementary identification" as introduced by Helene Deutsch, according to Racker [1953, p. 311]).

Many therapists view their induced countertransference feelings as caused by malicious manipulations on the part of the patient. This may well be true with patients who are revengeful and want the therapist to suffer as much as they. But in the main, the induced countertransference should be lableled as a product of an unconscious communication from the patient whose intent it is to re-create those conflictful interpersonal relations or intrapsychic problems which the patient has not mastered. In doing so, the patient gives the therapist the opportunity to establish a helpful ambience and to intervene in a therapeutic manner. The induction of the countertransference then may be seen as a *cooperative* effort on the part of the patient to engage the therapist, even though lack of contact and distance appears to be the compelling order of the therapeutic day. This view of the patient's communication is consistent with Searles' (1975) seminal view that the patient is attempting to help, not necessarily hinder, the therapist. Langs' (1975) and Sandler's (1976) emphases on the patient's attempts to facilitate a helpful therapeutic interrelationship are also relevant.

The "Anhistorical" Child

Related to the "Rip Van Winkle" child is the "Anhistorical" child. This is the child who variously replies with "I don't know," "I don't remember," "I don't care," and otherwise answers monosyllabically with a "yes" or "no." The presenting symptoms usually involve some behavioral or characterological disturbance with quasi- or pre-delinquent behavior, poor school achievement, strained peer relations, and unmanageability at home. The background usually involves neglect and exposure to a series of trauma, particularly violence between mother and father leading to a separation. In general, the child seems to live only in the moment, does not wish to recall the past, cannot anticipate and seemingly does not learn from his experience. It is as if he is wearing cognitive and emotional blinders, and is "anhistorical." The usual induced countertrans-ference is one of frustration, failure, incompetence, anger, "float-ing," and impotence. The therapist may feel that none of his training or experience has any significance, that he is professionally anhistorical.

Paul, a nine-year-old, bright-eyed, athletically built youngster, was referred for disruptive behavior in school and home. His mother, who was an interested but somewhat seductive young woman and who obviously enjoyed many of Paul's shenanigans, complained that Paul had not been functioning well in school, was apt to lie, cheat and steal, was the scourge of the neighborhood, and was uncontrollable at home. She described a stormy marital relationship with a sadistic man who eventually deserted her and their two children. Paul's disruptive behavior appeared coincidentally with the violent departure of his father.

In the initial interview, Paul denied any knowledge about the circumstances of his visit with me, indicated that he "sometimes" got into trouble in school, and that he would be willing to let me help him stay out of trouble. When I told him I could best help him if he could tell me the story of his life, his reply was, "I was born and here I am. That's it." any attempts to get him to elaborate were met with by vague, meaningless replies, evasion and insistence that he had nothing on his mind. He stubbornly claimed that he could not remember anything about his past — even the immediate past of the day. Backing away for several sessions, I allowed him to develop an interest in a racing car set and models. Any of my occasional questions were met with a stone wall of shrugs, "I don't know," and various other disclaimers. I noted to him that he liked action and not talk — that he was "a man of action." I also told him that he never appeared to worry and always seemed to have a good time. He agreed enthusiastically.

One day when he entered brightly and cheerfully as always, he asked me what I would like to do. Rather than reply "I'd like to listen to the story of your life," I asked him if he would be willing to help me.

Patient: (Surprise. Shrug. Smile.) I don't know.
Therapist: (Cheerfully.) That's wonderful.
Patient: What's wonderful?
Therapist: That you said you didn't know.
Patient: (Laughs, looks bewildered.)
Therapist: I really admire the fact that you don't know things.
Patient: What do you mean?
Therapist: Well, I noticed that you always have a clear mind and that your mind isn't cluttered up with a lot of junk like mine. Also, I admire the fact that you're a carefree guy who really enjoys life although you get into a little trouble once in a while. I have a problem that I think you can help me with. You see, my head is filled with a lot of worries, and I remember a lot of things I want to forget. This is very bad for my health and makes me feel lousy. So what I want you to do is help me be more like you, that is, not to care about anything or anybody and just forget about everything. (This was all said in a spirit of an anxious, cheerless, ruminative soul who wanted

some relief from his misery.) How about it?

Patient: (Playfully.) I don't know.

Therapist: That's the spirit. Suppose we just go on doing what we've been doing and I'll write down and then practice all the things you say and do so I won't know anything. Can you tell me anything else?

Patient: Not really.

Therapist: That's a very good one. I'll write it down along with the "I don't know."

For the next several sessions I kept a special sheet of paper ready to record any of his resistive maneuvers. We listed:

I don't care	Huh?
So what?	Eh!
Forget it	Could be
So?	Sometimes
Because	It doesn't matter
Who cares	

As I began to "practice" on him, he was at first pleased while displaying a somewhat tutorial and paternal air. Over the next few sessions, he began to object to my acting like him. At first smilingly, then with some determination, he tried to put a stop to my mirroring him.

Patient: What should we do today?

Therapist: I don't know.

Patient: (Despairingly.) Here we go again.

Therapist: What's wrong with my acting like you?

Patient: I don't know. Oh, I really hate it when you act like me.

Therapist: Why do you hate it?

Patient: I just do.

Therapist: That's wonderful — I'll write that down. I really like being like you. I can't understand why you don't like my being like you.

After persistent inquiry into his hatred of his mirrored self and a denied interpretation that he probably hates himself, Paul steadily became more interested in himself and could talk more meaningfully about his life. His behavior during this period, as reported by school and mother, improved considerably. When asked whether his behavioral improvement was connected with my acting like him, he demurred and said, "Well, maybe, but I just decided to change my attitude because people didn't like me and I kept getting in trouble."

Discussion. Therapists generally seem to be trained to maintain negative attitudes toward defenses. Defenses and resistances appear to be the despised enemies which need to be analyzed, interpreted, confronted, cracked and otherwise demolished — particularly when the patient is not overtly cooperative. This adversary and catabolic position appears to be inappropriate with patients whose ego defenses are weak and unstable. In essence, the above encounter amounts to pre-analytic and ego-supportive work. With the "anhistorical" child, we can hypothesize that the negative countertransference feelings are an accurate mirror of those feelings which the child's weak ego cannot endure. The therapist must not only endure these feelings, he should make a virtue of a necessity — that is, emphasize the positive aspects of the defense-resistance. After all, by the time the child has reached the therapist, hasn't the child's defensive behavior been criticized, demeaned, and punished at home and school? When the therapist finds a way to value the defense-resistance, a narcissistic transference (mirror transference in Kohut's (1977) terms) is established. That is, the child perceives that he and the therapist are the same along certain dimensions. The child then has the opportunity to project and externalize that part of him which he hates into the therapist. The child then can attack the hated introject and cease attacking his own ego. The child's ego and self-esteem is thus bolstered, especially when the therapist maintains a positive regard for the expelled introject and accompanying defense-resistances. With a strengthened ego, the child becomes less defensive and more reasonable. As the ego matures, the child then is more amenable to traditional psychotherapeutic approaches. Marshall (1972, 1976) supplies further examples of ego-strengthening devices and theoretical rationales.

Verbal reflections are of use where the trauma to the ego has occurred *after* the child has reached a point in his development where he can conceptualize and verbalize the trauma. Many workers use the cutoff concept of the oedipal stage and talk of preoedipal problems. No particular point in veridical time is relevant. Consideration should be given to the total development of the child; the development of concept formation, verbal expressiveness and symbolic processes with special emphasis on Piaget's stages. When the trauma occurs at a preverbal level — when action, thought, and verbalization are still fused — then verbal techniques alone are relatively useless. Only emotional communications appear to have any lasting impact.

"My Heart Belongs to Daddy"

A very common therapeutic situation which induces strong transference and countertransference reactions occurs with a teenage patient and a therapist of the opposite sex.

A fifteen-year-old girl who was physically well-endowed but considerably overweight appeared for her first interview with a large disheveled hat, dirty tattered blue jeans, grimy boots, and wrapped in a well-worn army field jacket. My immediate impression was that she was trying to disguise her innate physical beauty. She was surly and impudent in a way which suggested that she wanted to keep herself at considerable emotional distance. She barely alluded to her problems, which consisted of social withdrawal and isolation, depression, and excessive control by her parents.

Although I felt "put off" by this girl, I also experienced considerable feelings of being attracted to her along with sensual promptings, for beneath her benighted trappings I could see a very beautiful and warm young woman. Her inability to trust people along with my own emotional promptings immediately raised the unspoken question of whether we could trust me to use my feelings in a constructive manner.

Joyce felt there was something wrong with her since she was unable to trust anyone. My line of questioning, such as, "Why do you have to trust anyone?" "What's wrong with being yourself?" relieved some of the guilt relative to her mistrust and isolation. She agreed to return largely because she felt I did not tell her anything, that is, made no attempts to control nor seduce her.

In the next session she guiltily revealed that she did not trust me. I asked her, "Why in the world should you trust me — a complete stranger?" As Joyce groped to answer this question, she visibly relaxed and began to talk more freely about her circumstance. I was reminded at this time of Heimann's (1950) injunction to sustain and subordinate the emotional reaction. Over the next few sessions it became clear to me why I had not been sure that I could properly control my own erotic and seductive feelings. Joyce revealed that her father had maintained a paternalistic yet thinly disguised incestuous relationship with an emotionally disturbed sister. Moreover, in spite of the father's overt disapproval of Joyce's dating and "hanging out" with boys, he would attempt to "debrief" her after every social encounter. In addition, he would repeatedly remind her to think of him while on a date and consistently refer to her as his "best girlfriend." Joyce further intimated that her father saw her as a " young edition" of his wife whose beauty was now waning.

Joyce began to understand the strong pull of the father and realized that her social isolation was a reflection of her "loyalty" to her father and that her depression was a result of the internalized rage toward his demands as well as the guilt about her protest and rebelliousness. At one point in this exploration, she exasperatedly exploded with "I guess he wants me to be like the song, 'My Heart Belongs to Daddy'." It was clear then that my countertransference was parallel to the transference that the father was acting out on his daughter. An additional source of the countertransference emerged later in treatment after Joyce more comfortably examined her own very strong erotic feelings and later, her great capacity for orgasmic experience. That is, somehow, she had communicated and induced in me the strength of her own hidden sexual feelings.

Discussion. It has been standard procedure to match an adolescent with a therapist of the same sex. Various rationales, especially in terms of "supply a model for identification," have been established. However, with patients whose difficulties are of a preverbal nature, the sex of the therapist should make little difference. In treating regressed patients, the male therapist should have come to terms with the fact that he has never had the experience of carrying, giving birth, and suckling a child and that a Type IV countertransference may be relatively difficult to experience. Nonetheless, patients, if properly encouraged, will assist the therapist in developing and maintaining a thoroughgoing therapeutic stance (see the case of "A Mothering Man" below).

The Elective Mute

Greg, a seven-year-old, came into treatment because of his elective mutism with strangers and in school. Greg's parents, who were not very articulate and rather defensive, provided a limited developmental history and no clues to his mutism. Their silences and lack of spontaneity especially with the father present induced a feeling of frustration, annoyance, and lack of direction.

When Greg came into the initial interview he appeared to be a somber boy with searching eyes who would occasionally flash a quick, unreal smile. Since I realized that he would not talk to me, I told him it was not necessary to talk, but we would find some way of understanding each other — perhaps with our faces, particularly our eyes and mouth. He nodded in agreement and so began to play with the toys. There was no discernible pattern in his play except that he enjoyed crashing cars together. The ensuing weeks brought no change in the sessions and no change in his behavior outside of the sessions. I experienced mounting frustration and helplessness. Occasionally he would motion to me to join him in his play. Quite surprisingly, I found myself irritated with him and set limits prematurely and too firmly. Moreover, when he became absorbed in his play and ignored me, I experienced a sense of relief and drowsiness. I found myself condemning myself as being a poor therapist — uninterested and dull. I wondered why I ever accepted the case and wondered how I could get rid of him. At about this time, Greg's mother happened to mention that Greg's father liked to watch sports on TV and alluded to the fact that he would brook no interference with his pastime. She also intimated that he would go to sleep early, but she quickly and protectively added that he worked very hard during the day.

When Greg began to giggle or cry out in his play, I then ordered him not to make any sounds. At first he was taken aback, then smiled and giggled more openly. As I escalated my demands for quiet, he, just as deliberately and pleasurably, defied me and made various sounds with his mouth and toys. I fantasized myself as the father who wanted peace and quiet and thus began to experiment with various ways of quieting Greg. I sought to re-create the climate in which Greg's mutism evolved. The basic formula which brought squeals of delight from him was: "Shut up or I'll kill you!" As we repeated this theme several times I interpreted the parallel to our scene and what occurred with his father. We improvised and elaborated on the theme. For example, as I would make a gesture to grab him, he would pull out a gun and shoot me. Greg would literally fall off his feet in laughter as I feigned a convulsive death. Greg agreed to have the parents come in to view our game. They found remarkable similarities to what went on at home and agreed to some guidance in this area. At about this time, the school reported a "miraculous" change in Greg who not only began to talk, but was on his way to being a popular leader in his class.

The Daredevil

Joe was a fifteen-year-old who totally filled the diagnosis of "unsocialized aggressive reaction of adolescence." He had terrorized, angered and alienated all with whom he had contact. Certainly, many times he had angered me with his behavior in my office. Besides his aggressiveness toward others, Joe frequently would engage in near self-destructive acts particularly with his trail motorcycle. He was certain that he would not live until the age of twenty. After one particularly hair-raising accident where he suffered considerable cuts and bruises, he was bragging in a counterphobic manner about how much fun he had had and went on to talk about further dangerous stunts a la Evel Knievel.

Therapist: Do you want to kill yourself?

Joe: I don't care.

Therapist: How about my killing you?

Joe: How?

Therapist: Anyway you'd like. How about my throwing you off a cliff?

Joe: Nothing doing.

Therapist: Why not?

Joe: I don't want to die.

A few weeks later when Joe began to revive his self-destructive tendencies on his motorbike:

Therapist: Do you have any insurance?

Joe: What's that?

Therapist (Explains the concept of life insurance, premium payments and beneficiaries.)

Joe: So what?

Therapist: Well, suppose I take out a million dollar policy on your life and when you kill yourself, I'll collect a million bucks.

Joe: You dirty rotten son of a bitch. I wouldn't give you the satisfaction.

Therapist: What do you mean?

Joe: I wouldn't kill myself for you.

Therapist: You're going to kill yourself anyway — so why not?

Joe: Well I'm not going to kill myself period. Go fuck yourself!

Later in the session when Joe reverted to glorifying his death defying stunts.

Therapist: How about my advertising your new stunt for next weekend and I'll charge admission — say five bucks a head. People will pay anything to see someone risk their life and maybe get hurt. Maybe ten. You do your thing and I'll make some money on it.

Joe: You crazy son of a bitch. You're crazier than I am. I'm not going to do anything like that.

Therapist: Why not?

Joe: It's too crazy.

Therapist: You don't care if you hurt yourself or not and besides people pay lots of money to see other people get hurt.

Joe: Forget about it! Let's talk about something else.

Discussion. This intervention effectively quelled Joe's self-destructive acts on his motorcycle and led to Joe's despairing confession of his father's "craziness," drinking, threats, neglect, and abuse of him and his mother. Although a radical approach, this intervention was consciously and deliberately made with the following intent: (1) to establish a narcissistic transference relative to his murderous "crazy" impulses; (2) to obtain control of his harsh superego; (3) to allow for a projection onto me of his "craziness" and destructive impulses so that his ego could see more clearly what he was doing to himself. Interventions of this sort should only be made when the therapist is in full understanding and control of the therapeutic situation and the etiology of his countertransference. In Joe's situation my countertransference approach derived from the feelings of the sadistic mother and father who wished their son to be incapacitated. I appeared to Joe as reflecting his own internalized destructive feelings. Joe's ability to object to these representations was seen as a positive therapeutic step which probably occurred because I was successful in establishing a narcissistic transference. When he felt secure in the narcissistic transference, he could then use me as a helpful object.

In the treatment of delinquents it appears that the establishment of a narcissistic transference, as opposed to an object transference, may provide the foundation for a successful therapeutic relationship because these delinquents more easily tolerate a narcissistic relationship and cannot sustain an object relationship. When the delinquent perceives that the therapist is like himself, the narcissistic transference is established. The delinquent is at ease in this relationship because it re-creates the relatively comfortable relationship with the mother that preceded the traumatic separation-individuation phase. Within the security of the narcissistic-symbiotic relationship, the delinquent begins to experience the terrifying feelings that originally occurred when his symbiosis was broken and when he was not supported in his separation-individuation stage.

Furor Therapeuticus

An obsessive-compulsive child was being treated for his "thoughts" by a therapist in training. Because the therapy seemed to be hopelessly bogged down, the supervisor interviewed the child and asked him why the treatment was not going well. The child responded in effect, "Mr. T. has too many thoughts himself to really help me. Instead of paying attention to me, he just sits there and pays attention to his thoughts of curing me of my thoughts." When the child was asked how his therapist could really help him the boy said, "He should just listen and try to understand me." When the therapist in training was relieved of his *furor therapeuticus*, progress then occurred.

A Mothering Man

Joan, a seventeen-year-old, had been suicidally depressed. She had induced profound feelings of hopelessness, helplessness, and near immobilization in her therapist. While Joan was in a catatoniclike trance, her therapist asked how he could help her. She replied by commenting on a ray of light shining on the therapist's forehead. On inquiry, Joan determined that the light represented a ray of hope that the therapist could become a "mothering man" — her only possibility of survival. Joan wrote:

> Blue clouds given boundaries
> by white skies
> softened with light green leaves
> billowing in the spinnaker of birth
> sail over rough seas
> to reach its destiny.

Gray masses come thundering down
dampening all life
to be given;
forcing it away from
the bearer of individual lives

a ray of light struggles
through blue clouds
concealing itself
within the mind of
one mothering man
who painfully reveals
one dormant life
that was forced.

Over a long period of time Joan instructed the therapist about how the transformation could occur. Supervision by a woman also was helpful in potentiating the therapist's capacity to provide the emotional contact and care needed by Joan to grow. Later, Joan was able to document her mother's disregard for her while an infant and the father's inept but dutiful attention to her rearing.

IV: THE PARENTAL COMPLEXITY

The literature describing treatment approaches to parents is enormous. It spins off into various modalities such as group therapy, family therapy, and child guidance, and springs across the psychotherapeutic disciplines. However, a scan of the literature reveals that there is no clear-cut concept of countertransference toward parents. Nor is there any significant body of knowledge organized around the concept. Again, we may ask the question, "Why so little?" And again a suggested answer returns, "Because there's so much."

The complexity of the countertransference situation is increased probably exponentially, as the number of therapeutic adjunctive relationships is increased. The scope of the area therefore is so large that it cannot be adequately covered in the present chapter. Rather than attempt an extensive treatment of the subject, only a certain type of case will be presented — that of the symbiotic child and mother. This treatment situation is chosen because it is common, not fully explored in the literature and is fraught with grave counter-transference pitfalls. In tune with the general thesis of this chapter — that Type IV countertransference can enhance the therapy, some background material and one illustrative case will be presented which delineate the seeming countertransference obstacles and turn them into useful instruments.

The first problem is one of diagnosis. The initial telephone contact may not only provide important diagnostic clues, but may influence the mother's decision to accept the exploration of therapy. Quite typically, the mother indicates that her husband cannot or will not come in. Moreover, the mother gives the impression that she expects to be seen with her child. The fusion is apparent in the mother's absorption in the child or adolescent. Allusions to altered body boundaries such as "He gets under my skin" or "My heart beats for her" supply important clues. The simple amount of time that mother and child spend together, the presence of a school phobia or the mother's preoccupation with the child to the extent of the neglect of her own needs are other clues. Frequently there is a negative cast to the relationships where mother and child criticize, belittle, or otherwise claw at each other. One gets the feeling that they cannot let each other alone — that they cannot live with each other and they cannot live without each other. In passing, I may mention that this close binding relationship does not only occur between mother and child. I have seen several situations wherein the father, who spends considerable amount of time at home, is engaged in a symbiotic relationship.

The common response to the symbiotic dyad by schools (Sperling 1961), institutions, and even some therapists is "break them up," as if the symbiosis poses some threat to the observer. Some clinics correctly insist that the mother be in treatment, but by insisting that mother and child must have different therapists, the case may be lost. The inclination to "break them up" may be an important diagnostic and countertransference cue.

Another important indication of the degree of symbiosis is the force with which the mother controls the child and seeks to control the therapist and therapy. This control can seldom be successfully challenged early without deleterious effect. Moreover, the control may be only subtly manifested such as in the mother who develops a severe but medically puzzling gastroenteritis when her school phobic son began to reattend school. The control of the mother can be seen as a crucial, if not last ditch defense, and should be temporarily maintained and treated with the utmost respect. The initial countertransference reaction of the therapist is apt to be a rousing "No" or an indignant "Who do you think you are telling me how to treat your child?" These responses hark back to the therapist's individuation-separation phase and if not handled properly will result in therapeutic chaos. The experience of being controlled by the parent and the negativistic tendency of the therapist can have two implications. First, they may be the reverberations of the healthy impulse of the child in resisting the mother's untoward influence. Spitz (1957) has provided an excellent account of the developmental meaning of the child's "No." Second, the force of the resistance is a clue to the intensity of the mother's need for fusion, her need to control and her defensive vulnerability. Frequently the mother will reveal much later that she had been terrified of losing her child and of losing control of herself. Sometimes the mother, with her demands and volatility, can induce in the therapist the anxiety and terror against which she is protecting herself.

Where the child seems to be successfully opposing the symbiotic needs of the mother, it may be assumed that the mother is anxious about losing her symbiotic object and may be looking for someone with whom she can reestablish her symbiotic equilibrium. The therapist should be willing to establish that relationship with the mother. One way which usually relieves the mother's anxiety and allows a working relationship to form is to ask the mother for *her* opinion and guidance. As soon as the mother senses that the therapist will not upset the delicate balance, will not spirit away her child, and not cast her adrift, the mother becomes more cooperative. Similarly when the mother senses that the therapist is flexible, respects the symbiosis and is willing to treat them, the mother becomes more cooperative. The goal in the treatment of the symbiotic mother-child dyad is to provide therapy not only for the child but for the mother and the relationship. The goal is reached by the therapist becoming the symbiotic object for mother and child, respectively, and then resolving that relationship into an object relationship. Infrequently in the initial interview the mother will consider individual treatment for herself. Often, it may take years before the mother will accept help for herself. When the mother will not accept therapy or guidance, she may be willing to accept the role of "co-therapist" and "take lessons" from the child's therapist. The development of "filial therapy" by Guerney (1964), S. Marshall

(1978), and others is of interest in this regard. Freud (1909) established this therapeutic paradigm in his treatment of Little Hans.

As the mother (and child) become more involved in the therapeutic situation, the role of the father emerges slowly. At first the father seems conspicuous by the neglect afforded him. As mother and child weave the father into the sessions, he tends to be a vague, shadowy, and ambivalent figure. The father then tends to take on a more negative valence evoking in the therapist the question, "How can he be so neglectful or unfeeling or brutal etc." If the father has not been a part of the therapeutic scene, it is crucial to involve him for three reasons. One is that the therapist can really test his countertransference attitudes. Frequently the father is not what he is represented to be. The second is that the father may need help in becoming the object of the mother. The third is that the negative countertransference reactions of the therapist may be amplified and played back by the mother and child to the father to the point where the father is altogether pushed out of the therapeutic field. Grunebaum and Strean (1964) review the neglect of fathers in child guidance. Rubenstein and Levitt (1964) formulate some excellent hypotheses regarding the therapist's identification with the patient and the subsequent countertransference reactions to the patient's father.

In the following case the pathology of the family was blatant and seemingly begging for treatment. The parents recognized considerable marital maladjustment but closed this area off essentially saying, "If you try to investigate our marriage we will take our child out of treatment." They explained that they had had marital counseling and that a "satisfactory *modus operandi*" had been worked out. They implied that both were affectively cold and could live more or less emotionally separate lives together. According to Mrs. R., the daughter, Ruth, seemed to be a clinging, whining dependent eight-year old. Ruth certainly was deeply invested in her mother, largely as a function of a separation from her ill mother when Ruth had been eight months old. However, she was more deeply involved with peers and school than her mother perceived. Mrs. R., while seeming to be a haughty and detached person who could not abide Ruth's needs for closeness, actually derived considerable emotional satisfaction from her relationship with Ruth.

Accepting the caveat drawn by the parents, the therapist agreed to see Ruth once a week, the mother once a month, and the father as needed. The therapist felt that to separate mother and daughter by providing each with a different therapist would have created therapeutic havoc. The therapist slowly accelerated Mrs. R.'s schedule to once a week, which she begrudgingly accepted. The plan was relatively simple. The therapist tried to become Mrs. R.'s symbiotic object thus displacing Ruth. At the same time, the therapist would insinuate himself into Ruth's psychological structure as her symbiotic object.

The therapist's countertransference to the mother was one of feeling burdened and emotionally cold and distant. The therapist dreaded the sessions for there were long stony, uncomfortable silences as well as biting skepticism and criticism of the therapist. What was the meaning of the transference-countertransference? Mrs. R. was relating to the therapist as her own mother had related to her — with cold silences and neglect punctuated by sharp rejecting reproaches. The unconscious message was "I wish I could get rid of you, but I can't." Mrs. R. was also treating the therapist as she related to her daughter. And to complete the cycle, the therapist reverberated with a similar countertransference feeling — wanting to get rid of the mother.

In the midst of Mrs. R.'s complaints about Ruth's trying behavior, the therapist asked if it was feasible to get rid of Ruth. Mrs. R. dropped her severe mien and burst into an uncontrollable giggle. When she recovered, she attacked the therapist for his hardheartedness, then admitted she had thought about the idea, but had resigned herself to keeping her daughter. As Mrs. R. worked through her guilt, she also revealed that she felt that she had been a terrible mother. When the therapist joined her denigrating defense by telling her that he had known about her deficiencies for a long time, Mrs. R. sighed with relief about not having to keep up her pretenses with the therapist. In this more easy emotional flow, the therapist began to search for other ways to lessen the dullness and heaviness of the sessions. Mrs. R. was able to talk about her education and apprenticeship as a statistician and then began to unfold the story of her own life. As the therapist was able to shake free of his rejecting attitude and to see Mrs. R. in a more positive and accepting light, so there occurred a parallel in the mother-daughter relationship. It appeared that Mrs. R. had identified herself with the positive regard of the therapist which provided her with a role model in her reactions to Ruth.

From time to time the father was requested to come in with the mother in order to make sure that Mr. R. was supporting the therapy and to determine whether some inroad could be made into the marital impasse.

Ruth was terminated when she showed consistent signs of operating as a relatively autonomous person, that is, enjoying a sleep-away camp experience, maintaining good peer relations, yet enjoying a cooperative role in her family. Mrs. R. remained in therapy, overtly to help Ruth to consolidate her gains, but covertly to continue her own emotional growth. Mrs. R. terminated her own therapy when she had established herself as a professional. In effect, her symbiotic tie with Ruth was transferred to the therapist, worked through, and its residues displaced into her work situation.

V: SUMMARY

The lack of attention to countertransference in the treatment of children and adolescents appears to be due to several factors. The primary variable appears to be the variety and strength of affects evoked in the therapist which in turn produce anxiety, guilt, and a range of defensive reactions. Defenses against hostile and sexual feelings appear to be central.

Other important influences include: (1) the pedogogical-helper background of the early child analysts; (2) Anna Freud's denial of the existence of transference neurosis in children; (3) inattention to countertransference by Anna Freud and Melanie Klein; and (4) neglect by client-centered and behavior therapies.

Countertransference reactions have traditionally been treated as an anathema. However, in the past twenty-five years a few child therapists generally more cautious than adult therapists, have begun to explore the potential value of countertransference cues.

Four types of countertransference reactions are derived around the axes of two variables: (1) the source of the countertransference, i.e., patient induced or therapist derived; and (2) the extent of awareness of the countertransference by the therapist, i.e., conscious or unconscious.

Type I, wherein the therapist is dominated by his own unconscious reactions, is the most therapeutically pernicious while Type IV, wherein the therapist is aware of feelings induced by the patient, holds the most potential for therapeutic understanding and constructive intervention.

Several cases are presented which demonstrate how countertransferences, which originally impeded therapy, were used to facilitate progress. The range of countertransference reactions were: sleepiness, inadequacy, futility, boredom, anger, incompetence, sexuality, seductiveness, helplessness, disinterest, devotion to cure, immobilization, and hopelessness.

The involvement of the parents is seen as a complicating yet enhancing factor. As an example, the symbiotic mother-child situation is discussed. One case study which illustrates the use of pervasive feelings of rejection is provided.

References

Abbate, G.M. (1964). Report of panel: Child analysis at different developmental stages. *Journal of the American Psychoanalytic Association* 12:135-150.

Ackerman, N.W. (1959). Transference and countertransference. *Psychoanalytic Review* 46:17-28.

Aichhorn, A. (1935). *Wayward Youth*. New York: Viking Press.

———(1964). *Delinquency and Child Guidance: Selected Papers*, ed. O. Fleischmann, P. Kramer and H. Ross. New York: International Universitites Press.

Akeret, R.U., and Stockhamer, N. (1965). Countertransference reactions to college drop-outs. *American Journal of Psychotherapy* 19:622-632.

Bandura, A. (1956). Psychotherapist's anxiety level, self insight and psychotherapeutic competence. *Journal of Abnormal and Social Psychology* 52:333-337.

Bandura, A., Lipsher, D.H., and Miller, P.E. (1960). Psychotherapists' approach-avoidance reactions to patients' expression of hostility. *Journal of Consulting Psychology* 24:1-8.

Berlin, I.N. (1976). *Bibliography for Training in Child Psychiatry*. New York: Human Sciences Press.

Bick, E. (1962). Symposium on child analysis: I. Child analysis today. *International Journal of Psychoanalysis* 43:328-332.

Binswanger, L. (1957). *Sigmund Freud: Reminiscences of a Friendship*. New York: Grune.

Blos, P. (1974). Berta Bornstein, 1899-1971. *Psychoanalytic Study of the Child* 29:35-40.

———(1948). Emotional barriers in the understanding and treatment of children. *American Journal of Orthopsychiatry* 18:691-697.

———— (1951). On latency. *Psychoanalytic Study of the Child* 6:279-285.

Casuso, G. (1965). Report of panel: The relationship between child analysis and the theory and practice of adult psychoanalysis. *Journal of the American Psychoanalytic Association* 13:159-171.

Christ, A.E. (1964). Sexual countertransference problems with a psychotic child. *Journal of Child Psychiatry* 3:298-316.

Colm, H. (1955). A field theory approach to transference and its particular application to children. *Psychiatry* 18:329-352.

Corday, R.J. (1967). Limitations of therapy in adolescence. *Journal of Child Psychology* 6:526-538.

Cutler, R. (1958). Countertransference effects in psychotherapy. *Journal of Consulting Psychology* 22:349-356.

De Mause, L. (1974). The evolution of childhood. *History of Childhood Quarterly* 1:503-575.

Dorfman, E. (1951). Play therapy. In *Client-Centered Therapy,* ed. C.R. Rogers. Boston: Houghton Mifflin.

Eissler, K.R. (1949). Some problems of delinquency. In *Searchlights on Delinquency,* ed. K.R. Eissler. New York: International Universities Press.

Ekstein, R., Wallerstein, J., and Mandelbaum, A. (1959). Counter-transferences in the residential treatment of children: treatment failure in a child with a symbiotic psychosis. *Psychoanalytic Study of the Child* 14:186-218.

Feiner, A.H. (1977). Lowering the barriers to psychoanalysis. *Contemporary Psychoanalysis* 13:116-125.

Fiedler, F. (1953). Quantitative studies in the role of the therapist's feelings toward their patient. In *Psychotherapy: Theory and Research,* ed. O.H. Mowrer. New York: Ronald Press.

Freud, A. (1965). *Normality and Pathology in Childhood.* New York: International Universities Press.

Freud, S. (1909). Analysis of a phobia in a five-year-old-boy. *Standard Edition* 10:3-14.

Friend, M.R. (1972). Psychoanalysis of adolescents. In *Handbook of Child Psychoanalysis,* ed. B. Wolman. New York: Van Nostrand Reinhold.

Gardner, R. (1975). *Psychotherapeutic Approaches to the Resistant Child.* New York: Jason Aronson.

Geleerd, E.R. (1957). Some aspects of psychoanalytic techniques in adolescents. *Psychoanalytic Study of the Child* 12: 263-283.

Giovacchini, P.L. (1974). The difficult adolescent patient: counter-transferency problems. In *Adolescent Psychiatry,,* vol. 3, ed. S.C. Feinstein and P.L. Giovacchini. New York: Basic Books.

———(1975). Productive procrastination: technical factors in the treatment of the adolescent. In *Adolescent Psychiatry*, vol. 4, ed. S.C. Feinstein and P.L. Giovacchini. New York: Basic Books.

Gitelson, M. (1952). The emotional position of the analyst in the psycho-analytic situation. *International Journal of Psycho-Analysis* 33:1-11.

Green, M.R. (1972). The interpersonal approach to child therapy. In *Handbook of Child Psychoanalysis*, ed. B. Wolman. New York: Van Nostrand Reinhold.

Grunebaum, H.U., and Strean, H.S. (1964). Some considerations on the therapeutic neglect of fathers in child guidance. In *New Approaches in Child Guidance*, ed. H.S. Strean. Metuchen, N.J.: Scarecrow Press.

Guerney, B.G. (1964). Filial therapy. *Journal of Consulting Psychology* 28:304-310.

Heimann, P. (1950). On countertransference. *International Journal of Psycho-Analysis* 31:81-84.

Holmes, D.J. (1964). *The Adolescent in Psychotherapy*. Boston: Little, Brown.

Horwitz, L. (1974). *Clinical Prediction in Psychotherapy*. New York: Jason Aronson.

Jourard, S. (1971). *Self-disclosure: An Experimental Analysis of the Transparent Self*. New York: Wiley.

Kabcenell, R.J. (1974). On countertransference: the contribution of Berta Bornstein to psychoanalysis. *Psychoanalytic Study of the Child* 29:27-34.

King, C.H. (1976). Counter-transference and counter-experience in the treatment of violence prone youth. *American Journal of Orthopsychiatry* 46:43-52.

Kohrman, R., Fineberg, H.H., Gelman, R.L., and Weiss, S. (1971). Technique of child analysis: problems of countertransference. *International Journal of Psycho-Analysis* 52:487-497.

Kohut, H. (1977). *The Restoration of the Self*. New York: International Universities Press.

Langs, R.J. (1975). The patient's unconscious perception of the therapist's errors. In *Tactics and Techniques in Psychoanalytic Therapy, Volume II: Countertransference*. New York: Jason Aronson.

Lebovici, S. (1951). Countertransference in child analysis. *Psyche Stuttgut* 11:680-687.

Lebovici, S., Dratkine, R., Favreau, J.A., and Luquet-Parat, P. (1959). The psychoanalysis of children. In *Psychoanalysis of Today*, ed. S. Nacht. New York: Grune & Stratton.

Lebovici, S., Dratkine, R., and Kestemberg, E. (1970). Bilan de dix ans de practique chez l'enfant et l'adolescent. *Bulletin de Psychologie* 23:839-888.

Little, M. (1951). Countertransference and the patient's response to it. *International Journal of Psycho-Analysis*, 32:32-40.

Lorand, S. (1961). Treatment of adolescents. In *Adolescents*, ed. S. Lorand and H. Schneer. New York: Hoeber.

Marshall, R.J. (1972). The treatment of resistance of children and adolescents to psychotherapy. *Psychotherapy: Research Theory and Practice* 9:143-148.

———(1974). Meeting the resistances of delinquents. *Psychoanalytic Review* 61:295-304.

———(1976). "Joining techniques" in the treatment of resistant children and adolescents. *American Journal of Psychotherapy* 30:73-84.

———(1978a). The rise and fall of a milieu therapy program. *Residential and Community Child Care Administration* (In press).

———(1978b). The psychotherapy of antisocial children and adolescents. In *The Basic Handbook of Child Psychiatry*, ed. J. Nosphitz. New York: Basic Books.

Marshall, S. (1978). Filial therapy: the therapy of a mother-child symbiosis. Unpublished manuscript.

Masterson, J.F. (1972). *Treatment of the Borderline Adolescent: A Developmental Approach*. New York: Wiley-Interscience.

Menninger, K. (1958). *Theory of Psychoanalytic Technique*. New York: Basic Books.

Moustakas, C.E. (1953). *Children in Play Therapy*. New York: McGraw-Hill.

Pearson, G.H.J. (ed.) (1968). *A Handbook of Child Psychoanalysis*. New York: Basic Books.

Pichon-Riviere, E. (1952). Quelques considerations sur le transfert et le contre transfert dans la psychoanalyse d'enfants. *Revue Francais Psychoanalyse* 16:231-253.

Proctor, J.T. (1959). Countertransference phenomena in the treatment of severe character disorders in children and adolescents. In *Dynamic Psychopathology in Childhood*, eds. L. Jessner and E. Davenstedt. New York: Grune & Stratton.

Racker, H. (1953 [1957]) Meanings and uses of countertransference. *Psychoanalytic Quarterly* 26:303-357.

Reich, A. (1951). On countertransference. *International Journal of Psychoanalysis* 33:25-31.

_____(1960). Further remarks on countertransference. *International Journal of Psychoanalysis* 41:389-395.

Rheingold, J.C. (1967). *The Mother, Anxiety, and Death*. Boston: Little, Brown.

Rubenstein, B.O., and Levitt, M. (1957). Some observations regarding the role of fathers in child psychotherapy. *Bulletin of the Menninger Clinic* 21:16-27.

Sanders, W.B. (1970). *Juvenile Offenders for a Thousand Years*. Durham: University of North Carolina Press.

Sandler, J. (1976). Countertransference and role-responsiveness. *International Review of Psycho-Analysis* 3:43-47

Sarnoff, C. (1976). *Latency*. New York: Jason Aronson.

Searles, H.F. (1975). The patient as therapist to his analyst. In *Tactics and Techniques in Psychoanalytic Therapy, Volume II: Countertransference*, ed. P. L. Giovacchini. New York: Jason Aronson.

Slavson, S.R. (1952). *Child Psychotherapy*. New York: Columbia University Press.

Sperling, M. (1961). Analytic first aid in school phobia. *Psychoanalytic Quarterly* 50:504-518.

Spitz, R.A. (1956). Countertransference: comments on its varying role in the analytic situation. *Journal of American Psychoanalytic Association* 4:256-265.

Spotnitz, H. (1969). *Modern Psychoanalysis of the Schizophrenic Patient*. New York: Grune & Stratton.

Strean, H.S. (1970). *New Approaches in Child Guidance*. Metuchen, N.J.: Scarecrow Press.

Szurek, S. (1950). Problems around psychotherapy with children. *Journal of Pediatrics* 37:671-678.

Tauber, E. (1954). Exploring the therapeutic use of countertransference data. *Psychiatry* 17:331-336.

Tower, L.E. (1956). Countertransference. *Journal of the American
Psychoanalytic Association* 4:224-255.

Truax, C.B., and Carkhuff, R.R. (1967). *Toward Effective Counseling and Psychotherapy: Training and Practice.* Chicago:
Aldine.

Van Dam, H. (1966). Report on panel: Problems of transference in
child analysis. *Journal of the American Psychoanalytic
Association* 14:528-537.

Winnicott, D.W. (1949). Hate in the countertransference. *International Journal of Psycho-Analysis* 30:69-74.

Chapter 18

COUNTERTRANSFERENCE IN DISORDERS OF THE SELF

ERNEST S. WOLF, M.D.

In his address to the Nuremberg Psychoanalytic Congress, Freud (1910) for the first time took note of countertransference and described it as arising in the physician as a result of the influence of the patient on the physician's unconscious feelings. In subsequent years countertransference was widely discussed in the psychoanalytic literature, and there have been a number of excellent surveys of the topic. Gradually, and especially in recent years, there has been a shift in emphasis away from seeing countertransference as primarily an undesirable interference in the analytic process emanating from the psychoanalyst. Increasingly and at the same time, attention has been called to the uses of countertransference as a diagnostic and therapeutic tool in the conduct of psychoanalytic treatment. Such shifts are characteristic of the development of psychoanalytic science and they herald significant advances in psychoanalytic treatment and in psychoanalytic theory. Typically, what at first appears to be an obstacle in the path of psychoanalysis is transformed into one of the tools that facilitates the psychoanalytic process. It is a combination of clinical experience combined with novel theoretical conceptualizations that allows these transformations to occur. Thus, Freud turned the difficulties attending investigations in a hypnotic trance and the resistances to suggestions into the technique of free association. Similarly, transference was at first thought to be an almost insuperable obstacle to the pursuit of the psychoanalytic investigation. However, analysts learned to cope with the powerful emotional impact of transference reactions on patients as well as on themselves. Insights gained were conceptualized in an increasingly sophisticated theory of the transference and led to refinements in technique. Far from being an obstacle, the analysis of the transference has become an important tool in the working through process which leads to change in an analysis.

TRANSFORMATION OF THE CONCEPT

The transformation of psychoanalytic concepts of countertransference[1] from being primarily an obstacle to also becoming an aid in the conduct of treatment has been slow. On the one hand there are countertransference attitudes and actions which interfere with the initiation, unfolding, and resolution of the analytic process. On the other hand, there are countertransferences which become useful guides in the process of data collection through empathy and introspection. Moreover, some countertransference responses of the analyst are experienced by the analysand as deepening those aspects of the analytic ambience which facilitate the analytic process. Freud (1913), wrote Binswanger about this aspect of countertransference: "What one gives to the patient should never be direct affect but only consciously allotted and then more or less, as needed. Very much, under certain circumstances, but never out of one's own unconscious. This I take to be the formula. That is, each time one has to recognize one's countertransference and overcome it, only then is one free oneself. To give someone too little because one loves him too much is doing him an injustice and is a technical error. All this is not easy and, perhaps for this, one also has to be older" [author's translation].[2] Freud's formula states that the responses from the depth of the analyst which are under control allow the analyst to

1. In line with my preference, for heuristic reasons, to use words evocatively and confident that meaning emerges from usage, I shall forgo a precise definition of my use of the term *countertransference*.

2. Freud's telling statement was called to my attention by Heinz Kohut whom I want to thank for this and many other helpful suggestions.

give the patient a lot; but the responses from the therapist which are not under control lead to defensive maneuvers and to a nontherapeutic deprivation of the patient. The integration of these concepts into psychoanalysis has, indeed, not been easy, as Freud predicted. Perhaps, psychoanalysis first had to come of age.

A reconsideration of the theory and technical use of countertransference may be said to have begun seriously with Paula Heimann's pioneering study (1950). Other important contributors have been Winnicott (1949), Tower (1956), Racker (1968) and Sandler, Dare and Holder (1973). Yet, it would be misleading to think that countertransference theory and technique is now accorded its appropriate place in clinical psychoanalysis. While countertransference factors play as great a role in the course of analysis as the transferences, they are not yet allotted equal consideration in the clinical discussion of analytic cases. To be sure, there is a proliferating literature on the theoretical aspects of countertransference. Countertransference phenomena have been extensively studied with emphasis on precise definitions, and clear distinctions among competing definitions of countertransference, for example, between countertransference as the analyst's transference to the patient, and, countertransference as the analyst's reaction to the patient's transference. In addition, the latter has been differentiated from countertransference as the analyst's reaction to the whole patient rather than just to the patient's transference. Finally, distinctions were also suggested that would differentiate the analyst's transference reaction to the patient from a more totalistic point of view that encompasses all the emotional reactions of the analyst to the patient as countertransference. The clarification of these problems of proper classification within a theoretical framework make a valuable addition to the body of psychoanalytic theory and provide the clinician with a beginning guide to orienting himself in the complexities of the analyst-analysand relationships. But the translation of these theoretical clarifications into clinical action is retarded, in spite of the influential work of Heimann, Racker, and others, by the view that countertransference is essentially an inappropriate, if not pathological, phenomenon whose presence denotes some flaw which carries the flavor, even if ever so slightly, of moral opprobrium. Understandably, analysts hesitate to discuss publicly what even privately is recognized only against strong resistances.

Progress therefore has been slow. It has come from theoretical clarifications and from recognition of the potential usefulness of countertransference phenomena in the clinical psychoanalytic situation. Further progress can be expected from these same two directions, that is, from our widening theoretical framework which has added the psychology of the self to classical drive-and-defense psychology, and, from a further reduction in our own defensiveness as analysts as we become less prejudiced against recognizing our narcissistic motivations as potentially useful and not merely despised aspects of our personalities. Kohut's introduction of the concept self-object and increasing experience in the treatment of disorders of the self promise a significant contribution to the theory and clinical management of countertransference phenomena.

KOHUT'S DELINEATIONS

Self-Object Transferences in the Narcissistic Personality Disorders

Kohut's delineation of a new group of analyzable psychological disorders, their theoretical conceptualization, and the management of specific therapeutic problems associated with their psychoanalytic treatment evolved out of a frequently encountered difficulty in the psychoanalysis of apparently analyzable psychoneurotic patients. Though these patients often suffered intense intrapsychic conflicts, and though during the course of a properly conducted psychoanalysis they developed also intense transference-like states focused on the psychoanalyst, they did not respond as expected to the analysis of their intrapsychic conflicts. Characteristically, their suffering did not ameliorate or their acting out persisted and their transferences, whether intra-analytically to the analyst, or, extra-analytically to other transference objects, did not yield to the appropriate interpretations of the presumed underlying drive-and-defense constellation. These patients represented a very heterogeneous group whose behavioral profile varied greatly and included mildly anxious and shy people, depressed patients, bitter and angry persons, loudly arrogant people, as well as addicts, delinquents, and perverts. However, these patients had in common a particularly labile self-esteem regulation as evidenced by heightened sensitivity to slights, rejections, failures, and disappointments; more importantly, during the course of psychoanalytic treatment these analysands showed a propensity toward reactivating archaic narcissistic needs with which they turned to the analyst in the expectation of relief. Kohut described these transferencelike phenomena and termed them at first narcissistic transferences, later self-object transferences (Kohut 1966, 1968, 1971, 1972, 1977). Kohut also observed that these self-object transferences usually were analyzable in the standard psychoanalytic situation using classical psychoanalytic technique without the introduction of special parameters. Thus he could define a group of patients suffering from a specific syndrome, the narcissistic personality disorders, who were characterized neither by symptoms nor by behavior but by the development in the analysis of the pathognomonic self-objet transferences.

Mirror Transferences, Idealizing Transferences, and Corresponding Countertransferences

Kohut has described two kinds of self-object transferences, each representing the reactivation in the analytic situation of a specific childhood narcissistic need which had remained fixated and repressed or disavowed. Mirror transferences are the reactivated archaic needs of the child for narcissistic enhancement, for acceptance and confirmation of the child's greatness, perfection, and worth. Idealizing transferences are the reactivated needs of the child to share in the calmness and strength of an admired parent by merging with the image of calm omnipotence and unfailing omniscience. In a properly conducted psychoanalysis, that is, in a psychoanalytic ambience (Wolf 1976) which is neither moralistic nor educational but open to the assertion of archaic narcissistic needs, the transferences will emerge spontaneously, albeit slowly against the resistances and caution built up during years of exposure to rebuffs or neglect.

Corresponding to the two types of self-object transferences which unfold during the analysis, Kohut (1968, 1971) noted that two types of countertransferences might be evoked. In the more archaic versions of the mirror transferences, for example, the analyst is exposed to the experience of his not being acknowledged by the patient as a separate object since the patient experiences the analyst as a part of the patient, a part which is totally merged into the patient's self-experience. The experience, therefore, of not being responded to as having an existence of his own evokes in the analyst certain reactions, countertransferences, which depend to some extent on the particualr narcissistic vulnerability of the analyst. The most common countertransference reaction here is that the analyst feels bored, sleepy and finds it difficult to listen to the patient's need to expand himself in self-centered soliloquy. Other countertransference reactions are frequently observed by analysts who have become alert to their own sensitive narcissistic responses: they may notice becoming irritable or they may suddenly become aware that they have lost empathic contact with what is going on inside the analysand. Sometimes, the first awareness of the countertransference comes with acting out, for example, finding oneself prematurely ending an analytic session, or noting that a sharp tone of disapproval or an ironic twist or a depreciating reminder to the patient of some obvious reality have almost inobtrusively slipped into one's interpretations. Usually, it is the patient who first notes these countertransferences and it is the patient's reactions that draw the analyst's attention to them.

Instead of the intense need to merge there may unfold during analysis other varieties of the mirror transferences and these will tend to evoke in the analyst corresponding varieties of countertransferencereactions. To cite one example, certain analysands need to strengthen their very shaky self-image by seeing and hearing it enacted, so to speak, in front of their own eyes and ears: they are driven to demand that the analyst have the same opinions, values, feelings, interests, joys, sorrows, etc, as the analysand. The discerning reader will recognize that these transferences — a variety of mirror transference termed alter-ego or twinship transference by Kohut — are the reactivation during analysis of childhood needs for self-confirmation, particularly those needs that may have been acted out in the fantasy of an imaginary playmate. Here again the evoked countertransference depends as much on the specific narcissistic vulnerability of the analyst as on the demand of the analysand for a specific needed response. For example, an analyst may become aware of his countertransference reaction in noting how he asserts his separate identity by giving learned opinions to certain analysands. Even a correct and necessary interpretation can be given in the spirit of this need to assert one's separate and superior judgment to the consternation of the analysand. Becoming aware of the analysand's dismay serves the analyst as a pointer to his countertransference.

The second major type of self-object transference described by Kohut was termed by him the idealizing transference. As expected, specific countertransference reactions to the idealizing transferences are also frequently observed. The idealizing transferences represent the reactivation of the patient's archaic need to have available to him a calm, strong, reliable object, and, accordingly, those reactivated needs are experienced by the analyst not only as demands on his admired calm strength but also as an intensely stimulating idealization of his person. It is the latter stimulation, particularly, which tends to evoke the analyst's countertransference as the analyst attempts to escape the uncomfortable narcissistic resonances within himself by reducing the stimulation through some reality-oriented or even self-deprecatory comment. Equally important are the analysand's defenses against the idealizing transference and the countertransference evoked by these defenses. For example, the first manifestation of a beginning idealizing transference often is seen in the appearance of an overtly depreciating attitude toward the analyst, that is, the patient's defense against the transference. Analysts, in spite of having been analyzed, are only rarely so free of narcissistic vulnerabilities that they will not react with some feeling of being slighted or hurt, a feeling which may precipitate a countertransference action unless detected and understood by the analyst.

The Psychology of Disorders of the Self

Kohut's recognition of the self-object transferences, the delineation of a new group of analyzable disorders (the narcissistic personality disorders), the clarification of certain common countertransference reactions, together with theoretical revisions of the theory of narcissism and recommendations for psychoanalytic treatment — all these were major advances in psychoanalysis which widened the therapeutic scope and deepened the theoretical understanding. Kohut's emphasis on the separate development of narcissistic libido as distinguished from object libido became the major theoretical revision in the theory of narcissism. Narcissism, that is, the cathexis of the self with narcissistic libido, was no longer conceptualized as a transient phase during the development from infancy to maturity, but was now seen to follow its own line of development from archaic infantile modes to full maturity. However, experience in the treatment of the narcissistic disorders inevitably led to deeper understanding of the core psychopathology and made it increasingly difficult to explain the structural essence of these disorders within the framework of classical drive-and-defense psychology. What emerged was the insight that the self, its structure, its weaknesses and defects, its need for external and internal bolstering, was at the center of these disorders. Conceptualizing the vicissitudes of defects of the self in terms of insufficient cathexis or conceptualizing the intense aggressions that were observed in terms of an untamed aggressive drive did not account for the observed data and required an uncomfortable stretching of classical drive-and-defense psychology. The introduction by Kohut (1971) of the concept self-object and of the self/self-object model for the structure of the self were the decisive steps leading to a more comprehensive understanding of the disorders of the self (a more fitting term than the previous designation of narcissistic personality disorders) and provided the basis for a psychoanalytic psychology of the self.

The Self-Object

To be more specific, a self-object is an object which is experienced as part of the self. For example, the infant experiences the totality of his mother's psychological caretaking presence as part of his self. This may be visualized more dramatically by imagining the infant's experience of unpleasure and tension resulting from the absence of the psychologically sustaining self-object. Absence spells discomfort, even extremely so, and responsive presence means an experience of bliss. The need for the life-sustaining psychological presence of self-objects, like the need for the life-sustaining physical presence of oxygen and other nutriments, remains throughout life, though the psychological self-objects can gradually be present at greater distances and can, with increasing maturity, be represented by symbols which substitute for the person whose presence was needed originally. For example, self-object constancy is reached when the child's capability for symbolic representation has achieved a point of solidity where the self-object's visual or auditory physical presence is no longer needed to maintain the functional psychologic presence of the self-object. By the time adulthood is attained the symbolic yet functional presence of self-objects usually has been taken over by a multitude of partial self-objects, such as one's whole family, community, membership in various groups, etc. (Wolf 1976b). All these partial self-objects in their aggregate totality provide the experience of a functional psychological self-object presence needed to sustain the well-being, the cohesion, the vigor and the harmony of the self. One need only empathically imagine the mental state of a person suddenly removed from his sustaining self-object environment, for example, being suddenly transported without friend or family into a totally alien culture, in order to get a glimpse into the painful state of deficiency of self which is precipitated by the sudden loss of the self-object environment.

DEVELOPMENT OF SELF-OBJECT TRANSFERENCES

The recognition of the centrality of the self and its self-object relationships leads to a clarification of some of the complexities of transference and countertransference in the psychoanalytic treatment of disorders of the self. First, it seems clear that the self-object transferences consist of more than the reactivation of archaic forms of the persisting need for self-objects. Amalgamated with the reactivated archaic needs are the expectable age-appropriate self-object needs[3] of the analysand which include a proper respect for the analysand's extra-analytic obligations and interests that may easily be mistaken for resistances. Second, the analytic situation facilitates regression and as a result the more archaic forms of needs for self-objects become very prominent during the course of an analysis. Some intensification and archaization of the self-object transferences are therefore observable in any psychoanalysis. The fear and shame connected with these painful regressions accounts for some of the nonspecific resistances to the regressive pull experienced by many analysands, particularly during the beginning phases of an analysis. The tactful explanation and, above all, the analyst's ability to understand the patient's very legitimate reluctance to undergo an initial increase in the feeling of disconcerting helplessness will facilitate the proper unfolding of the analytic process and launch a direction setting tone of empathic acceptance combined with calmly reasoned explanations of the experienced

3. The age-appropriate self-object needs are specific for each patient depending on his life history, experiences, culture, social class, etc., and are not, therefore, to be thought of as pathological, though, of course, fixation *may* be evidence for injury to the self. It is more useful to describe these self-object needs as having reached various degrees of development along a line from infancy to maturity. A maturely developed self-object need, e.g., for a mirroring milieu which will acknowledge mature ambitions, or for an idealizable ethic that transcends human limitations, is not a sign of psychopathology.

phenomena. Third, analysts often become aware introspectively of an equally nonspecific reaction to the patient's initial reluctance. The analyst's reaction is derived from his healthy narcissistic involvement in his analytic work and from a misperception of the analysand as "resisting the analysis." This reaction often manifests as impatience with the analysand. However, once the analysis has proceeded beyond its early phase the reactivated archaic needs for a responsive self-object become the predominant self-object transference manifestations. They represent in a more or less distorted form the specific needs that had remained unresponded to by the specific interactions between the nascent self and the self-objects of early life.

Controlled Self-Object Countertransferences are Sources of Empathic Data

Next I want to examine the phenomena of countertransference within the framework of a psychoanalytic psychology of the self. The analyst, just like the analysand, enters the analytic situation with certain needs for self-objects. To be sure, it is expected that the analyst's own analysis has allowed him to work through the more archaic forms of his needs for self-object responses, and that he has internalized sufficient structure to give cohesion, vigor, and harmony to his self. In other words, it is expected that sufficient structure has formed the matrix for the integration of his ambitions with his skills and talents under the guidance of an internal value system; that the defects in his self have been covered or filled in by sufficient compensatory structures (cf. Kohut 1977) so that his needs for responsiveness from archaic self-objects have modified into less intense needs that can be relieved by more distant and more symbolic self-object representatives. Moreover, it is to be hoped that the analyst in his professional as well as in his private life finds the opportunity for relationships of intimacy and creativity commensurate to his needs. Still, after all is said and done, there always remain unfulfilled longings to be mirrored and unfulfilled strivings to merge into an idealized imago. As the analyst begins analytic work with a new analysand he will, if he is to gain empathic contact with the analysand, allow himself some controlled regression. Only in this way can he attain the state of evenly suspended attention which Freud recommended as the proper posture for the analyst. This state of regression, though mild and controlled, does intensify the analyst's residual needs for a self-object and thus makes it possible for the analysand temporarily to become a self-object for the analyst. In other words, aspects of the analysand are experienced as part of the analyst's self and become available for introspective examination. It is by virtue of such controlled self-object counter-transferences that empathic data, that is, data obtained by vicarious introspection, become available to the analyst. Self-object counter-transferences, therefore, are an indispensable part of psychoanalytic treatment since they provide the major channel for those empathically collected data which make the formulation of psychoanalytic hypotheses possible (Kohut 1959). It is to be stressed, however, that it is balanced, controlled[4] empathy which is in the service of treatment and not archaic, uncontrolled empathy. For example, in being empathic with the pain of a patient's narcissistic injury, the analyst may, via his controlled response, help the patient recognize the legitimacy of feeling outraged over the injury and threat to the self; yet, the analyst would not be helpful if his uncontrolled archaic empathy allowed residues of his own deeply buried narcissistic rage to find an outlet through subtly encouraging the patient's acting out.

Obviously, the controlled regression and the reactivation of the analyst's need for responses from archaic self-objects make the analyst also more vulnerable since his self is more fragile in the somewhat regressed state. In this more vulnerable state of the self the analyst may react to the impact of the analysand's self-object transferences with untoward countertransference reactions that I have already discussed above in connection with mirror and idealizing transferences. These reactions are more easily understood by consideration of the self-object nature of these countertransferences. For example, the boredom and withdrawal in reaction to an analysand's intense need for merging with the self-object can now be recognized as the defensive withdrawal of the analyst's vulnerable self from the engulfing propensities of the analysand's

4. "Control" in the context of a psychology of the self is not synonymous with control of the id by the ego. Rather, control means that in a cohesive self the constituents are present in a balanced integration which constrains the constituent parts. Conversely, loss of cohesion wrenches the constituent parts of the self out of the integrating and constraining matrix, resulting in their appearance as "uncontrolled" disintegration products. In this view, control is not seen as the ego's sublimation of a drive or as the neutralization of a charge by an opposite countercharge but may be visualized as analogous to the process that transforms the qualities of the atoms which constitute a molecule into the qualties of that molecule.

merger transference. To give another example, an analysand's self-depreciation and concomitant idealization of the analyst as an idealized self-object is not only overstimulating to the residual grandiosity of the analyst's regressed vulnerable self, but, and equally important, the analysand's self-depreciation diminishes his availability as a temporarily needed idealizable self-object for the analyst. The need for a minimum of availability of the analysand as an at least potentially idealizable self-object — a source of potential countertransference reactions — should not be dismissed lightly or even critically rejected. This particular self-object need may evoke anger at the analysand in the analyst who feels injured in his self by the disappointment in his patient; on the other hand, when properly controlled, the need to idealize the analysand is a self-object countertransference that may provide that modicum of confirmation to the analysand's potential which, analogous to a healthy mother's conviction of her baby's perfection, is legitimately needed in order to overcome the destructive deficits left by the failure of the self-objects of early childhood. If one could not possibly respect one's analysand as a unique and valued human being with whom one can work towards a worthwhile achievement, then one should probably not analyze him. Cognitive understanding alone is no more sufficient than love alone is.

MINI-COUNTERTRANSFERENCE PHENOMENA: A CLINICAL EXAMPLE

The countertransference reactions which I have discussed so far are relatively gross phenomena that may facilitate or may hinder the initiation of the analytic process, the spontaneous unfolding of the transferences, and the empathic contact of the analyst with the analysand. The importance of these countertransferences is self-evident. There is, in addition, another category of countertransference phenomena — I will term them mini-countertransferences — which are characterized by the subtlety in which they cause disruptions in the established analytic process. An example will illustrate.

The analysand was a thirty-eight-year-old physician during the third year of his analysis. The patient had come into treatment because of recurrent episodes of severe depression. The first depressive episode had been precipitated when the patient and his wife had been summoned to a school conference with his son's teacher. The teacher had complained that the youngster presented a behavioral problem to the school. Significant in this analysand's past history was the loss of his mother because of illness during the patient's infancy. Following this loss, there had occurred several years of institutionalization. As a matter of fact, his childhood was almost empty of sustaining psychological relationships except for the idealized institutional authorities and for a kindly and admired grandfather with whom he had sufficient contact to establish a meaningful relationship. In the structure of this patient's self then there remained a central defect associated with insufficient confirming-mirroring responses from the caretaking self-objects of his early institutional years. However, he had learned to elicit a modicum of confirming responses from the institutional authorities by being a good boy, an eagerly compliant and helpful child. He thus was able to build a precariously established compensatory structure (cf. Kohut 1977) which was strengthened by the relationship with the grandfather and that covered the defective part of his self, allowing him to function in life with a measure of healthy zest, joy, and creativity until the sudden breakdown into depression. Before that breakdown the patient had arranged to maintain and strengthen the compensatory structure of his self by maintaining institutional affiliation (e.g., medical school, hospital, professional societies) where by being a good student or active member he could continue to receive the sustaining responses from the self-objects now represented by the institutional authorities.

When his son — with whom the patient in normal parental manner was identified because he experienced him as part of his self — then suddenly was the object of severe criticism by the school authorities, and the patient was helpless in doing anything to effect the usual gratifying compliance with the idealized yet dreaded authorities, his compensatory structure collapsed, and the core pathology of empty depression came to the fore.

During the analysis we worked to ameliorate somewhat the core defect by analyzing the depressive episodes precipitated by weekends and other disruptions in the continuity of the relationship to the analyst as mirroring-confirming self-object. While there was some reduction in sensitivity to separation, the main work of the analysis and its main effectiveness was in the area of analyzing and thereby reconstructing and strengthening the damaged compensatory structures. The patient derived additional strength from an elucidation of the protective function of the compensatory structure vis-a-vis the depressive core.

I will now illustrate the subtly intertwined roles of transference and countertransference in the working-through process. The patient had a close friend who was taken seriously ill and though the patient initially attempted to prescribe for his friend, he recognized, with interpretive help from me, that his excessive involvement was motivated more by his need to be the good boy who takes care rather than by considerations of his friend's welfare. One day, soon thereafter, the patient told me that he had prevailed upon his friend to accept the care of another physician who then had promptly hospitalized his friend. For various reasons my attention at the time had been drawn to the aspect of separation from his friend and to the institutionalization of his friend in a hospital. My comments, therefore, were directed toward clarifying my patient's reactions to the separation, an issue which had always been a sensitive one. He listened politely and I did not notice any particular affective reaction. Next day, however, he complained of waking up with a great deal of anxiety and now he was feeling depressed. Moreover, this always well-dressed man that day was wearing a clashing color combination that struck me as unusually disharmonious. His voice was testy and I recognized that the patient was in a state of what we had come to call a "mini-fragmentation."

Asking myself where I had failed, perhaps the previous day, to properly understand and respond to the patient, I could not come to any answer until my patient remarked that I had not said anything about how well he had coped with delivering his friend to the hospital. Then I recognized what had happened. The patient, after my previous interpretations about his motivation for taking care of his friend, had decided that I would be pleased if he withdrew from taking care of the friend. I had become for the patient like the institutional authority of his childhood and when he told me, apparently proudly, that he had been a good boy and let another physician help his friend, he expected a confirming acknowledgment. Such an acknowledgment would have meant to him acceptance by the self-object as worthy to share in the idealized self-object's power and righteousness. At the same time and at a deeper level he was also exhibiting himself proudly as the perfect good boy for which he demanded confirming responses from a mirroring self-object. Having recognized the dynamics of the transference disruption, I could interpret it to the patient, who almost immediately calmed down. His mini-fragmentation subsided.

The Working-Through Process: Transmuting Internalization

Episodes like this one, when repeated innumerable times, make up the working through process of a psychoanalysis. In the above example, it was a mini-countertransference reaction on my part, brought about by a fixation on the separation issue rooted in my own archaic self-object needs, which blinded me to being empathically in touch with the patient's self and his self-object needs. I had responded to a *part,* the anxious part concerned with separation, instead of to the whole person.

These mini-countertransference reactions are unavoidable and probably occur much more frequently than is recognized by even the most perceptive analysts. They represent an example of recurring opportunities for turning an apparent obstacle to the analytic process into a powerful vehicle for analytic cure. For it is through the back-and-forth of the mini-disruptions and mini-fragmentations caused by mini-countertransferences that the stage is set to make the interpretations and genetic reconstructions which, by changing a traumatic frustration into an optimal one, allow the process of transmuting internalization to add new structure to the self and thereby to strengthen it. These wholesome processes take place in consequence of disruptions that occur spontaneously as part of the analyst's inevitable and countertransference determined failures which are then properly explained to the patient (cf. Kohut 1977, p. 32). Any deliberate disruption or planned manipulation of the analytic relationship would, of course, be perceived as the dishonest maneuver that it is and destroy the basis for mutual trust without which analytic work cannot flourish.

THE BIPOLAR ANALYTIC CONFIGURATION

Before ending this discussion, I would like to take a brief look beyond the issues of transference and countertransference by focusing on the analysis as a process that has a beginning, a middle, and an end. When does an analysis begin? When an analysand first decides to be analyzed? When he first starts working with the analyst? When there is a discernible transference neurosis? I would like to propose some tentative answers to these questions. An analysis begins when the analysand's attempt to make the analyst a self-object is met by the reciprocal self-object strivings of the analyst so that both analyst and analysand become engaged in a stable, coherent, mutually reciprocal self-object configuration. In this configuration the analyst's self, including parts of the analysand as a self-object, makes up one pole, and the analysand's self, including parts of the analyst as self-object, makes up the other pole. This bipolar configuration is one of internal tension as the poles are pulled together via an interposed energic field of self-object bonds while, at the same time, the individual selves of both analyst and analysand move into different directions according to their own individual life plans. Such a bipolar configuration is analogous to the structure of an individual self as proposed by Kohut (1977). This analytic selflike configuration emerges during the analytic process and is contributed to by the selves of two people, analyst and analysand. It is a temporary structure which lasts while the analytic process continues. However, as is well known, once started the analytic process often persists beyond the formal termination of an analysis. Similarly, the analytic configuration seems to have a life of its own that may extend beyond the formal analytic sessions. For the emergence of a stable working analytic relationship means that the internal forces have come together in a stable configuration which has a direction of its own. This direction and the to-be-attained goal of the analysis, though fully determined by the pattern of its constituent parts, is not predictable by either analyst or analysand. Yet, in retrospect, at the end of an analysis, it becomes clear that it could not have aimed at a different conclusion. Attempts to interfere with the natural course of an analysis will tend to derail or even destroy it.

The stability of the bipolar analytic configuration expresses the continuity of the reciprocal self/self-object relationship. However, though continuing, the self-object experience does change in a successful analysis. The analysand's self gradually experiences the analyst as self-object in a less archaic mode; he sees the analyst more as a real object representing sought-after qualities. It is these qualities then, sometimes very sophisticated ones, which are needed as self-objects and for the sake of which the relationship with the carrier of these qualities is valued. For his part, the analyst's experiencing the analysand as a self-object also changes in response to the growing cohesion of the analysand's self. The analysand is seen as increasingly autonomous and it is precisely the quality of autonomy that becomes the self-object instead of the person of the analysand. In general, the changes in the nature of the self-object experience parallel the transformations that make up the developmental line for self-objects, and it is empathic sensitivity which keeps selves in tune with their self-objects and vice-versa.

Propelling Power of an Analytic Configuration

An analytic configuration, once it has sprung into active existence, is a powerful structuring of psychological relationships. Neither analyst nor analysand can easily ignore it or withdraw from it; in other words, both experience some relative helplessness vis-a-vis the propelling direction of the analysis. Not only do they both feel a commitment to the analysis, but they also feel that as individuals they seem to have little influence on where the analysis is going. For example, the analysand may wish to focus on the analysis of certain psychosomatic symptoms with the hope of getting some early symptom relief. He may find, however, that the unfolding analytic material leads away from symptoms to other kinds of associations, for example, current or past experiences of disconcerting intrusions by others into his fragile self, with exacerbations of distressing somatic symptoms. Working through these traumas of intrusion probaby will firm up his self-structure to the point of amelioration of somatic symptomatology eventually. In the meantime the analysand often feels helpless and may think of the analysis as besides the point of his real concerns. The analyst, for his part, is similarly unable to set the direction of the analysis. Out of theoretical convictions or because of a personal bent he may try to interpret a particular line of material that is, in fact, only peripheral to the affective center of the present moment. For instance, in the case of the psychosomatic symptoms just cited as an example, the analyst chose to interpret a particular somatic symptom, a flare-up of a backache, as determined by the conflict between a desire for and a fear of a homosexual attack by the analyst. This might well have been a partially correct interpretation, but it was off-center; it stressed a nonfocal side issue at the expense of recognizing the vulnerability of a total self to disintegrating intrusions by self-objects.

However, my purpose here is not to add another example of a countertransference, this time one determined by putting theory above clinical empathy. Rather, I want to emphasize that the analysis, beyond transference and countertransference, becomes a repetition of the ambience of childhood. The self/self-object milieu of the formative years is recreated by the analysis for both analyst and analysand. In the above example, the analysand at that moment experienced the analytic ambience, that is, most any activity of the analyst, as if it were again the intrusion of a psychotically insensitive mother into his self; and the analyst, at that moment, was reliving the frustrations of his inability as a youngster to explain what he meant to his elders and, in the present situation, took recourse to theory in order to receive a confirming understanding from his self-object.

Transference and Countertransference as Manifestations of Self/Self-Object Relations

I will summarize. The phenomena that clinically we have come to know as transference and countertransference — and that have been defined in various ways — can be conceptualized as the manifestations of self/self-object relations when viewed within the framework of a psychology of the self. These phenomena are difficult to isolate in either self or self-object but are compounded as much of the self's self-object needs as of the self-object's responsiveness to these needs. But beyond the needs themselves they are influenced by the perceptions of these needs, by the balance between introspective awareness and empathic in-tuneness. Transferences and countertransferences represent the state of the self and of the self-objects. A strong, cohesive, vigorous, and harmonious self is likely to be well in touch with its own needs and likely to be empathically sensitive to the self-object needs of another self. An analyst is well served by his self being in such a healthy and mature state; he will be equipped with a wide choice of selective responses with which to aid his analysand in the analytic task. An injured self is not likely to be either empathic with itself nor with others but, condemning both, will try to protect what integrity it has left against real or fancied assault from the outside. The more injured the self, the more fragmented and imbalanced its structure, the more it is in need of integrating responses. Responses addressed to the total self facilitate integration and cohesion; responses addressed to details, *pars pro toto*, are likely to hasten further disintegration.

During the analytic process one is constantly tempted to concentrate attention on this conflict or that individual self-assertion, on this defense or that resistance, on this transference or that countertransference, while at the same time easily forgetting the total context which gives meaning to these dynamic phenomena. As scientists it is our tendency to avoid the complex and mysterious whole which we never can grasp in its totality and to focus our efforts on the parts which are explainable so that by sharing our understanding we feel confirmed in our uncertain selves. In this way we add, bit by bit, to our knowledge, much of it useful. But occasionally we catch an elusive glimpse of a larger configuration, a more total Gestalt, which illuminates all the bits of accumulated data and gives them added meaning. It is for this larger vision that we need to keep our eyes open.

References

Freud, S. (1910). The future prospects of psycho-analytic therapy. *Standard Edition* 11:139-151.

_____ (1913). Letter to Ludwig Binswanger of February 20, 1913. In Ludwig Binswanger, *Erinnerungen an Sigmund Freud*. Bern: Franke Verlag, 1956. p. 65.

Heimann, P. (1950). On countertransference. *International Journal of Psycho-Analysis* 31:81-84.

Kohut, H. (1959). Introspection, empathy and psychoanalysis. *Journal of the American Psychoanalytic Association* 7:459-483.

_____ (1966). Forms and transformations of narcissism. *Journal of the American Psychoanalytic Association* 14:243-272.

_____ (1968). The psychoanalytic treatment of narcissistic personality disorders. *Psychoanalytic Study of the Child* 23:86-113.

_____ (1971). *The Analysis of the Self*. New York: International Universities Press.

_____ (1972). Thoughts on narcissism and narcissistic rage. *Psychoanalytic Study of the Child* 27:360-400.

_____ (1977). *The Restoration of the Self*. New York: International Universities Press.

Racker, H. (1968). *Transference and Countertransference*. New York: International Universities Press.

Sandler, J., Dare, C., and Holder, A. (1973). *The Patient and the Analyst: The Basis of the Psychoanalytic Process*. New York: International Universities Press.

Tower, L. (1956). Countertransference. *Journal of the American Psychoanalytic Association* 4:224-255.

Winnicott, D.W. (1949). Hate in the countertransference. *International Journal of Psycho-Analysis* 30:69-74.

Wolf, E.S. (1976a). Ambience and abstinence. *Annual of Psychoanalysis* 4:101-115.

―――― (1976b). The family as self-object. *Proceedings of the Annual Meeting of the American Political Science Association*, September 1976.

CONTRIBUTORS

L. Bryce Boyer, M.D. is associate director, Psychiatric Residency Training, Harrick Memorial Hospital, Berkeley, California, and was chairman, Interdisciplinary Colloquium on Psychoanalytic Methods and Questions in Anthropological Fieldwork, American Psychoanalytic Association, 1970-1977.

Lawrence Epstein, Ph.D. is a supervising analyst, supervisor of psychotherapy, and member of the faculty, William Alanson White Institute. He was formerly assistant clinical professor of psychiatry at Albert Einstein Medical College of Yeshiva University and currently is clinical professor in the Post-Doctoral Program of Psychotherapy at Adelphi University.

Arthur H. Feiner, Ph.D. is a fellow, training, and supervising analyst, and supervisor of psychotherapy at the William Alanson White Institute. He is the editor of *Contemporary Psychoanalysis*.

Michael Fordham, M.D. is a graduate of Cambridge University, studied medicine and surgery at Saint Bartholomew's Hospital, London. He was a Commonwealth Fellow in child psychiatry, and formerly chairman of the Society of Analytical Psychology, and chairman of the Medical Section of the British Psychological Society and subsequently its Honorary Fellow. He has been chairman of the psychotherapy section of the Royal Medico-Psychological Association, and when it became The Royal Society of Psychiatry, was elected a Founder Fellow.

Peter L. Giovacchini, M.D. is clinical professor, Department of Psychiatry, University of Illinois College of Medicine, and is in the private practice of psychoanalysis.

León Grinberg is a supervising and training analyst, and professor at the Institute of Psychoanalysis, Buenos Aires. He was president of the Argentine Psychoanalytic Association and, at present, is full member of the Buenos Aires Provisional Psychoanalytic Association. He was vice president of the International Psycho-Analytical Association, and also chairman of the Training Council of the Latin

American Psychoanalytical Societies. He has been full visiting professor at Madrid University, and supervisor and professor to the Madrid Psychoanalytical Study Group.

Robert Winslow Hunt, M.D. is director, Continuing Care Services, Vanderbilt Clinic, Presbyterian Hospital. He is on the faculty, Columbia Psychoanalytic Center for training and research, New York City.

Amnon Issacharoff, M.D. is a training and supervising analyst, and supervisor of psychotherapy, William Alanson White Institute. He is assistant clinical professor in psychiatry, New York Medical College; lecturer, College of Physicians and Surgeons, Columbia University.

Robert Langs, M.D. is editor-in-chief of the *International Journal of Psychoanalytic Psychotherapy* and associate professor of psychiatry at the Mount Sinai School of Medicine, New York. He is a graduate of the Downstate Psychoanalytic Institute, Brooklyn, New York.

Robert J. Marshall, Ph.D. was formerly staff psychologist-chief, Clinical Psychology Section, Veterans Administration Hospital, Montrose, New York; psychologist Lincoln Hall, Lincolndale, N.Y.; chief psychologist, Westchester Psychiatric Group, Yorktown Heights, New York. At present he is in the private practice of psychoanalysis and psychotherapy, at the Northern Westchester Center for Psychotherapy, Yorktown Heights, New York.

Joyce McDougall, D.Ed. a graduate of Otage University, Dunedin, New Zealand, came to London in 1950 where she studied child psychoanalytic work at the Hampstead Clinic. She trained for adult psychoanalytic work at the Institute of Psychoanalysis in Paris, France, and is now a supervising and training analyst of the Paris Psychoanalytical Society.

Donald Meltzer, M.D. is a qualified psychoanalyst (London): adult-1957, child-1958, training analyst-1962. He was director of child psychiatry, Washington University School of Medicine and consultant psychiatrist, USAF. He is in the private practice of adult and child psychoanalysis in Oxford, England.

Harold F. Searles, M.D. is a training and supervising analyst of the Washington Psychoanalytic Society. He is a clinical professor of psychiatry at Georgetown University School of Medicine, and for twenty years was a consultant in psychiatry at the National Institute of Mental Health. From 1949-1964 he worked at Chestnut Lodge Sanitarium in Rockville, Maryland. He practices psychoanalysis in the Washington D.C. area.

Hyman Spotnitz, M.D., Med, Sc.D. is engaged in the private practice of psychoanalytic psychiatry (individual and group) in New York City. He is a life fellow of the American Psychiatric Association and of the American Orthopsychiatric Association; fellow of the American Group Psychotherapy Association, American Association for the Advancement of Science, and New York Academy of Medicine; and honorary president of the Manhattan Center for Advanced Psychoanalytic Studies.

Edward S. Tauber, M.D. is a fellow, training and supervising analyst, William Alanson White Institute; past president, William Alanson White Psychoanalytic Society; charter fellow, The American Academy of Psychoanalysis; adjunct professor of psychology, New York University, Department of Psychology; research consultant, Department of Neurology and Psychiatry, Montefiore Hospital and Medical Center; visiting professor, Department of Pharmacology, National University of Mexico.

Earl G. Witenberg, M.D. is director, fellow, training and supervising analyst, William Alanson White Institute. He is past president of The American Academy of Psychoanalysis; associate clinical professor of psychiatry, Albert Einstein College of Medicine.

Ernest S. Wolf, M.D. is a graduate of the Chicago Psychoanalytic Institute where he is on the faculty and is a training and supervising analyst. He is an Associate Professor of Psychiatry at Northwestern University School of Medicine. Primarily in the private practice of psychiatry and psychoanalysis, he has been Director of Student Mental Health at Northwestern University, and Associate Director of the Center for Psychosocial Studies of Chicago.

INDEX

Index

473